STEPPING INTO AutoCAD®

A Guide to Technical Drafting Using AutoCAD

Mark Merickel

With Technical Assistance From Rusty Gesner

 New Riders Publishing, Thousand Oaks, California

STEPPING INTO AutoCAD®

A Guide to Technical Drafting Using AutoCAD

By Mark L. Merickel

Published by:

New Riders Publishing
Post Office Box 4846
Thousand Oaks, CA 91360 USA

First Edition 1986
Second Edition 1987
Third Edition 1988
Fourth Edition 1989

2 3 4 5 6 7 8 9

Printed in the United States of America

Library of Congress Cataloguing-In Publication Data

```
Merickel, Mark.
STEPPING INTO AutoCAD : a guide to technical drafting using
AutoCAD / Mark Merickel : with technical assistance from
Rusty Gesner
      p.      cm.
   ISBN 0-934035-51-2 : $29.95
   1. AutoCAD (Computer program)    I. Gesner, Rusty.   II. Title.
T385.M439  1989
620'.00425'02855369--dc20
                                               89-12163
                                                 CIP
```

Warning and Disclaimer

Trademarks

About the Authors

Mark Merickel

Mark Merickel has taught drafting at the secondary and community college level for fifteen years. He has industrial training and hands-on experience with both mainframe and microcomputer-based drafting and design systems. For the last ten years, he has been a pioneer and leader in bringing CAD/CAM curriculum into public education. Mr. Merickel is a frequent guest lecturer and speaker on CAD/CAM in industrial and educational forums.

Mr. Merickel holds a B.A. in Drafting and Design, an M.A. in Industrial Technology, and secondary, vocational, and community college teaching credentials for the state of California. He is currently a Ph.D. candidate in Vocational/Technical Education at Oregon State University, Corvallis.

Rusty Gesner

B. Rustin Gesner is director of technical applications for New Riders Publishing and heads its technical office in Portland, Oregon. He is responsible for many of the New Riders books and software products. He has used AutoCAD since Version 1.1 and writes about AutoCAD from the standpoint of a long-time user.

Prior to joining New Riders, Mr. Gesner was president of CAD Northwest, Inc., Portland, Oregon, where he sold, installed, and supported AutoCAD systems. Mr. Gesner is a registered architect. Before forming CAD Northwest, he was a practicing architect in Portland. He attended the College of Design, Art and Architecture at the University of Cincinnati, and Antioch College.

Acknowledgments

Thank you, Colleen, for the editing and support that make my writing efforts worthwhile.

Thanks to Autodesk, and especially to Joe Oakey, manager of the educational department, for continuing encouragement and support.

Thank you to Richard Erickson of Hayward, California, for assistance with geometric dimensioning and tolerancing (GDT), and ANSI Y14.5 technical support.

Thanks to Dorothy Kent for allowing us to use command definition material from the AutoCAD REFERENCE GUIDE.

Thanks also to Rusty Gesner for text contributions and technical editing, to Pat Haessly for ANSI Y14.5 Menu System and AutoLISP development, to Christine Steel for text editing and page layout, and to Kevin Coleman for illustration and testing. Special thanks to Cliff Schatz for reviewing exercises and ANSI Y14.5 standards.

STEPPING INTO AutoCAD was designed and illustrated using Microsoft Word, provided by Microsoft Corporation; Xerox Ventura Publisher, provided by the Xerox Corporation; and AutoCAD, provided by Autodesk. Pages were output on a NEC LC890 Postscript laser printer. Cyco International provided Flying Dutchman (file transfer software) and AutoManager (drawing management and viewing software). Symsoft provided copies of Hotshot and Hotshot Plus. KETIV Technologies, Inc., provided other invaluable computing equipment.

Production

Lead Editor: Christine Steel
Technical Editor: Rusty Gesner
Page Design: Christine Steel, Carolyn Porter
Illustration: Kevin Coleman
Paste-Up: Todd Meisler
SIA Disk Development: Pat Haessly, Rusty Gesner, Ken Billing

Table of Contents

CHAPTER 3   Prototype Drawings

PART II. DRAFTING IN TWO DIMENSIONS

CHAPTER 4   2D Drafting and Dimensioning

APPENDIX C   AutoCAD SYSTEM VARIABLES

APPENDIX D   AutoCAD Command List

Introduction

STEPPING INTO AutoCAD is designed to assist the technical drafter with quickly putting AutoCAD to work. With each release, AutoCAD becomes more powerful. This book is your guide to efficiently and productively using its many tools, options, and techniques.

Using AutoCAD for Technical Drafting and Design

The goal of a drafter or designer is to communicate ideas clearly. To avoid ambiguity and resulting production errors, drafters and designers need to be able to accurately use the tools of the trade to convey design intent. AutoCAD and this book are two important tools in producing superior drawings with minimal effort.

STEPPING INTO AutoCAD assists you with choosing the right tool for the job, whether you are doing traditional two-dimensional drafting or three-dimensional design and modeling.

2D vs. 3D — Choosing the Right Tool for the Job

AutoCAD offers an extremely wide variety of commands. With a little practice, you will soon be using simple AutoCAD drafting techniques to develop projects in both two and three dimensions. Besides speed and efficiency, the decision of whether to draw in 2D or 3D should be based on factors such as:

- Whether the drawing conveys technical or visual information;

- Whether parts are being designed as well as drafted; and

- Whether the drawing information will be used in post-processing operations, such as N.C. machining or rendering with AutoShade.

If a simple two-dimensional drawing will do the job, why spend the time generating three-dimensional drawings? On the other hand, if three dimensions are useful, then use them. STEPPING INTO AutoCAD will guide you through commands and drafting techniques for 2D, 3D, and various combinations of both.

STEPPING INTO AutoCAD and GDT

In two dimensional drafting, geometric dimensioning and tolerancing (GDT) is essential to communicating the design concept.

STEPPING INTO AutoCAD has a strong emphasis on the use of GDT according to ANSI Y14.5M-1982 standards and accepted industry practice. Our discussion of GDT includes how to use and customize AutoCAD's dimensioning according to industry standards, how to create and use GDT symbols, and how to automate the process of doing GDT with our optional menu system (more about that later).

How the Book Is Organized

STEPPING INTO AutoCAD is a hands-on tutorial. It is designed to teach you how to use AutoCAD for production machine drafting, engineering drawing, and related disciplines. It is organized to guide you through operations that demonstrate the command "tools" and techniques you would use to complete a typical technical project.

You can work through the book from cover to cover or, if you are an experienced AutoCAD user, you may wish to skip around and choose sections containing information which is new to you.

STEPPING INTO AutoCAD has four major parts and four appendices:

Part I

ORGANIZING AutoCAD provides you with the basics for organizing an AutoCAD workstation for engineering drafting and design. It begins with a discussion of equipment and operating systems and goes on to introduce the basic AutoCAD commands. In Part I, you'll learn how to set up a prototype drawing as a foundation for future drawings.

Part II

DRAFTING IN TWO DIMENSIONS shows you how to create, edit, and dimension 2D drawings. It discuses setting up 2D production drafting projects, using AutoCAD's drafting command tools to develop production drawings, developing a library of standard drafting symbols, and dimensioning and tolerancing engineering drawings in keeping with ANSI Y14.5M-1982 industrial dimensioning standards.

Part III

DRAFTING IN THREE DIMENSIONS covers 3D extrusion drafting (sometimes called 2-1/2D), and introduces 3D use of the user coordinate system. Part III applies AutoCAD to designing 3D models with polygon mesh surface techniques, then shows you how to capture and assemble 2D drawings from 3D images.

Part IV

CUSTOMIZING AutoCAD explains how to install and use the Y14.5 Menu System (from the book's companion disk) to do GDT in your production work, and points you down the road to further AutoCAD customization for even greater productivity.

APPENDICES

Appendix A contains a brief explanation of MS-DOS commands, file handling, AUTOEXEC.BAT and other batch files, and text editor selection. Appendix B covers tips and problems with setup, memory, and errors you may encounter. Appendix C is a useful, annotated table of AutoCAD's system variables. Appendix D contains brief descriptions of all AutoCAD commands, and a few AutoLISP-defined 3D commands.

Read This — It's Important

We've tried hard to make STEPPING INTO AutoCAD as easy to use and follow as possible. To avoid errors and misunderstandings, we recommend that you read the following sections before jumping into the book.

How Exercises Are Shown

The sample exercise which follows demonstrates our format for commands and instructions. Exercises use the full width of the page, with commands, instructions, and computer feedback (prompts) positioned at the left margin. In the sequence presented below, commands or operations which you are expected to enter are shown in bold text. Since commands may be entered in various ways (keyboard, screen menus, pull-down menus, and tablet menus, to name a few), the command name is shown following the Command: prompt as if it were entered from the keyboard. This should not restrict the way you enter commands; you may type them or use a menu. It is only intended to provide you with the command name used at that point in the exercise. When we *want* you to use a menu, the menu label is shown as in the Select [DRAW] [DTEXT] example below.

Prompts which follow the commands are shown as they will appear on the screen, although for simple commands and repetitive sequences, the command dialogue may be abbreviated, or replaced with a simple instruction. For example, object selection sequences are often abbreviated as a single Select objects: prompt and an instruction.

Example Exercise

```
Command: LINE
from point:                            Toggle <F9> on, pick point ①.
To point:                              Toggle <F8> on, pick point ②.
To point: @2,0                         Enter coordinate value.
To point: <RETURN>                     To Command prompt.
Command:

Select [DRAW] [DTEXT]                  Select from menu.
DTEXT Start point or Align/Center/Fit/Middle/Right/Style:    Pick point ③.
Height <0.20>: .4
Rotation angle <0>: <RETURN>
Text: NOTES, UNLESS OTHERWISE SPECIFIED:    Enter text.
Text: <RETURN>
```

Input that you should type is shown in bold. For readability, we show leading zeros on numbers in the text, like 0.5, however you should omit the leading zeros when you input to AutoCAD, like the .4 shown above.

The section to the right of the commands and prompts is reserved for our comments and instructions. They are for your information in completing the command and are not intended to be entered literally.

All you need to do in an exercise is to follow the command sequence, refer to the in-line instructions, and input any text shown in bold. The <RETURN> is shown only where there is no other input, but we assume you will use returns as needed to enter your input. Keys are presented like <^D> for the Control-D combination, or <F6> for function key six.

Exercises are accompanied by illustrations and *screen shots* of what you should see on your screen at key points. Bubbles like ① are shown in many illustrations to refer to key points or positions on the exercise drawing. An example of an illustration bubble is shown below.

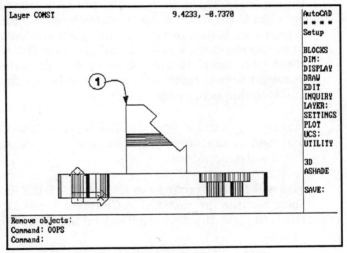

Sample Screen Shot With Bubble Icon

In most cases, STEPPING INTO AutoCAD allows you to jump from chapter to chapter, especially if you have the SIA DISK. But there are a few operations which need to be done in earlier chapters so that later exercises will work properly. These are identified in the text. In particular, you need to start with the setup sections of Chapter 1.

Things to Watch For

The printing font used in the exercises and program listings doesn't distinguish clearly between zero and the letter O, or the number one and lower case letter L. You need to watch these closely:

0   This is a zero.
O   This is an upper case letter O.
1   This is the number one.
l   This is a lower case letter L.

The Optional STEPPING INTO AutoCAD Drafting Disk

To help you save time and effort, we offer an optional SIA DISK with this edition of STEPPING INTO AutoCAD. The disk contains both the customized ANSI Y14.5 Menu System and completed drawing files from the exercises. These drawing files can save you valuable time and let you get right to the heart of the exercises by eliminating repetitive or tedious setup tasks. Some exercises in later chapters depend on drawings created in earlier chapters. The SIA DISK gives you the option of being able to do these later exercises using drawing files from the SIA DISK. This way, you don't have to spend time making drawings that teach you commands and techniques you may already know.

However, you do not need the disk to work through the book. The book is designed so that every exercise can be performed by a new user in a step-by-step approach.

You will find an order form for the SIA DISK in the back pages of the book. See the instructions in Chapters 1 and 12 for installing the SIA DISK to make the drawing files and the Y14.5 Menu System files ready to use.

How to Use the SIA DISK's Exercise Drawings

Exercises which use pre-developed drawings from the SIA DISK are designated in the exercise description. The exercises provide simple icons, shown in the sequence below, telling you when to use files from the SIA DISK.

Do "this" if you have the SI DISK. This is the *disk* icon.

 Do "this" if you do not have the SI DISK. This is the *no-disk* icon.

The Y14.5 Menu System

The SIA DISK also contains the Y14.5 Menu System. The system's geometric dimensioning and tolerancing tools simplify drawing setup and enable you to draft and dimension according to the ANSI Y14.5M-1982 standards. The Y14.5 Menu System lets you set decimal precision, limits, tolerances, and generate ANSI Y14.5 symbols in both decimal inch and SI metric standards.

The Y14.5 Menu System uses screen menus, tablet menu, pull-down menus, or any combination of these menus. Whichever your system supports, you will increase your drafting productivity with the drafting functions and AutoLISP routines available on the SIA DISK's Y14.5 program.

Prerequisites for STEPPING INTO AutoCAD

Although this book has been written for a wide range of AutoCAD users, there are a few considerations which should be followed.

DOS Version

We recommend that you use PC or MS-DOS 3.0, or later.

UNIX, Macintosh, and Other Operating Systems

AutoCAD is designed so that all of its drawing and support files are compatible with every system capable of running AutoCAD. No special files or preparations should be necessary if you have an operating system other than PC or MS-DOS, except you will need a DOS system to copy the files from the SIA DISK. STEPPING INTO AutoCAD has not been tested on other operating systems, but because all of AutoCAD's files are compatible with any system running AutoCAD, it should work with little trouble. The exercises are shown in DOS format; if you are working on another operating system, your prompts or file handling procedures will vary.

AutoCAD Version and Equipment

You do not need a fast and fancy system to run AutoCAD. However, if your system is not running at IBM-AT speed or faster, you may find some operations a little slower than you like. This especially applies to the 3D polygon mesh surface models. You will need 640K of RAM. A mouse or digitizing tablet is virtually essential.

Run the following sequence in AutoCAD to check your version, and to verify that AutoLISP is enabled for the setup and Y14.5 Menu System exercises.

Checking Your AutoCAD Version

```
Command: (ver)
"AutoLISP Release 10.0"
```
Type (ver) and enter a <RETURN>.
Or your version number.

➡ *NOTE: If you got a bad command message, check to see that AutoLISP is not disabled by insufficient memory, or by the AutoLISP option on the configuration menu under "Configure operating parameters."*

If you have a release that is earlier than AutoCAD Release 10, don't be alarmed. Most STEPPING INTO AutoCAD exercises are compatible with Release 9. But you will see some discrepancies and you will have to substitute some of the following commands and techniques:

Use VIEW and ZOOM in place of multiple viewports.

Use CHANGE in lieu of CHPROP commands.

Recalculate your coordinates to compensate for offset UCS's where used (this should not be necessary for the slight offset of the BDR UCS).

Other Release 9 alternatives are included in Chapter 9 on 3D, but Chapters 10 and 11 require Release 10 or later.

If you wish to use the Y14.5 Menu System with earlier versions of AutoCAD, it may be necessary for you to edit some menu functions and revise commands such as CHPROP.

Earlier editions of STEPPING INTO AutoCAD for AutoCAD versions earlier than Release 9 are available from New Riders Publishing.

Stepping Right In

Let's step right into AutoCAD by turning to Chapter 1 and organizing your DOS system environment for productive drafting.

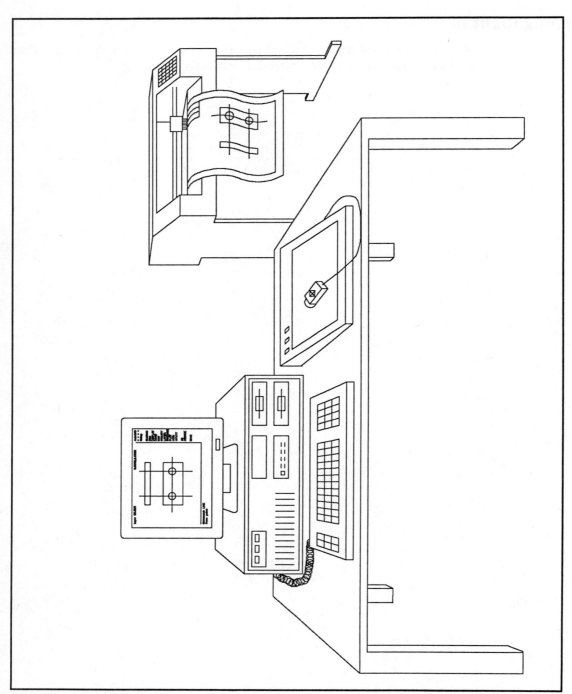

Typical AutoCAD Workstation

CHAPTER 1

System Management

GETTING TO KNOW YOUR WORKSTATION

AutoCAD is a computer-aided drafting (CAD) tool with which you can design and draft virtually any object. The more you use AutoCAD, the more you will realize its power. AutoCAD's power and your drafting skills provide two variables for efficient production drafting. A third variable is system management. Managing your AutoCAD working environment is the key to drafting productivity. No matter how fast or creative you are, you will never realize the full potential of AutoCAD without good system setup and management.

This chapter discusses the parts of an AutoCAD workstation (platform) typically used for production drafting and design. We'll show you how to set up your Disk Operating System (DOS) and AutoCAD drafting environments. We'll also provide instructions for loading the optional STEPPING INTO AutoCAD Disk (SIA DISK). The SIA DISK contains drawing files to make our exercises easier, and includes a production ANSI Y14.5 menu system with all the macros, symbols, and dimensioning tools you need to perform standard ANSI Y14.5 drafting. More about the SIA DISK and how to order it is in our Introduction.

A Typical AutoCAD System

AutoCAD can be used on many different workstation configurations. As the number of AutoCAD-supported workstations increases, so does the number of available options. We happened to develop this book on a 386-based computer, but STEPPING INTO AutoCAD can be used with any of the computers that support AutoCAD Release 10. Most of the exercises (except for those in 3D) will also work on any computer that operates AutoCAD Release 9. Let's look at some typical AutoCAD production drafting workstations.

AutoCAD on DOS-Based Systems

The 16-bit IBM-AT and compatibles, and the 32-bit Intel 80386 microprocessor-based computers which run PC-DOS or MS-DOS operating systems are the most widely used systems for computer-aided drafting. The IBM-AT class machines have been the traditional workhorses of production drafting. However, as costs fall and the need for processing power increases, 386-based machines (which are up to four times faster than the IBM-AT) have become the main micro-CAD platform.

AutoCAD on UNIX-Based Systems

Engineering workstations, like the SUN 3, SPARCstation, and 386i, are becoming popular AutoCAD industrial drafting and design platforms. These computers run a variety of 32-bit micro-processors, from the Intel 80386, to the Motorola 68020 and 68030, to specialized RISC processors. They use UNIX, a multi-tasking operating system which is not limited to the current 640K RAM (Random Access Memory) constraints of MS-DOS. These UNIX platforms are powerful, flexible, and fast, but the UNIX operating system is more complex than good old MS-DOS.

AutoCAD has also been ported to Xenix 386, a type of UNIX that can run AutoCAD on 386-based AT compatibles much faster than the DOS version.

AutoCAD on Other Operating Systems

AutoCAD has been ported to several other hardware/operating system combinations. These include IBM's Operating System/2 (OS/2), the Macintosh II, DEC VMS, and Apollo AEGIS. Although the operating systems and user environments of these platforms can differ substantially, AutoCAD looks and performs nearly identically on each one. And AutoCAD Release 10's binary file format allows access to files between these systems without the need for file conversion.

General System Components

In addition to a processor, your computer needs a math co-processor and sufficient RAM to run AutoCAD. The co-processor should match the processor in type and speed. RAM requirements vary with the operating system. DOS requires at least 640K, but you'll see an improvement in performance with one to four Mb of additional RAM. Other operating systems need two to eight Mb of RAM. See your AutoCAD Installation and Performance Guide for more information and performance tips.

Your computer also needs a hard disk with at least 20 Mb of space for DOS and up to 100 Mb for UNIX, depending on your flavor of UNIX. If you don't have a lot of RAM, a fast disk access time (less than 30 milliseconds) will noticeably improve AutoCAD's performance.

A typical micro-CAD workstation also needs input and output devices. The absolute minimum is a mouse and a video graphics display. Options include a digitizer tablet and a plotter or printer. The components of the CAD workstation may vary in their general appearance, but their functions remain the same. A typical configuration is shown at the beginning of the chapter.

Let's look briefly at the workstation components, starting with the display.

Graphic Controllers and Displays

The main output device is the video display screen which shows the graphics and text produced with the computer. The screen displays your AutoCAD drawing along with the screen menu area where you can select drawing commands.

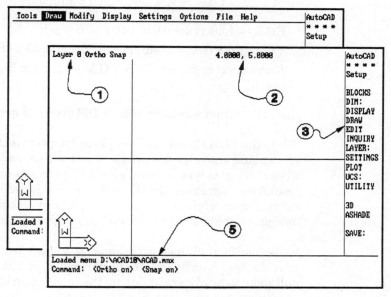

Typical AutoCAD Screen Display

The illustration is annotated to show the:

① ② Status line, which displays status and coordinate information,

③ Screen menu,

④ Pull-down menu bar, which accesses pull-down menus, icon menus, and dialogue boxes, and the

⑤ Command line(s).

We'll examine the elements of the AutoCAD screen in detail later, but for now, let's focus on the display hardware. The display has two components: the video card (often called a video graphics controller) that generates the image; and the video display (often called a monitor) that displays the image. These components must be matched to each other's capabilities.

Display Resolution

The resolution of the video card determines the quality of the image you see on your system's display. Screen resolutions are measured in dots (pixels) along the X and Y axes. AutoCAD supports video cards exceeding 1024 x 1024 pixel resolution. Some common resolutions are:

EGA — Low resolution, 640 x 350 pixels.

VGA and **PGA** — Medium resolution, 640 x 480 pixels.

Enhanced or *Super* **EGA/VGA** — Medium high resolution, 800 x 600 pixels.

High resolution would be 1024 x 768 pixels or greater.

While the EGA (Enhanced Graphics Adaptor) is the minimum resolution you should consider for production drafting and design applications, a VGA card costs no more and yields 37 percent greater resolution. Higher resolution increases detail, reduces the jaggedness of diagonals and curves, and eliminates many pans and zooms. Most drafters and designers prefer medium to medium-high resolution.

Video cards that use a technology known as *display list processing* provide significantly greater performance, but at a higher cost. They pan and zoom in hardware, reducing the calculations that AutoCAD performs to display images.

Some video cards require (or offer the option of) a two-monitor display, where one monitor displays text and the other displays graphics. Two monitors can increase your efficiency if you find yourself flipping frequently between the AutoCAD text and graphics screens.

As the types of microcomputer-produced graphics continue to increase, so do the video formats which drive these graphics. Your monitor must match the output format of your video card. The easiest way to accomplish this is with the handy-dandy one-monitor-fits-all display.

Autosync Monitors

The autosync monitor is a device which does not require you to closely match input bandwidths and synchronization rates. Instead, an autosync monitor analyzes the video signal received and, if it is within its range, adjusts to match the graphics card. Besides simplifying your choices, this makes it possible for you to upgrade your video card without having to change your monitor.

If you do not use an autosync monitor, you will have to be careful to match the specifications of your monitor with those of your video card.

Ghosting or Cursor Trails

All monitors with the same display resolution are not necessarily created equal. When monitors are used for production drafting, you should make every attempt to use those which minimize eye strain. Two causes of eye strain are phosphor persistence and flickering. Unfortunately, these are conflicting problems and the cure for one makes the other worse. Phosphor persistence or ghosting is when a moving cursor *smears* or leaves a *cursor trail* in its wake. This can be bothersome when you spend a lot of time tracking cursor positions across the screen.

You will find flicker most noticeable when you look at the monitor out of the corner of your eye. Flicker is worsened by *interlaced* video, a technology that increases resolution at low cost. Interlaced displays usually compensate by increasing the scan rate or by using long-persistence phosphors which increase cursor smear. It is impossible to find a monitor which does not flicker, but try to select a display with the least amount of flicker and an acceptable amount of cursor smearing.

AutoCAD's Advanced User Interface

AutoCAD's Release 10 AUI (Advanced User Interface) is required for pull-down menus, icon menus, and dialogue boxes. These AUI features make AutoCAD's drawing and editing commands easier to access. If you are setting up an AutoCAD workstation, we recommend that you choose a graphics card which supports the AUI. However, the AUI is not necessary for use with STEPPING INTO AutoCAD. You can use this book with either the standard AutoCAD screen menu interface or with the AUI.

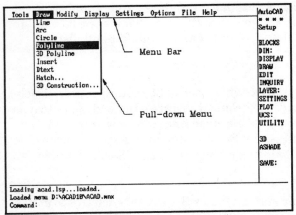

AutoCAD's AUI Pull-Down Menu

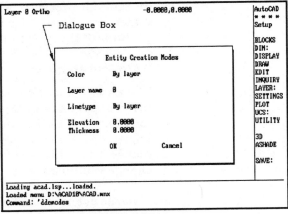

AutoCAD's AUI Dialogue Box

You can tell whether your workstation supports the AUI by checking the POPUPS system variable (type SETVAR POPUPS<RETURN> in AutoCAD). If POPUPS is 1, you can use AUI features; if it is 0, you need an ADI driver to get AUI. Many graphics controllers provide support for AutoCAD's AUI through ADI drivers. ADI is a generic device interface supported by AutoCAD which requires drivers supplied by the hardware manufacturer. Some third-party developers also provide ADI drivers for older video boards; ask your dealer. An ADI version 4.0 or later driver will also improve the performance of AutoCAD's multiple viewport windows.

➡ *NOTE: Some ADI drivers, particularly older ones, do not (or cannot) support AUI. Check before you buy.*

Input Devices

The keyboard is the most familiar input device. You will spend most of your time at a CAD workstation using it and other input devices such as a digitizer or mouse.

Keyboard

You can use the workstation's keyboard to enter drawing commands or text. You also can use the keyboard to enter precise data, such as coordinates or dimensions. AutoCAD supports several shortcut toggle

and function keys for quick access to frequently used features. The keys used for these features vary with the system; however, the IBM-style assignments are the most common. (See your AutoCAD Installation and Performance Guide if you do not have an IBM or compatible system.) AutoCAD has assigned these features to the following function and control keys:

FLIP SCREEN — <F1> controls AutoCAD's flip screen function. Flip screen toggles between AutoCAD's graphics and text screens. If you need to check the data you have entered into AutoCAD, you can toggle to the text screen and the information will be displayed.

COORDS — <F6> or <^D> controls coordinate display, toggling the status line's coordinate read-out on and off. When on, the coordinate read-out continually changes, displaying the current location of your drawing cursor (the two perpendicularly crossed lines that follow the movements of your pointing device).

GRID — <F7> or <^G> controls a grid display made up of an array of dots on the screen that act like electronic graph paper.

ORTHO — <F8> or <^O> controls an *orthographic* drawing function, an aid for drawing lines. When ortho is toggled on, you can draw only horizontal or vertical lines.

SNAP — <F9> or <^B> controls a *snap to* drawing aid. When snap is on, it constrains the cursor to moving in precise increments.

TABLET — <F10> or <^T> toggles the tablet between tracing mode and the normal screen-pointing drawing mode.

DELETE — <^X> is the delete key and cancels the current input, allowing you to re-enter your input.

CANCEL — <^C> cancels commands. One to three <^C>s will get you out of any AutoCAD command.

The Control key is used in combination with other keys. These are abbreviated like <^D>, read Control-D, which means hold down the Control key while you strike the letter D.

Using the Numeric Pad for Cursor Control

Although you usually control your drawing cursor with your mouse or digitizer pointing device, it is possible to control your drawing cursor with keys on the keyboard. These keys are located on the numeric keypad at the right of the IBM keyboard:

MENU — <INS> toggles screen menu (not pull-down) cursor control over to the cursor keys on or adjacent to the numeric keypad.

SCREEN — **<HOME>** toggles screen drawing cursor control over to the cursor keys on or adjacent to the numeric keypad.

ABORT — **<END>** returns cursor control to the mouse or digitizer pointing device.

← → ↑ ↓ — are the arrow direction keys that move the cursor.

FAST SLOW — **<PG-UP>** and **<PG-DOWN>** increase or decrease screen drawing cursor speed.

When you have positioned your cursor with these keys, use the <RETURN> key to enter it.

Mice and Digitizer Tablets

The mouse is a fairly inexpensive input device which controls the AutoCAD cursor. Most mice provide one to three buttons which you use for cursor and command interaction. The left-most (or only) button is the *pick* button. It enters a point or selects a menu item. The other buttons are controlled by the AutoCAD menu. Generally, the button on the right performs a <RETURN> just as the keyboard would, and the middle button, if used, pulls down POP1, the first pull-down menu.

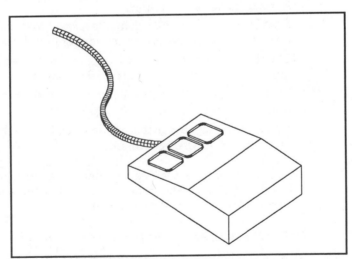

Typical Mouse

The digitizer is an electronic drawing board. The digitizer's pointing device tracks positions and sends signals to direct the drawing screen's cursor. Most digitizers come with either a *stylus* or a *puck* with three to sixteen selection buttons. Both of these pointing devices give you cursor control. The button functions are controlled by the AutoCAD menu.

AutoCAD provides a tablet menu template which may be attached to the digitizer's surface. You can use the tablet to pick graphic points and to *select* AutoCAD drawing and editing commands. You can further enhance the AutoCAD menu with customized menus like the Y14.5 tablet menu on the SIA DISK. You will need either a digitizer tablet or AUI support to use the Y14.5 menu.

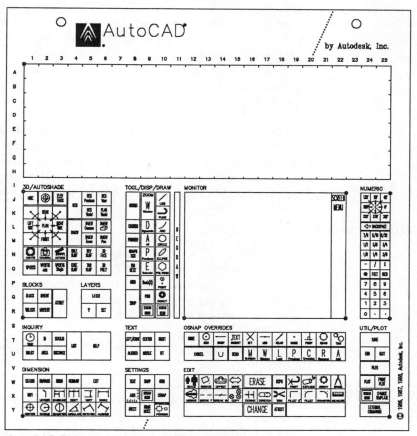

AutoCAD Release 10 Standard Tablet Menu

The advantage of using a digitizer as a pointing device is that AutoCAD commands, as well as drawing symbols, can be located on the tablet menu along with the screen drawing area. You can input your data without lifting the pointing device from the digitizer's surface. This lets you rapidly alternate between picking coordinate points and choosing commands or symbols. Also, AutoCAD's TABLET command enables you to use the digitizer tablet to trace existing drawings.

Sorting Them Out

There are a few considerations to bear in mind when selecting input devices. First, since digitizers and mice will both input data, you should select an input device based on your drafting style. Although the cost of a mouse is considerably below that of a digitizer, most drafters prefer a digitizer and stylus/puck. A digitizer is required if you must trace drawings. It has a high degree of accuracy, and supports the use of AutoCAD's tablet menu overlay, or other customized production drafting tablet overlays like the ANSI Y14.5 overlay available with this book. A few dollars saved up front may cost you far more in lost productivity. However, if you prefer keyboard and screen or pull-down menu input to tablet menus and have no need to trace, you may find a mouse to be perfectly suitable.

Like many CAD hardware components, digitizers and mice have become commodity items, so stick to proven brand names. Although most input devices support AutoCAD, not all do. The one steadfast rule for acquiring AutoCAD workstation hardware is, "Seeing is believing." If you can, try out the hardware under your actual working conditions.

Output Devices

In addition to the video display output, you need *hard copy* output. Your choice of output devices will depend on the quantity, size, and accuracy needed for your drawings. AutoCAD supports a wide variety of hard copy devices, ranging from pen plotters to dot matrix printers to laser printers. You can use any of these with our exercises.

Let's take a look at a few typical AutoCAD output devices.

Pen Plotters

Plotters output accurate hard copies of your drawings in a variety of sizes with reasonable speed and cost. The most common types of pen plotters are the flatbed (usually up to 17 x 11 inches) and the grit wheel (up to 36 x 48 inches and larger) plotters. On the flatbed, the paper is stationary while the pen moves in the X and Y axes. On the grit wheel plotter, the grit wheels move the paper forward and back, perpendicular to the pen's side-to-side movement.

The plotter is truly the beast of burden in the CAD industry, turning out hard copy after hard copy. It pays to purchase a plotter with a proven track record. You need to weigh plotter cost against the line quality, speed, and the number and type of pens. No matter what the cost of the plotter, test your potential purchase by using it to plot a benchmark drawing. Consider the following factors when you evaluate plotters:

- Accuracy

- Resolution

- Repeatability

- Maximum pen speed

- Pen acceleration (time to reach maximum speed)

- Pen down delay (time for ink to flow before accelerating)

Acceleration is usually more important than maximum speed, since most pen and media combinations do not plot well at high speeds.

Pens

Whether you are using single or multiple pen plotters, the pens you use must work properly to perform the plotting job. Many types of plotter pens are available, from disposable to jewel-tipped. The pens you choose will depend on your management style and on which pens are available for your plotter. Here are some common plotter pen types:

Ceramic Disposable Pens — moderate cost, good quality, durable, consistent at slow speeds, paper or mylar.

Felt Tip Pens — low cost, good check plot pens, paper only.

Fiber Tip Pens — low cost, consistent at moderate speeds, good check plot pens, paper only.

Disposable Liquid Ink Pens — moderate cost, very good quality, consistent at moderate speeds, paper or mylar.

Roller Ball Pens — low cost, good quality, consistent at moderate speeds, paper only.

Pressurized Ballpoint Pens — fast, consistent on most media, long life, trouble-free, available for few plotters.

Refillable Liquid Ink Pens — user care and maintenance required for consistent plots, high initial cost (jewelled tips preferable) but moderate cost with reuse, best quality, paper or mylar.

When you configure AutoCAD for plotting, you can set pen speed to match the pen type (ink) and media used for plotting. Four inches per second (ips) is considered a slow pen speed; 16 ips is considered a moderate pen speed. Any pen speed over 20 ips is considered fast and will require pens which support rapid movement.

Printer Plotters

Printers are gaining wide acceptance in the CAD field as output devices for producing small, low-cost *check* plots. Since many CAD workstations are commonly used for other functions like word processing or spread sheet programs, printers are commonly available. Printers usable as printer plotters by AutoCAD include dot matrix, thermal, laser, and ink jet.

Dot Matrix Printers

Dot matrix printers are low cost and reliable. They produce printer plots which are inexpensive in per-sheet cost with reasonable speed. Their major drawback is resolution. Low resolutions may be acceptable for text, but produce unacceptable jagged edges for technical drawings. Dot matrix printers vary from 60 to 360 dpi (dots per inch). Most printers exceeding 200 dpi will yield satisfactory plots, but the higher resolutions generally require more time. Exceptions are printers which can be configured as plotters using ADI drivers to yield high resolution at speeds faster than pen plotters.

Ink Jet, Thermal, and Laser Printers

Non-impact printers include ink jet, thermal, and laser printers. The availability and price of non-impact printers have improved dramatically in the last few years. Laser printers are most commonly used, offering high resolution (300 to 400+ dpi). With their prices continually coming down, laser printers are an excellent output device for an AutoCAD workstation. Some laser printers emulate pen plotters, reducing the time it takes to get a drawing plotted. Ink jet printers offer color, high resolution, and reasonable cost, but at slower speeds. Thermal printers offer beautiful colors, but at lower resolutions. Whichever you choose, be sure AutoCAD supports it, or that the manufacturer provides an ADI driver.

Disks and Disk Drives

Disk drives are usually housed in the same case as the CAD workstation computer. The disk drive reads and writes information to a magnetic disk. The information on the disk can be read by the computer as many times as necessary. The computer can also write new information to the disk's unused space. You can replace old information with new information by having the computer write over it. When this occurs, the old information is permanently erased from the disk.

Hard Disk Drives

The most common device for storing data on an AutoCAD system is a hard disk. Hard disks operate in the range of millisecond access rates. The density and number of disks and read-write heads determine the data capacity of a hard disk unit. Hard disk capacity is measured in megabytes (one Mb is 1,024,000 bytes or 1000K). The capacity is steadily increasing. Today's technology offers hard disk storage in the range of 10 to 300+ Mb. We assume that you are running AutoCAD on a workstation with a hard disk and a diskette drive.

Diskettes

Removable diskettes are 3 1/2 or 5 1/4 inches in diameter and may store from 360K (low density) to 1.2 or 1.44 Mb (high density) of data. Three and one-half inch cartridge diskettes are encased in durable hard plastic, while the 5 1/4 inch floppy diskettes are flexible and require extra care in handling. It pays to handle all diskettes with caution. Bending your floppies or exposing them to heat, moisture, or magnetic forces can damage them. An individual *bit* (1/8 of a byte) of information occupies a very small portion of the disk. As a result, a scratch or even a fingerprint on the magnetic surface can cause major read or write errors.

Backup Systems

There are two typical ways to back up the data on your CAD system's hard disk. The first is to copy data files from your hard disk to diskettes. This process requires that you periodically back up selected files either by using DOS commands or by using a commercial disk backup program. If you are backing up an entire hard disk or multiple hard disks, a commercial backup program will quickly pay for itself in time saved. The second method is to use a *streaming tape cartridge* backup system. A good streaming tape cartridge system can back up a 20 Mb hard disk in approximately three minutes. When comparing backup programs or tapes, consider portability (from computer to computer), speed, and whether you can retrieve individual files or only the entire set.

Removable Mass Storage

There are also removable high capacity (10 to 44 Mb) cartridge disks, which can serve as both working media and backup. The best known of these is the Iomega Bernoulli Box.

Setting Up AutoCAD in a DOS Environment

DOS stands for Disk Operating System, either PC-DOS or MS-DOS. DOS is a collection of programs for operating your computer. These programs process commands to manage files, information, and input/output devices. DOS allows the computer to communicate with its hardware. You need DOS to set up your AutoCAD environment. Although AutoCAD performs well under DOS, it is continually fighting a 640K RAM limit imposed by MS-DOS. MS-DOS is written to directly address up to 640K of RAM. AutoCAD is a very large program, and drawing files can also get large. AutoCAD must swap portions of program code, drawings, and temporary files in and out of this 640K. When this happens, AutoCAD writes temporary disk files, slowing the performance of the system considerably. One way to avoid this problem is to add extended or expanded RAM to the workstation.

Extended and Expanded Memory

To get around the memory limitations of DOS, you can enhance your workstation by adding extended or expanded memory. Expanded memory can be added to any PC/XT, AT, 386-AT, or PS/2 class computer, however extended memory requires an AT or 386 machine. Unless you also need expanded memory for other programs, extended memory is preferable for AutoCAD. Either can be used by AutoCAD as *extended I / O page space,* to substitute for swapping data to disk. This greatly increases AutoCAD's performance. See your AutoCAD Installation and Performance Guide and the README.DOC file for information on installation and setting DOS environment variables to control this additional memory.

AutoLISP is the AutoCAD programming language used by the SIA DISK's Y14.5 menus, by many third-party programs, and even by several items on the standard AutoCAD menu. AutoLISP also competes for DOS's limited 640K of memory, using up to 128K of it. With Extended AutoLISP (Release 10), you can load AutoLISP into extended (but not expanded) RAM. This prevents AutoLISP from running out of RAM, and speeds it up by eliminating swapping. Extended AutoLISP has a fringe benefit — it uses about 80K *less* of the 640K RAM than normal AutoLISP, freeing up more memory for the rest of AutoCAD. See your AutoCAD Installation and Performance Guide for more information.

There are several ways to set up a hard disk. The following information will help you set up your hard disk to run AutoCAD.

Loading DOS Programs on a Hard Disk

We assume that your hard disk has been installed, formatted, and contains the DOS *system* files needed to *boot* DOS from the hard disk. This means that when you turn on the computer (with the diskette drive empty), the C> or C:\> DOS command prompt appears. In addition to system files, DOS includes utility programs (external commands) like FORMAT and DISKCOPY. These should be in a subdirectory named C:\DOS (or a name of your preference) that is on your *path* (a path setting which tells DOS what directories to search for programs and external commands). We also assume that you are familiar with directories, subdirectories, and the following DOS commands:

DIR — lists files and subdirectories

COPY — copies files

COMP — compares files

DISKCOPY — copies diskette

DISKCOMP — compares diskette

FORMAT — formats (prepares) disk for data

MD — makes directory (subdirectory)

CD — displays current directory

CD *name* — changes to directory *name*

If you do not have a directory on your path which contains the DOS utility files, make a subdirectory and copy the DOS files into it from the DOS diskette. The path is one of several settings made by two files that the computer reads when it starts up. These are the CONFIG.SYS and AUTOEXEC.BAT files. You need to verify several settings in these files and modify them if necessary. You can modify them with the DOS EDLIN text editor, or any other text editor that produces plain ASCII files such as Norton's Editor. Most word processors have an ASCII *non-formatted* or *non-document* mode. We will assume that you have a program editor available. If you do not have an ASCII editor available, or if you are not sure that your editor is suitable, see Appendix A for information on selecting and testing text editors. Appendix A also shows an alternative COPY CON method for creating text files.

If you are unfamiliar with these DOS concepts and commands, see Appendix A and your DOS manual for more information. Refer to Appendix B for tips on troubleshooting problems.

For STEPPING INTO AutoCAD, you will need a CONFIG.SYS file and an AUTOEXEC.BAT file containing the lines shown in the next section. (These files apply only to DOS systems.)

The CONFIG.SYS File

The CONFIG.SYS file installs *device drivers* that tell the computer how to talk to devices, including RAM disks, expanded memory, and some disk drives and video cards. It also includes instructions that will improve your system's performance and increase your environment space for customization.

The CONFIG.SYS file must be located in the root directory so it will be read automatically when your computer boots up. You may never even know it is there. If you have a CONFIG.SYS file, check and modify it if needed. If you don't have one, create one. Your file should include the following lines:

```
BUFFERS=32
FILES=24
SHELL=C:\COMMAND.COM /P /E:512
```

CONFIG.SYS

The BUFFERS line allocates more RAM to hold your recently used data. Use a number from 20 to 48. The FILES line allocates more RAM to keep recently used files open. This reduces directory searching and increases data access speed. The SHELL line ensures adequate space for DOS environment variables. The /E:512 is for DOS 3.2 or 3.3. Substitute /E:32 for DOS 3.1 or 3.0. The SHELL and FILES lines are required to give enough environment and file space for this book's setup. The numbers for FILES and BUFFERS are minimal, and larger values may improve disk performance even more. However larger values decrease the RAM available to AutoCAD and other functions, so you may have to compromise, particularly if you get Out of RAM errors with AutoCAD, or cannot load AutoLISP.

AUTOEXEC.BAT

The AUTOEXEC.BAT file will automatically set up your system when you turn the computer on. At their simplest, DOS batch files are lines of commands that are executed as if typed at the DOS command prompt. Like CONFIG.SYS, AUTOEXEC.BAT must be in the root directory. Examine your AUTOEXEC.BAT file. It should contain the following lines:

```
PROMPT $P$G
PATH C:\;C:\DOS;
```

AUTOEXEC.BAT

PROMPT PG causes the DOS prompt to display your current directory path such as C:\ACAD> instead of C>, so you don't get lost in subdirectories.

PATH is essential for automatic directory access to programs and DOS commands. The C:\ root and C:\DOS paths are needed for this book's setup. Each path is separated by a semicolon. If your DOS files are in a different directory, substitute your directory name. You should use whatever is relevant to your setup. Your path will probably contain additional directories.

If your AUTOEXEC.BAT doesn't include prompt and path lines, edit or create the file in your root directory.

➤ *NOTE: The CONFIG.SYS and AUTOEXEC.BAT changes will not take effect until you reboot your computer. If you changed or created these files, test them by either warm booting (pushing the <Ctrl>, <Alt>, and <Del> keys simultaneously) or by turning the computer off and then restarting it.*

Setting Up AutoCAD

The AutoCAD program comes on several diskettes. These program disks (except for the sample drawings and programs on the Bonus Disk) must be copied onto your formatted hard disk to run AutoCAD.

Creating a Subdirectory for AutoCAD

The best method for managing a hard disk is to keep your root directory small and to organize your data and program files in some logical order. We recommend keeping your AutoCAD files in a subdirectory. Here is how to create one.

Making an AutoCAD Subdirectory

```
C:\> MD \ACAD       Makes the directory.
C:\> CD \ACAD       Changes the current subdirectory to \ACAD.
C:\ACAD>
```

The PROMPT PG in your AUTOEXEC.BAT causes the prompt to show the directory, like C:\ACAD>.

If you do not already have AutoCAD copied to and configured in your ACAD directory, do so now. See your AutoCAD Installation and

Performance Guide for complete instructions. Once you have the AutoCAD program files in the ACAD subdirectory of your hard drive, the files will remain when you turn the computer off.

Configuring AutoCAD

When you enter ACAD for the first time, AutoCAD will tell you that it is not yet configured and will prompt you through its configuration menu. Step through the configuration menus and menu options as they are presented, and select the hardware devices which make up your workstation. If you have any difficulty with this process, see your AutoCAD Installation and Performance Guide for more information. If you use an ADI device driver, see the manufacturer's instructions.

Starting AutoCAD

If you have just installed and configured AutoCAD, test it with the following. If you have previously installed and configured it, skip this test. For this test, we'll change to the \ACAD subdirectory first, then start AutoCAD.

Starting AutoCAD

C:\> **CD \ACAD**	Change current directory to \ACAD.
C:\ACAD> **ACAD**	Start AutoCAD.

You can start AutoCAD from any directory by typing \ACAD\ACAD, assuming your AutoCAD program directory is named ACAD. (If not, substitute your AutoCAD directory, such as \ACAD10\ACAD if your directory is named ACAD10.)

If it has been configured, the AutoCAD program first displays the main menu. The main menu lets you create new or edit existing drawings, plot drawings, install (configure) AutoCAD, and gives you several utility options.

```
              A U T O C A D
Copyright (C) 1982,83,84,85,86,87,88 Autodesk, Inc.
Release 10 c2 (99/99/99) IBM PC
Advanced Drafting Extensions 3
Serial Number:  99-999999

Main Menu

   0.  Exit AutoCAD
   1.  Begin a NEW drawing
   2.  Edit an EXISTING drawing
   3.  Plot a drawing
   4.  Printer Plot a drawing

   5.  Configure AutoCAD
   6.  File Utilities
   7.  Compile shape/font description file
   8.  Convert old drawing file

Enter selection: 1

Enter NAME of drawing: TEST
```

Main Menu With Option 1 Selected

We'll come back later and explore the main menu options; for now let's jump right into the drawing editor by selecting option 1 from the main menu. Call your first drawing TEST and AutoCAD will put you into the drawing editor. AutoCAD drawings have names like TEST.DWG, but AutoCAD supplies the file name's .DWG extension. You can use characters, numbers, and most symbols in your drawing names, but avoid using spaces.

Creating a New Drawing

`Enter selection:` **1**	The first main menu selection.
`Enter NAME of drawing:` **TEST**	
	The AutoCAD drawing screen appears.
	Play around and try a few commands if you like. Read the following explanation before you end with the QUIT command.
`Command:` **QUIT**	Exits to the main menu without saving the drawing.

AutoCAD's first screen in the drawing editor displays an area for drawing graphics, with a screen menu running down the right side. The initial screen menu is called the root menu. If you look at the bottom of the AutoCAD screen, you'll see a `Command:` prompt line. This is AutoCAD's communication channel, where you can enter commands and read messages from AutoCAD.

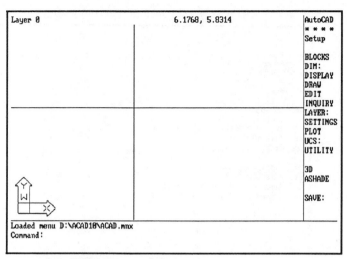

AutoCAD Screen With Crosshairs

As you move your pointing device across the desk top or pad, the crosshairs on the screen move too. When you move the crosshairs into the menu area, a menu item lights up.

If you have just installed and configured ACAD, and you have a digitizer tablet, use the AutoCAD TABLET command's CFG option to configure the tablet menu. See Chapter 12 for instructions.

If everything is working, let's set up for using the book.

Setting Up for STEPPING INTO AutoCAD

STEPPING INTO AutoCAD's exercises and the optional SIA DISK are designed so that you can work through the book's exercises without interfering with your normal AutoCAD setup and workflow. To avoid potential conflict, you'll need to set up a separate directory and AutoCAD configuration for our exercises.

Let's create the SI-ACAD subdirectory.

Making the SI-ACAD Subdirectory

C:\ACAD> **CD **	Changes to the root directory.
C:\> **MD SI-ACAD**	Creates the STEPPING INTO AutoCAD subdirectory.
C:\> **CD SI-ACAD**	Makes SI-ACAD the current directory.
C:\SI-ACAD>	

The SI-ACAD Subdirectory in a UNIX Environment

On a UNIX system, create the SI-ACAD subdirectory in your *home directory*. Throughout the book, you will have to substitute appropriate UNIX commands and paths for the DOS commands and paths shown. The following table shows UNIX and DOS equivalents.

DOS	UNIX	Purpose
CD \	cd ~	Change to root (DOS) or home (UNIX) directory.
MD \SI-ACAD	mkdir ~/si-acad	Make book's directory.
DIR filename	ls -l filename	List directory for filename.
DIR *.	ls -d */	List directories.

Some UNIX systems may vary from these examples. Depending on your system, AutoCAD may be installed in /usr/acad, /files/acad, or ~acad directories. Check with your UNIX system administrator if you aren't sure how AutoCAD is set up.

DOS doesn't care whether file names are upper or lower case, but UNIX file names are case-sensitive. Most UNIX file names are lower case. If you use UNIX, input your file names in lower case letters.

If you are using a UNIX text editor, you will find that the SIA DISK's text files end each line with a <^M> (a <RETURN>) and each file with a <^Z> due to their DOS text format. You may need to strip the <^M> and <^Z> characters in order to modify them in your editor.

SIA DISK Installation

Besides saving you typing and drawing setup time, the SIA DISK provides starting drawings for the chapter exercises, letting you bypass material and jump into the book where you want. If you don't have the disk yet, read along.

Before starting, make a backup copy of the disk using DISKCOPY. Store the original in a safe place, and use your copy as the working disk. If you have the SIA DISK, follow the instructions below to load the disk files onto your hard disk.

Installing the SIA DISK Files in the SI-ACAD Subdirectory

Put the copy of the SIA DISK in drive A:

`C:\> ` **`CD \SI-ACAD`**	Make sure it is the current directory.
`C:\SI-ACAD> ` **`A:SI-LOAD`**	The files are listed one by one as they are copied.

In addition to drawings for the book's exercises, the SIA DISK contains the Y14.5 menu files with drafting symbols, macros, and AutoLISP routines. These are installed and explained in Chapter 12.

To install the SIA DISK on a UNIX system, you can install it on a DOS system first. Then copy the files by disk or across the network (if any) into your ~si-acad directory.

To keep any changes we make from affecting your normal AutoCAD setup, let's create a separate configuration.

Copying the AutoCAD Configuration and Overlay Files

Before using AutoCAD with STEPPING INTO AutoCAD, copy the configuration files from your AutoCAD program subdirectory to the SI-ACAD subdirectory. Using the SI-ACAD subdirectory keeps the Y14.5 program files from interfering with your existing AutoCAD configuration and files.

Creating an SI-ACAD Configuration

`C:\> ` **`CD\SI-ACAD`**

`C:\SI-ACAD> ` **`COPY \ACAD\ACADP?.OVL`**	Copies plotter and printer configuration.
`C:\SI-ACAD> ` **`COPY \ACAD\ACADD?.OVL`**	Copies digitizer and display.
`C:\SI-ACAD> ` **`COPY \ACAD\ACAD.CFG`**	Copies the main configuration file.

This example assumes your hard disk is drive C and that ACAD is your AutoCAD subdirectory name. If not, substitute your drive letter or subdirectory name.

Now you need to create a simple SIA.BAT batch file to start AutoCAD. This SIA.BAT file avoids conflicts with your current AutoCAD setup and keeps the book's files out of your ACAD directory.

Automating AutoCAD Startup With SIA.BAT

The SIA.BAT file is a batch file like the AUTOEXEC.BAT batch file. Individual batch files like SIA.BAT can be executed to run multiple commands and settings at the DOS prompt with a single command. Batch files are particularly useful for setting up and starting programs. SIA.BAT will load and run the AutoCAD program, saving you from having to type in loading instructions each time you run AutoCAD.

The SIA.BAT file listed below automates loading and starting AutoCAD. It tells AutoCAD where to find its support and configuration information, and changes to the SI-ACAD directory so that your drawings will be stored there by default.

```
SET ACAD=\acad          Support variable.
SET ACADCFG=\SI-ACAD    Configuration variable.
CD\SI-ACAD              Changes to \SI-ACAD subdirectory.
\acad\ACAD %1 %2        Starts AutoCAD.
SET ACAD=               Deletes variables upon exiting.
SET ACADCFG=
CD\                     Changes back to the root directory.
```

SIA.BAT File

The \acad\ACAD %1 %2 line runs ACAD from the current directory, in this case \SI-ACAD. The %1 %2 are placekeepers that pass along any command line parameters, such as you might use to execute an AutoCAD script file.

Use your ASCII text editor to create SIA.BAT in your root directory. See Appendix A if you need help with text editors. Omit the right-hand comments; they are not part of the file.

➡ *NOTE: If your AutoCAD directory is not named \ACAD, then substitute your directory name everywhere \acad is shown in lower case letters in the program listing above.*

Creating the SIA.BAT File in the Root Directory

C:\SI-ACAD> **CD**   Change to the root directory.

Use your ASCII text editor to create the SIA.BAT file as shown above, with any needed modifications.

Let's review the SIA.BAT file and see how it works. At the same time, we'll create a default ACAD.DWG file to ensure we are all using the same startup drawing.

Testing SIA.BAT and Creating a Default ACAD.DWG

You can start a STEPPING INTO AutoCAD session from any directory on your hard drive by simply typing \SIA.

Starting AutoCAD With SIA

C:\> **\SIA**

As soon as you type \SIA from the DOS prompt, the batch file takes control of your computer. The directory is changed to SI-ACAD and the AutoCAD program displays the main menu for you. Now you need to prepare a temporary prototype drawing so that your initial STEPPING INTO AutoCAD sessions are set to the default settings. Later, in Chapter 3, we will create more elaborate prototypes.

When you begin a new drawing, AutoCAD looks for a drawing called ACAD.DWG. AutoCAD uses this drawing to establish the default working environment for your new drawing. Initially, we'll assume your prototype drawing is the same as when you took AutoCAD out of the box. In order to make sure this is true, you need to create a new ACAD.DWG in your SI-ACAD directory. The following exercise creates the new prototype drawing. The equal sign following the drawing name tells AutoCAD to make the ACAD.DWG with its original default settings.

Creating a Prototype Drawing

Enter selection: **1**
Enter NAME of drawing: **ACAD=**

The AutoCAD drawing screen appears.

Command: **END**   Enter END command to save and exit.

The main menu re-appears.

The default prototype drawing ACAD.DWG has been added to the SI-ACAD subdirectory.

➥ *NOTE: If you have not just installed and configured ACAD, your initial drawing setup may be configured to some other drawing. If you are not sure that it is set to ACAD.DWG, then check it now and change it to \SI-ACAD\ACAD if needed. To do so, chose item 5 in the main menu to reconfigure AutoCAD, then choose item 8 in the configuration menu and specify \SI-ACAD\ACAD as the prototype file of your initial drawing setup.*

If you have any errors or problems in configuration or setup, see your AutoCAD Installation and Performance Guide and Appendix A.

Automating AutoCAD With a UNIX Script

The syntax and process of creating the UNIX equivalent of the SIA.BAT file depends on your particular system environment. Consult your system administrator and refer to your AutoCAD Installation and Performance Guide for syntax. UNIX users can omit all memory settings, such as ACADFREERAM and LISPHEAP; however ACAD and ACADCFG need to be set. You also need to add the appropriate entries to change directories and to start up AutoCAD.

Summary

In this chapter, you have learned how to set up and manage your system to take full advantage of the power of AutoCAD. You have configured your hardware and software for compatibility and efficient drafting. The system has been tested, and you are now ready to proceed to Chapter 2, to begin drafting with AutoCAD. Let's step right in . . .

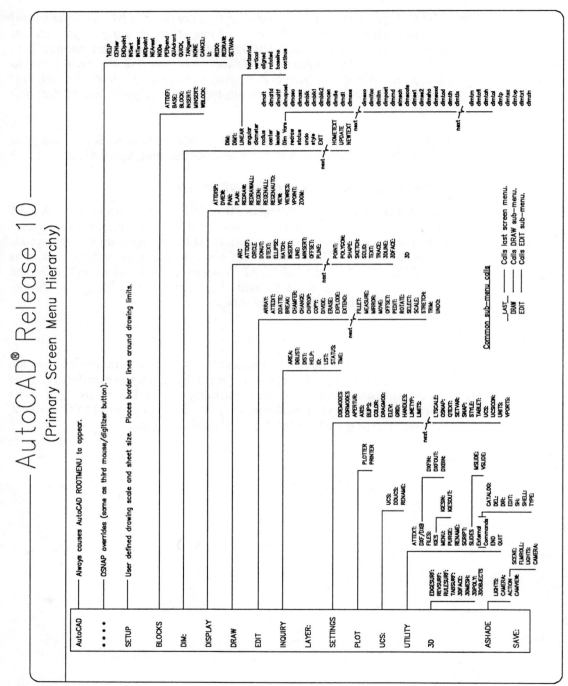

AutoCad's Standard Screen Menus

Starting a Drafting Project

COMMANDS, MENUS, AND DIALOGUE BOXES

AutoCAD is organized into several major parts, including the main menu, the configuration menu, the plotting dialogue, the file utilities menu, and the drawing editor. Each part is typically a collection of related tools. You'll spend most of your time drawing and editing in the drawing editor, but to get there (or anywhere else) you have to go through the main menu.

AutoCAD's Main Menu

The main menu is a sort of guide to AutoCAD's entire tool chest. With it, you can enter any of AutoCAD's major program parts and execute several utility functions.

```
        A U T O C A D
Copyright (C) 1982,83,84,85,86,87,88 Autodesk, Inc.
Release 10 c2 (99/99/99) IBM PC
Advanced Drafting Extensions 3
Serial Number:  99-999999

Main Menu

   0.  Exit AutoCAD
   1.  Begin a NEW drawing
   2.  Edit an EXISTING drawing
   3.  Plot a drawing
   4.  Printer Plot a drawing

   5.  Configure AutoCAD
   6.  File Utilities
   7.  Compile shape/font description file
   8.  Convert old drawing file

Enter selection:
```

The Main Menu — AutoCAD's List of Tools

Using AutoCAD's Main Menu Options

To start a drafting project, choose Begin a NEW Drawing from the main menu. The main menu provides a table of contents from which you can make various selections. For example, to begin a new drawing, you select number 1. To call up and edit an existing drawing, you select number 2. Here is a list of all the selections:

0. **Exit AutoCAD** — The 0 returns you to the operating system. Use this option whenever you need to leave the AutoCAD program.

1. **Begin a NEW drawing** — Enter 1 to open AutoCAD's drawing editor for creating a new drawing. AutoCAD will prompt you to name the new drawing.

2. **Edit an EXISTING drawing** — Enter 2 to open AutoCAD's drawing editor for editing an existing drawing. AutoCAD will prompt you for the name of the existing drawing file.

3. **Plot a drawing** — This tool lets you make hard copies of a drawing on a plotter without entering the drawing editor. After entering this option, AutoCAD prompts for the drawing file name and plotting parameters. See Chapter 3.

4. **Printer plot a drawing** — This tool makes hard copies of a drawing on a printer plotter without entering the drawing editor. See Chapter 3.

5. **Configure AutoCAD** — This option takes you to the AutoCAD configuration menu. If you install a new input or output device, or if you reinstall AutoCAD, use the configuration menu tools to adjust or reset your workstation's configuration file.

6. **File utilities** — AutoCAD provides access to several DOS functions in the file utilities tools. AutoCAD will prompt you to supply the DOS format needed for each utility. These tools are listed below.

7. **Compile shape/font description file** — Use this tool before using a custom shape (a type of symbol) or custom text font. AutoCAD's standard text fonts are already compiled.

8. **Convert old drawing file** — This choice is required only for drawings made with AutoCAD version 2.5 or earlier.

With the exception of configuration, all of these options require a file name.

Drawing File Names

Once you choose Begin a NEW Drawing, Edit an Existing Drawing, or either of the plotting selections, AutoCAD prompts you for a drawing file name. Drawing file names can be up to eight characters long. You may only use letters, digits, dollar signs "$", hyphens "-", and underscores "_". Drawing files are automatically given a file extension of DWG, so you do not need to type .DWG after the name. AutoCAD will also accept a subdirectory prefix attached to your drawing name, such as \DRAWINGS\PART. Using a prefix causes AutoCAD to save the drawing in the designated subdirectory, in this case the subdirectory named DRAWINGS.

If you need to copy a drawing into a different subdirectory, you can use the AutoCAD file utilities menu.

File Utilities Menu

The following lists the file utilities tools. Their DOS command counterparts are shown in the square brackets.

0. **Exit File Utility** Menu

1. **List Drawing files** [DIR *.DWG] — Examines a disk or subdirectory, listing drawing files on the disk you specify.

2. **List user specified files** [DIR] — Lists files (of any type) in a designated disk or subdirectory. You can specify the files just like you do with the DOS command DIR, using wildcards (* or ?) if needed.

3. **Delete files** [DEL or DELETE] — Removes unwanted files from a disk or subdirectory. The file name must match the name on the disk exactly. It may include drive and/or directory, but not wildcards.

4. **Rename files** [REN or RENAME] — AutoCAD lets you rename files. The file name must match the name on the disk exactly. It may include drive and/or directory, but not wildcards.

5. **Copy file** [COPY] — You can copy files from one disk and/or directory to another or make a backup copy of a particular file. Wildcards are not permitted.

The file utilities menu can also be accessed from within AutoCAD's drawing editor by using the FILES command.

FILES

> FILES *activates the file utilities menu. It provides an alternative to DOS (or your operating system) for managing your files.*

Once you are in the drawing editor, you have a whole set of menu tools at your disposal.

AutoCAD's Drawing Editor Menus

Either the `Begin a NEW drawing` or the `Edit an EXISTING drawing` selection takes you into the drawing editor, where you do the bulk of your CAD work.

The AutoCAD program is command-driven. Commands draw lines, enter data, or add dimensions. Everything you do in the drawing editor is done by issuing one of AutoCAD's more than 140 commands. That's a lot of commands to keep track of, so AutoCAD lets you organize commands into sets accessed by several menus. Because drafting and designing are personal processes and many of us are not used to typing commands into a computer, AutoCAD provides five alternative ways to enter drawing commands: screen menus, keyboard, tablet menus, pull-down menus, and icon menus. You can fully customize any or all of the menus, but AutoCAD starts you out by providing a standard menu with tools you can use right away.

AutoCAD's standard menu has several hundred major menu items. Most of these access scores of commands or major command options. Menus are a convenient way to organize and group commands so they can be easily found and selected for execution. When a menu item is selected, it sends a command, a series of commands, a subcommand, or other input to AutoCAD for execution. AutoCAD receives the command or other input in the same way, regardless of whether it is typed at the keyboard or chosen from a menu.

The most commonly used menu is the screen menu.

The Screen Menu

In the drawing editor, you will find the screen menu on the right-hand side of the screen.

The first group or page of menu items in AutoCAD's drawing editor is known as the root menu. Most items on the root menu lead to further collections of tools. Each collection of menu items is referred to as a menu page. Some pages lead to still more pages. [DRAW] and [EDIT], two of the most frequently used items, take you to tools for drawing and editing. Menu item selection is usually made by highlighting an item with the pointing device and pressing the pick button.

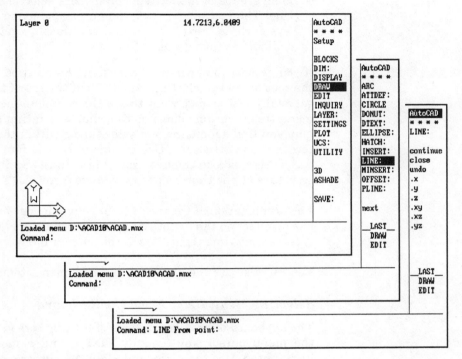

AutoCAD's Screen Menu Paging

Screen Menu Rules

Although menus are customizable and flexible, the standard AutoCAD menu observes several conventions:

- A selection followed by a colon executes the AutoCAD command and usually presents a selection of subcommands.

- A selection without a colon following it is a *key* to other menu pages, but does not itself execute any commands.

- Subcommands are always listed in lower case letters.

- Selecting [AutoCAD] at the top of the menu page will always return you to the root menu.

- Selecting [* * * *] will present object snap options.

- Shortcut key selections are at the bottom of many menu pages. They allow you to return to the [_LAST_] (previous) menu page or to the [DRAW] and [EDIT] menu pages.

- Some groups of menu items offer more selections than can fit on one page. The bottoms of many menu pages have a selection of shortcut keys such as [next], [previous], and [last] to get to all the selections available to such groups.

If you get lost somewhere in the menu system, you can always return to the root menu by selecting [AutoCAD] at the top of the menu page. If you get really lost or just want to see the complete menu organization, the menu tree diagram shown as this chapter's facing page illustration will help you find submenus and sets of tools within the standard AutoCAD screen menu structure. Use the menu tree to familiarize yourself with AutoCAD's screen menus and commands. Seeing the entire menu structure at one time helps to visualize AutoCAD's menu sequences.

The organization of the menu is for convenience of command access, but has no effect on the AutoCAD command structure. Any command can be typed at any time regardless of the current menu page.

You can also use the keyboard to access menu items.

Selecting Menu Items From the Keyboard

The keyboard offers two methods of making screen menu selections. Hit the menu cursor key (usually <INS>) and a menu selection will be highlighted. Use the <UP> and <DOWN> cursor arrow keys to move the highlighted bar to the desired item. Then press the <INS> key again to execute the selection.

The second method is to start typing the name of the menu selection at the COMMAND: prompt. As you type, the first menu item that begins with characters matching what you've typed will be highlighted. Most selections are highlighted by the time you've typed one or two characters. After your selection is highlighted, press the <RETURN> or the space bar to execute the selection.

The Button Menu

Using AutoCAD efficiently requires some sort of pointing device such as a tablet cursor or a mouse. There are usually a number of buttons on these pointing devices. A typical mouse has two or three buttons; a tablet cursor can have up to sixteen buttons. AutoCAD reserves one button as a pick or select button. The remaining buttons are predefined in the

ACAD.MNU file but may be reassigned to different functions through menu customization. The standard assignments are:

BUTTON	FUNCTION	BUTTON	FUNCTION
1	<RETURN>	6	<^G> toggle grid
2	pull down Tools menu	7	<^D> toggle coords
3	<^C> cancel	8	<^E> toggle isoplane
4	<^B> toggle snap	9	<^T> toggle tablet
5	<^O> toggle ortho		

You can access as many of these as you have buttons available.

A digitizer tablet provides greater efficiency than a mouse because it gives you immediate access to any number of tablet menu items.

The Tablet Menu

AutoCAD's tablet menu overlay can be used with any digitizer tablet that supports the AutoCAD program. Menu items are assigned a box and position on the template. They are grouped into related sets of tools. You can select any item by putting your pointing device directly on top of the box and pushing the *select* button.

Tablet menus perform the same functions as screen and button menus. Many tablet menu selections open a corresponding screen menu page to help you select a subcommand. The tablet menu can also show graphic images that identify the selection. Tablet menus offer a few advantages over some of the other menus. Tablet menu selections provide immediate access to tools without flipping through menu pages. The entire tablet is customizable, or you can just add your own items to Tablet Area 1 at the top of AutoCAD's standard tablet menu. The SIA DISK's ANSI Y14.5 tablet menu, fitting into Tablet Area 1, is shown below.

AutoCAD's Tablet Menu Showing the ANSI Y14.5 Menu

Pull-Down Menus

Pull-down menus are similar to screen menus. If your video hardware supports pull-down menus (supports the AUI), you will see a menu bar when you move your pointing device to the top of the graphic screen. You need a mouse or some other pointing device to access the pull-down menus. You can't access them from the keyboard. The menu bar presents a list of labels indicating the selections available in each pull-down menu.

Ten pull-down menus are available for you to use and customize. AutoCAD's standard menu is pre-programmed to use the first eight. To access the tools in a pull-down menu, you must first make them visible by opening it. To open a pull-down menu, highlight the menu bar label and press the pick button on your pointing device. This pulls it down (some people say pops it up) over the graphic screen and presents you with a list of items that can be selected in the same manner as screen menus. Once you make a selection, the command is executed and the pull-down is closed.

The pull-down menu illustration on the following page will help you find submenus and sets of tools within the standard AutoCAD pull-down menu structure.

Many pull-down selections are designed to present dialogue boxes, icon menus, and multiple commands. Multiple commands repeat until they are canceled or another command selection is made. Like the tablet menu, many pull-down menu selections open an appropriate screen menu page to help you select a subcommand. Also like the tablet menu, pull-down menus offer advantages over screen menus. Your choices may be quicker since you don't have to flip through multiple menu pages. If you need to use a command several times in a row, you can do it easily from the pull-down menus.

AutoCAD® Release 10
(Menu Bar and Pull-Down Menus)

Tools	Draw	Modify	Display	Settings	Options	File	Help	AutoCAD
OSNAP	Line	Erase	Redraw	UCS Dialogue...	Ashade...	Save	Help	****
CENter	Arc	Move	Zoom Window	UCS Options...	Fonts...	End		SETUP
ENDpoint	Circle	Copy	Zoom Previous	UCS Previous		Quit		BLOCKS
INSert	Polyline	Properties	Zoom All	Drawing Aids...	Icon Menus	Plot		DIM:
INTersection	3D Polyline	Break	Zoom Dynamic	Entity Creation...		Print		DISPLAY
MIDpoint	Insert	Fillet		Modify Layer...	Icon Menus			DRAW
NEArest	Dtext	Mirror	Pan					EDIT
NODe	Hatch...	Trim	Dview Options...	Dialogue Box				INQUIRY
PERpendicular	3D Construction...	Extend	Vpoint 3D...					LAYER:
QUAdrant		Stretch	Plan View (UCS)	Dialogue Box				SETTINGS
QUICK,	Icon Menus	Edit Polylines	Plan View (World)					PLOT
TANgent				Dialogue Box				UCS:
NONE	Icon Menus		Set Viewports...					UTILITY
				Dialogue Box				3D
FILTERS...			Icon Menus					
Cancel				Icon Menus				ASHADE
U			Icon Menus					SAVE:
Redo								
List			Icon Menus					

Sub Menu

Menu Bar and Pull Down Menus

Dialogue Boxes

AutoCAD offers a convenient technique for viewing and executing certain complex commands or groups of settings — the dialogue box. You can call up a dialogue box by making a menu selection or by entering its command name. DDUCS, for example, calls the UCS dialogue box. (All dialogue commands begin with DD.)

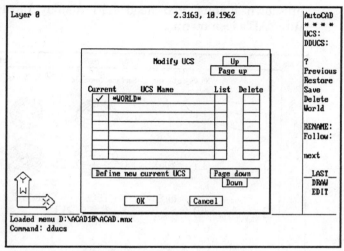

AutoCAD's UCS Dialogue Box

Dialogue boxes pop up over the graphics screen. You can make changes by pointing to a setting and pressing the pick button on your pointing device. You may then enter new values, give names, turn toggles on or off, and execute commands. Each dialogue box provides an [OK] and a [Cancel] box. When you are satisfied with the dialogue box's settings, just point to [OK] and press your pick button. These are the dialogue box commands:

DDEMODES (Entity MODES) accesses the dialogue box for setting current layer, color, linetype, elevation, and thickness.

DDLMODES accesses the layer dialogue box. This dialogue box differs from the previous box in that complete control of layers is made available to you.

DDUCS accesses all the settings and functions of the UCS commands.

DDRMODES (dRaw MODES) accesses the screen drawing aids dialogue box. It contains snap, grid, axis, ortho, blipmode, and isoplane.

DDATTE accesses the attribute editing dialogue box.

Dialogue boxes are a dynamic and efficient way to change settings. As with the pull-down menus, you can only access dialogue boxes if your video devices support the AUI.

Icon Menus

An icon menu displays your menu selections as graphic images on the screen. This provides visual cues to aid in selecting the correct item. Like pull-down menus, you need AUI display hardware support to use AutoCAD's icon menus.

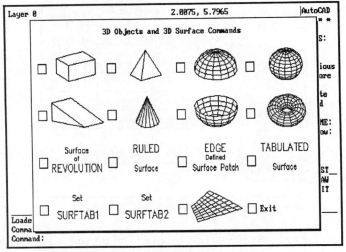

AutoCAD's Icon Menu for 3D Objects

AutoCAD uses slide files (compact, quick-displaying screen image vector files) to construct icon menus. Four, nine, or sixteen images, each containing one menu item, are displayed at a time. You can select an item on an icon menu by highlighting the small square to the left of its icon image and pressing the pick button on your pointing device. AutoCAD executes the selection like any other menu selection. Icon menus can page through other icon menus the same way the screen menu pages through other menu pages. The preset icon menus showing hatch patterns and text styles are a very effective use of icon menus. The images provide more information than a brief descriptive label could.

Sometimes the quickest way to issue commands or options is to type them at the keyboard.

Giving Commands to the Drawing Editor

Once you know your way around AutoCAD's commands, it can be quicker to type them than to wade through pages of menus. You can execute any command or option in AutoCAD by simply typing the command or option name followed by a <RETURN>. Usually one key letter is enough to enter an option, but command entry requires typing the entire command name. For example, let's look at the ARC command.

Entering Commands From the Keyboard

Command: **ARC**	Enter the full command name.
Center/<Start point>: **C**	Just the first letter.
Center:	Pick a point.
Start point:	Pick a point.
Angle/Length of chord/<End point>: **A**	Just the first letter.
Included angle: **45**	Type the number.

Entering a command puts the program into a data entry mode. In this mode, you are prompted to specify the data needed to complete the command. After you input the data, AutoCAD executes the function. The command prompt line will change to reflect your data entry. When AutoCAD is finished executing the command, it will return to the command mode and display the Command: prompt again.

Defaults and Entering Values

Defaults are displayed at the command line in angle brackets such as these< >. Defaults may be accepted by pushing the <RETURN> key or space bar, or they may be overridden by entering different values or information. Other command options are separated by forward slashes and displayed with their key letters in upper case characters. If you prefer, you can type the entire option key name, but you only need to type the character(s) displayed in upper case. Numerical data and coordinates (the X,Y,Z coordinates relative to the drawing's 0,0,0 base point) can also be typed. Enter points, angles, and distances by picking them with your pointer (digitizer, mouse, or keyboard cursor), as we will show later in the chapter.

Transparent Commands

Some commands can be used transparently, while you are in the middle of other commands. To do so, an apostrophe must precede the command name, like 'EXAMPLE. Transparent commands won't work while you are using the TEXT, DTEXT, ATTDEF, SKETCH, PLOT, PRPLOT, VPOINT,

DVIEW, or DIMensioning commands. You can't use transparent commands if the drawing requires a regeneration. When we give a command definition for a command which can be used transparently, we'll indicate transparency with a leading apostrophe, for example:

' ZOOM   *The apostrophe indicates that ZOOM can be used transparently.*

Data Entry Errors

If the data you enter does not match the type of data required by a command, AutoCAD will generally forgive it and reprompt with a message like one of the following.

```
Unknown command
Point or option keyword required
*Invalid*
```

AutoCAD's Responses for Unacceptable Data Entries

When you are reprompted, you get another chance to enter the correct data. You can type '? or 'HELP to get help, or you can cancel out of the command. To cancel a command, select cancel from the screen menu or hold down the Control key while you strike the <C> character. Some commands require two or three <^C>s to fully cancel.

You can also *undo* an error, kind of like a graphic or command level backspace.

Undoing Incorrect Points or Values

If you enter a wrong value, simply press the backspace key to fix it. If you've already hit <RETURN> or picked a wrong point, you can select [Undo] or type U and a <RETURN> in most commands. For example, in the LINE command, undo will remove the last line developed so you can simply continue from the previous point. You may undo all lines back to the original line *starting point*. Once a command has been completed, you can select [Undo] or type U at the command prompt to undo the entire previous command (or menu item).

Let's see menus, commands, and input in action as we take you on an AutoCAD tour.

A Tour of AutoCAD

The following drafting exercise takes you on an introductory tour of AutoCAD. Read through the exercise, or better yet, journey along using your AutoCAD program to develop the PART drawing. We'll step you through starting, quitting, saving, and ending drawing sessions, we'll look at AutoCAD's drawing editor, dialogue, and some drafting command tools, and we'll show you how to get help when you need it.

Setup Parameters and Values

The PART drawing uses the parameters shown in the table below. All of the parameters except LIMITS are defaults, so you need not set them.

AXIS	GRID	SNAP	
.5	1	.2	
UNITS	Decimal 0.00.		
LIMITS	0,0 to 17,11.		
Layer Name	State	Color	Linetype
0	CURRENT	7(White)	CONTINUOUS

Parameters for the PART Drawing

Remember, this is just a tour. If this is your first experience with AutoCAD, relax and enjoy it.

Beginning the Drawing

To begin our tour of AutoCAD, let's enter the drawing editor by beginning a NEW drawing. From now on we'll assume that you always use the SIA.BAT batch command you created in Chapter 1 to start AutoCAD.

Beginning the PART Drawing

C:\ **SIA**	Start AutoCAD with the batch command.
Enter Selection: **1**	Begin a NEW drawing from the main menu.
Enter NAME of drawing: **PART**	

AutoCAD's Automatic Drawing Setup

The initial menu page is the root menu. It contains the [Setup] routine which steps you through a series of drawing unit, scale, and sheet size selections. Let's choose a B-size drafting sheet. To set your drawing up, use your pointing device to highlight and make the following menu selections.

Setting Up a B-Size Drawing Sheet

Select **[Setup]**
Select the Units from the screen menu: *Select* **[decimal]**
Select the Scale from the screen menu: *Select* **[FULL]**
Select the Paper size from the screen menu: *Select* **[B- 11x17]**

You can select any of the units, scales, and sheet sizes presented in the menu and shown on the illustration below. You may also choose other sheet sizes. If you need to set up a drawing sheet size which is not listed on the screen menu, simply select [other] and enter the new drawing parameters. You are prompted to provide the coordinate position of the lower left corner and the upper right corner of the drawing sheet. You must specify these positions in the current unit values.

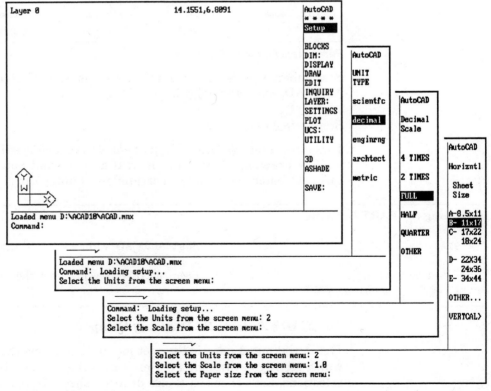

AutoCAD's Setup Menu Choices

After you select [B- 11x17] as a sheet size, AutoCAD generates the drawing area to the limits of 0,0 as the lower left corner and 11,17 as the upper right corner. The [Setup] routine then generates a sheet size border at the drawing limits and returns you to the root menu. Behind the scenes, this setup procedure uses an AutoLISP routine to get input from you and to execute several AutoCAD commands. It uses the UNITS and LIMITS commands to set up the drawing, then uses the INSERT command to insert the border. The border is stored in another drawing file named BORDER.DWG. Let's take a look at the UNITS command.

Drafting in Different Units

Many drafting and design disciplines use AutoCAD. These include scientific, mechanical, engineering, and architectural drawing. Since each of these disciplines may use different units to describe a drawing, AutoCAD gives you several drafting unit choices. The choices are accessed by the UNITS command.

UNITS

> *The UNITS command controls the format and display for the input of coordinates, distances, and angles. You specify the system of units, the precision, the system of angle measurement, the precision of angle display, and the direction of angles.*

AutoCAD's available types of units include:

Scientific — defines units in scientific notation.

Decimal — defines units in decimals. You specify the digits to the right of the decimal. These units may be interpreted for any decimal unit, including metric units.

Engineering — defines units in feet and inches. Inches are displayed in decimal inches.

Architectural — defines units in feet and inches. Fractions of inches are displayed in real fractions.

Fractional — defines units in inches and fractional parts of inches.

With the exception of engineering and architectural modes, these systems can be used with any basic unit of measurement. For example, decimal mode is perfect for metric units as well as for decimal English units. AutoCAD's default is decimal notation with four digits to the right of the decimal point. Let's use the UNITS command to set decimal units to two digits to the right of the decimal.

Setting Decimal Units

```
Command: UNITS                                    Flips to text screen.
Systems of units:      (Examples)

    1. Scientific       1.55E+01
    2. Decimal          15.50
    3. Engineering      1'-3.50"
    4. Architectural    1'-3 1/2"
    5. Fractional       15 1/2
Enter choice, 1 to 5 <2>: <RETURN>       Accept default to keep decimal units.
Number of digits to right of decimal point (0 to 8) <4>: 2    Set to 2 digits.
```

The UNITS command continues by allowing you to set the system for measuring angles. This can be set for disciplines such as machine, architectural, and civil (surveying) drafting.

Selecting the System of Measuring Angles

```
Systems of angle measure:       (Examples)

    1. Decimal degrees           45.0000
    2. Degrees/minutes/seconds   45d0'0"
    3. Grads                     50.0000g
    4. Radians                   0.7854r
    5. Surveyor's units          N 45d0'0" E

Enter choice, 1 to 5 <1>: <RETURN>                Accept default for decimal degrees.
Number of fractional places for display of angles (0 to 8) <0>: <RETURN>

Direction for angle 0:
    East    3 o'clock  =  0
    North  12 o'clock  =  90
    West    9 o'clock  =  180
    South   6 o'clock  =  270
Enter direction for angle 0 <0>: <RETURN>
Do you want angles measured clockwise? <N> <RETURN>    For counterclockwise.
Command: <F1>                                          To flip back to graphics screen.
```

Some drafters choose not to accept AutoCAD's default position (direction) for angle 0. Change angle direction with the UNITS command by entering new values instead of accepting the defaults shown above.

➡ *NOTE: No matter what units you set, you can always enter your input in decimal form.*

UNITS controls the display, input, and dimensioning formats, but not the actual accuracy of your data. You can always enter input with greater accuracy than the units you have selected can show; however the display will be rounded off. For example, with the above settings, 0.3125 will be accepted at its full accuracy but the coordinates display and prompts will round it off to 0.31. Don't let that cause you to make mistakes. When we do dimensioning in a later chapter, we'll see some techniques for adjusting units.

There are a number of other accuracy or positioning tools available for drawing.

Positioning Tools (Drawing Aids)

Positioning tools are drawing aids which are used for locating specific points on a drafting sheet or part. Drafters have always been concerned with developing accurate graphic representations of parts or projects. Accurate has taken on a new meaning with AutoCAD. The geometry which makes up a part can now be drawn to the accuracy of fourteen decimal positions (that's .00000000000001). To maintain this kind of accuracy, AutoCAD offers some very precise positioning tools.

Ortho, grid, snap, and axis are four positioning tools that you should learn to set and use immediately. The state of the grid and axis is visually obvious on the drawing editor's screen. The *status line* above the drawing area displays the status of snap and ortho, in addition to showing you which drawing layer is current. Use either the screen menu or the dialogue boxes to set them.

Setting Drawing Aids Using the Screen Menus

If your system does not support pull-down menus, you can set the drawing aids using the screen menus or by typing the individual commands. Even if you set your drawing aids with the dialogue box, read the following for more information on each setting.

Although we don't need to set it at this time, you probably noticed the ortho toggle.

ORTHO

> *ORTHO constrains your drawing lines, polylines, and traces to horizontal and vertical lines. ORTHO mode controls the angle at which you pick the second point in many drawing and editing commands. ORTHO is a toggle, and the default setting is off.*
> ON/OFF <Off>:

Ortho may also be toggled transparently by using the dialogue box or by keying <^O> or <F8> on the IBM-style keyboard.

Grid sets a series of dots (a grid) on the current viewport at user-defined intervals.

GRID

> *GRID, a drawing aid, displays dots at any user-defined increment. It helps you to keep the space you are working in and the size of your drawing entities in perspective. GRID dynamically toggles off and on, as well as accepts numeric values. The default settings are 0.0000 and off.*
> Grid spacing(X) or ON/OFF/Snap/Aspect <0.00>:

The grid is a drafting aid that assists you with locating positions or distances on the drawing screen. The grid can be set at equal X-Y spacing, on or off, and at an aspect ratio (differing X-Y spacing). Avoid spacing grid dots too close together; your screen display will be slow or impossibly dense. A snap option setting of zero makes the grid equal to the snap value, and adjusts it every time snap is changed. For the best use of grid and snap, set them to different values. It is common to set the grid to larger increments (.5, 1, 1.5, and so on) and then set the snap to smaller increments (.1, .2, .3, and so on). If you enter a number and an X, such as 4X, then the grid is set to that number times the snap setting. Grid may be toggled transparently by using the dialogue box or by keying <^G> or <F7> on the IBM-style keyboard.

Setting a 1-Inch Grid Spacing

```
Select [SETTINGS] [GRID:]
Command: GRID                              Or just type GRID.
Grid spacing(X) or ON/OFF/Snap/Aspect <0.00>: 1
```

Axis is another excellent drafting alignment tool. It works similar to grid.

AXIS

> *AXIS creates ruler marks, or ticks, on the bottom and right side of your screen. These marks are used as a visual drawing aid. The default setting is off and the default value is 0.0000.*
> Tick spacing(X) or ON/OFF/Snap/Aspect :

Setting a .5-Inch Axis

Select **[SETTINGS] [AXIS:]**
Command: **AXIS**   Or just type AXIS.
Tick spacing (X) or ON/OFF/Snap/Aspect <0.00>: **.5**

Axis and grid are only visual aids, and don't actually affect accuracy. Snap lets you snap to (or pick) the grid dots or increments of the grid as an aid to positioning your cursor.

SNAP

> *SNAP lets you move the crosshairs at any defined increment. This command is dynamic. You can constantly modify the increment value and turn the setting on and off. The default setting is 1.0000 and off.*
> Snap spacing or ON/OFF/Aspect/Rotate/Style <1.00>:

With snap on and equal to your grid spacing, your cursor will only move from one grid dot to another grid dot. This helps you to quickly and accurately locate a position on the drawing. You can set snap to any spacing, aspect ratio, rotation, or style (isometric or normal), as well as on or off. Snap may be toggled transparently by using the DDRMODES dialogue box or by keying <^D> or <F9> on the IBM-style keyboard.

Setting a .20-Inch Snap Spacing

Select **[SETTINGS] [next] [SNAP:]**
Command: **SNAP**   Or just type SNAP.
Snap spacing or ON/OFF/Aspect/Rotate/Style <1.00>: **.20**

If you pick a point with snap off, AutoCAD takes the coordinates of the pointer's pixel position and does not round the point input to match the displayed value. Although it may display as 0.25,0.25, a point might really be 0.2487123,0.2512345 in the drawing data base. Using snap when picking points forces them to the exact increment values. You use CAD for accuracy, so use snap or another form of precise point entry like those explained below.

Setting Drawing Aids With a Dialogue Box

The drawing aids dialogue box is a quick and convenient way to select drawing aid commands and make changes to their status.

'DDRMODES | *Dynamic Dialogue dRawing MODES controls the settings of drawing aids like snap, grid, and axis with a dialogue box.*

If your system supports AUI, use DDRMODES to set snap, grid, and axis. They may also be set by their individual command names or by calling them from the screen menu. One advantage of using 'DDRMODES instead of individual commands is that it can be used transparently, although some settings may not take effect in the middle of some commands.

Using Dialogue Boxes

Pull down **[Settings]**
Select **[Drawing Aids...]** The dialogue box appears.
Command: **'ddrmodes** Or just type DDRMODES.

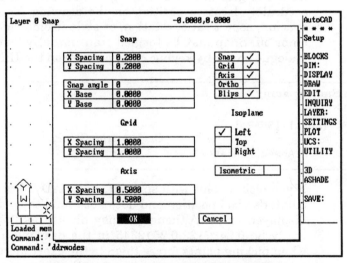

Setting Exercise Drawing Aids Using Dialogue Box

The box at the upper right, with snap, grid, ortho, axis, and blips, is a group of toggles. A check mark indicates that it is toggled on. To change a toggle, move your pointer to highlight the check box next to the setting label and click on it. Specific values for snap, grid, and axis may be set by highlighting the input boxes next to their key labels, such as the [1.00] next to [X Spacing]. Once highlighted, you can type in the desired input value. If you start to type or click on the input box, a pair of [Cancel] and [OK] boxes appear. To accept the input, hit a <RETURN>, or click on [OK].

Click on [Cancel] to abort the setting. The permanent [Cancel] and [OK] *buttons* at the bottom of the dialogue box similarly accept or cancel the entire screenful of settings.

Let's set snap, grid, and axis.

Setting Drawing Aids With the Dialogue Box

Select **[Grid | X Spacing | 0.00]**	Click on input box next to grid X spacing label.
Enter **1**	Enter a value of 1 and <RETURN>.
	The Y spacing changes to match.
Toggle **[Grid]**	Click on grid toggle at upper right.
Select **[Snap | X Spacing | 1.00]**	
Enter **.2**	Enter a value of 0.2 and <RETURN>.
	The Y spacing changes to match.
Toggle **[Snap]**	
Select **[Axis | X Spacing | 0.00]**	
Enter **.5**	
	The Y spacing changes to match.
Toggle **[Axis]**	
Select **[OK]**	OK at the bottom accepts it all.

Your PART drawing should now look like the illustration shown below.

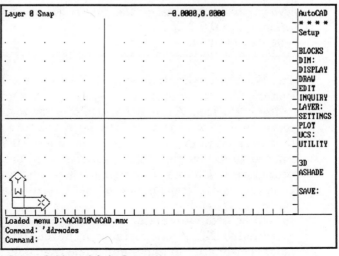

Snap, Grid, and Axis Set

Points and Coordinates

The point is the key element of the AutoCAD drawing database. AutoCAD stores points in the Cartesian coordinate system with coordinate values such as 1,2.5,0. In the default orientation of the 2D Cartesian coordinate system, positive X axis values go to the right and negative X values go to the left of the 0,0 base. Positive Y is up (on the screen) and negative Y is down. If you go 3D, positive Z is towards the viewer and negative Z is into the screen. This default orientation can be changed, but the three axes will always maintain the same relative orientations to each other.

The axis, grid, and coords displays on the status line give you some indication of where the 0,0 base is located and what portion of the coordinate system is currently displayed. AutoCAD also provides another convenient orientation tool, the UCS icon.

The User Coordinate System Icon

When you first enter the drawing editor, the UCSICON is shown at the lower left of the screen. This indicates the orientation of the current coordinate display. You can set this icon to position itself at 0,0,0 or you can suppress its display altogether with the UCSICON command.

UCSICON

> *The UCSICON marker graphically displays the origin and viewing plane of the current UCS. The default setting for the icon is on and Noorigin (displayed at the lower left corner). The ORigin option displays at 0,0,0, if possible.*
> ON/OFF/All/Noorigin/ORigin <ON>:

The World Coordinate System (WCS) is AutoCAD's default coordinate system. The world coordinate system is designated by a "W" near the center of the icon. AutoCAD also allows you to define any number of user coordinate systems (UCS's). A user coordinate system is a local system that is offset in any or all axes from the 0,0,0 WCS base. It can also be rotated to any angle in 3D space. We will present techniques for this procedure in Chapter 9, Extrusion Drafting and Dimensioning, and in Chapter 10, 3D Drafting in the User Coordinate System.

In any coordinate system, you may specify points with Cartesian coordinates (X,Y,Z axis distance from the 0,0,0 base) like 1,2,3 or with polar coordinates (distance and angle from 0,0 in the X,Y plane only) like 2<45 for 2 units at 45 degrees. For 2D drawing, the Z value may be omitted. We will omit Z values until we get into 3D. Cartesian coordinates may be *absolute* offsets from the 0,0,0 base, or *relative* to a previous point. Polar coordinates are always relative to the last (previous) point.

Absolute Coordinates

You may specify absolute coordinate values in the X,Y (or X,Y,Z) axis directions. For the starting point of a line, for example, enter the distance in the X axis direction from the 0,0 position, and the distance from 0,0 in the Y axis direction. The values for X,Y are separated by a comma. AutoCAD will automatically designate the Z as zero if no Z value is entered. You may designate coordinate values in positive or negative axis directions (X,Y or -X,-Y). The default is positive, so you must precede a negative direction with a minus sign. The positive and negative absolute coordinate directions are illustrated below.

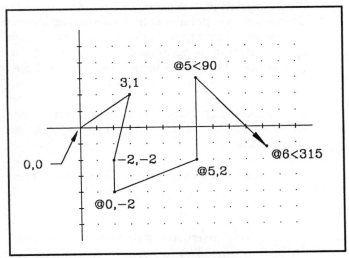

Absolute, Relative, and Polar Coordinates

Relative Coordinates

You can specify relative Cartesian coordinates by preceding the coordinate value with the @ (at) symbol. This tells AutoCAD to interpret the value as an offset relative to the last point entered, not relative to 0,0. For example, once you have established a line's starting point, you locate the endpoint relative to the start point, like @1.5,0. This would draw a 1.5-unit-long line in the X direction with no Y offset. You may specify relative Cartesian coordinates with either a default positive or negative direction for any axis.

Polar Coordinates

Polar coordinates are always specified, by their distance and angle, relative to the last point. Precede the polar coordinate with an @ symbol, followed by the linear distance value, the angle symbol <, and an angle value. You may not specify Z polar coordinate values. Polar coordinates can be entered with either a positive or negative distance or angle, although negative distances may be confusing.

The Coordinate Read-Out — Where's the Cursor?

The coords read-out on the status line displays the cursor location. Its default displays the last point picked in X,Y coordinates, such as 2.0000,3.0000. When you toggle coords with <^D> or <F6>, the read-out continually updates to display the current location of the cursor. When toggled at the command prompt, it updates in X,Y coordinates. Coords displays polar coordinates when appropriate, and X,Y coordinates otherwise, when toggled once in most commands. The second time it is toggled during a command will cause it to display absolute X,Y coordinates. One more toggle and the read-out returns to its original status.

As you draw, toggle coords as needed and watch the read-out. This is an efficient way to locate and pick points, as long as your snap is set appropriately.

Let's put all of this into practice and draw a part.

Drafting a Part

The following instructions show how to use the LINE command to draw the part outline. You can draw a continuous series of lines by picking a starting point with your pointing device, and then selecting any number of sequential endpoints. As you draw each line, it *rubberbands* from the last point selected. The exercise shows you the absolute, relative, and polar coordinate inputs you need to draw the part. For variety in point input, the PART Drawing illustration provides dimensions if you wish to pick points, with snap and coords to guide you.

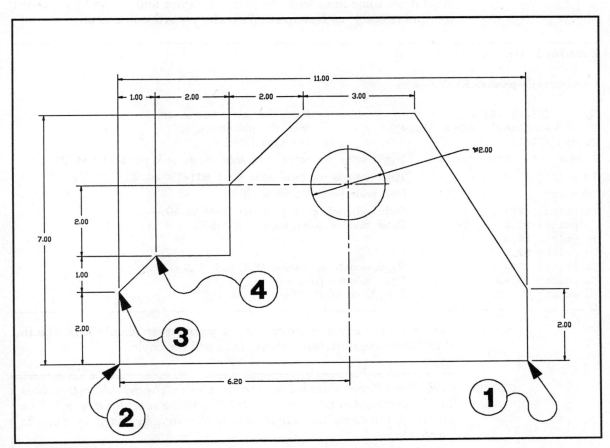

PART Drawing

Ready to Draw

Let's draw the first few lines. When you select either the screen or pull-down menu LINE items, the screen menu pages to a set of tools for drawing lines.

LINE | *LINE lets you draw straight line segments. You can enter 2D or 3D points by entering a From point and a series of To points. Entering C closes a series, U undoes the last segment, and <RETURN> at the From point prompt continues the previous line or arc.*
| `From point:   To point:`

We'll draw some lines with the pointing device and others by keyboard coordinate entry, with snap on. We'll also try ortho on and off.

Drawing Lines

Continue in the previous PART drawing.

Select **[DRAW] [LINE:]**	From the screen menu, or
Pull down **[Draw]** *Select* **[Line]**	from the pull-downs, or
Command: **LINE**	just type LINE.
From point: **<F8>**	Toggle ortho on, make sure snap is on, pick point 14,2 at ①.
To point: **<F6>**	Toggle coords on, pick polar point @11<180 at ②.
To point:	Pick polar point @2<90 at ③.
To point: **<F8>**	Ortho off, pick polar point @1.41<45 at ④.
To point: **@2,0**	Enter relative point, then <RETURN>.
To point: **@0,2**	
To point: **@2,2**	
To point: **<F6>**	Toggle coords to absolute X,Y, pick 11,9.
To point: **@3,-5**	Enter relative point.
To point: **C**	Type C or select [Close].

Except for the circle and dimensions, your screen should look like the PART Drawing illustrated above. Let's add the circle.

CIRCLE

> *The CIRCLE command is used to draw circles. The default method uses a <Center point> and <Radius>. If DRAGMODE is set to on or auto (the default), you can determine the size of the circle by dragging it on the screen.*
> 3P/2P/TTR/<Center point>:

When you select CIRCLE from the screen or pull-down menus, AutoCAD presents a menu page with five options for creating circles. These options are: Three Point (3P), Two Point (2P), CENter-RADius (CEN,RAD), CENter-DIAmeter (CEN,DIA), and Tangent - Tangent - Radius (TTR).

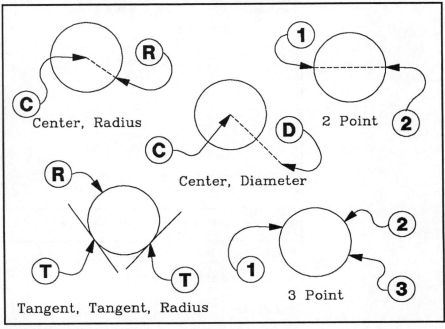

AutoCAD's Circle Options

When you select one of these menu options, it executes the CIRCLE command and provides the input parameters to prompt you for the type of circle you selected. If you enter CIRCLE by typing characters at the command line, you can enter the desired parameters manually, for example entering a D for diameter. After you establish the first point of the circle, move the cursor in any direction and you will see a varying circle attached to it. This action is called *dragging*. With snap on, you can drag the circle to the desired size and accurately pick the radius. Let's try it.

Drawing a Circle

```
Select [DRAW] [CIRCLE] [CEN,RAD:]          From the screen menu, or
Select [Draw] [Circle] [CEN,RAD:]          from the pull-down menu,
Command: CIRCLE                            or just type CIRCLE.
3P/2P/TTR/<Center point>:                  Pick point 9.2,7.
Diameter/<Radius>: <F6><F6>  Toggle coords to polar, pick polar point @1 or just type 1.
```

It is important to note that you can either type specific radii or diameter values, or you can *show* values by picking points to designate the size of the circles.

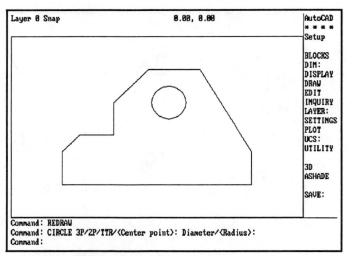

PART Drawing With the Circle Added

Now let's add some annotations.

Text Tools

Drafting projects commonly require text for title block information and drawing notes.

TEXT	*TEXT lets you enter text in your drawing. An older command than DTEXT, TEXT does not dynamically show your text characters on the screen as you enter them. It places the text string when you end the text input.* `Start point or Align/Center/Fit/Middle/Right/Style:`

DTEXT	*The DTEXT (Dynamic TEXT) command prompts for the same text parameters as the TEXT command, but DTEXT draws the text characters on the screen as you type them. DTEXT displays a rectangular character box to show where the next character will be placed.*

QTEXT	*QTEXT (Quick TEXT) sets a mode that causes the screen to draw boxes in place of text strings and attributes. This saves time when redrawing or regenerating the screen. The box or rectangle is the height and approximate length of the text string. The default setting is off.*

DTEXT is generally the preferred text entry command for two reasons. First, it displays characters as they are entered. Second, you can enter multiple lines of text in one command by using a <RETURN> to step down to each new line. Move the DTEXT box and pick a point if you want to start a new line at a new location. The DTEXT box will be repositioned at the new location and you may continue to enter text.

When you execute the TEXT or DTEXT commands from one of the AutoCAD menu choices, you get a menu page that includes several different justification formats. These include Left <default>, Align, Center, Fit, and Middle. You can also designate the size (Height) and Rotation angle you want.

Let's use DTEXT, left justified, and override the default height value. Place the text anywhere you like.

Adding Text to a Drawing

Select **[DRAW] [DTEXT:]**	From the screen menu, or
Select **[Draw] [Dtext]**	from the pull-down menu,
Command: **DTEXT**	or just type DTEXT.
Start point or Align/Center/Fit/Middle/Right/Style:	Pick default left alignment point.
	Pick the point in the circle, to experiment.
Height <0.20>: **.4**	Set text height large enough to see.
Rotation angle <0>: **<RETURN>**	Zero is horizontal.
Text: **JUST TESTING**	Enter the text with a <RETURN>.
Text:	You get a new box and prompt for a new line.
	Backspace until all the text is gone.
	Pick new point 1,10 for the real text, as illustrated.
Text: **NOTES, UNLESS OTHERWISE SPECIFIED:**	Enter the text with a <RETURN>.
Text: **1. INTERPRET DRAWING PER ANSI Y14.5M-1982**	Enter the text.
Text: **<RETURN>**	To end text entry.

Your screen should look like the illustration below.

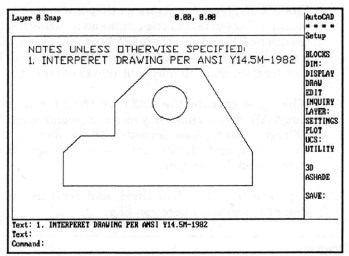

Text Added to the PART Drawing

Text Control Codes

There are certain characters or symbols that are not available on the standard keyboard. You can enter the following characters and symbols from the keyboard by preceding their specified code letters with double percent symbols.

%%O	— Toggles overscore mode
%%U	— Toggles underscore mode
%%D	— Draws "degrees" symbol
%%P	— Draws "plus/minus" tolerance symbol
%%C	— Draws "diameter" dimensioning symbol
%%%	— Forces a single percent sign
%%nnn	— Draws special character with number "nnn"

Let's enter the diameter and the plus-or-minus codes.

Entering Special Characters From the Keyboard

```
Command: DTEXT
DTEXT Start point or Align/Center/Fit/Middle/Right/Style:    Pick a start point.
Height <0.40>: <RETURN>
Rotation angle <0>: <RETURN>
Text: %%C2.00%%P.03                                          Enter the text.
Text: <RETURN>                                               To end text entry.
```

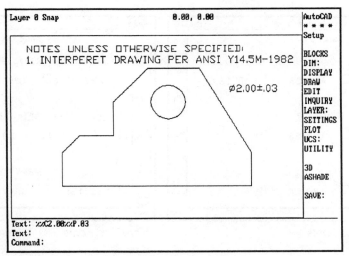

The Codes Generate the Symbols

The default text style that we have been using, called STANDARD, is efficient but crude. You have many other choices.

Using Various Text Styles

AutoCAD's text appearance is determined by the current *style*. A style is defined by a text font (a set of character definitions) and modified by a number of style parameters that are set with the STYLE command.

STYLE

> *The STYLE command lets you create new text styles, modify existing styles, and obtain a listing of defined styles. The style name is arbitrary; you can use up to 31 characters to name a style. A style is named by assigning it a text font. Font files have the .SHX extension.*
> Text style name (or ?) <ROMANC>:

AutoCAD provides many different fonts to choose from, and you can define an infinite number of style variations from them. Fancier fonts look better but take longer for AutoCAD to regenerate. You might want to use a fancy font for a title block or logo. You can see all of the supplied fonts with the [Options] [Fonts...] pull-down menu selection. It displays a three-page icon menu of preset style definitions, each matching the name of its font. Most of these are shown in the illustration below.

```
Layer 0 Snap              9.00, 11.40        |AutoCAD
                                             |* *
N                  Select Text Font          |P
1                                            |KS
     ROMAN SIMPLEX   ROMAN DUPLEX   MONOTXT   |
  ☐   ABC123    ☐   ABC123    ☐   ABC123     |LAY
                                             |
                                             |IRY
                                             |R:
     ROMAN COMPLEX   ROMAN TRIPLEX           |INGS
  ☐   ABC123    ☐   ABC123    ☐ Next        |ITY
                                             |
                                             |
                                             |DE
     ITALIC COMPLEX  ITALIC TRIPLEX          |
  ☐   ABC123    ☐   ABC123    ☐ Exit        |:
Text:
Text:
Command:
```

Some Available Text Fonts

```
Layer 0 Snap              12.40,6.00        |AutoCAD
                                            |* *
N                  Select Text Font         |P
1                                           |KS
     GOTHIC ENGLISH  GOTHIC GERMAN  GOTHIC ITALIAN
  ☐   ABC123    ☐   ABC123    ☐   ABC123   |LAY
                                            |
                                            |IRY
                                            |R:
     GREEK SIMPLEX   GREEK COMPLEX          |INGS
  ☐   ΣΩ        ☐   ΣΩ        ☐ Next       |ITY
                                            |
                                            |
                                            |DE
     SCRIPT SIMPLEX  SCRIPT COMPLEX         |
  ☐   ABC123    ☐   ABC123    ☐ Exit      |:
Text:
Text:
Command:
```

More Text Fonts

Setting a Text Style (Fonts)

Pull down **[Options]** *Select* **[Fonts...]** **[ROMAN COMPLEX]**   From the icon menu, or
Select **[SETTINGS]** **[next]** **[STYLE]** **[fonts]** **[Romanc]** **[Romanc]**   from the screen menu, or just
Command: **STYLE**   type STYLE, then ROMANC.
Text style name (or ?) <STANDARD>: **ROMANC**   Style is supplied if you use menus.
New style.
Font file <txt>: **ROMANC**   Font is supplied if you use menus.
Height <0.00>: **<RETURN>**   Default the options.
Width factor <1.00>: **<RETURN>**
Obliquing angle <0>: **<RETURN>**
Backwards? <N> **<RETURN>**
Upside-down? <N> **<RETURN>**
Vertical? <N> **<RETURN>**

ROMANC is now the current text style.

Of course, you can set any of the options to distort the style as desired.
The height option is noteworthy. If set to zero, the text commands prompt
for and control height. If the style height is set to any other value (a fixed
height style), it controls height and the text commands do not prompt for
it.

Let's generate some fancy text on the PART drawing, this time using the
TEXT command.

Generating ROMANC Text

```
Command: TEXT
Start point or Align/Center/Fit/Middle/Right/Style: R     Right justified.
End point:                                                Pick a point.
Height <0.40>: <RETURN>
Rotation angle <0>: <RETURN>
Text: Drawn By: YOUR NAME                                  Substitute your name.

Command: <RETURN>                                         Repeats TEXT command.
TEXT Start point or Align/Center/Fit/Middle/Right/Style: <RETURN>    The default.
Text: Date: June 15, 1989
```

After adding the fancy text, your completed PART drawing should look
like the illustration below.

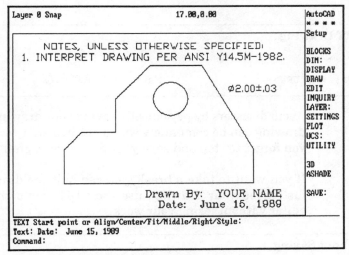

Fancy Text Completes the Drawing

When you use a text command, the previous text (if any) is highlighted.
Using <RETURN> to default at the start point prompt accepts the
previous style, justification, height, and rotation without reprompting,
and positions the new line under the previous one.

Many styles can be defined, but only one style can be current. To change
current styles, use the Style option of the text commands or use the
STYLE command and default its options.

Saving, Quitting, and Ending

Saving will do exactly what the name implies. It will save your drawing to the disk. You can save the drawing under the default directory and name, in this case PART in the directory SI-ACAD. You may also direct the file to be saved under any other existing directory and file name (such as \SIA-DWG\PARTY). After the drawing is saved, you will remain in the drawing editor to continue with your project.

END/QUIT/SAVE

> *The END command updates (saves) the drawing file and exits to AutoCAD's main menu. The old drawing file becomes the new .BAK file. QUIT exits the drawing editor without updating the drawing file. SAVE updates the drawing file and leaves you in the drawing editor for further editing. SAVE also creates a .BAK file.*

Saving Your PART Drawing

```
Command: SAVE
File name <PART>: <RETURN>            Saves as PART.DWG.
```

Avoid disasters by periodically saving your drawing file. A day's worth of drawing can be completely wiped out in a split second of power outage if you forget to stop and save your file every so often.

If you want to take a break, you can quit the drawing editor. Since you just saved your drawing, use the QUIT command to exit the drawing editor without losing your work.

QUIT to Exit Without Saving

```
Command: QUIT                                    Type QUIT.
Really want to discard all changes to drawing? Y   Enter Y for yes.
```

We'll use the END command at the end of the chapter.

HELP — Getting It When You Need It

As you begin using more AutoCAD commands, there may be occasions when you get lost. Help is available almost anytime you need it.

'HELP or '?

> *HELP lists available commands and provides specific information about the operation of individual commands.*
> Command name (RETURN for list):

To invoke help when you are at a Command: prompt, type HELP or just a question mark. You will be prompted for what you want help with. A <RETURN> displays a listing of available topics. Try it.

Using the HELP Command

Continue in the previous drawing, or edit an EXISTING drawing named PART.

```
Command: HELP                                    Or just type a ?
Command name (RETURN for list): <RETURN>
Press RETURN for further help. <RETURN>
Press RETURN for further help. <RETURN>
Press RETURN for further help. <RETURN>
```

This will cycle you through four screens of commands and general help.

```
AutoCAD Command List  (' = transparent command)

APERTURE   CHANGE     DIVIDE     EXPLODE    IGESOUT
ARC        CHPROP     DONUT      EXTEND     INSERT
AREA       CIRCLE     DOUGHNUT   FILES      ISOPLANE
ARRAY      COLOR      DRAGMODE   FILL       LAYER
ATTDEF     COPY       DTEXT      FILLET     LIMITS
ATTDISP    DBLIST     DVIEW      FILMROLL   LINE
ATTEDIT    DDATTE     DXBIN      'GRAPHSCR  LINETYPE
ATTEXT     'DDEMODES  DXFIN      GRID       LIST
AXIS       'DDLMODES  DXFOUT     HANDLES    LOAD
BASE       'DDRMODES  EDGESURF   HATCH      LTSCALE
BLIPMODE   DDUCS      ELEV       'HELP / '? MEASURE
BLOCK      DELAY      ELLIPSE    HIDE       MENU
BREAK      DIM/DIM1   END        ID         MINSERT
CHAMFER    DIST       ERASE      IGESIN     MIRROR

Press RETURN for further help.
```
Commands

```
AutoCAD Command List  (' = transparent command)

MOVE       PRPLOT     ROTATE     STRETCH    UNITS
MSLIDE     PURGE      RSCRIPT    STYLE      'VIEW
MULTIPLE   QTEXT      RULESURF   TABLET     VIEWPORTS
OFFSET     QUIT       SAVE       TABSURF    VIEWRES
OOPS       REDEFINE   SCALE      TEXT       VPOINT
ORTHO      REDO       SCRIPT     'TEXTSCR   VPORTS
OSNAP      'REDRAW    SELECT     TIME       VSLIDE
'PAN       'REDRAWALL 'SETVAR    TRACE      WBLOCK
PEDIT      REGEN      SHAPE      TRIM       'ZOOM
PLAN       REGENALL   SHELL/SH   U          3DFACE
PLINE      REGENAUTO  SKETCH     UCS        3DMESH
PLOT       RENAME     SNAP       UCSICON    3DPOLY
POINT      'RESUME    SOLID      UNDEFINE
POLYGON    REVSURF    STATUS     UNDO

At the "Command:" prompt, you can enter RETURN to repeat the last command.

Press RETURN for further help.
```
More Commands

```
You can enter points, or coordinates, in any of the following ways:

   Absolute:  x,y
   Relative:  @deltax,deltay
   Polar:     @dist<angle

For the commands that accept 3D points, you can include a Z coordinate
in the absolute and relative formats:

   Absolute:  x,y,z
   Relative:  @deltax,deltay,deltaz

If you omit the Z coordinate, the current elevation is used.

X/Y/Z filters can be used to compose a full point from the X, Y, and
Z components of intermediate points.  For instance, the filter ".X"
will instruct AutoCAD to use just the X coordinate of the following
point.  The Y (and possibly Z) values will then be requested.

See also:  Section 2.7 of the Reference Manual.

Press RETURN for further help.
```

Point Entry

```
Object selection:  ("Select objects:")

   (point)  = One object
   Multiple = Multiple objects selected by pointing
   Last     = Last object
   Previous = All objects in the Previous selection-set
   Window   = Objects within Window
   Crossing = Objects within or Crossing window
   BOX      = Automatic Crossing (to the left) or Window (to the right)
   AUto     = Automatic BOX (if pick in empty area) or single object pick
   SIngle   = One selection (any type)
   Add      = Add mode: add following objects to selection-set
   Remove   = Remove mode: remove following objects from selection-set
   Undo     = Undo/remove last

When you are satisfied with the selection-set as it stands, enter RETURN
(except for "Single" mode, which does not require an extra RETURN).

See also:  Section 2.9 of the Reference Manual.

Command:
```

Object Selection

You can also get help on any specific command.

Getting Help on a Specific Command

To get help on individual commands, enter the command's name at the HELP command name prompt, or use 'HELP or '? transparently in the middle of other commands. Let's take a look at help for the CIRCLE and LINE commands.

HELP With the CIRCLE Command

```
Command: HELP
Command name (RETURN for list): CIRCLE

Command: LINE
From point: '?

Press RETURN to resume LINE command.
Resuming LINE command.
From point: <^C>

Command: <F1>
```

Enter HELP or ?

Displays a screenful of CIRCLE information.

Or enter 'HELP.
Displays a screenful of LINE information.

Cancel it.

Toggle to return to the graphics screen.

```
The CIRCLE command is used to draw a circle. You can specify the circle
in several ways. The simplest method is by center point and radius.

Format:     CIRCLE 3P/2P/TTR/<Center point>: (point)
            Diameter/<Radius>: (radius value)

To specify the radius, you can designate a point to be on the
circumference. You may enter "DRAG" in response to the "Diameter/<Radius>"
prompt to specify the circle size visually. If it is more convenient to
enter the diameter than the radius, reply to the "Diameter/<Radius>" prompt
with "D".

The circle can also be specified using three points on the circumference
(reply "3P" when prompted for the center point), or by designating two
endpoints of its diameter (reply "2P"). For these methods, you can "drag"
the last point or specify object snap "Tangent" points.

In addition, you can draw a circle by specifying two lines (and/or other
circles) to which the circle should be tangent, and a radius. Enter "TTR"
for this option.

See also:  Section 4.3 of the Reference Manual.

Command:
```

Displaying Help for the CIRCLE Command

You can customize your HELP file by adding drafting standards or other information to it. For more details on customizing the HELP file, refer to the book, CUSTOMIZING AutoCAD.

Inquiry — Drafting Inspection Tools

Most drafting projects conform to rigorous standards of accuracy. Use the following inquiry commands to inspect a drawing for correct parameters and geometry or to get information about existing objects.

AREA — Calculates an area and perimeter.

DBLIST — Data base listing of all entities (see LIST).

DIST — Measures the distance between two points.

ID — Identifies X,Y,Z of a pick point.

LIST — Lists drawing information on selected entities.

STATUS — Provides screen and parameter status.

TIME — Provides information on drawing time.

The inquiry tools are especially useful for specific design tasks such as checking the tolerances of mating parts. They always display their results in whatever units format you have set up. Let's take a closer look at a few of AutoCAD's inquiry (or *inspection*) tools.

> AREA
>
> *The AREA command lets you calculate an area by picking a series of points or by selecting entities (circles and polylines). In addition to the area, you are also given the perimeter, and line length or circumference. You can keep a running total by adding and subtracting areas. The default picks points to define the area.*
> `<First point>/Entity/Add/Subtract:`

You can add or subtract areas to determine an area of unusual shape. Let's let AutoCAD calculate the areas of our circle and of our entire part.

Calculating Area and Perimeter

Continue in the previous drawing, or edit an EXISTING drawing named PART.

```
Select [INQUIRY] [AREA:]
Command: AREA                                           Or just type AREA.
<First point>/Entity/Add/Subtract: A                   Enter A or select [Add].
(ADD mode) Next point:                                  Pick each perimeter point in turn.
(ADD mode) Next point: <RETURN>                         Finish and calculate.

Area = 55.00, Perimeter = 32.07
Total area = 55.00

<First point>/Entity/Subtract: S                        Or select [Subtract].
<First point>/Entity/Add: E                             Entity selection mode.
(SUBTRACT mode) Select circle or polyline:              Select the circle.
Area = 3.14, Circumference = 6.28
Total area = 51.86

(SUBTRACT mode) Select circle or polyline: <RETURN>     Exit entity mode.
<First point>/Entity/Add: <RETURN>                      Finished.
```

You can continue to add or subtract any number of entities or sets of points within a single AREA command.

```
Command:
```

> DIST
>
> *DISTANCE is an inquiry command that determines the length of an imaginary 2D or 3D line, its angle in the XY plane, its angle from the XY plane if 3D, and the delta XY (or XYZ) between two points.*
> `First point:    Second point:`

Measuring the Distance Between Two Points

```
Command: DIST
First point:                                    Pick any point.
Second point:                                   Pick any point.
Distance = 2.79,   Angle in X-Y Plane = 21,   Angle from X-Y Plane = 0
Delta X = 2.60,   Delta Y = 1.00,   Delta Z = 0.00
```

Of course, your results will vary depending on the points you picked.

ID | *ID identifies the absolute X,Y,Z coordinates of any selected point.*
`Point:`

Checking the Position of a Point

```
Command: ID                                     Pick any point.
 X = 14.60      Y = 7.40      Z = 0.00          Your point will vary.
```

LIST/DBLIST *The LIST command provides information on selected entities within a drawing. The DBLIST (database) command provides information on all entities within a drawing. These commands list layer assignment, XYZ position relative to the current UCS, and color and linetype (if not the default BYLAYER).*

You can list information about specific entities. When you select the LIST command, you are prompted to select which entity to list. You can select an individual entity or you can select multiple entities. The selection will return a lengthy list of information that includes linetypes, layers, locations, lengths, angles, and perimeters.

Let's list information for a line, circle, and text, as shown below. When you have completed the selections, AutoCAD will return a text screen with information similar to ours.

Listing Information About Entities

Continue in the previous drawing, or edit an EXISTING drawing named PART.

```
Command: LIST
Select objects:                         Pick the bottom line on part.
1 selected, 1 found.
Select objects:                         Pick the circle.
1 selected, 1 found.
Select objects:                         Pick the top text string.
1 selected, 1 found.
Select objects: <RETURN>                To end selections.
                                        AutoCAD flips to text screen.


            LINE      Layer: 0
        from point, X=    14.00  Y=     2.00  Z=     0.00
          to point, X=     3.00  Y=     2.00  Z=     0.00
   Length =    11.00,  Angle in X-Y Plane =    180
          Delta X =   -11.00, Delta Y =    0.00, Delta Z =    0.00


            CIRCLE    Layer: 0
     center point, X=     9.20  Y=     7.00  Z=     0.00
     radius      1.00
     Circumference =       6.28,   Area = 3.14


            TEXT      Layer: 0
     Style = STANDARD   Font file = txt
        start point, X=     1.00  Y=    10.00  Z=      0.00
     height       0.40
        text NOTES, UNLESS OTHERWISE SPECIFIED
     rotation angle        0
        width scale factor      1.0000
   obliquing angle        0
 generation normal
```

If a long listing scrolls off the screen, you can press <^S> to halt the scroll. Depressing any key will continue the listing process. If you have a printer, you can press <^Q> before executing the command to echo the data to the printer. Another <^Q> turns the printer echo off.

Next, we'll check the status of our current drawing with the STATUS command.

STATUS

> *STATUS gives you current information on drawing limits, extents, the drawing aids settings, and some system information. The status report is a text screen.*

AutoCAD will return a text screen with information as shown below. Some of the status information we present may be different from yours because of differences in workstation configurations. Other information, such as number of entities, may also vary. All entities created are counted, even if erased.

Checking the Status of Your Drawing

Command: **STATUS**   AutoCAD flips to text screen.

```
33 entities in PART
Limits are        X:      0.00      17.00   (Off)
                  Y:      0.00      11.00
Drawing uses      X:      0.00      17.00 **Over
                  Y:      0.00      11.00 **Over
Display shows     X:      0.00      17.00
                  Y:      0.00      16.15
Insertion base is X:      0.00   Y:      0.00   Z:      0.00
Snap resolution is X:     0.20   Y:      0.20
Grid spacing is   X:      1.00   Y:      1.00

Current layer:     0
Current color:     BYLAYER -- 7 (white)
Current linetype: BYLAYER -- CONTINUOUS
Current elevation:        0.00  thickness:        0.00
Axis on  Fill on  Grid on  Ortho off  Qtext off  Snap on  Tablet off
Object snap modes: None
Free RAM: 12488 bytes        Free disk: 9123840 bytes
I/O page space:  81K bytes   Extended I/O page space: 1024K bytes
```

Command: Toggle <F1> back to graphic screen.

Take some time to look over your drawing's status. Information like this can provide the answers to many questions you may have regarding your drawings in the future.

You will find the TIME command useful in checking the progress of drawings.

TIME

> *TIME displays the following: current date and time; date and time the drawing was created; date and time the drawing was last updated; and the current amount of time in the drawing editor. In addition, you can set an elapsed timer. The default setting has the elapsed timer on.*

Let's check the time in your PART drawing.

Checking the Time

```
Command: TIME                    AutoCAD flips to text screen.

Current time:           01 Jan 1989 at 19:34:40.940
Drawing created:        01 Jan 1989 at 18:34:04.920
Drawing last updated:   01 Jan 1989 at 18:45:34.180
Time in Drawing Editor: 0 days 01:00:35.960
Elapsed timer:          0 days 01:00:35.960
Timer on.
Display/ON/OFF/Reset: <RETURN>
```

Your times will, of course, vary from ours. We've almost reached the end of our tour.

END — Saving and Exiting the Drawing Editor

If you created a masterpiece during this tour of AutoCAD and wish to save the drawing as you exit the drawing editor, the END command will do the job in one step.

END to Save and Exit

```
Command: END                              Type END.
```

Your drawing should now be saved to the SI-ACAD directory of your hard disk. For real security, you will want to back up your work on diskettes.

Copying Your Drawing to a Backup Diskette

The sequence below uses the DOS COPY command to copy the PART.DWG file from the subdirectory named SI-ACAD to a formatted diskette in drive A. Then, since this isn't a *real* drawing, you might want to erase the drawing file(s) on the hard drive with a DELETE command.

Backing Up With the DOS COPY Command

```
Enter selection: 0          Enter 0 to exit to DOS.
                            The SIA.BAT batch file resets the AutoCAD variables and returns you to the
                            root directory.

C:\SI-ACAD>SET ACAD=
C:\SI-ACAD>SET ACADCFG=
C:\SI-ACAD>CD \
```

Put a formatted diskette in drive A.

```
C:\> COPY SI-ACAD\PART.DWG  A:        Copy it to drive A.
C:\> DIR A:                           Lists the file(s) on drive A.
 Volume in drive A has no label
 Directory of  A:\

PART     DWG    4704   6-02-89   5:18p    Your data will vary.

C:\> COMP SI-ACAD\PART.DWG A:         Verify the copy.
C:SI-ACAD\PART.DWG and A:PART.DWG
Eof mark not found
Files compare ok
Compare more files (Y/N)? N

C:\> DEL SI-ACAD\PART.DWG A:          Clean up — delete the drawing on drive C.
```

As you proceed through the book, back up the drawings you want to save. For your work drawings, you should have at least two current copies in existence, and make additional backups at regular intervals.

For your trip through this book, delete the drawings you don't want to keep so your hard disk won't get cluttered.

Summary

Menus are powerful tools within AutoCAD, and using them efficiently will increase your drafting productivity. You have seen that many commands may be executed from the screen, tablet, pull-down, and icon menus, or from being typed at the command prompt. AutoCAD gives you a great deal of flexibility in command entry. With a little practice, you will soon find your preference.

This has been only a brief tour of AutoCAD's menu options, electronic drawing sheet, positioning tools, inquiry commands, and file handling procedures. As you progress through STEPPING INTO AutoCAD, your ability to use AutoCAD for technical drafting and design will continue to expand. In Chapter 3, we'll develop drafting prototypes for efficient drawing and hard copy output. You will see how you can save valuable time by developing, and re-using, prototype drawings with preset drafting parameters and annotations.

Let's get started on that prototype drawing . . .

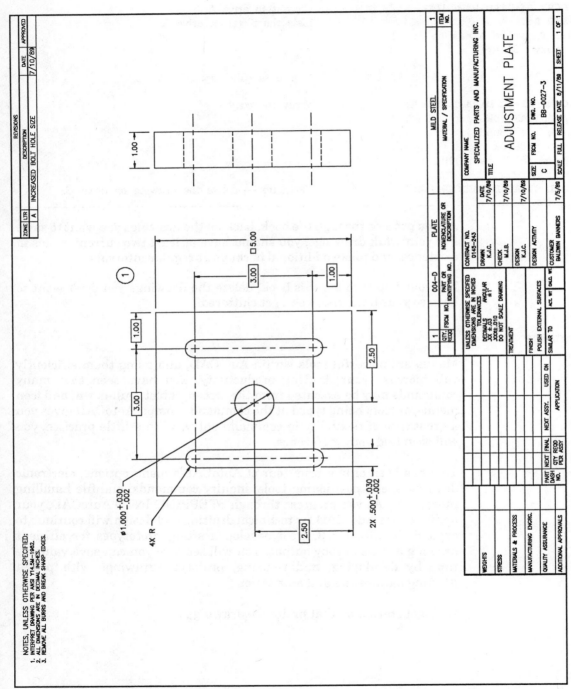

Prototype Title Block With PLATE Drawing

CHAPTER 3

Prototype Drawings

BORDERS, TITLE BLOCKS, AND MORE

Information is often repeated from drawing to drawing. This standard information can include pre-printed borders and title blocks for various sheet sizes, and pre-printed or sticky-back legends, general notes, and BOM's (bills of materials). AutoCAD's *prototype* drawings allow you to automate routine elements in your CAD drawings. A prototype drawing is simply an existing drawing that is used as the starting point for a new drawing. You can have any number of prototypes, and one can be preset in the configuration menu as the default prototype. Others can be called from the main menu when you start a new drawing.

But prototype drawings can provide more than just pre-drawn borders and title blocks. AutoCAD has many settings, drawing layers, dimensioning settings, viewport configurations, and other system variables. If one of your objectives for using AutoCAD is to reduce drafting time, it is not efficient for you to spend valuable work time setting up drawing parameters each time you begin a new project. By creating a series of prototype drawings, you will have a system already geared to fit your 2D or 3D drafting and design needs every time you start a drawing.

The main aspects of drawing setup are *system settings* such as drawing size, snap, grid, coords, ortho, text styles, and dimensioning setup, and standard *graphic elements* such as title blocks and borders. There are several methods for controlling these components, including prototype drawings, startup menus, and automatic AutoLISP routines that set up your drawing. The best system is a combination of all three methods, which can automate the handling of multiple sheet sizes and plot scales. However, for simplicity, we'll start with a single multi-purpose prototype drawing which incorporates both system settings and graphic elements.

This will be a generic 2D prototype, not specific to any particular industrial discipline. In keeping with our theme, the sheet size, border, drawing arrangement, title block format, supplemental data block format, standard tolerance block, treatment block, finish block, parts list, and revision block are all defined according to ANSI Y14.1 standards.

➡ *NOTE: The exercise shows you how to develop a prototype in decimal inch measurements. If you need to draft in ISO-SI metric, you will find that with a few size and variable modifications, this exercise provides an excellent guide to the creation of metric prototypes.*

Creating a Generic Drafting Prototype

This chapter shows you how to create a C-size (22 x 17) prototype drawing, which we'll name PROTO-C. This prototype is designed for use in this book's exercises. It is an example of a typical startup prototype, which you can copy and modify to suit the needs of your particular application. The most straightforward part is making the drawing settings.

Standard Drawing Settings

Settings commonly made in most drawings include snap, grid, units, text height, and style, all of which we used in the previous chapter. We will also set the drawing size, zoom the screen, and make the other settings shown. The following table is typical of how we display groups of settings as a guide to drawing setup.

COORDS	GRID	LTSCALE	SNAP
DIST<ANGLE	1.0/ON	0.375	0.0625/ON
TEXT HEIGHT	**APERTURE**	**PICKBOX**	
0.1255	5	2	
UNITS	Decimal, all defaults.		
STYLE	ROMANS		
LIMITS	0,0 to 22,17		
ZOOM	0.8		
VIEW	ALL		

Prototype Drawing Settings

If you have the SIA DISK, it includes a ready-to-use prototype drawing named PROTO-C. However, unless you are familiar with all of the above settings as well as dimension variables, layers, colors, linetypes, views, and UCS's, perform the following exercises anyway for practice, but don't save the results. You can skip the repetitive parts. If you are familiar with this material, just read along to see if you can pick up anything new.

 If you don't have the SIA DISK, you will need to create the PROTO-C prototype drawing before proceeding to the next chapter.

Starting the Drawing and Setting the Limits

The first step is to use the LIMITS command to make a C-size drawing sheet. A C-size sheet is 22 x 17 inches, so we will set up our drawing area as 22 x 17. This will work fine for full scale. We will deal with other scales at the end of this chapter.

LIMITS

> *LIMITS determines your drawing area or boundaries, defined by the absolute coordinates of the lower left and upper right-hand corners. With the LIMITS command, you can modify these values or turn limits checking on and off. The default settings are from 0,0 to 12,9 with limits checking off.*
> ```
> ON/OFF/<Lower left corner> <0.0000,0.0000>:
> Upper right corner <12.0000,9.0000>:
> ```

The limits checking feature is enabled by turning limits on. When limits checking is on, you cannot enter points outside the drawing limits. This avoids the problem of accidentally drafting entities outside the drawing sheet. We won't turn limits checking on yet because we will later set up a scratch area for temporary drawing and parts development that is deliberately outside the drawing sheet.

➡ *NOTE: Some versions of AutoCAD Release 10 become slow in object snapping and entity selection if you draw outside the limits. This was fixed in the AutoCAD Release 10 c7 and later versions. Updates are available from your dealer. Your version is shown in the header of the main menu.*

Let's start the drawing and set the limits. Use the equal sign in the drawing name to ensure that you start with the default settings you want.

Getting Started and Setting Limits

`C:\> `**`SIA`**   Use SIA.BAT to start AutoCAD for all of our exercises.

   Begin a NEW drawing named TEMP=, or just read along.

   Begin a NEW drawing named PROTO-C=.

```
Command: LIMITS
ON/OFF/<Lower left corner> <0.0000,0.0000>: <RETURN>
Upper right corner <12.0000,9.0000>: 22,17
```
                                        Enter the new sheet size.

The corner values for the LIMITS command may be any value. For example, instead of using 0,0 for the lower left corner, you could use a negative coordinate.

Because we will use the default settings, we don't need to set units. The precision (number of digits to the right of the decimal point in the UNITS command) controls how many digits the coordinate read-out displays and dimensions. If you set it to three digits, the read-out will look like this: X.XXX. Although only three digits display, you may enter more precise values. For example, if you entered .0625, AutoCAD would record the exact value in the drawing database even though the displayed value would be rounded off to .063 units.

The default is four places precision (0.0000). We can easily control precision as needed by setting the LUPREC (Linear Units PRECision) and DIMRND (DIMension ROUNDing) system variables. We generally recommend leaving precision set to a large number like four. The extra places won't hurt anything and may help to avoid errors that can occur when the coords display roundoff misleads you into thinking an inaccurate but rounded off number is accurate. The DIMRND system variable can control the precision of dimensioning independently of display units precision.

Setting System Variables With SETVAR

When you use commands such as SNAP, GRID, and LIMITS, AutoCAD stores the settings as *system variables*. A system variable is a stored setting with a name by which it can be accessed and changed. AutoCAD has over 130 system variables. For example GRID affects two variables: GRIDMODE and GRIDUNIT. GRIDMODE is a grid on/off setting represented by 1 for on and 0 for off. (All system variables use 1 for on and 0 for off.) GRIDUNIT is a point or coordinate value, such as 1.0000,1.0000 for a one-unit square grid. The values are always shown in current units, although you can enter them in decimal form with any precision, regardless of current units.

'SETVAR

> *SETVAR retrieves and modifies system variables. Most system variables are also modified through AutoCAD commands. A few system variables are "read-only." Enter a ? for a listing of all variables.*
> ```
> Variable name or ? <default>:
> ```

Most system variables affected by AutoCAD's many commands can be changed directly with the SETVAR command. While SETVAR is often used in menus, it has one great advantage in everyday drafting: 'SETVAR is transparent, so you can use it in the middle of nearly any other command. For example, you can't use SNAP in the middle of a LINE command, but you can use 'SETVAR transparently.

Example: Setting SNAPUNIT

```
To point: 'SETVAR                    The quote makes it transparent.
>>Variable name or ?: SNAPUNIT       >> indicates suspension.
>>New value for SNAPUNIT <0.1250,0.1250>: .1,.1
Resuming LINE command.
To point:                            It uses the new 0.1 unit snap.
```

When used in the middle of another command, SETVAR suspends that command temporarily, giving you a double angle bracket prompt (>>) to indicate suspension.

Another reason to use SETVAR is simplicity. For example, the UNITS command steps through a long series of options, but each has its own system variable. You can use SETVAR to change one variable without having to deal with related settings. We could easily change the precision of linear units to three by using SETVAR LUPREC.

Example: Setting Linear Units of Precision (LUPREC)

```
Command: SETVAR
Variable name or ?: LUPREC
New value for LUPREC <4>: 3
```

The similar AUPREC variable sets the precision of angular units. Try it on your own.

Let's set some system variables. Although we could set snap, grid, and similar settings with their commands or through menu and dialogue boxes, let's use SETVAR instead. The following is a list of the variables we will set with SETVAR. The use of some of these settings will become clearer in later exercises or chapters. For a complete list of system variables, refer to Appendix C.

APERTURE — sets the object snap "target" size in pixel units. See the OSNAP command definition for details.

COORDS — 0 for off (updates only when a point is picked), 1 for continuous X,Y update, and 2 for continuous dist<angle display update.

GRIDMODE — turns the grid on (1) and off (0).

GRIDUNIT — a coordinate value representing the X,Y grid spacing.

PICKBOX — sets the object selection box size in pixel units. When selecting objects, the pick box is displayed on the screen instead of the cursor to aid in picking objects or entities. The pick box must touch the entity you wish to pick, but too large a size will touch entities you don't want.

SNAPMODE — turns the snap on (1) and off (0).

SNAPUNIT — a coordinate value representing the X,Y snap spacing.

TEXTSIZE — sets the current text height.

TEXTSTYLE — sets the current text style.

UCSICON — turns the USC icon display on and off, and allows you to make it display at the 0,0,0 origin point.

SNAP has several other variables which control rotation, style, and base point. You can offset the snap grid to any increment base point, rotate it to any angle, and set it to isometric style. The grid and axis follow snap's style, angle, and base point.

➡ *The aperture and pick box are sized in pixels above and below the cursor crosshairs, so a setting of 5 yields a total height of 10 (five above and five below). You may like your aperture and pick box larger or smaller than the settings we show, depending on your video resolution. The greater your resolution, the larger your preference will probably be.*

Let's set the variables listed above.

Changing Settings With System Variables

Continue in the PROTO-C drawing.

```
Select [SETTINGS] [next] ['SETVAR:]
Command: SETVAR                                    Or just type SETVAR
Variable name or ?: APERTURE
New value for APERTURE <5>: 5


Command: <RETURN>                                  To repeat the command.
SETVAR Variable name or ? <APERTURE>: COORDS
New value for COORDS <0>: 2


Command: <RETURN>
SETVAR Variable name or ? <COORDS>: GRIDMODE
New value for GRIDMODE <0>: 1
```

```
Command: <RETURN>
SETVAR Variable name or ? <GRIDMODE>: GRIDUNIT
New value for GRIDUNIT <0.0000,0.0000>: 1,1

Command: <RETURN>
SETVAR Variable name or ? <GRIDUNIT>: PICKBOX
New value for PICKBOX <3>: 2

Command: <RETURN>
SETVAR Variable name or ? <PICKBOX>: SNAPMODE
New value for SNAPMODE <0>: 1

Command: <RETURN>
SETVAR Variable name or ? <SNAPMODE>: SNAPUNIT
New value for SNAPUNIT <1.0000,1.0000>: .0625,.0625

Command: <RETURN>
SETVAR Variable name or ? <SNAPUNIT>: TEXTSIZE
New value for TEXTSIZE <0.2000>: .125

Command: <RETURN>
SETVAR Variable name or ? <TEXTSIZE>: TEXTSTYLE
TEXTSTYLE = "STANDARD" (read only)

Command: <RETURN>
SETVAR Variable name or ? <TEXTSTYLE>: UCSICON
New value for UCSICON <1>: 3
Command: REGEN                                    Regenerate the screen.
```

You probably noticed some inconsistency in the execution of these settings. If used transparently with 'SETVAR, some will take effect immediately, some after the next bit of input, and some will not take effect until after the current command is ended. Some settings do not display until you *regenerate* (recalculate and redisplay) the screen, even if they take effect immediately. Read the command definitions below, and experiment as you work through our exercises to find what is useful and when.

REGEN/REGENALL

> *REGEN causes the current viewport to be regenerated (recalculated and redrawn); REGENALL regenerates all viewports. When a drawing is regenerated, the data and geometry associated with all entities is recalculated. REGEN and REGENALL are not transparent commands. You can cancel a regeneration with <^C>.*

REGENAUTO

> *REGENAUTO lets you control some (not all) regenerations. Some changes, such as block redefinitions, linetype scale changes, or redefined text styles, require a regeneration before they are made visible. Sometimes, particularly when making multiple changes, you do not want to wait for these regenerations. You can set REGENAUTO off and use the REGEN command to regenerate the screen when you are ready to look at the results.*
> ON/OFF <On>:

'REDRAW/ 'REDRAWALL

> *REDRAW cleans up the current viewport. REDRAWALL cleans up all viewports. Blips are removed and any entities or parts of entities that seem to have disappeared during editing are redrawn. Grid dots are redrawn if the grid is on. These are transparent commands. (If the grid is on, you can get the same effect by toggling the grid with two <F7>s or <^G>s.)*

Some variables, such as TEXTSTYLE, cannot be changed by SETVAR. These *read-only* variables can be changed only by the commands that control them. We'll have to use the STYLE command to set TEXTSTYLE.

Setting Text Style

```
Command: STYLE
Text style name (or ?) <STANDARD>: ROMANS
New style.
Font file <txt>: ROMANS
Height <0.00>: <RETURN>                 Default the options.
Width factor <1.00>: <RETURN>
Obliquing angle <0>: <RETURN>
Backwards? <N> <RETURN>
Upside-down? <N> <RETURN>
Vertical? <N> <RETURN>
ROMANS is now the current text style.

Command: SAVE                           Save for safety, unless you have the SIA DISK.
File name <PROTO-C> <RETURN>
```

AutoCAD uses over 30 system variables to control dimensioning.

Getting the Prototype Ready for Dimensioning

We'll explore dimensioning with AutoCAD in detail later, but while we are creating the prototype drawing, we need to preset some variables. Dimensioning variables consist of three main types: those that control dimensioning scale of components, those that control dimensioning style such as tolerancing, and those that toggle dimensioning options on and off. You can set dimensioning variables with SETVAR, but the AutoCAD DIM command mode allows them to be controlled directly, simply, and transparently.

To set up the prototype drawing to control dimensioning variables according to ANSI Y14.5, the following dimension variables should be reset. For a complete listing and description of all dimensioning variables, refer to the system variables table in Appendix C.

DIMASZ — controls arrow size from base to point (it also controls text fit).

DIMCEN — controls circle/arc center tick marks and center extension lines. The positive default of 0.09 causes AutoCAD to generate only a .09 long tick mark at the center of the circle/arc. A zero value causes no marks or lines to be drawn. A negative value defines the length of the tick mark and the distance which the extension lines project past the circle/arc perimeter.

DIMDLI — controls the dimension line increment (spacing between dimension lines) for continuous and base line dimensions.

DIMEXE — specifies how far the extension line extends beyond the dimension line.

DIMEXO — specifies the extension line offset from the dimension origin points.

DIMTXT — controls height of dimensioning text.

DIMZIN — controls whether or not leading and trailing zeros will be generated. See your AutoCAD Reference Manual for complete details.

Use the following instructions to set each of the dimension variables described above.

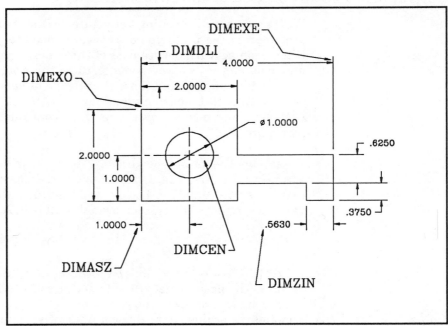

Effects of Default Dimensioning Settings

Setting Dimension Variables

Continue in the PROTO-C drawing.

```
Command: DIM                      Dimensioning command mode has its own DIM: prompt.
DIM: DIMASZ
Current value <0.1800> New value: .125     Arrow size.
DIM: DIMCEN
Current value <0.0900> New value: -.1      Draw both center mark and center lines.
DIM: DIMDLI
Current value <0.3800> New value: .5       Dimension line increment.
DIM: DIMEXE
Current value <0.1800> New value: .125     Extension line extension.
DIM: DIMEXO
Current value <0.0625> New value: .125     Extension line offset.
DIM: DIMRND
Current value <0.0000> New value: .001     Round to three places.
DIM: DIMTXT
Current value <0.1800> New value: .125     Text height.
DIM: DIMZIN
Current value <0> New value: 4             Suppress leading zeros on decimals.
DIM: EXIT                          Or you can use <^C> to exit.
Command: SAVE                      Unless you have the SIA DISK.
```

There is also an overall size variable named DIMSCALE that controls all of these size-related dimensioning variables. For a full size plot scale, we'll leave DIMSCALE set to 1. Scaling is explained at the end of this chapter.

➡ *NOTE: The above settings will be our defaults, We will adjust DIMCEN, DIMDLI, and others which have been left at AutoCAD's standard defaults as we need them.*

We can also include graphic elements, such as a border and title block, in our prototype.

Creating a Border and Title Block

To plan your title block, you need to consider the border that your plotter can accommodate. Most plotters can't (and you wouldn't normally want them to) plot all the way to the edges of the paper. You need to allow room for a border that fits within the *available plot area* of your particular plotter (or printer). The AutoCAD PLOT and PRPLOT commands display what this available area is. Let's check it. (To do this check, your AutoCAD must be configured for a plotter or printer-plotter.)

Checking the Area of Your Plotter

```
Command: PLOT                                    Or PRPLOT to check a printer-plotter.
What to plot -- Display, Extents, Limits, View, or Window : <RETURN>
```

The current plotting parameters are displayed . . .

```
Do you want to change anything? <N>: Y
```

Plotting entity color, pen number, linetype, and pen speed are presented . . .

Hit several <RETURN>s and you get:

```
Standard values for plotting size

Size    Width    Height          Your sizes will vary with your plotter.
A       10.50     8.00
B       16.00    10.00
C       21.00    16.00
D       33.00    21.00
MAX     44.72    23.30

Enter the Size or Width,Height (in Inches) <MAX>: <^C><RETURN>
```
                                    Cancel, then return to continue.

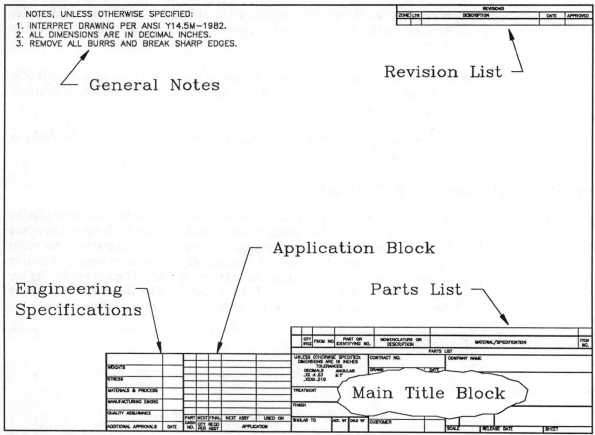

NOTES, UNLESS OTHERWISE SPECIFIED:
1. INTERPRET DRAWING PER ANSI Y14.5M—1982.
2. ALL DIMENSIONS ARE IN DECIMAL INCHES.
3. REMOVE ALL BURRS AND BREAK SHARP EDGES.

General Notes

Revision List

Application Block

Engineering Specifications

Parts List

Main Title Block

The Complete Sheet

The above list shows typical maximum areas available for various size plot sheets, in our case an HP DraftPro plotter. Let's consider a C-size sheet.

The C-size area shown above is 21.00 wide by 16.00 high. This is the maximum effective plotting area that you can plot without clipping any portion of the drawing. In other words, the largest full scale object that this plotter can plot on a C-size sheet is 21 x 16. So we need to design our border to fit within that area. If your plotter has a smaller maximum effective plotting area, you'll have to adjust the border dimensions in the following exercises. If larger, you could expand them, but it might be simpler to just leave them at 21 x 16. In our case, the ANSI standard C-size sheet had to be changed to account for the C-size effective plotting area of the HP DraftPro plotter.

We'll be using polylines and lines to draw our prototype's border and title block.

Drafting a Polyline Border

The border, title block, weight block, application block, parts list, and revision list are drawn using AutoCAD's PLINE command. When completed, the prototype will match the illustration above. First we'll draw the simple outer border with a polyline. Polylines are different from ordinary lines in several ways.

PLINE

> *A polyline is a series of line and arc segments that are interconnected because they share the same vertices and are processed as a single entity. The PLINE command draws 2D polylines. PLINE starts with a From point prompt. After entering the first point, you can continue in line mode or arc mode. Each mode has its own set of prompts. To edit polylines, you can use PEDIT as well as most of the regular edit commands.*

Example Polylines

In Chapter 10, we will encounter 3D polylines and the 3DPOLY command, but for now we'll consider only 2D polylines. A single polyline can have any combination of straight or arc line segments. The joints between segments are called vertices. Arcs are circular, but other curves can be approximated by combinations of straight and arc segments. The PEDIT command offers automatic curve fitting, splines, and other ways to modify existing polylines. You can also modify polylines by inserting, moving, or deleting vertices, or joining several lines, arcs, and polylines into one polyline. A segment can have any width or even be tapered. The default width is 0. Because a polyline is a connected sequence of line and arc segments, the entire polyline may be treated as one object.

The entities created by the DONUT, ELLIPSE, and POLYGON commands are polylines. The AREA command finds the enclosed area of a polyline. The FILLET and CHAMFER commands globally modify all the vertices of a polyline.

Use the following coordinates to draw the border centered on the sheet (limits), with a 0.02 width polyline on layer 0. Don't worry if you can't see the points as you draw. You can type your coordinates outside the current view, then zoom out to see your work when finished.

Drafting the Border

Continue in the PROTO-C drawing.

```
Command: PLINE
From point: .53125,.53125                                  Select a starting point.
Current line-width is 0.00
Arc/Close/Halfwidth/Length/Undo/Width/<Endpoint of line>: W       Width.
Starting width <0.0000>: .02
Ending width <0.0200>: <RETURN>                            Defaults to starting width.
Arc/Close/Halfwidth/Length/Undo/Width/<Endpoint of line>: @0,15.9375   Relative point,
                                                                       up 15.9375.
Arc/Close/Halfwidth/Length/Undo/Width/<Endpoint of line>: @20.9375,0   Right.
Arc/Close/Halfwidth/Length/Undo/Width/<Endpoint of line>: @0,-15.9375  Down.
Arc/Close/Halfwidth/Length/Undo/Width/<Endpoint of line>: C           Closes and exits.
```

Why didn't we just draw from 0,0 to 21,16 or from .5,.5 to 21.5,16.5? We started at approximately .5,.5 to center the border in the 22 x 17 limits, but we had to offset it a bit more, to .53125,.53125. If we had drawn a full 21 x 16 border, its center line would be right on the plot extents, and the outer half of the polyline width would be outside the maximum plotting area. The outer half of the width would get clipped, not plotted. So we shrank our border by 1/16 inch and offset it by 1/32 inch to fit within the limits. This makes the border size 20-15/16 inches, convenient for later snapping.

Zooming to the Whole View

AutoCAD lets you display any range of coordinates (any portion of your drawing) on the screen. You can magnify the view or shrink it. The command is called ZOOM.

We'll examine all of the ways to control ZOOM as we proceed through this and later chapters. For now, we'll just zoom out to see the entire drawing.

' ZOOM

> *The ZOOM command magnifies (zooms in) or shrinks (zooms out) the display in the current viewport. It does not physically change the size of the drawing, but lets you view a small part of the drawing in detail, or look at a greater part with less detail. Entering a number for magnification is considered an absolute value in drawing units. Placing an X after the value defines the magnification relative to the current display.*
> ```
> All/Center/Dynamic/Extents/Left/Previous/Window/
> <Scale(X)>:
> ```

Viewing the Drawing With ZOOM

```
Command: ZOOM
All/Center/Dynamic/Extents/Left/Previous/Window/<Scale(X)>: A          A for All.
Regenerating drawing.                                      And it displays the whole drawing.
```

To make drawing easier, we'll use the UCS command to align the border with our snap and coordinate system.

Setting a User Coordinate System

We placed the 0,0 point of our limits at the corner of our electronic 22 x 17 drawing sheet and sized our border in 0.0625 (1/16) increments. The rest of the title block is also in 0.0625 increments. It would be great if our border and title block aligned with our 0.0625 SNAPUNIT setting, or if 0,0 were at the corner of the border instead of the sheet. But the border is offset to 0.53125,0.53125. We can compensate for this with the UCS command.

UCS

> *The UCS (User Coordinate System) command lets you redefine the location of 0,0 and the direction of X,Y. The default UCS is the WCS (World Coordinate System). You can set your user coordinate system with the UCS command or with the DDUCS dialogue box.*
> ```
> Origin/ZAxis/3point/Entity/View/X/Y/Z/Prev/Restore/
> Save/Del/?/<World>:
> ```

Although the UCS is intended primarily for 3D work, it is also valuable in 2D to align the coordinate system with drawing points. With it set to the corner of our border, all drawing points can be entered relative to that new 0,0 corner instead of to the limits corner (which is now -.53125,-.53125).

We'll examine the UCS command and the DDUCS dialogue box in detail in the 3D chapters. For now, just offset the UCS's 0,0 origin, and save the new UCS with the name BDR.

Setting and Saving a UCS

Continue in the PROTO-C drawing.

```
Command: UCS
Origin/ZAxis/3point/Entity/View/X/Y/Z/Prev/Restore/Save/Del/?/<World>: O
Origin point <0,0,0>: .53125,.53125       The corner of the border.
Command: <RETURN>                          Repeat the command to save the UCS.
UCS
Origin/ZAxis/3point/Entity/View/X/Y/Z/Prev/Restore/Save/Del/?/<World>: S
?/Name of UCS: BDR                         Saves it to name BDR, for border.
```

Until the UCS is changed again, 0,0 is at the corner of the border and the lines we will draw are on our snap increment.

We drew the border on the default layer, layer 0. Other parts of the title block will be drawn on other layers.

Organizing With Layers, Linetypes, and Colors

If you are familiar with overlay drafting, AutoCAD's layers will seem familiar. AutoCAD allows you to organize your drawing into any number of layers. You are always drawing on a layer, whether it is the default layer 0 or a layer that you have created with the LAYER command.

LAYER

The LAYER command controls layers which act like transparent drawing overlays. You can create (with the Make or New options) an unlimited number of layers and give them names up to 31 characters long. You can set any layer active (current), turn layers on (visible) or off (invisible), freeze or thaw layers, and control their colors and linetypes. When a layer is frozen, it is disregarded by AutoCAD, and will not be plotted, calculated, or displayed. You draw on the current layer. The default settings for new layers are white with continuous linetype. You can also control layers with the DDLMODES dialogue box.
`?/Make/Set/New/ON/OFF/Color/Ltype/Freeze/Thaw:`

Most drawings, including the drafting exercises in this book, require multiple drawing layers. This section shows you how to create drawing layers with specific names, linetypes, and colors. It also shows you how to change the current layer, turn layers on and off, and freeze and thaw them. We will need the following layers for our title block and for other drawing purposes.

Purpose	Layer Name	State	Color	Linetype	Pen
Floating	0	ON	7 (White)	CONTINUOUS	Med
Main title block	TITL-CX	ON	7 (White)	CONTINUOUS	Med
Border, title outline	TITL-OT	ON	7 (White)	CONTINUOUS	Med
Engineering spec. block	SPEC-CX	ON	7 (White)	CONTINUOUS	Med
Outline engr. spec.	SPEC-OT	ON	7 (White)	CONTINUOUS	Med
Part application	APPL-CX	ON	7 (White)	CONTINUOUS	Med
Outline part usage	APPL-OT	ON	7 (White)	CONTINUOUS	Med
Part inventory	PART-CX	ON	7 (White)	CONTINUOUS	Med
Outline part inventory	PART-OT	ON	7 (White)	CONTINUOUS	Med
General notes	NOTES	ON	5 (Green)	CONTINUOUS	Med
Other text	TEXT	ON	5 (Green)	CONTINUOUS	Med
Construction lines	CONST	ON	6 (Magenta)	CONTINUOUS	None
Object lines	OBJECT	ON	2 (Yellow)	CONTINUOUS	Bold
Center lines	CL	ON	1 (Red)	CENTER	Thin
Hidden lines	HL	ON	3 (Green)	HIDDEN	Med
Hatches & fills	HATCH	ON	4 (Cyan)	CONTINUOUS	Thin
Phantom lines	PL	ON	4 (Cyan)	PHANTOM	Thin
Dimension lines	DIM	ON	1 (Red)	CONTINUOUS	Thin
Dashed lines	DL	ON	1 (Red)	DASHED	Thin

The Prototype's Layers

The four center columns (Layer Name, State, Color, and Linetype) are AutoCAD's layer data. The Purpose and Pen columns are information we've added to better understand layer usage. AutoCAD supports a number of linetypes which can be assigned to layers for screen display and plotting. If you have a color display, layers will display in the colors assigned to them. Normally you do not plot in colors, but AutoCAD makes plotter pen assignments by color. We've established three pen line weights and assigned them to the seven colors shown in the above Color and Pen columns. Yellow is bold; red and cyan are thin; green and white plot medium; magenta is not plotted; and blue is not used because it is hard to see on many displays.

There are five layers with similar pairs of names. The extension -CX (for CompleX) indicates that the major complexity of an item's entities go on that layer. The outline of the item goes on the corresponding -OT (for

OuTline) layer. For example, the border we just drew will be changed to the TITL-OT layer, and we will add a simple outline of the main title block's perimeter to it. However, the text and interior lines of the title block will be placed on the TITL-CX layer. This allows you to freeze the TITL-CX layer so AutoCAD doesn't waste time calculating and displaying it as you pan and zoom your drawing. The TITL-OT layer provides an outline to help you keep track of the area available for drawing objects.

This is only one of many ways to organize layers. See CUSTOMIZING AutoCAD, also from New Riders Publishing, if you want more information and alternatives.

Using the Modify Layer Dialogue Box

You can invoke the LAYER command at the keyboard, through the screen, tablet, or pull-down menus, or you can use the DDLMODES dialogue box, making the settings shown in the preceding table and the following illustration.

'DDLMODES

> *DDLMODES (Dynamic Dialogue Layer MODES) presents a dialogue box to control layer options. The options include setting the current layer, creating new layers, renaming layers, and modifying layer properties (color, linetype, on / off, freeze, and thaw).*

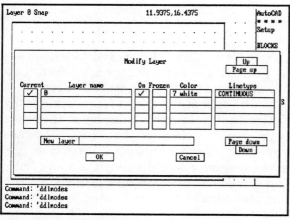

Modify Layer Dialogue Box

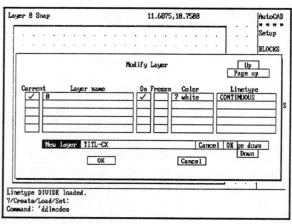

Enter the Layer Name

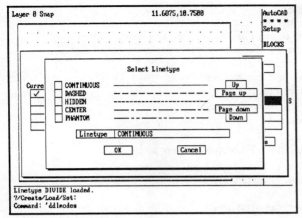

Selecting Layer Linetypes

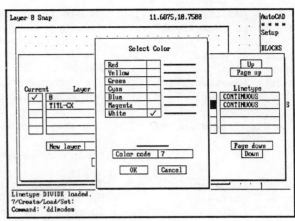

Selecting Layer Colors

We need to load more linetypes with the LINETYPE command. Then we'll set up the layers and take a closer look at their colors and linetypes.

Use either the Creating Layers With DDLMODES exercise below, or just read through it and use the Creating Layers With the LAYER Command exercise which comes next.

Creating Layers With DDLMODES

Continue in the PROTO-C drawing.

```
Command: LINETYPE
?/Create/Load/Set: L              Load linetypes.
Linetype(s) to load: *            Asterisk wildcard for all linetypes.
File to search acad: <RETURN>     The standard linetype file.
Linetype DASHED loaded.           It lists those loaded.
Linetype HIDDEN loaded.
Linetype CENTER loaded.
Linetype PHANTOM loaded.
Linetype DOT loaded.
Linetype DASHDOT loaded.
Linetype BORDER loaded.
Linetype DIVIDE loaded.
?/Create/Load/Set: <RETURN>       Exit.
```

To use the *Modify Layer* dialogue box:

Pull down	**[Settings]**	
Select	**[Modify layer...]**	Or type DDLMODES.
Highlight	**[New layer]**	Actually, you highlight the box *next* to [New layer].
Enter **CL**		And <RETURN> or select [OK] to accept the layer name.
Select	**[7 White]**	The default color box in the new layer's row.
Select	**[Red]**	And select [OK] to accept it.
Select	**[Continuous]**	The default linetype box in the new layer's row.
Select	**[Center]**	And select [OK] to accept it.
Highlight	**[New layer]**	And start process over for next layer.
		Set up layers as shown in the Prototype's Layers table.
Select	**[Page up]**	To scroll back to the TITL-CX layer.
Select	**[Current]**	Set layer TITL-CX current.
Select	**[OK]**	To exit Modify Layer dialogue box.

To change a layer's name, highlight the old name and enter the new name, with a <RETURN> or [OK] to accept it.

After all layers are set up and the modify layer dialogue box displays the layer status correctly, click [OK] to exit the dialogue box. The name of the new current layer, TITL-CX, should appear at the top left of the screen on the status line.

Using the Layer Command

The LAYER command can do anything DDLMODES can do. Using LAYER is often more efficient for one or two quick settings. It also has the advantage of being able to apply settings to multiple layers, with wildcard name entry. LAYER's options include:

? — Lists all existing layers.

Make — Makes a new layer and sets it current.

Set — Sets an existing layer current.

New — Creates one or more new layers, but doesn't set them current.

ON and OFF — Turns one or more existing layers on or off (invisible).

Color and Ltype — Assigns a new color or linetype to one or more existing layers.

Freeze and Thaw — Freezes and thaws one or more existing layers.

Except for Make and Set, the LAYER options accept multiple layer names. You may enter all the layer names you wish, separating each name by a comma, for example: OBJECT, HL, CL. You can also use wildcards when naming layers for the on, off, color, linetype, freeze, and thaw options. A name such as PART??? would apply to both PART-CX and PART-OT.

If you didn't use DDLMODES to set up the prototype drawing's layers, use the following exercise. You can use tablet and screen menus, or just type the command, options, and layer names.

Creating Layers With the LAYER Command

```
Select [LAYER:]
Command: LAYER                                          Or type LAYER.
?/Make/Set/New/ON/OFF/Color/Ltype/Freeze/Thaw: M        Or select [Make].
New current layer <0>: TITL-CX                           Creates it and sets it current.
?/Make/Set/New/ON/OFF/Color/Ltype/Freeze/Thaw: N        Or select [New].
New layer name(s): TITL-OT,SPEC-CX,SPEC-OT,APPL-CX,APPL-OT,PART-CX,PART-
OT,NOTES,TEXT,CONST,OBJECT,CL,HL,HATCH,PL,DIM            Enter the new names.
?/Make/Set/New/ON/OFF/Color/Ltype/Freeze/Thaw: L        Or select [Ltype].
Linetype (or ?) <CONTINUOUS>: CENTER                    Or select [center].
Layer name(s) for linetype CENTER <TITL-OT>: CL
?/Make/Set/New/ON/OFF/Color/Ltype/Freeze/Thaw: C        Or select [Color].
Color: R                                                Or select [red] or enter a 1.
Layer name(s) for color 1 (red) <TITL-OT>: CL,DL,DIM    Makes all three layers red.
```

Continue assigning the rest of the colors and linetypes illustrated below.

```
?/Make/Set/New/ON/OFF/Color/Ltype/Freeze/Thaw: <RETURN>  Exits the LAYER command.
```

We didn't have to preload the linetypes we used. Unlike DDLMODES's modify layer dialogue, the LAYER command automatically attempts to load linetypes as needed.

If you have the SIA DISK's Y14.5 Menu System, it includes a menu section for turning the prototype layers on, off, and invoking their other options.

That was a lot to set up. Let's list the layers to be sure they're right.

Listing Layers

Check the status of your layers with the **?** layer option. The listing order of the layers depends on the order in which they were created.

```
 Layer name    State    Color      Linetype        SPEC-CX       Frozen   7 (white)  CONTINUOUS
                                                    SPEC-OT       Frozen   7 (white)  CONTINUOUS
0              On       7 (white)  CONTINUOUS       APPL-CX       Frozen   7 (white)  CONTINUOUS
TITL-OT        On       7 (white)  CONTINUOUS
SPEC-CX        Frozen   7 (white)  CONTINUOUS       APPL-OT       Frozen   7 (white)  CONTINUOUS
SPEC-OT        Frozen   7 (white)  CONTINUOUS       PART-CX       Frozen   7 (white)  CONTINUOUS
APPL-CX        Frozen   7 (white)  CONTINUOUS       PART-OT       Frozen   7 (white)  CONTINUOUS
                                                    NOTES         Frozen   5 (green)  CONTINUOUS
APPL-OT        Frozen   7 (white)  CONTINUOUS       TEXT          On       5 (green)  CONTINUOUS
PART-CX        Frozen   7 (white)  CONTINUOUS
PART-OT        Frozen   7 (white)  CONTINUOUS       CONST         On       6 (magenta) CONTINUOUS
NOTES          Frozen   5 (green)  CONTINUOUS       OBJECT        On       2 (yellow) CONTINUOUS
TEXT           On       5 (green)  CONTINUOUS       CL            On       1 (red)    CENTER
                                                    HL            On       3 (green)  HIDDEN
CONST          On       6 (magenta) CONTINUOUS      HATCH         On       4 (cyan)   CONTINUOUS
OBJECT         On       2 (yellow) CONTINUOUS
CL             On       1 (red)    CENTER           — Press RETURN for more —
HL             On       3 (green)  HIDDEN           PL            On       4 (cyan)   PHANTOM
HATCH          On       4 (cyan)   CONTINUOUS       DIM           On       1 (red)    CONTINUOUS
                                                    DL            On       1 (red)    DASHED
— Press RETURN for more —                           TITL-CX       On       7 (white)  CONTINUOUS

                                                    Current layer: OBJECT

                                                    ?/Make/Set/New/ON/OFF/Color/Ltype/Freeze/Thaw:
```

Listing the Layers   *Page Two of Layer List*

Listing Layers

```
Command: LAYER
?/Make/Set/New/ON/OFF/Color/Ltype/Freeze/Thaw: ?       Enter ? to list them.
Layer name(s) for listing <*>: <RETURN>               Return for all.
                                                       You get the listing illustrated above.
?/Make/Set/New/ON/OFF/Color/Ltype/Freeze/Thaw: <RETURN>  Exits.
Command: SAVE                                          Unless you have the SIA DISK.
```

If any of your names, colors, or linetypes are wrong, correct them now and then SAVE your drawing.

Changing the Current Layer

Although we set the TITL-OT layer current with the Make option, you can also set a new layer current (active) with the Set option, like this:

Example: Setting the Current Drawing Layer

```
?/Make/Set/New/ON/OFF/Color/Ltype/Freeze/Thaw: S      Or [Set].
New current layer <0>: HL
?/Make/Set/New/ON/OFF/Color/Ltype/Freeze/Thaw: <RETURN>
Command:
```

Next, we'll see how color and linetype control can be independent of layers.

Colors and Linetypes

Every AutoCAD entity has layer, color, and linetype properties. The defaults for color and linetype are BYLAYER, which means the color and linetype are controlled by what is assigned to its layer. Although color and linetype may be assigned independent of layers, we generally recommend that you use specific layers to control specific linetypes and entity colors. Layer control simplifies drawing management, standardization, and passing drawings between consultants and suppliers whose linetype and color/pen conventions differ from yours. For example, if you've set up thin lines for the red layer, but a consultant uses blue for thin, he can just reset the red layers to blue instead of changing the color of every affected entity separately. (When entities are blocked into symbols and parts, changing their individual colors and linetypes can be very difficult.)

But when you occasionally need the flexibility of individual colors or linetypes, you have that option through the COLOR and LINETYPE commands, or through the DDEMODES Entity Creation Modes dialogue box.

' DDEMODES

> *The DDEMODES (Dynamic Dialogue Entity creation MODES) dialogue box shows the current settings for layer, color, linetype, elevation, and thickness. You can change any of these variables. Layer, color, and linetype present another dialogue box when selected.*

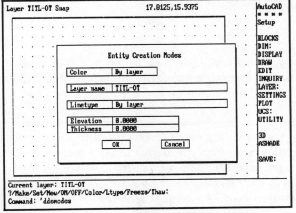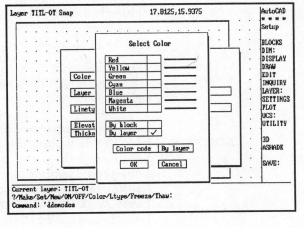

DDEMODES Entity Creation Modes Dialogue Boxes

Entity Colors

Color adds more than aesthetic appeal to your work. As your drawings become more complex, different colors increase entity recognition and expand drafting productivity. Individual color assignments are called entity colors. AutoCAD uses seven standard named colors. Other colors may be made available by specifying their numbers if your graphics card and monitor support additional colors.

```
               Standard COLOR Designations
   1 Red          3 Green       5 Blue         7 White
   2 Yellow       4 Cyan        6 Magenta
```

These colors may be assigned by the COLOR command.

COLOR

> *The COLOR command controls the color of new entities, overriding the default layer color. To change the color of existing entities, use the CHPROP command. To control layer colors, use the LAYER command. Use a color number or name to set a new color. You can also set the current entity color with the 'DDEMODES dialogue box. The default setting is BYLAYER.*
> `New entity color <BYLAYER>:`

If you set the new entity color to 1 (red), then all new entities will be drawn in red, regardless of layer, until you change it again. Linetype is similarly controlled.

Entity Linetypes

Line colors and types may be controlled in two ways: by layer and by using the LINETYPE command to assign a default linetype independent of layer.

LINETYPE

> *LINETYPE assigns linetypes to entities, loads linetype definitions stored in library files, and creates new linetype definitions. Linetypes are based on dash-dot line segments. You can control the linetypes of new entities explicitly or by their layer assignment. You can also set linetype with the 'DDEMODES dialogue box. The default setting is BYLAYER.*
> `?/Create/Load/Set:`

LINETYPE's options are:

? — The **?** option lists all linetypes in a linetype definition file (not those in the drawing).

Load — Loads one or more linetypes. You can use the **?** and ***** wildcards to load several or all linetypes at once.

Set — Sets the linetype for all new entities, regardless of layer.

The illustration below shows AutoCAD's predefined linetypes.

AutoCAD's Predefined Linetypes

Although the LAYER command loads linetypes as needed, DDLMODES, DDEMODES, and the LINETYPE Set option all require that the linetype be loaded first. If you need additional linetypes, you can create them through customization. For more information on this process, refer to the AutoCAD Reference Manual, or to the New Rider's books INSIDE AutoCAD and CUSTOMIZING AutoCAD.

Linetype patterns may appear continuous if the line segment is very short, so polyline curves and short segment series do not work well with broken linetypes. A scale that is too large or too small for the display or plot may also make a broken linetype appear continuous.

Linetype Scale

Non-continuous linetypes are controlled by the LTSCALE system variable and command. You can vary the plotted and displayed scale by changing this linetype scale factor, which applies to all non-continuous linetypes contained within the current drawing.

LTSCALE

> *LTSCALE (LineType SCALE) determines the dash and space settings for linetypes. The LTSCALE is a global value. All linetypes (except for continuous) are multiplied by the LTSCALE. The default setting is 1.0000.*
> ```
> New scale factor <1.0000>:
> ```

An LTSCALE of 0.375 works well for full scale drawings. Drawings which will be plotted to other scales should be set to 0.375 times their plot scale. The LTSCALE should be set for plotting, not screen display. You sometimes need to adjust it temporarily to differentiate lines on screen. If you do, remember to reset it before plotting. The following instructions set LTSCALE to an acceptable value for full scale output.

Setting the Linetype Scale Factor

Continue in the PROTO-C drawing.

```
Command: LTSCALE
New scale factor <1.0000>: .375
```

With the layers, colors, and linetypes set, we are ready to complete the prototype drawing's title block.

Title Block Format

You can avoid the necessity and expense of purchasing pre-printed title blocked sheets by developing your own title blocks on your prototypes. The title block presented in this exercise contains the following parts.

Contract Number Block	Treatment Block
Drawn Block	Finish Block
Approval Blocks	Similar To Block
Design Activity Name and Address Block	Weight Blocks
Drawing Title Block	Application Block
Size Block	Part Dash Number
Quantity Required Per Assembly	Drawing Number Block
Next Assembly and Used On	Scale Block
Additional Approvals Block	Release Date Block
Sheet Block	Parts List
Standard Tolerance Block	

All of these parts are shown on the title block illustrations and are sized and located according to ANSI Y14.1 standards.

If you have the SIA DISK, your PROTO-C file includes all of these blocks, with most on frozen layers.

If you don't have the SIA DISK, you can draw the entire title block or you can skip part of it. Only the main title block, the parts list, and the revision list are necessary for later exercises, although all parts are shown in our illustrations.

To allow layers to be turned off or frozen, the major parts of the title block are created on different pairs of layers. Draw the outline of each area on the ????-OT layers, and the complex portions (internal lines and text) on the ????-CX layers. This lets you turn complex lines and text off by freezing their layers, which will speed up your drawing regenerations and redraws. If you want to freeze or turn off both parts of a pair, use a wildcard, such as TITL??? for TITL-CX and TITL-OT.

Drawing the Main Title Block

Let's draw the main title block as shown in the following illustration. Set the corresponding layer current as you draw each part of the title block. The bold lines are controlled by polyline width instead of the layer's color/pen setting, so medium lines, bold lines, and text can be on the same layer. Medium lines can be either zero-width polylines, or you can just use the LINE command for them.

All lines are on the 0.0625 snap of the UCS that you saved under the name BDR, but you may have to adjust the snap increment to 0.3125 to enter some of the text. You may find a 0.5-unit grid easier to work with. Use SNAP and GRID to adjust them. Snap and grid should be dynamic. Modify them as needed. You will find it easier to draw if coords are toggled (<^D> or <F6>) to show DIST<ANGLE. You can type the coordinates, or just pick the DIST<ANGLE shown on the coords line with your cursor. All the lines are at right angles, so toggling ortho on (<^O> or <F8>) will also make drawing easier.

First, we'll zoom in to the area we want to draw in. We'll use a ZOOM Window option, which allows us to specify the area by its corners. Then we'll draw the title block outline (the bold top and left lines) on layer TITL-OT.

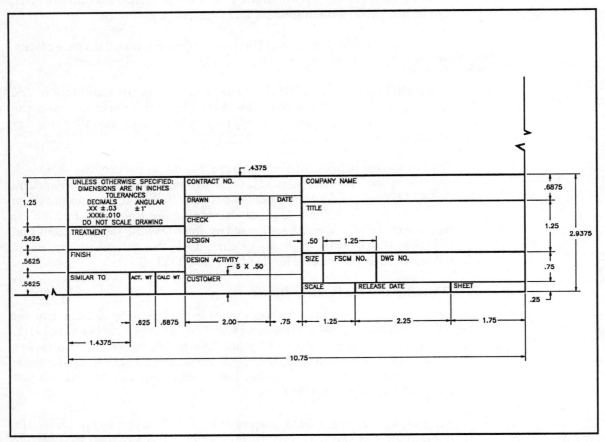

Main Title Block

Drawing the Main Title Block Outline

Continue in the PROTO-C drawing.

```
Command: ZOOM
All/Center/Dynamic/Extents/Left/Previous/Window/Scale(X): W      Window.
First corner: 10,-.5                                            Pick or type.
Other corner: 22,8
```

Make sure layer TITL-OT shows current on the status line.

```
Command: PLINE
From point: 20.9375,2.9375          2.9375 above the lower right corner.
Current line-width is 0.0200
<F8>                    Width is .2, coords show DIST<ANGLE, and ortho is toggled on.
```

```
Arc/Close/Halfwidth/Length/Undo/Width/<Endpoint of line>: @10.75<180
Arc/Close/Halfwidth/Length/Undo/Width/<Endpoint of line>: @2.9375<270
Arc/Close/Halfwidth/Length/Undo/Width/<Endpoint of line>: <RETURN>     To exit.
```

That puts the outline on layer TITL-OT. Now let's put the rest on layer TITL-CX. There are a number of parallel lines to draw. The OFFSET command will give us an easy way to draw one line and copy it by an offset distance.

OFFSET

> *OFFSET lets you copy an entity parallel to itself, once you establish an offset distance. You can offset a line arc, circle, or polyline by giving an offset distance or a through point.*
> `Offset distance or Through <Through>:`

OFFSET is particularly powerful when you have a series of parallel but otherwise identical lines to draw.

Temporarily reset your UCS to the lower left corner of the title block to make point entry easier. You can use an @ (the shorthand character for last point) to enter the point, since it is the end of the last polyline drawn.

Drawing the Complex Main Title Block

```
Command: UCS
Origin/ZAxis/3point/Entity/View/X/Y/Z/Prev/Restore/Save/Del/?/<World>: O
Origin point <0,0,0>: @        The corner of the title block.
                               Now all points are relative to the title block corner, our new 0,0.

Command: LAYER               Set layer TITL-CX current.

Command: PLINE               Draw the line between the "UNLESS OTHERWISE SPECIFIED"
                             and the "CONTRACT NO." boxes.
From point: 2.75,0
Current line-width is 0.0200
Arc/Close/Halfwidth/Length/Undo/Width/<Endpoint of line>: @2.9375<90
Arc/Close/Halfwidth/Length/Undo/Width/<Endpoint of line>: <RETURN>
Command: OFFSET              Copy the line to the right.
Offset distance or Through <Through>: 2.75
Select object to offset:     Pick the last polyline.
Side to offset?              Pick point to the right, and it copies it.
Select object to offset: <RETURN>    To exit.

Command: PLINE               Draw the rest of the bold lines.
                             Use OFFSET where efficient.
Command: LINE               Draw and offset the thin lines.
```

We need text to complete the title block. Most text is 0.1 high, but you will have to temporarily set text height to 0.08 for the "ACT. WT" and "CALC WT" boxes. Most is left justified, but use C (for Center) justification for the "UNLESS OTHERWISE SPECIFIED," "DATE," and "FSCH NO." boxes. Don't draw the dimensions; they are just there to guide you. Temporarily set snap to .03125 when needed. Zoom in on the parts if it makes entering the text easier. The ZOOM command's P (for Previous) option will return you to the current view.

Adding the Title Block Text

```
Command: DTEXT
Start point or Align/Center/Fit/Middle/Right/Style: C
Center point: 1.375,2.75
Height <0.1250>: .1
Rotation angle <0>: <RETURN>
Text: UNLESS OTHERWISE SPECIFIED
Text: DIMENSIONS ARE IN INCHES
Text: TOLERANCES
Text: DECIMALS        ANGULAR
Text: <RETURN>                    Or pick another center text point and enter more text.

Command: <RETURN> Enter the tolerances with left justified text.
DTEXT Start point or Align/Center/Fit/Middle/Right/Style:  Pick under "DECIMALS."
Height <0.1000>: <RETURN>
Rotation angle <0>: <RETURN>
Text: .XX %%p.03      %%p1%%d     Generates the plus/minus and degree symbols.
Text: .XXX%%p.010
Text: DO NOT SCALE DRAWING
Text: TREATMENT
                                 And pick another point to enter more text.
Text: <RETURN>                   Return to accept it all.

                                 Enter the rest of the text. Watch the .1 and .08 heights!
```

That completes the main title block. Now let's use the same techniques to draw the parts list illustrated below.

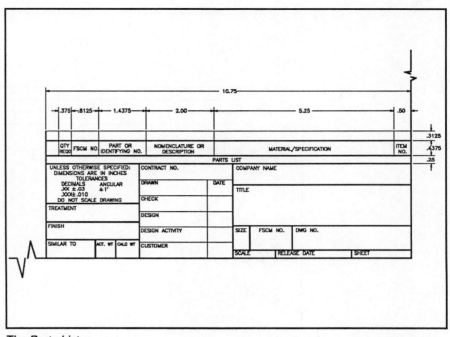

The Parts List

Drawing the Parts List

Command: **LAYER**   Set layer PART-OT current.
Command: **ZOOM**   Use Previous if needed to get the whole title block.
Command: **PLINE**   Draw the bold lines.
Command: **LINE**   Draw the other lines.

Command: **LAYER**   Set layer PART-CX current.
Command: **DTEXT**   Add the text.

The revision list should always be visible on all drawings, so we'll put it on layer TITL-OT, along with the main title block outline.

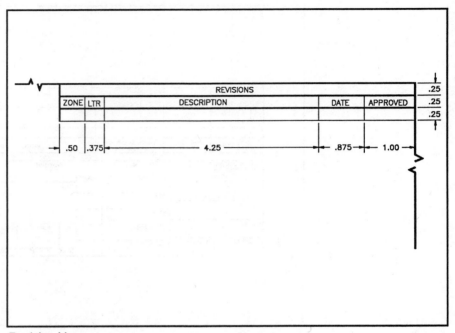

Revision List

Zoom to the upper right corner of the drawing and create a revision block as shown above.

Creating the Current Revision List

Command: **LAYER**	Set layer TITL-OT current.
Command: **ZOOM**	Zoom A for All to the whole sheet.
Command: **<RETURN>**	
ZOOM	Zoom W for Window, to the upper right corner.
Command: **PLINE**	Draw the bold lines.
Command: **LINE**	Draw the other vertical lines.
Command: **DTEXT**	Add the text, 0.1 high, M for middle justification.

The border, too, will always be visible. We drew it on layer 0, but it would make more sense if it were on the TITL-OT layer. We can fix this with the CHPROP command, which changes the properties of existing entities.

Changing Layers, Colors, and Linetypes

CHPROP

> *CHPROP redefines the layer, color, linetype, and 3D thickness properties of existing entities. Use CHPROP instead of CHANGE to change entity properties.*
> Change what property (Color/LAyer/LType/Thickness) ?

Changing the Border's Layer

```
Command: CHPROP
Select objects: 1 selected, 1 found.                  Pick the border polyline.
Select objects: <RETURN>                              Done selecting.
Change what property (Color/LAyer/LType/Thickness) ? LA
New layer <0>: TITL-OT                                And it changes layer.
Change what property (Color/LAyer/LType/Thickness) ? <RETURN>    To exit.

Command: SAVE                                         Unless you have the SIA DISK.
```

The rest of the title block is optional.

OPTIONAL: Title Block Completion

If you want to create a complete ANSI Y14.1 sheet, you can add an application block and an engineering specifications block, as illustrated.

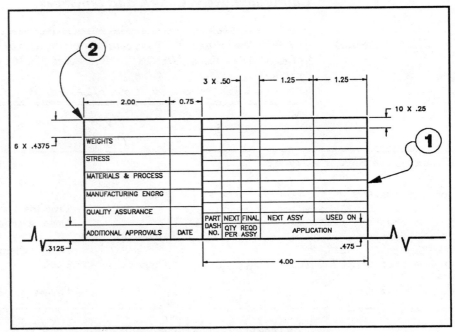

OPTIONAL: Application and Engineering Specifications Blocks

① Application Block

> Set layer APPL-OT current.
>
> Draw the top and left line with PLINE.
>
> Set layer APPL-CX current.
>
> Use LINE and OFFSET to create the rest of the lines.
>
> Use DTEXT, 0.1 high and middle justified to add the text.

② Engineering Specifications Block

> Set layer SPEC-OT current.
>
> Draw the top and left line with PLINE.
>
> Set layer SPEC-CX current.
>
> Use LINE and OFFSET to create the rest of the lines.
>
> Use DTEXT, 0.1 high and middle justified to add the text.
>
> SAVE, unless you have the SIA DISK.

Standards for General Notes

General notes can apply to a specific part being drawn or they can be standardized to apply to all of your drawings. If you have standard general notes, you can make them a part of your prototype drawing. In any case, general notes should conform to the following standards:

- Notes should be clear, concise, and imperative.

- Notes should be parallel to the bottom edge of the border.

- Notes should be in standard upper case text and not underlined.

- Locate general notes in upper left of B,C,D,E,F sheets, and do not exceed an 8-inch width.

- Punctuate according to rules of English grammar and avoid non-standard abbreviations.

- Sequence notes by fabricating or manufacturing process.

Use the following instructions to add general notes to the PROTO-C drawing. When applying this to your own work, both parts lists and general notes begin on Page 1 and continue as necessary. When the parts list is so long that it extends into the general notes, start the general notes on Page 1 and continue them on subsequent pages.

OPTIONAL: Adding General Notes to the Prototype

Add the example notes as illustrated.

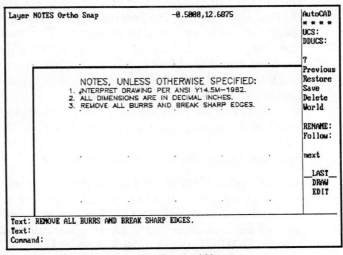

OPTIONAL: Prototype with General Notes

① **Adding General Notes**

Set layer NOTES current.

Zoom to the upper left corner of the drawing.

Use 0.125-high, centered text for the "NOTES, UNLESS OTHERWISE SPECIFIED" heading.

Use 0.125 DTEXT with the default left justification for the rest of the notes.

SAVE, unless you have the SIA DISK.

Controlling Layer Status

You can control which layers will be off (calculated but not displayed), frozen (not calculated or displayed), or thawed and on (displayed normally). If you want to display only the object lines of a drawing, turn off or freeze layers like CONST, HL, CL, TEXT, and DIM. You can enter multiple layer names with wildcards or on one line with names separated by commas. Turning off or freezing unneeded layers increases your drafting speed and efficiency because unnecessary information is not displayed or plotted. You may control the status of layers by using either the screen menu, tablet menu, or the layer dialogue box.

If you try to draw on a layer that is off, your lines will disappear. AutoCAD protects you from accidentally turning the current layer off by giving a "Really want layer 0 (the current layer) off? <N>" message. Simply respond yes if you *do* want it off.

During normal drawing, you don't need to see the *interior* lines and text of the title block, application block, parts list, and engineering specifications block. Turn these layers off or, better still, freeze them by freezing ????-CX. Their -OT outline layers will still display so you can see what space the blocks occupy. If, when starting a new drawing, you want to freeze both layers for the application block, parts list, and engineering specifications block, you can do so by specifying APPL-??, PART-??, SPEC-??. Then, to later call up different parts of the title format, simply thaw or turn on its layer. What could be easier?

Startup Layer Status for the Prototype

Set the status of layers on your prototype drawing so that it is ready for drafting upon initial startup. The following exercise shows how we like to set up the drafting prototype. We freeze layers which are commonly unused during initial drawing tasks. You could turn them off instead. We also set OBJECT as our default current layer.

Setting the Prototype Layers

```
Command: LAYER
?/Make/Set/New/ON/OFF/Color/Ltype/Freeze/Thaw: S
New current layer <>: OBJECT                              Set layer OBJECT current.
Layer ?/Make/Set/New/ON/OFF/Color/Ltype/Freeze/Thaw: F
Layer name(s) to Freeze: ????-OT,SPEC-??,APPL-??,PART-??,NOTES
Layer ?/Make/Set/New/ON/OFF/Color/Ltype/Freeze/Thaw: <RETURN>
Command: SAVE                                            Unless you have the SIA DISK.
```

The OBJECT layer is now current. When you begin a new drawing from PROTO-C, OBJECT will be the active drawing layer. Only the border, revision block, and main title block outline will be visible; the rest of the title layers are frozen to speed up display and regeneration time. Put important text, like the drawing name and number, on the TITL-OT layer to keep it visible.

The last thing we want to add to our prototype drawing is a scratch UCS and a couple of views to make drawing easier.

Setting Up Views and UCS's

It would be convenient if you could draw in a scratch area on any layer, without interfering with other things in your drawing. Then you could experiment or develop parts in clear space, and move them into your main drawing when done. You can do this with the help of UCS. You have already offset the UCS origin and saved a UCS. To make a scratch area, we'll create a SCRATCH UCS as illustrated below.

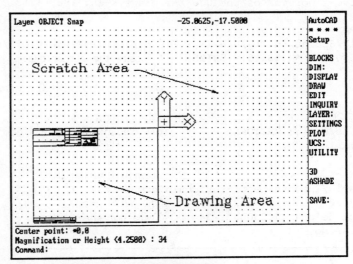

SCRATCH, WORLD, and BDR UCS's

The SCRATCH UCS has its origin at the WCS (world coordinate system) coordinates of -.53125,-.53125, exactly the opposite offset of our BDR UCS origin. SCRATCH has its X and Y axes rotated 180 degrees from the WCS, so they are also exactly opposed to BDR's X and Y axes. When you draw in the SCRATCH UCS, it appears just as normal as the BDR UCS, with its own local axes. After you draw a part there, you can move it into the real drawing by simply rotating it 180 degrees about the WCS 0,0 origin. Because the positive coordinates of SCRATCH extend in the opposite directions of the positive coordinates of BDR, they won't get in each other's way during normal drawing.

Once we create the UCS, we can orient our display view to it with the PLAN command, which will be fully explained in the 3D chapters. For now, we just need PLAN to do its default, which is like a ZOOM All oriented to the current UCS.

Let's set it up. Although we are still in our temporary offset UCS, we can specify WCS coordinates by prefacing them with an asterisk, like *0,0 for the WCS origin.

Creating a SCRATCH UCS

Continue in the PROTO-C drawing.

```
Command: UCS
Origin, ZAxis/3point/Entity/View/X/Y/Z/Prev/Restore/Save/Del/?/<World>: 3
Origin point <0,0,0>: *0,0                    The WCS origin.
Point on positive portion of the X-axis <-9.7188,-0.5313,0.0000>: *-1,0,0   The WCS -X.
Point on positive-Y portion of the UCS X-Y plane <-10.7188,-1.5313,0.0000>: *0,-1,0
                                              The WCS -Y.
Command: <RETURN>
UCS Origin/ZAxis/3point/Entity/View/X/Y/Z/Prev/Restore/Save/Del/?/<World>: O
Origin point <0,0,0>: *-.53125,-.53125        Opposite the border offset.

Command: UCS                                  Save the UCS with the name SCRATCH.

Command: PLAN                                 Flip it right side up.
<Current UCS>/Ucs/World: <RETURN>            Set display to current UCS.
Regenerating drawing.

Command: ZOOM                                 Zoom out to see it.
All/Center/Dynamic/Extents/Left/Previous/Window/<Scale(X): C
Center point: *0,0                            The WCS origin.
Magnification or Height <4.2500> : 34         Twice our sheet size.
Regenerating drawing.
```

Now your drawing should match the above illustration, without our annotation.

The PLAN and ZOOM commands we just did each caused the drawing to regenerate. We can eliminate the need for one of these commands by saving a view.

Saving Views

Once the drawing gets complex, it pays to eliminate unnecessary regenerations. We can replace the PLAN and ZOOM commands we just did with a single VIEW command.

'VIEW

> *The VIEW command lets you save, name, and restore the current display or a windowed area. The view name can be up to 31 characters.*
> `?/Delete/Restore/Save/Window:`

Let's save the upper right part of our display as the view SCRATCH. Then, when we go to our SCRATCH UCS, we can also restore our SCRATCH view, eliminating the PLAN and ZOOM steps.

Saving the SCRATCH View

```
Command: VIEW
?/Delete/Restore/Save/Window: W
 View name to save: SCRATCH
First corner: -1,-1                    In the current SCRATCH UCS coordinates.
Other corner: 22,17
Command: <RETURN>
VIEW
?/Delete/Restore/Save/Window: R
 View name to restore: SCRATCH         Zoom to it.
```

The saved and restored SCRATCH view should match the left-hand illustration below. Let's also save a view of the real drawing, as shown in the illustration below right.

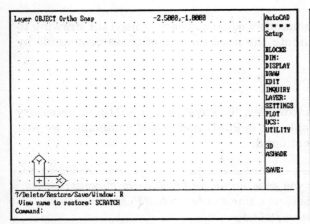

The SCRATCH View

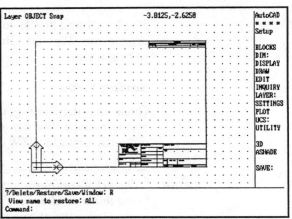

The View ALL

Saving a View ALL

Once AutoCAD has regenerated a view of the drawing, you can zoom to smaller views and pan (move the view from side to side) *within* that regenerated area without suffering another regen. Panning and zooming then occur at redraw (redisplay without recalculation) speed, which is much faster than regeneration. A ZOOM All always regenerates (often twice, to find the drawing extents). We can eliminate many of these regenerations by saving a view ALL. We'll make view ALL about 20 percent bigger than the border to allow a little buffer. This buffer will eliminate accidental regenerations caused by a pan or zoom extending slightly beyond the edge of the border.

Let's zoom out to a view that is a little bigger than the entire drawing, and save it as ALL. We'll use a zoom scale factor of 0.8, so the drawing extents fill 80 percent of the screen. (By contrast, a scale of 0.8**X** would fill 80 percent of the screen with the *current* view.) We'll also have to restore BDR, our prototype's default UCS, and use PLAN to orient the UCS view. While we're at it, let's make a BDR view.

Creating View ALL

```
Command: UCS            Restore BDR.
Command: PLAN           To current UCS.

Command: VIEW           Save view All.
?/Delete/Restore/Save/Window: S
  View name to save: BDR
```

```
Command: ZOOM
All/Center/Dynamic/Extents/Left/Previous/Window/Scale(X): 0.8
Regenerating drawing.
```

Command: **<RETURN>**	Test the views, but don't change UCS's.
VIEW	Restore view SCRATCH.
	You get a blank screen and an upside down UCS icon.
Command: **VIEW**	Restore view ALL.

That completes our prototype setup. Before we end the drawing session, let's check some of the settings we toggled.

Final Check and Ending the Prototype

As we worked, we changed snap, ortho, layers, and other settings. Check your settings against the following table and the layer table earlier in this chapter. Change them if you need to. Then END your drawing. If you have the SIA DISK, you don't need to END because you already have a final PROTO-C drawing.

GRID	SNAP	COORDS	TEXT HEIGHT	ORTHO
1.0/ON	0.0625/ON	DIST<ANGLE	0.125	Off

Prototype Drawing Settings

Checking and Ending PROTO-C

Continue in the PROTO-C drawing.

Command: **LAYER**	Check the layers, colors, and linetypes.
	Check the frozen layers. Make sure OBJECT is current.
Command: **SETVAR**	Set TEXTSIZE back to 0.125.

Check and adjust the other settings in the above table.

Command: **END**	Save and exit to the main menu.

You have a finished C-size prototype. To use it in new drawing startups, simply enter the new drawing name equal to it, like **newname=PROTO-C**, or you can configure it as the default.

Configuring and Testing PROTO-C

Your AutoCAD setup probably uses the default name ACAD.DWG as its automatic prototype drawing. New drawings will start up using this default prototype drawing unless you instruct AutoCAD to use a different default. Because most of our exercises use the PROTO-C prototype drawing, we'll make it the default.

 Use the following instructions to set up a separate configuration in the SI-ACAD directory for STEPPING INTO AutoCAD's exercises. This way, you can change the default without affecting your normal AutoCAD setup. Do this whether or not you have the SIA DISK. Start from the main menu.

Configuring PROTO-C as the Default Drawing

```
Enter selection: 5                          Configure AutoCAD.
Press RETURN to continue: <RETURN>

Enter selection <0>: 8                       Configure operating parameters.
Enter selection <0>: 2                       Initial drawing setup.
Enter name of default prototype file for new drawings
or . for none <ACAD>: PROTO-C

Enter selection <0>: <RETURN> <RETURN> <RETURN>     Three times to save and
                                                    exit to main menu.

Enter selection <0>: 1        Begin a NEW drawing named TEST.
                              It should start up identically to the PROTO-C you saved.

Command: QUIT                 And if okay, exit to DOS.
```

Now all new drawings will start identically to PROTO-C unless you specify a different prototype with an equal sign.

Organizing Multiple Prototypes

As the number of your AutoCAD drafting and design projects increases, you may need to create a series of prototype drawings. This series may include prototypes which are designed for various sizes and scales of output, SI metric standards, and possibly first-angle projection. Good file management is essential to maintaining a productive drafting and design environment. Whether you need one or one hundred different prototypes, a few organizational considerations will help keep them straight.

Name your prototypes informatively. The name is only a handle for recalling the prototype, but it can also provide information about the prototype. For example, the drawing in this exercise is a PROTOtype,

C-size, thus the name PROTO-C. The nomenclature or code you use to name and keep track of your prototype drawings is strictly up to you.

Group prototypes along with other support files in an AutoCAD support directory. You can use the SET ACAD=*directory* environment setting to tell AutoCAD to look in that directory for support files.

AutoCAD can automatically load your default prototype drawing. The factory default is ACAD.DWG, but you can assign any name. In the configuration menu, choose "2. Initial drawing setup" under the "8. Configure operating parameters" submenu.

Having a different prototype for each sheet size is okay. A different prototype for each combination of sheet size, title block design, and plot scale is simple and reasonable if you only have a few combinations, as we do in our exercises here. However, this simple approach gets unwieldy if you have a lot of combinations. If you used four different sheet sizes, each with three different title blocks, and you plotted to five different scales, you would need 60 prototypes. That's a management and maintenance nightmare.

There's a better way.

Simplifying and Automating Drawing Setup

While a simple, combined sheet size, scale, title block prototype is fine for our exercises, you should set up an automated system for real work. Many of the settings we have mentioned for prototyping are scale-dependent, for example, snap, grid, and text height. The simple approach of one prototype for each combination of sheet size and plot scale yields an unwieldy number of combinations.

If you have the SIA DISK's ANSI Y14.5 Menu System, the use of prototypes is greatly simplified. The Y14.5 Menu System contains routines for setting up both decimal inch and SI metric production drafting prototype drawings. The Y14.5 Menu System uses just one prototype for each sheet size, and automatically adjusts the scale-related settings for the desired plot scale. We chose to include the title blocks in the prototypes, but they could be kept in separate files and inserted at the appropriate scale by the menu if your application requires various title blocks.

Let's examine the relationship of prototype to plot scale.

Scaling for Plotting

Because many prototype settings are scale-dependent, we need to understand how scaling is done in CAD drawings to deal with them. In manual drafting, you draw most representations of objects smaller than their real world size so you can fit them on a sheet of paper (or other media). In CAD, you draw within an unlimited world, set by your drawing limits. This makes drawing much easier because you don't have to scale objects down to draw them. You simply draw in real-world units.

But you need to consider the final product. In most cases, the final product is the drawing, which must fit on a real sheet of paper. So at plot time, you have to scale the drawing by the same scale factor that you would have used to draw it if you had drawn it manually. You need to draw text and symbols at a size that will look right in the plot when scaled by this *plot scale* factor.

Scale Factor Settings

When you set the scale factor of an AutoCAD drawing, it affects several drawing parameters. These include sheet size, line width, text size, dimensioning, symbol size, and linetype scale.

Of the drawing parameters presented above, sheet size is the most important. AutoCAD calls the sheet size setting *limits*. To determine our limits for a particular sheet size, we need to know what scale it is intended for. For example, consider a C-sized, 22 x 17 sheet:

SIZE	SCALE	LIMITS	DRAWING AREA	PLOT SCALE
C-22x17	FULL	0,0 to 22,17	15 x 8	1
C-22x17	0.5=1	0,0 to 44,34	30 x 16	2
C-22x17	0.25=1	0,0 to 88,68	60 x 32	4
C-22x17	0.125=1	0,0 to 176,136	120 x 64	8

C-Size Scales and Sizes

The important thing in determining limits is the *drawing area* needed to represent the object. The "DRAWING AREA" column in the table is approximate, based on our PROTO-C and allowing for title block, dimensions, and notes. When drawing, you back in to this table. You know about how big the object to be drawn is, and you know what scale and/or sheet size you'd *like* to fit it onto. The table will tell you if it fits or if you have to try a different sheet size or scale.

Let's determine the sheet size, scale, and limits of a 40-inch diameter flange drawn real world size. The drawing's two orthographic views will take up about 60 by 40 inches. According to the drawing size column in the table, it requires a scale of 0.125=1 to fit on a C-size sheet with its available drawing size of 120 x 64. It is a simple matter of calculation and title block design to extend the above table to other sheet sizes and scales.

Adjusting Settings and Graphics for Scale

Once you determine drawing scale, adjust your scale-dependent drawing settings. For example, if you want text to be 0.125 on the plot at a scale of 0.125=1 (1:8), then multiply 0.125 text height by 8, and draw it one unit high. All scalar dimension variables must be similarly adjusted. The DIMSCALE system variable makes this easy. Just reset DIMSCALE to the plot scale factor shown in the above table, and AutoCAD multiplies it against the other dimensioning variables when you draw dimensions. Other settings like grid and snap, and graphics like polyline thicknesses, are also multiplied by this same factor. In fact, the Y14.5 Menu System uses DIMSCALE as a global scale factor for all settings and symbols. Symbols, like bubbles, are scaled proportionately to text, so a 0.25-inch bubble should be drawn 2 inches (0.25 x 8) to plot at 0.25 inches. Graphics such as title blocks should also be inserted or rescaled by the same plot scale factor.

When you use PROTO-C to start a new drawing at other than full scale, you will need to adjust these settings. The STEPPING INTO AutoCAD Y14.5 Menu System automates this for you. See Chapter 11 for more information on the use of the Y14.5 Menu System. You can also develop your own custom startup routines. See the books CUSTOMIZING AutoCAD and INSIDE AutoLISP, both from New Riders Publishing, for these techniques.

Summary

This chapter has shown you how to develop a generic prototype drawing that you can adapt to your own drafting application(s) or use as a springboard for additional prototypes that fit your specific needs.

Chapter 4 uses your new prototype drawing as a starting point for its exercises. In Chapter 4, you will be introduced to some new commands and techniques which are used for precision drafting and editing. The chapter also shows you how to dimension engineering drawings to industrial standards. Let's move on to Chapter 4 and put your new prototype to work.

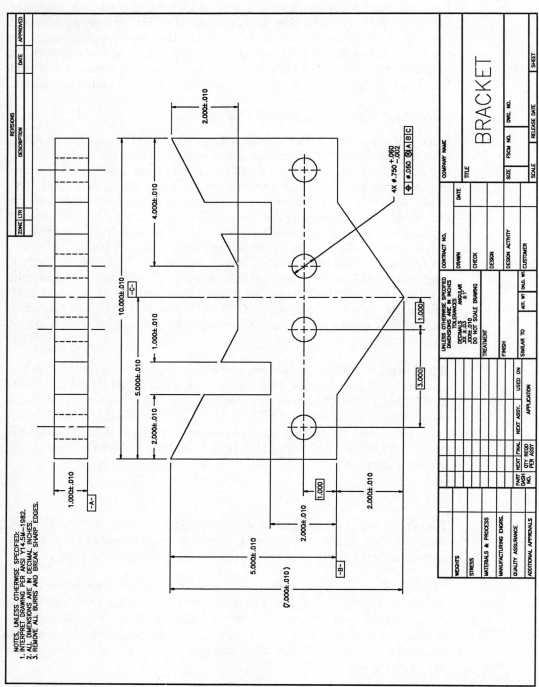

The BRACKET Drawing

CHAPTER 4

2D Drafting and Dimensioning

THE BASIC TECHNIQUES

Much has been said recently of 3D CAD drafting capabilities. However, many parts and objects can be adequately and efficiently drafted in 2D. In fact, most shop drawings only require fully dimensioned two-dimensional drawings to produce a part in a non-automated manufacturing facility. If 2D drafting will supply the necessary information, then 2D is the right tool for the job.

This chapter shows you how to draft a dimensioned 2D orthographic drawing of the mounting bracket shown on the facing page. It teaches you many of AutoCAD's commands at the same time, including APERTURE, BREAK, DIM, ERASE, EXTEND, MIRROR, OOPS, OSNAP, REDO, TRIM, UNDO, VIEWRES, and VPORTS. It also explains AutoCAD's object selection and expands upon the ZOOM and UCS commands.

Drawing this chapter's mounting bracket will show you how editing commands which erase, break, trim, and mirror entities complement the entity creation commands. We will set up multiple viewports and use ZOOM to manipulate the drawing screen. We will also work with the settings, linetypes, and layers from last chapter's prototype drawing. In the chapter's second half, we will introduce you to AutoCAD's array of dimensioning features.

We will be using the PROTO-C prototype drawing developed in Chapter 3, which has all the necessary parameters set. If you do not have the SIA DISK, you need to complete the PROTO-C drawing and configure it as the default prototype before starting this exercise.

The SIA DISK already has both the PROTO-C drawing and the finished BRACKET drawing. Use them to do either or both parts of the chapter. You may also choose to use some of the Y14.5 Menu System menu selections, if you have installed the program and reviewed its use as explained in Chapter 12.

If you don't have the SIA DISK, you'll need to develop the BRACKET drawing in the first part of the chapter in order to dimension it in the second part.

Setting Up With Multiple Viewports and ZOOM

A *viewport* is the currently active portion of the drawing screen. Up to now, we have been using the default single viewport. The screen may be divided into one, two, three, or four rectangular viewports. The following exercise uses two vertical viewports to display different views of the BRACKET drawing. We will edit the drawing close-up in a zoomed viewport while we view the entire drawing in the other.

VPORTS

The VPORTS command lets you divide your screen into several viewing areas. Each viewport can display a different view of your drawing. Each viewport contains its own drawing display area and can have independent magnification, viewpoint, snap, grid, viewres, ucsicon, dview, and isometric settings. You can independently ZOOM, REGEN, and REDRAW in each viewport. DOS-based systems let you define up to four viewports at any one time. Other systems let you define up to sixteen.
Save/Restore/Delete/Join/Off/?/2/<3>/4:

Follow the instructions below to divide the screen into two viewports. If pull-down menus are available, you can use the viewports icon menu.

Setting Multiple Viewports

 Begin a NEW drawing named **TEMP=**.

 Begin a NEW drawing named **BRACKET=**.

Layer OBJECT should be current.

Pull-down **[Display]** *Select* **[Set viewports...]**   And pick the box by the twin vertical icon,

Command: **VPORTS**   or type the command and responses.
Save/Restore/Delete/Join/Off/?/2/<3>/4: **2**
Horizontal/<Vertical>: **<RETURN>**   Default to vertical.

Click your pointer in the left viewport to make it active.

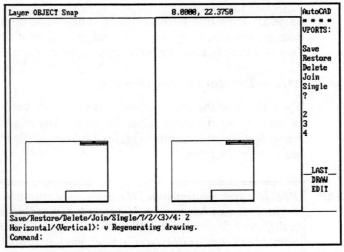

Bracket Displayed in Both Viewports

When you first set multiple viewports, they all display the current drawing. However, only one of these viewports can be active. To set a viewport current, move your cursor to that viewport and push the pick button on your pointing device. AutoCAD will display a bold border around the current viewport. Additionally, the cursor will display in the active viewport. An *arrow* will display in the nonactive viewport(s).

Many of AutoCAD's commands may be started in one viewport and then continued in a different viewport. For example, you can select the LINE command and attach the line's starting point to an entity in the active viewport. Then activate a viewport with a higher magnification (zoom) and attach the endpoint of the line to an easily recognized position. This is a useful technique in 2D and 3D computer drafting.

The VPORTS command subdivides the current viewport. You can merge two viewports into one rectangular viewport with the JOIN command. By combining subdivision and joining, you can create non-standard viewport configurations. Viewport settings can also be named, saved, and restored so you don't have to rebuild a particular viewport configuration.

Once you have configured the viewports, use PAN and ZOOM to make them display what you want.

Controlling the Screen Display With PAN and ZOOM

As your drawings become larger and more detailed, you will need to manipulate the magnification and locations of drawings on the screen. Two commands that perform these operations are PAN and ZOOM.

PAN — Displacing the Drawing

If you think of the viewport as a window into your drawing, think of PAN as moving the drawing around behind that window. You can move your drawing diagonally, sideways, up, or down while maintaining the current zoom magnification.

'PAN

> *PAN lets you scroll around the screen without altering the current zoom ratio. It is similar to repositioning paper on a drafting board to access a different drawing part. You do not physically move entities or change your drawing limits; you move your display window across your drawing. PAN is a transparent command. The default setting provides a displacement in relative coordinates.*
> ```
> Displacement: Second point:
> ```

The PAN command uses the *displacement* value between two points. You can enter the points from the keyboard or pick them with the pointing device. The *first point of displacement* is where you move the drawing from and the *second point of displacement* is where you move the drawing to. The cursor trails a line from the first point, showing the pan path, as you pick the second.

Let's use PAN to reposition the border drawing in the center of the left viewport.

Panning the Drawing Up

```
Command: PAN
Displacement:              Pick the center of the border area.
Second point:              Pick the center of the left viewport.
Regenerating drawing.
```

The drawing should be centered in the left viewport. Now use ZOOM to move in for some close work in the right viewport.

ZOOM — *Taking a Closer Look*

Let's examine the ZOOM command in more detail. ZOOM magnifies or reduces any part of an active viewport. Zooms are generally used to increase the viewing resolution of drawings. It is easier to draw or edit specific entities when a part of the drawing is magnified. You can zoom in the following ways:

number — Zooms to a specified scale, relative to the ZOOM All view.

numberX — Zooms to a specified scale, relative to the current viewport.

ZOOM All — Displays the entire drawing or limits, whichever is larger.

ZOOM Extents — Displays the entire drawing as large as possible, ignoring limits.

ZOOM Window — Displays the rectangular area defined by two diagonally opposite corner points. Once you pick the first corner of the window, you will find a box attached to the cursor. Drag the box to enclose the portion of the drawing to be magnified, then pick the second corner.

ZOOM Center — Zooms relative to a center point and view height.

ZOOM Left — Zooms relative to a user-selected left corner point and view height.

ZOOM Previous — Restores the previous zoom. It can be repeated up to ten views back.

ZOOM Dynamic — Interactively displays the entire drawing as you choose a window to zoom to.

The ZOOM Center and Left commands allow you to default to the current center or left corner point by hitting <RETURN>. They then present the current view height as a default. Let's try a ZOOM Center.

Using ZOOM Center

Click on the right viewport to activate it.

```
Command: ZOOM
All/Center/Dynamic/Extents/Left/Previous/Window/<Scale(X)>: C    Center.
Center point: 9,8
Magnification or Height <21.2500> : 11    The corner of the title block is still visible.
```

Your screen should match the Right Viewport Zoomed illustration below.

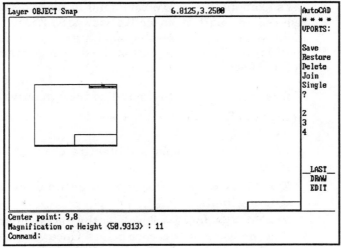

Layer OBJECT Snap   6.8125,3.2500   AutoCAD
                                                           * * * *
                                                           VPORTS:

                                                           Save
                                                           Restore
                                                           Delete
                                                           Join
                                                           Single
                                                           ?

                                                           2
                                                           3
                                                           4

                                                           LAST
                                                           DRAW
                                                           EDIT

Center point: 9,8
Magnification or Height <50.9313> : 11
Command:

Right Viewport Zoomed

ZOOM Dynamic requires a bit more explanation.

ZOOM Dynamic — Choosing Your View

ZOOM Dynamic interactively magnifies or reduces any part of the
drawing, using three boxes and an hourglass to que you for input. The
viewport temporarily redraws to show the extents of the entire drawing.
The four *corner markers* indicate the currently generated area within
which you can pan and zoom without a regeneration. The *hourglass*
comes on to tell you when a regeneration would be required. The fixed
solid box is the *current view box*. Use the movable solid *new view box* to
show where you want to go. It is initially sized and located to duplicate
the current view box. When the X displays at the center of the new view
box, you can drag its position. When an arrow displays at the side of the
new view box, you can drag its size. It always resizes in proportion to the
viewport. You can switch between the X to move and the arrow to resize
by clicking your pick button. Exit the command and execute the zoom by
pressing the <RETURN> key or the space bar.

This dynamic operation is an excellent tool for simultaneous ZOOM and
PAN operations. Let's fill the left viewport a bit better with the border.

Using ZOOM Dynamic

Click on the left viewport to activate it.

```
Command: ZOOM
All/Center/Dynamic/Extents/Left/Previous/Window/<Scale(X)>: D
```
Click to get the resizing arrow.
Drag to about the width of the border and click to get the X to move.
Move side to side and watch the hourglass.
Repeat the resizing if needed to fill the box with the border.
Center the box on the border and <RETURN> to execute the zoom.

```
Command: SAVE
```
Save it.

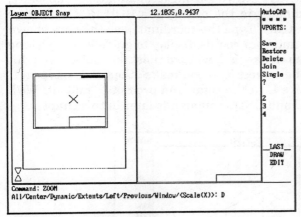

ZOOM Dynamic Screen

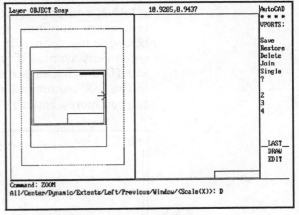

Changing the New View Box Size

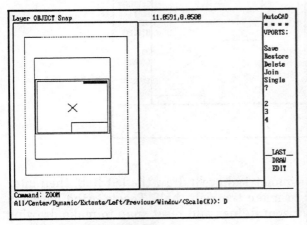

Locating the New View Box

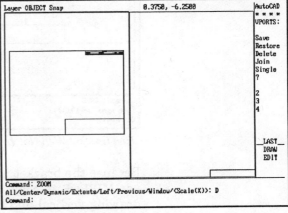

The Resulting Display

While the ZOOM Dynamic selection screen is displayed, your drawing will be doing a redraw. With more complex drawings, this may take a little time but you need not wait for the entire drawing to regenerate before you select a ZOOM Dynamic new view box size and position. As soon as you can establish where and how large you wish to zoom, you may execute the zoom.

The right viewport is the primary working viewport. This places the magnified image of the bracket close to the screen menu where selections are easy to make. You can watch the entire drawing update in the left viewport after every operation.

Coordinate Entry for the Bracket

We will develop the BRACKET drawing using a combination of absolute, relative, and polar coordinates in the prototype's BDR UCS and other temporary coordinate systems. Type the coordinates as they are shown below, or use snap, grid, and your coords display to guide you in picking equivalent points. If you make a keyboard mistake before you hit <RETURN>, backspace and correct it. If you make other errors, type a U in the LINE command, or a U at the command prompt to undo it. We'll tell you more about the U and UNDO commands later in this chapter.

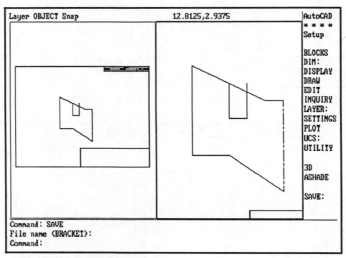

Half Bracket With Notch

Because the bracket is symmetrical, we'll draw the left half, then later use MIRROR to copy it to make the right half. Toggle ortho on when drawing vertical and horizontal lines and reset snap to make drawing easier.

Drawing the Front View and Notch

Continue in the previous BRACKET or TEMP drawing.
Activate the right viewport.

Command: **SNAP**	Set to 0.125.
Command: **LINE**	Draw the left half profile.
From point: **12,4**	Type or pick the absolute starting point.
To point: **@-3,2**	Continue typing or picking the following coordinates.
To point: **@2<180**	
To point: **@5<90**	
To point: **@4,-2**	
To point: **@1<0**	
To point: **C**	Close with center line and exit command.
Command: **CHPROP**	Move the last line to layer CL.
Select objects: L	L for Last.
1 found.	
Select objects: **<RETURN>**	
Change what property (Color/LAyer/LType/Thickness) ? **LA**	
New layer <OBJECT>: **CL**	
Change what property (Color/LAyer/LType/Thickness) ? **<RETURN>**	
	Depending on your display, it may still *appear* continuous.
Command: **LINE**	
From point: **9,10**	The starting point of the notch.
To point: **@2<-90**	Or pick 2<270.
To point: **@1<0**	
To point: **@2<90**	
To point: **<RETURN>**	To end the LINE command.
Command: **SAVE**	Save it.

Your drawing should look like the Half Bracket With Notch illustration.
We'll trim the notch a little later.

Viewing Drawings and Linetype Scale

If your center lines are not showing proper lengths and gaps, you can
change the value of the LTSCALE variable. But keep in mind that the
on-screen appearance of linetype spacing and the final product, which is
the plotted output, may differ. Set the LTSCALE factor to achieve the best
results in **plotted** form. You can experiment with this setting to achieve
a desired linetype scale. We find 0.5 to be the best setting for 1:1 scale.
You can set it temporarily to make viewing easier, but remember to reset
it before plotting. The VIEWRES command (later in this chapter) also
affects the screen appearance of linetypes.

Working in a Temporary UCS

Repositioning the coordinate system origin sets a new 0,0 home base. This makes it simple to position or create entities relative to the new 0,0 origin. You will find this technique very useful for both 2D and 3D drafting.

Because the bracket is symmetrical, let's position the UCS at its bottom point.

Changing the Origin of the UCSICON

```
Command: UCS
Origin/ZAxis/3point/Entity/View/X/Y/Z/Prev/Restore/Save/Del/?/<World>: O
Origin point <0,0,0>: 12,4            The Z value is unnecessary for 2D.
```

Your drawing will now display the UCS icon at the new origin, the bottom center of the bracket, as shown in the following illustration.

Next, let's add the drill holes.

Drawing Drill Holes With Circles

The bracket has four holes in it. We will construct two of these holes. The other two will be generated later when we mirror the other half of the bracket.

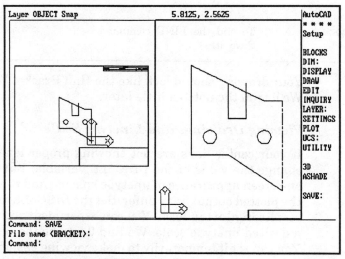

Bracket With Circles

You can draw circles in several ways. Try the default center point and radius, as well as the diameter option. Drag and pick the radius and diameter with the aid of snap and coords, or type the values shown. Try toggling ortho on (<^O> or <F8>) if you drag and pick.

Making the Circles on the Bracket

```
Command: CIRCLE
3P/2P/TTR/<Center point>: -4,3          Relative to the new UCS.
Diameter/<Radius>: .375                 Half of the 0.75 diameter value.
Command: <RETURN>
CIRCLE 3P/2P/TTR/<Center point>: -1,3
Diameter/<Radius>: D
Diameter: .75                           Enter the circle diameter.
Command: SAVE
```

Your drawing should look like the Bracket With Circles illustration. Your circles may look octagonal, although they'll plot with full resolution. AutoCAD simplifies the display of curves to save time. You can control the screen resolution with the VIEWRES command.

VIEWRES

> *VIEWRES controls fast zooms and the display resolution of arcs, circles, and linetypes. The default setting is for fast zooms with a resolution factor of 100 percent. Fast zoom allows most zooms and pans at redraw, not regeneration, speed.*

See your AutoCAD Reference Manual, or the New Riders books INSIDE AutoCAD or AutoCAD REFERENCE GUIDE for more information.

Now let's explore how the editing commands can help you draw.

Editing — More Than an Eraser

AutoCAD's editing commands correct mistakes. They also serve as important drafting tools to modify drawings. Your drafting production will be greatly enhanced by understanding AutoCAD's editing commands. The simplest is ERASE.

ERASE

> *ERASE deletes entities from the drawing.*
> ```
> Select objects:
> ```

ERASE hardly needs demonstration or explanation. The only trick is selecting what you want to erase. AutoCAD calls that *object selection,* and it is common to most editing commands.

Object Selection

The basic concept of AutoCAD's object selection is the *selection set,* made up of the group of objects that you select. Once you have the desired set, you <RETURN> to exit object selection and execute the editing command at hand.

There are several methods for selecting objects. They include:

pick point — Selects a single object, which must be within the pick box range (pixel size) of the pick point.

Last — Selects the last object created.

Previous — Selects all objects in the previously completed selection set.

Window — Selects all objects that are visibly contained within a window indicated by two opposite corner points.

Crossing — Selects all objects either within or crossing the window.

Multiple — Allows multiple selections by any method before adding them to the selection set.

Add — Adds the selections that follow to the selection set.

Remove — Removes the selections that follow from the selection set.

Undo — Undoes the previous selection operation (add or remove).

BOX — Combines Window and Crossing for one selection. If you pick points left to right it works like Window, but if you pick right to left it works like Crossing.

SIngle — Exits object selection automatically after successful selection by any one of the above methods, eliminating the need to enter a <RETURN>.

AUto — Combines BOX and picking by point for the selections that follow.

You may use any combination of these modes when building a selection set. You need only enter the upper case portion of the names listed above. Most video displays distinguish between Window and Crossing by showing the crossing box with a dashed line and the window box with a solid line.

Each object selection returns a message like "n found" or "n selected, n found" as it adds the selection to the selection set. When an entity has been selected, most displays highlight it. The highlighting method varies.

It can be a color change, or blinking or dashed lines. Highlighting adds to the selection time, but you can turn it off when selecting complex objects. Use SETVAR to set HIGHLIGHT to 1 for on or 0 for off.

You *can* use BOX, SIngle, and AUto manually, however there is no real advantage to doing so. Manually, if you know what and how you want to select, you can enter W or C as easily as BOX or AU, and you can <RETURN> as easily as entering SI. BOX, SIngle, and AUto are intended to be built into menu items to make object selection more automatic. For example, most pull-down [Modify] menu items use SIngle and AUto modes combined.

Combining SIngle and AUto modes works like this: if you pick a point which is on an entity, it is selected and object selection is completed without a <RETURN>. But if you pick a point which is *not* on an entity, it goes into BOX mode, allowing either a Window or Crossing selection. The choice is determined by where you pick the second opposite corner point. If the second corner is to the right, it attempts to select a Window. If it is to the left, it attempts a Crossing window. If it fails to find an object, it repeats. As soon as any object is selected, it completes and exits object selection.

➤ *NOTE: Sometimes SNAP gets in the way of object selection, preventing you from getting the cursor right on or adjacent to the point or window you want to select. Toggle SNAP off when needed, but be sure to toggle it back on when drawing or you may draw inaccurately.*

Using Object Selection With ERASE

Let's try using ERASE with several of the object selection modes.

Selecting and Erasing Entities

Continue in the BRACKET or TEMP drawing.

Command: **ERASE <F9>**	Or <^B> to toggle snap off.
Select objects:	Pick any point on the red center line.
1 selected, 1 found	The line is highlighted.
Select object: **<RETURN>**	Completes object selection and executes ERASE command. The line disappears.
Command: **ERASE**	Try Window and Crossing.
Select objects: **W**	Window both circles.
First corner:	Pick left point ①.
Other corner:	Drag and pick point ②.
2 found	Only the circles highlight.

Select objects: **C**	Select the notch with Crossing.
First corner:	Pick right point ③.
Other corner:	Drag and pick point ④.
3 found	All three lines highlight.
Select object: **<RETURN>**	Completes object selection and executes ERASE command.
	The circles and lines disappear.
Command: **<F9>**	Or <^B> to toggle snap back on.

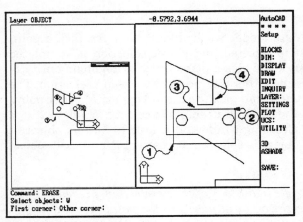

Window Selects Circles

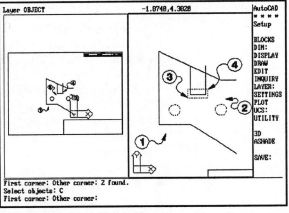

Crossing Selects Notch Lines

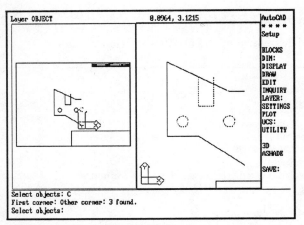

Circles and Lines Are Highlighted

Circles and Lines Are Erased

The selected circles and lines are gone, but actually we need them back.

Replacing Mistaken Erasures With OOPS

If you erase the wrong entities, AutoCAD has an OOPS command to replace them.

OOPS

> OOPS restores the last entity, or group of entities, deleted by the most recent ERASE command.

We need to get back the circle and line that you just erased. Let's retrieve them with OOPS.

Oopsing an Entity Back

Command: **OOPS**	Brings back the circles and notch lines.
Command: **OOPS**	A second OOPS does nothing.

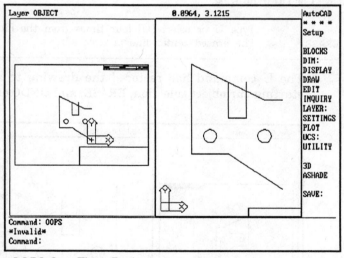

OOPS Gets Them Back

If OOPS only steps back one ERASE command, how do we get the previously erased center line back? We use the U or UNDO commands, which offer more flexibility and control in reversing commands.

The U, UNDO, and REDO Commands

If you perform another command operation after incorrectly erasing entities, you still have a few tricks up your sleeve. The U and UNDO commands can be used to save the day.

U/UNDO

> *The U and UNDO commands let you step back through your drawing, reversing previous commands or groups of commands. UNDO keeps track of the previous commands in a temporary file. This file is cleared at the end of each drawing editor session, or when you plot. U undoes a single command or group per execution. UNDO offers additional controls.*
> ```
> Auto/Back/Control/End/Group/Mark/<number>:
> ```

The U command can undo one command at a time until your drawing is back to the state at which you started the current working session (or just after the last plot), but we won't go back that far. Let's use U to restore the center line.

Using the U Command

Continue in the BRACKET or TEMP drawing.

```
Command: U
OOPS OOPS ERASE ERASE
```
Type U or select [U] four times from the [Tools] pull-down menu. The erased center line is restored.

The U command has restored the drawing to where we were before starting our object selection, ERASE, and UNDO experimentation.

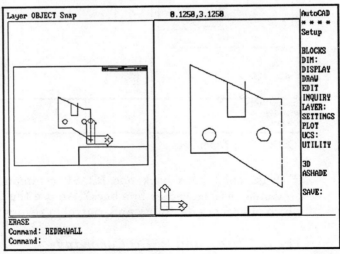

Easy Undoes It

When U or UNDO undoes a command (or group), the name of the command (or the word GROUP) being undone will be displayed for your information at the command prompt. A *group* can be a group of commands executed by a menu item, or a group you create with the UNDO options shown below. If you get carried away and undo too much, you can use the REDO command.

UNDO Options and the REDO Command

The UNDO command allows you to undo several commands at one time, and provides special functions such as:

Auto-Undo — Used to group commands in menus.

Back — Undoes back to the last marked place in the drawing.

Control — Controls the range of the UNDO and U commands: One only allows one command to be undone; All is the normal default; and None disables U and UNDO.

End — Ends a grouping of commands.

Group — Starts grouping a series of commands.

Mark — Establishes a marked position in the drawing for the Back option to find.

<number> — Specifies the number of preceding operations to be undone as one step.

A standout drafting feature of the UNDO command is the mark. If you have completed one phase of a drafting project and are about to begin a new one, you can set a mark. Then if the next phase is experimental, or just plain doesn't work out, you can UNDO Back to the place in your drawing where you set the mark. Be careful though; without the mark, you may UNDO back to the beginning of the current drawing session.

REDO | *REDO simply reverses the last U or UNDO command. A group, the UNDO Back, or <number> options are treated as a single REDO operation.*

UNDO and REDO are helpful editing tools to have in your AutoCAD tool kit. Apply them as needed in our exercises and in your drafting projects. There will be many occasions when you try a command or a series of commands that do not turn out the way you would like. This is where the U, UNDO, and REDO commands will prove invaluable.

Let's move on to some more constructive editing tools.

Breaking Entities

AutoCAD lets you *break* entities into smaller pieces. You can break lines, arcs, or circles by specifying the entity to break, the point to break from, and the point to break to.

BREAK

> *BREAK enables you to split or erase portions of lines, arcs, circles, 2D polylines, and traces. When you select an object to break, the default assumes your pick point is also your first break point.*
> ```
> Select object: Enter second point (or F for first point):
> ```

When breaking circles, BREAK creates arcs, removing the counterclockwise portion between the two pick points.

The first pick point is the default first break point, but if it is at an intersection, it may pick the wrong entity. The F option gets around this, letting you reselect your break point. Let's try it.

Breaking Lines

Continue in the BRACKET or TEMP drawing.

```
Command: BREAK                                    Break the diagonal line to open the notch.
Select object:                                    Pick point ①.
Enter second point (or F for first point): F      To reenter first point.
Enter first point:                                Pick point ②.
Enter second point:                               Pick point ③.

Command: SAVE
```

The diagonal is now two lines, opening the notch.

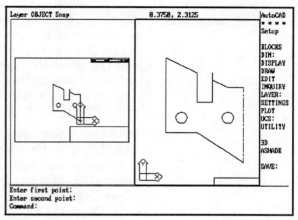

Pick Line and Points to Break   Notch Is Opened

If the first or second break point is not on the entity, the nearest point on the entity will be used. This will be perpendicular to the break point for lines, and at the point of the tangent that would form a perpendicular for arcs and circles. If the break point is off the end of a line or arc, the entire end will be broken off, leaving only one line or arc.

You probably had no trouble picking the exact intersections of the lines since they were convenient snap points in our exercise drawing. In the real world, points like these are often at some odd geometric spacing so you can't snap accurately, or the snap increment required may be so small as to be impractical without zooming way in. AutoCAD's object snap offers an alternative way to accurately pick points on existing geometry.

Object Snap

Object snap aids point picking by allowing you to specify several modes of geometric points on existing entities. It then filters the point pick and *osnaps* it to the nearest point that matches the geometric mode used. For example, you can osnap to the exact intersection of two lines, circles, or arcs with the INT mode. Think of it as snapping to attachment points on entities.

You can use object snap in the middle of any point entry by entering the modes(s) desired before picking the point. Object snap normally searches all objects crossing the aperture and selects the closest potential snap point of the specified type(s). The *aperture* is a box added to the crosshairs during osnap mode to indicate the range of the osnap search area.

APERTURE

> *The APERTURE command controls the size of the target box located in the middle of the crosshairs during object snap selection. You can change the size in pixels of the aperture box. The default setting is 10 pixels for most displays. The setting is half the height of the box, or the number of pixels above or below the crosshairs.*
> `Object snap target height (1-50 pixels) <10>:`

You can enter the object snap modes by typing their first three letters and a <RETURN>, or by selecting them from a menu. The [* * * *] from any of the screen menu pages or the [Tools] selection from the pull-down menu presents lists of object snap overrides. In the following mode listing, *line* and *arc* apply to a line or arc polyline segment as well as to a line or arc entity. There are 12 different modes:

CENter — Snaps to the center point of an arc or circle. Pick it on its circumference or arc.

ENDPoint — Snaps to the closest endpoint of a line or arc. (Use ENDP instead of END to avoid having it accidently interpreted as the END command.)

INSert — Snaps to the insertion point of a shape, text, or block entity.

INTersec — Snaps to the intersection of any combination of two lines, circles, or arcs. For this object snap mode, both objects must cross the aperture on the screen.

MIDpoint — Snaps to the midpoint of a line or arc.

NEArest — Snaps to the point on a line, arc, circle, or point entity that is closest to the crosshairs.

NODe — Snaps to a point entity.

PERpend — Snaps to the point on a line, circle, or arc that is perpendicular from the previous point or to the next point.

QUAdrant — Snaps to the closest quadrant (0, 90, 180, and 270 degree) point of an arc or circle.

TANgent — Snaps to the point on a circle or arc that, when connected to the previous or next point, forms a line tangent to that object.

QUIck — Overrules the normal object snap search of all objects crossing the aperture. When many items are visible on the screen, this search can result in a noticeable delay. If you use **QUI** mode along with other object modes, it osnaps to the *first* qualified point found instead of searching all possibilities for the nearest. The point found will generally be one of the most recent entities.

NONe — Suppresses or turns off osnap.

Let's try a few of these in a repeat of the previous BREAK command.

Breaking a Line Using Object Snap

Continue in the BRACKET or TEMP drawing.

```
Command: <F9>                         Toggle snap off to see that OSNAP is in control.
Command: U                            Undo the previous BREAK.

Command: BREAK
BREAK Select object: NEA              NEArest.
to                                    Position cursor so aperture corner only crosses the top diagonal,
                                      then pick.
Enter second point (or F for first point): F
Enter first point: END                ENDpoint.
of                                    Position cursor so aperture crosses top of left vertical notch line,
                                      then pick.
Enter second point: INT               INTersection.
of                                    Position cursor so aperture crosses both diagonal and other
                                      vertical notch lines, then pick.
Command: <F9>                         Restore snap.
Command: U                            Undo the BREAK command.
```

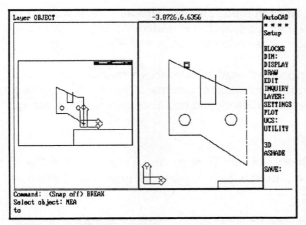

Pick Line to Break

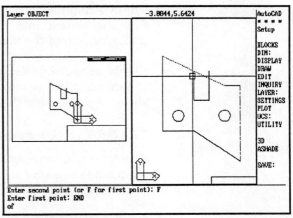

END of First Point of Break

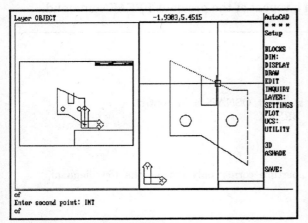

INTersection of Second Point

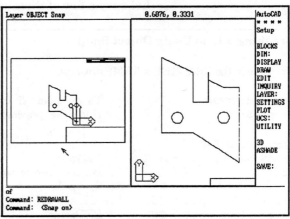

Broken Notch

There are only three ways to create accurate drawings in AutoCAD: snapping to a snap increment; entering coordinates (absolute, relative, or polar); and osnapping to existing geometry. Use whichever method best suits the situation throughout this book and in all your work. Anything else is only approximate.

These osnap modes can be combined. You can choose INT, END, MID to find the closest intersection, endpoint, or midpoint, or you can use END, QUI to find the most recent endpoint.

Single or multiple osnap modes used in the above manner are called osnap *interrupts* or *overrides*, or *transient* osnaps. If you need to make a series of picks using the same mode(s), you can also set a running osnap.

The OSNAP Command

OSNAP sets a *running* object snap mode or modes. Your specified object snap mode remains active, affecting all point picks until you change or override it.

OSNAP

> *OSNAP (Object SNAP) lets you preset one or more running object snap modes. The default setting is off or NONe. You can override a running mode by entering a different transient osnap mode or modes when a point is requested. The STATUS command displays the current running osnap mode.*

OSNAP allows you to make multiple object snap selections without having to re-select after every use. You can still use other transient modes, or NONe to temporarily suppress the running mode.

Trimming a Drawing

We could use BREAK to trim off the other vertical notch line, but instead we'll undo the previous break and use the TRIM command to do both breaks. The TRIM command provides you with a multiple breaking tool that can greatly increase your drawing cleanup speed and accuracy.

TRIM

> *TRIM makes it possible for you to clip entities that cross a boundary or cutting edge. You can have more than one cutting edge. Entities like lines, arcs, circles, and polylines can act both as boundary edges and as objects to trim.*
> Select cutting edge(s)... Select object to trim:

As its name implies, the TRIM command *trims off* selected entities precisely at user-defined cutting edges, like a combined BREAK and OSNAP would do. You may use any of the entity selection methods to define the cutting edges.

We'll use TRIM to precisely trim the unnecessary line segment which crosses the bracket's notch.

Trimming Crossing Lines

```
Command: TRIM
Select cutting edge(s)...
Select objects: C                    Select all three lines with Crossing.
First corner:                        Pick point ①.
Other corner:                        Pick point ②.
Select objects: <RETURN>             Done selecting edges.

Select object to trim:               Pick point ③ on diagonal.
Select object to trim:               Pick end of right vertical at ④.
Select object to trim: <RETURN>      Exit.
```

The two verticals trimmed the diagonal and the diagonal trimmed the right vertical. The bracket should now appear as shown in the following illustration.

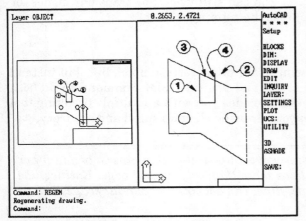

Pick Points for Trim

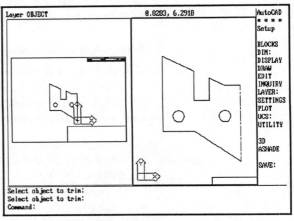

Notch Is Trimmed

The TRIM command has a cousin, the EXTEND command.

Extending Lines

While the TRIM command trims entities *at* a boundary edge, the EXTEND command extends existing entities *to* a boundary edge.

EXTEND | *EXTEND lengthens the endpoints of a line, open polyline, and arc to a boundary edge. Boundary edges include lines, circles, arcs, and polylines. You can have more than one boundary edge, and an entity can be both a boundary edge and an entity to extend.*

To create the top view of the bracket, we only need to draw two horizontal lines, then TRIM and EXTEND the rest. We'll draw its left half, then mirror it to create the other half.

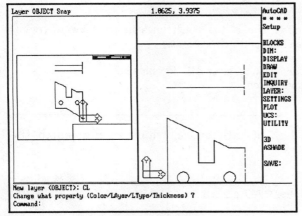

Panned View With Top and Center Lines

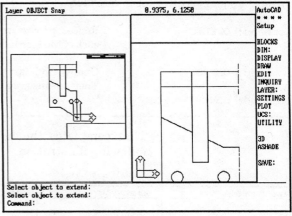

Vertical Object Lines Extended .

Drawing the Top View With TRIM, EXTEND, BREAK, and OFFSET

Continue in the BRACKET or TEMP drawing.
Make the right viewport active.

Command: **PAN**	Or DVIEW to see the bracket and the top border line.
Command: **LINE**	Draw the two horizontals as illustrated above.
Command: **LINE**	Draw top center line as shown.
Command: **CHPROP**	Change top center line to layer CL for center.
Command: **EXTEND** Select boundary edge(s)...	Extend the three vertical object lines upward.
Select objects:	Pick the new top horizontal line.
Select objects: **<RETURN>**	
Select object to extend:	Select each vertical near its top end.
Select object to extend: **<RETURN>**	
Command: **TRIM** Select boundary edge(s)...	Trim the in-between portions of the vertical object lines.
Select objects:	Pick new bottom horizontal and both top diagonal lines.
Select objects: **<RETURN>**	
Select object to trim:	Pick each vertical in the middle.
Command: **OFFSET**	Create the circle center lines in the top view.
Offset distance or Through <Through>: **T**	Through.
Select object to offset:	Select top center line.
<F8>	Or <^O> toggles ortho on.
Through point:	Align vertical crosshairs exactly on center of circle and pick.
Select object to offset:	Pick new line at same point.

Through point:	Align on center of other circle and pick.
Select object to offset: **<RETURN>**	
Command: **OFFSET**	Repeat process to offset one of the notch lines in top view to create each of the four hidden lines of the circle edges.
Command: **CHPROP**	Change the last four lines to layer HL for hidden. They become green and hidden.
Command: **SAVE**	

That completes the left half of both views, which should match the following illustration.

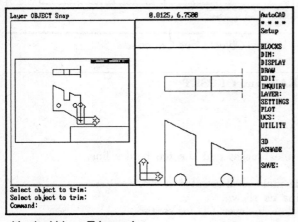

Vertical Lines Trimmed

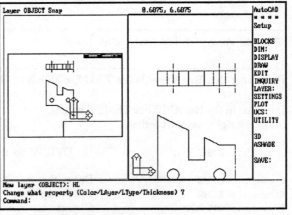

The Completed Left Half

We can complete the right half in a single MIRROR command. But first, change back to a single viewport to make it easier to work on the whole thing.

Changing Back to a Single Viewport

Command: **VPORTS**	
Save/Restore/Delete/Join/SIngle/?/2/<3>/4: **SI**	SIngle.
Command: **ZOOM**	Zoom Window or Dynamic to fill screen with the border.

When you change back to a single viewport, the image from the last current viewport fills the screen. Depending on whether it was the left or right, you had to zoom in or out to fill the screen. Changing viewports should become as common a drafting process as setting snap, grid, or osnap. Whenever you find yourself needing to view your drawing in another format, reset VPORTS.

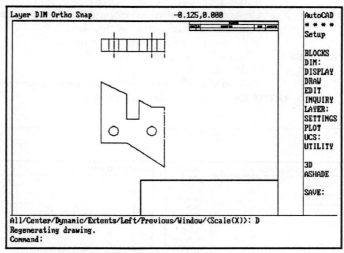

The Single Viewport Display

Mirroring the Bracket

AutoCAD lets you mirror any entity or group of entities. This is a great time saver for drawing symmetrical objects such as gaskets and brackets.

MIRROR

> *The MIRROR command creates mirror images of a selected group of entities. You can keep the original group of mirrored entities or you can delete it. The default does not delete the originals. MIRROR can also reflect text or keep it right-reading when mirroring an image, controlled by the MIRRTEXT system variable. The default setting for MIRRTEXT is 1 (on) to mirror (reflect) text.*

The MIRROR command creates an exact mirror image, including layers and linetypes, about a line at any angle specified by picking two points. The MIRROR command gives you the opportunity to delete the original entity if you simply want to flip the entity. In the following exercise, we're going to retain the old object while we duplicate it to create the right side of the bracket.

Mirroring the Bracket

Command: **MIRROR**	Make sure ORTHO and SNAP are on.
Select objects: **C**	Crossing window of everything but main center lines.
First corner:	Pick first corner point for window.
Other corner:	Pick second corner point for window.
Select objects: **\<RETURN\>**	When all objects have been selected.
First point of mirror line:	Pick point on main mirror line.
Second point:	Pick any point above or below, near main mirror line.
Delete old objects? \<N\> **\<RETURN\>**	Do not delete.
Command: **END**	

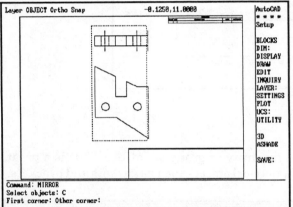

Crossing Window for Mirror

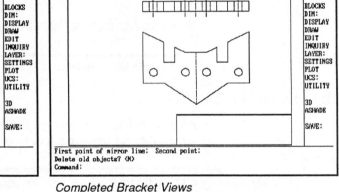

Completed Bracket Views

Upon completion, your drawing should look like the Completed Bracket Views illustration above.

Very few drafting projects are complete without dimensioning. The remainder of this chapter will guide you through the use of a few of AutoCAD's dimensioning commands and techniques.

Dimensioning Engineering Drawings

Dimensioning plays an important role in communicating size descriptions and other information. Dimensions should provide a complete and unambiguous description of a part. The size description communicates information to manufacturers regarding what materials to use, the size and location of all features, and special instructions or specifications. With the product itself at stake, it is critical that dimensioning be performed according to an industry-wide standard so drawings will provide a *single interpretation* of how a part is to be produced. Drawings and exercises in STEPPING INTO AutoCAD conform to the Geometric Dimensioning and Tolerancing (GDT) standard of ANSI Y14.5M-1982 wherever possible.

The objective of this part of the bracket exercise is to guide you through a few of AutoCAD's basic dimensioning features. This means that instead of fully dimensioning the bracket, we will use it to show specific introductory dimensioning techniques. For additional practice of the skills you acquire from this exercise, you can complete the bracket's dimensioning on your own.

AutoCAD'S Built-In Dimensioning

AutoCAD's automatic dimensioning maintains complete integrity with drawing accuracy. Dimensioning is a separate mode within AutoCAD, indicated by a `Dim:` prompt which replaces the `Command:` prompt. When in *dimensioning mode,* numerous dimensioning subcommands and dimensioning system variables are available, but AutoCAD's drawing and editing commands are not.

DIM/DIM1

> *DIM activates the dimensioning mode. The command prompt changes to* DIM:, *and only the subcommands associated with dimensioning are active. DIM1 activates the dimension mode for a single command and then returns you to the regular command prompt.*

We assume that you are already familiar with dimensioning terms such as dimension lines, extension lines, and leaders. If you are not, refer to INSIDE AutoCAD, from New Riders Publishing, or the AutoCAD Reference Manual for definitions and examples.

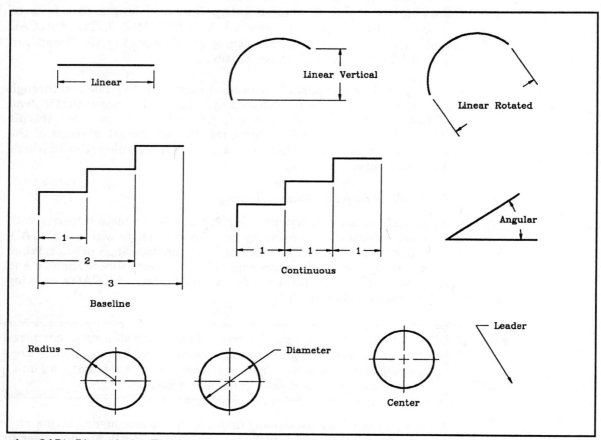

AutoCAD's Dimensioning Types

Once in dimensioning mode, you need only type the first three letters, like HOR for HORizontal, to execute AutoCAD's dimensioning commands. AutoCAD's dimensioning commands fall into seven different categories:

■ LINEAR DIMENSIONING COMMANDS

ALIgned draws the dimension line parallel to the extension line origin points or to a selected entity.

BASeline dimensions are measured from the same first point. Once you have created the first linear dimension, BASeline dimensions the rest of the entities at a set increment from the last dimension line using the same first point of origin of the extension line. All you provide is the second extension point for each.

CONtinue dimensions are generated in a series or chain. Once you have created the first linear dimension, CONtinue dimensions the rest of the entities, each chained to the previous. If the dimension text does not fit, the dimension line will be incremented from the last. All you provide is the second extension point.

HORizontal draws the dimension line horizontally.

ROTated draws the dimension line at an angle that you define.

VERtical draws the dimension line vertically.

■ ANGULAR DIMENSIONING COMMANDS

ANGular measures the dimension angle between two non-parallel lines.

■ RADIUS DIMENSIONING COMMANDS

RADius dimensions circles and arcs by placing a radius line (half a diameter line and containing one arrow head) through the center of the circle or arc.

■ DIAMETER DIMENSIONING COMMANDS

DIAmeter dimensions circles and arcs by placing a dimension line through the center of the circle or arc.

■ ASSOCIATIVE DIMENSIONING COMMANDS

HOMetext moves associative dimension text to its default location.

NEWtext enables you to revise associative dimension text, adopting the current dimension variable settings.

UPDate modifies associative dimension entities to adopt the current dimension variables.

■ DIMENSIONING UTILITY COMMANDS

CENter constructs a dimensioning center mark or center lines for circles and arcs.

EXIt will return you from dimensioning mode to the command prompt. You can also press <^C> to exit.

LEAder, made up of arrow head, lines, and text, is drawn from where the arrow head is placed to where you want the dimension text or notes to be placed.

REDraw refreshes the current viewport display.

STYle lets you change the text style of your dimensioning text.

STAtus lists the current settings of the dimension variables.

Undo, while in the dimensioning mode, voids the latest dimensioning operation. You can undo one step at a time until you reach the beginning of the current dimensioning mode session.

■ DIMENSIONING VARIABLES

Dimensioning variables are system variables that control the formats for your dimensions, such as arrow head or tick mark size, text location, and size. Some of the variables contain values while others act as on and off switches. They can be accessed by SETVAR, or as dimensioning subcommands. (See the complete list in the Appendix C system variables table.)

Associative Dimensioning

AutoCAD's default is *associative dimensioning*. Nonassociative dimensioning generates each dimension as a set of individual line, solid, and text entities. To update, you have to select and erase each entity and redo the dimensioning command. Associative dimensions are single entities, with control points at the dimension points picked. When you modify an object by stretching or scaling it, the associative dimension automatically updates as if the dimension lines are linked to the object. This allows dimensions to be automatically updated when you edit the geometry of a drawing. DIMASO is the dimension variable that controls associative dimensioning. Associative dimensioning will be explored in Chapter 5.

Customizing Dimensioning

It is easy to do standard automatic dimensioning with AutoCAD. However, no single style of dimensioning meets everyone's standards. Therefore, AutoCAD provides numerous dimensioning system variables with which you can alter dimensioning style. We set the dimension variables required to make AutoCAD conform to ANSI Y14.5 standards in last chapter's prototype drawing. Let's review what these settings are, why they are needed, and how they work.

DIMASZ — 0.125 sets the size of the dimension line arrows, and affects the fit of text between extension lines.

DIMCEN — -0.1 draws 0.1-inch circle/arc center tick marks with extension lines projecting 0.1 past the circle/arc perimeter.

DIMDLI — 0.5 sets the spacing between dimension lines for successive continuous and baseline dimensions. (We'll adjust this as needed when we dimension.)

DIMEXE — 0.125 sets the extension line to extend 0.125 inches beyond the dimension line.

DIMEXO — 0.125 sets the extension line to begin with a 0.125-inch offset from the dimension origin points.

DIMTXT — 0.125 sets our choice of standard height for dimensioning text.

DIMZIN — 4 suppresses any leading zero before a decimal point for values of less than one inch.

We will also use several other variables to control options such as tolerances. There are several situations where you need to work around AutoCAD to get the proper results. That's because:

■ AutoCAD places diameter dimension text at the center of a circle, if it fits. To force the dimension text to be placed outside the circle, you can pad the text string with invisible leading or trailing spaces.

■ AutoCAD tends to force *limited space dimensions* (dimensions whose text size or text string length does not fit between the extension lines) outside the extension lines. AutoCAD insists on 4.3 times the DIMTXT setting plus the text height or string length between extension lines before it will place the text between the extension lines. Often, you will want to force a slightly tighter fit to gain room for additional dimensions. There are two ways to work around this. First, you can use the MOVE command (if associative dimensioning is off) or the STRETCH command (if associative dimensioning is on) to relocate the text after the fact. Second, you can set the DIMTIX dimensioning variable to 1 (on). DIMTIX forces all dimension text "between" extension lines, even if it overlaps them.

Occasionally, AutoCAD will cross extension lines. If it becomes absolutely necessary for you to cross an extension line with a dimension line, use the BREAK command to produce a visible gap on each side of the dimension line.

Recommended Spacing for Dimensions

Dimensioning with AutoCAD sometimes requires more space than traditional drafting, so allow enough room around your views to make your drawing dimensions readable. Here are a few guidelines for spacing dimensions on AutoCAD drawings.

■ The space between the first dimension line and the part outline should be at least 0.375 inches (10mm), preferably a minimum of 0.5 inches.

■ The space between succeeding parallel dimension lines should be at least 0.25 inches (6mm), preferably 0.5 minimum. For automatic continuing and baseline dimensioning, this is preset to 0.5 by DIMDLI.

If possible, equally space all dimension lines and try to match the space between the first dimension line and the part.

■ Try to space your dimension lines at snappable locations. This makes it easy to keep dimension lines equal distances apart and in line with each other.

In the following section, we will use a combination of linear, diameter, and dimensioning variables to dimension the bracket.

Dimensioning the Bracket

We won't demonstrate all of AutoCAD's dimensioning subcommands but will concentrate on linear dimensioning. Other subcommands and more advanced dimensioning techniques are in the following chapters.

The first step in dimensioning the bracket is to set the current layer to DIM, which uses red continuous lines. If you are using the Y14.5 Menu System, you can select [DIM] from the tablet to set the layer. Once the DIM layer is set, we will draw the center lines on the circles in the front view.

You can issue dimensioning commands by typing them as shown below, or by using the screen or tablet menus. To access the screen menu, select [DIM:] from the root menu. Then select the type of dimensioning you want, using [next] to get to the associative options. The linear options and dimensioning variables are also grouped as separate pages, accessed by [LINEAR] and [Dim Vars]. Throughout the following exercises, zoom and pan as needed to see what you are doing.

Let's try it. If you have the SIA DISK, you have the BRACKET drawing ready to dimension. If you don't have the disk, you need the BRACKET drawing drawn in the first half of this chapter.

Generating Circle Center Lines

Enter Selection: **2.**	Edit an EXISTING drawing named BRACKET.
Command: **LAYER**	Set DIM current.
Command: **SNAP**	Set to 0.125.
Command: **DIM**	
Dim: **CEN**	CENter.
Select arc or circle:	Pick one of the circles. Center lines appear.
Dim: **<RETURN>**	
CEN Select arc or circle:	Pick the second circle. Continue with the other two circles.

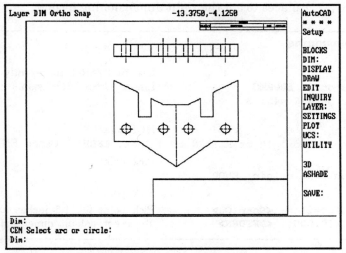

Pick the Circles for Center Lines

The four circles have center marks and lines.

Fixing Dimensioning Errors

If you make a mistake, type **U** or select [undo] to remove the last
dimension and remain in dimensioning mode. Once you exit Dim mode,
you can use ERASE to delete individual dimensions, but a U or an UNDO
will obliterate everything done in the dimensioning mode session. If
associative dimensioning is not on, each dimension entity becomes a set
of separate lines, solids, and text which must be erased individually.

Linear Dimensioning

Linear dimensions can be HORizontal, VERtical, ALIgned, ROTated,
BASeline, and CONtinue (chain). The key to successful dimensioning lies
in the order of point selection which controls the direction, orientation,
and location of the dimension. If at first you don't succeed, **U** and try
again.

Generally, you first designate the length of the dimension line by picking
its starting and ending points. Accuracy is as important here as in
drawing, so use snap or osnap as needed. In the sequence below, use
object snap to locate the two points (for this drawing, snap would work as
well if you zoom in). Use a snap point to pick the position of the dimension
line. The dimension text will be placed at the center of the dimension line.

Let's start with the top horizontal dimension. First set LUPREC to three places to get the right dimensioning format.

Horizontal Dimensioning

Dim: **'SETVAR**	Use SETVAR transparently.
>>Variable name or ?: **LUPREC**	Linear Units PRECision.
>>New value for LUPREC <4>: **3**	
Dim: **HOR**	HORizontal.
First extension line origin or RETURN to select: **ENDP**	Osnap ENDPoint.
of	Pick point ①.
Second extension line origin: **ENDP**	
of	Pick point ②.
Dimension line location: **<Snap On>**	Pick point ③, 1.5 inches above the object.
Dimension text <10.000>: **<RETURN>**	To accept default dimension text.

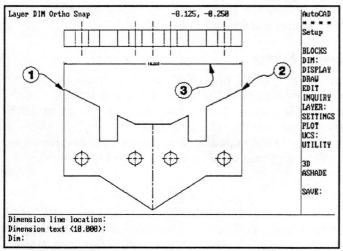

Horizontal Dimension

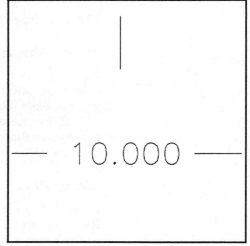

Detail of Dimension Text

Notice that AutoCAD's default dimension is uni-directional and in decimal units representing inches. Dimensions are created with three places to the right of the decimal point because LUPREC set the linear units of precision to 3. If you are using the Y14.5 Menu System, you can easily change the dimensioning precision by selecting [.XX], [.XXX], or [.XXXX] from the tablet.

Next, we'll add tolerances to our dimension.

Drafting With Tolerances

To draw dimensions with tolerances or limits, we simply set positive (+) and negative (-) tolerance values and toggle the required tolerance or limits variables on or off. The dimensioning variables for plus and minus limits and tolerancing are:

> **DIMTOL** — On (1) for tolerances appended to dimension, off (0) for none.
>
> **DIMLIM** — On (1) for a pair of limit dimensions in lieu of single dimension, off (0) for normal.
>
> **DIMTP** — The Tolerance (limits) Plus value.
>
> **DIMTM** — The Tolerance (limits) Minus value.

You can set these variables from the screen menu dimension variables page by selecting [DIM:] [Dim Vars] [next] [next], by typing their names at the Dim: prompt, or with the Y14.5 Menu System. With the Y14.5 program, select [SET TOLERANCE PLUS], [SET TOLERANCE MINUS], and [TOLERANCE ON/OFF] or [LIMITS ON/OFF] from the tablet. The menu also provides many of the common tolerance values in easy selections, like [.001], [.002], or [.003].

➥ *NOTE: DIMTOL and DIMLIM cannot both be on simultaneously. When you turn one on, it turns the other off.*

Make the following settings to set tolerancing.

Setting Tolerances

```
Dim: DIMTOL
Current value <Off> New value: ON

Dim: DIMTP
Current value <0.000> New value: .01

Dim: DIMTM
Current value <0.000> New value: .01
```

Updating Dimensions

If associative dimensioning is on, we can use the UPDATE subcommand to update any existing dimension to the current settings. How about updating the previous horizontal dimension?

Updating a Dimension With Tolerances

`Dim:` **UPD**	UPDate.
`Select objects:` **L**	The last dimension.
`Select objects:` **<RETURN>**	Now it sports ± tolerances.

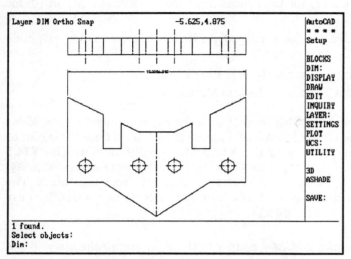

Horizontal Dimension With ± Tolerance

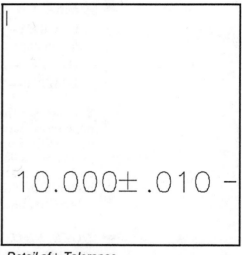

Detail of ± Tolerance

Notice that if the DIMTP and DIMTM values are equal, a single ± tolerance is appended. If they differ, separate plus and minus values are appended, one above the other.

Selecting Entities to Dimension

Instead of establishing dimensions by picking points, most dimensions (of a line, arc, or circle) can also be determined by selecting an entity. To do so, enter a <RETURN> when you see the prompt, `First extension line origin or RETURN to select`. Then use normal object selection to select the entity to be dimensioned. AutoCAD extracts the points needed from the entity in AutoCAD's drawing database, and all you need to pick is the dimension text location. The dimension value will then be generated based upon the entity's database information. It's a lot easier than osnap, and just as accurate.

Let's try this, along with tolerances, on the next dimension.

Vertical and Continue Dimensions With Tolerances

VERtical works like HORizontal. Let's dimension the bracket's thickness by selecting the lift end line entity.

Vertical Dimensioning by Entity Selection

Dim: **VER**   VERtical.
First extension line origin or RETURN to select: **<RETURN>**   To select entity.
Select line, arc, or circle: Pick line at ④.
Dimension line location: Pick point ⑤.
Dimension text <1.000>: **<RETURN>**   Notice the default <1.000> doesn't show tolerances.

But the dimension is generated with ±.010 tolerance.

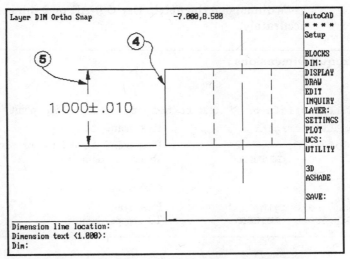

Vertical Dimension With ± Tolerance

Let's continue with CONtinue.

Continuous (Chain) Dimensions

CONtinue dimensioning lets you place dimensions in a continuous chain. You start with a single linear dimension, such as HORizontal. Then, use CONtinue (or the [CONTINU] screen item) to add a series or chain of subsequent dimensions. For each CONtinue dimension added to the chain, AutoCAD uses the endpoint of the last dimension as a first point for the next dimension, so you are prompted only for the endpoint of the new extension line. AutoCAD neatly aligns these dimensions into a chain.

➡ *NOTE: CONtinue defaults to continue from the last dimension created. If you want to continue an older previous dimension, you can use UPDate to make it become the "last" dimension.*

In the following exercise, we will continuously dimension the horizontal location and size of the notch from the left-hand edge of the bracket. You need to dimension from left to right to get the format of the continuous dimensions shown below, because the one-inch dimension text for the notch will be placed outside the extension lines. For limited-space dimensions such as this, the location of the dimension text is determined by the direction of your second extension line origin pick. In this example, chain dimensioning from right to left would overlap with unacceptable results. With practice, you will be able to avoid problems caused by limited-space dimensions.

Let's dimension the notch. Use OSNAP, or zoom in to where you can snap accurately.

Continuing Horizontal Dimensions

```
Dim: HOR
First extension line origin or RETURN to select:        Pick point ⑥.
Second extension line origin:            Pick point ⑦.
Dimension line location:                 Pick point ⑧, 0.5 inches above the object.
Dimension text <2.000>: <RETURN>         To accept default.

Dim: CON                                 CONtinue.
Second extension line origin:            Pick point ⑨.
Dimension text <1.000>: <RETURN>         To accept default.
```

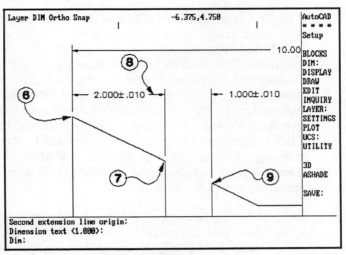

Horizontal Continued Dimensions

When you use toleranced chain dimensioning to dimension engineering drawings, you may develop an accumulation of tolerance error. The maximum variation between two features is equal to the sum of the tolerances of the intermediate distances. Toleranced chain dimensioning should only be used when accumulation is acceptable to the design intent.

Controlling Dimension Text

Whenever AutoCAD prompts you for dimension text, it presents a default value in angle brackets. Thus far, we have always accepted this default text with a <RETURN>, but you may sometimes want to adjust the dimension text. You have the option of entering your own text, which will then override the default as the dimensioning text.

There is another, even more powerful dimensioning text option. You can combine AutoCAD's default dimensioning text with your own text, without retyping AutoCAD's default text. To do so, you imbed a pair of angle brackets in the text string that you input. These angle brackets indicate the location for the default text, and are replaced by the default text when the dimension is drawn. For example, if the default presented is <.750> and you want to dimension it as 4 x .750, then you would enter 4 x < > as your dimension text, or you could get (.750) by entering (< >) as text.

Let's try this with a baseline dimension.

Baseline Dimensioning

BASeline is similar to CONtinue. Baseline dimensioning allows you to dimension multiple locations from one baseline. As with CONtinue, use any linear dimensioning form to create the base dimension. Its first extension line establishes the starting datum point — the baseline. Subsequent BASeline dimensions use this line as their first extension line, prompting you only for the second extension line origin. AutoCAD automatically draws each baseline dimension line at a spacing from the previous dimension line equal to the value of the DIMDLI (Dimension Line Increment) variable, which was set to 0.5 inch in the prototype drawing. You can change it with the SETVAR DIMDLI, the DIMDLI dimensioning subcommand, or the Y14.5 Menu System [Dim Vars] screen or pull-down menus.

Dimension the left side of the front view with a VERtical and BASeline dimension. Use dimension text override to make the 7.000 reference dimension. Use OSNAP, or zoom in to where you can snap accurately. You'll have to temporarily adjust the dimension line increment, DIMDLI, to avoid text overlap.

Baseline Dimensions

```
Dim: VER
First extension line origin or RETURN to select:        Pick first point ①.
Second extension line origin:                           Pick second point ②.
Dimension line location:                                Pick a point three inches from object.
Dimension text <5.000>: <RETURN>
Dim: DIMLIM                                             Set to off.
Dim: DIMDLI                                             Increase dimension line increment.
Current value <0.500> New value: 1

Dim: BAS                                                BASeline.
Second extension line origin:                           Pick point ③.
Dimension text <7.000>:                                 Override the default text.

Dim: DIMDLI                                             Restore dimension line increment.
Current value <1.000> New value: .5
```

You will find yourself making frequent adjustments to DIMDLI to get just the results you want.

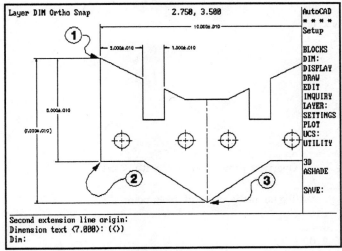

Vertical Baseline Dimensions

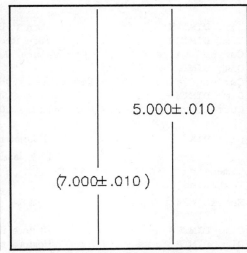

Detail of Baseline Dimension Text

Let's circle back and try a diameter dimension.

Diameter Dimensions With Limits

We started with center marks and lines in the circles. The last dimension to be drawn is the diameter dimension for the front view's third circle from the left. Because we are dimensioning a hole, we will generate the dimension with differing upper and lower tolerances. To do so, you simply set new values for DIMTP and DIMTM.

Because this circle already has the circle center lines on it, you should temporarily set the value of the DIMCEN dimensioning variable to zero. This prevents the creation of additional circle center lines when you use DIAmeter to dimension the circle. Use SETVAR, the DIMCEN dimensioning subcommand, or the Y14.5 Menu System [Dim Vars] screen or pull-down items to set it, then use DIAmeter to draw the dimension.

Diameter Dimensioning Circles

```
Dim: DIMLIM                    Turn it back on.
Dim: DIMCEN                    Turn it off.
Current value <-0.100> New value: 0
Dim: DIMTP
Current value <0.060> New value: .06
Dim: DIMTM
Current value <0.060> New value: .002


Dim: DIA                       DIAmeter.
Select arc or circle:          Pick leader location at ④.
Dimension text <.750>: 4X ◇              Override dimension text with < >s.
Text does not fit.
Enter leader length for text: <F8>       Toggle ortho off and pick point ⑤.


Dim: DIMCEN                    Restore it to -.1.
Dim: DIMTP                     Restore to .010.
Dim: DIMTM                     Restore to .010.


Dim: EXIT                      Or <^C> to exit Dim mode.

Command: ZOOM                  Use ZOOM Dynamic to get a full view of the drawing.
Command: UCS                   Restore the BDR UCS.

Command: END                   Unless you want to do the following optional bracket completion.
Command: SAVE                  If you want to do the following optional bracket completion.
```

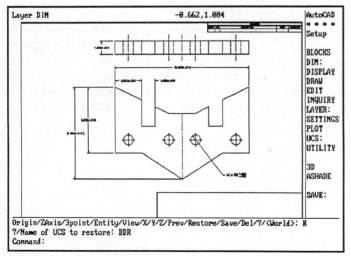

Circle With Diameter Dimension

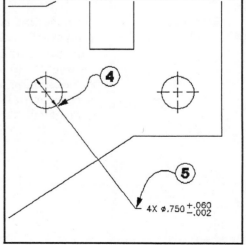

Detail of Diameter Dimension

That completes the dimensioning exercises for this chapter. At this point, your drawing should match the following illustration.

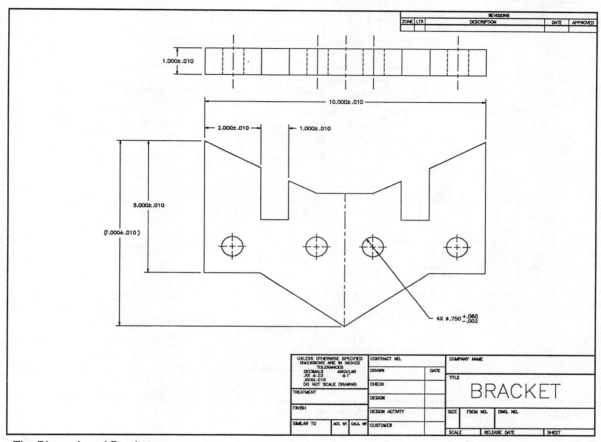

The Dimensioned Bracket

OPTIONAL: Completing the Bracket

If you wish, you can complete the dimensioning of the bracket and thaw some of the title block layers. If you find the datum and feature control symbols a bit tedious, you'll be glad to know you'll find better methods in Chapters 7 and 8, and in the Y14.5 Menu System which is explained in Chapter 12. The completed bracket is shown below.

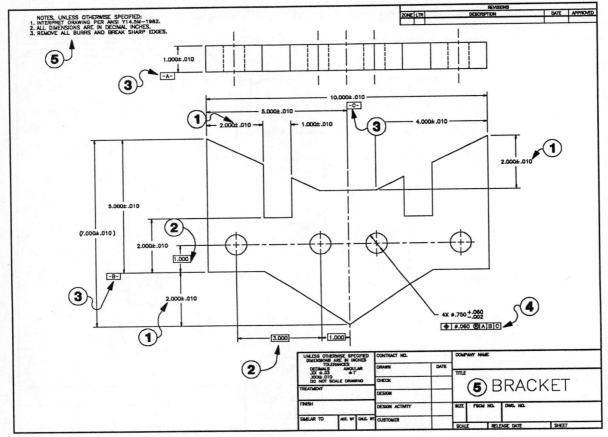

The Completed Bracket With Title Text and Notes

① **Linear Dimensions** — Use HORizontal and VERtical to complete the normal dimensions.

② **Basic Dimensions** — Turn off DIMLIM to generate the dimensions, then zoom in and add the box with a polyline. Create one box, and use the COPY command to replicate it.

③ **Datum Feature Symbols** — Draw or copy the boxes like the basic dimensions, then use DTEXT to add all of the dashes and identifying letters.

④ **Feature Control Frame** — Draw the frame with lines or polylines and add circles. Add the text with DTEXT, and relocate the cursor as needed. Use %%c to get the diameter symbol in the text string.

⑤ **Title Block** — Use LAYER to thaw layer TITL-CX and NOTES, and set TITL-CX current. Add any title text you desire.

Finally, END the drawing and exit AutoCAD.

Summary

With the completion of the BRACKET drawing, you have been introduced to many of the techniques used to develop 2D engineering drawings. The BRACKET exercise has shown you how to set up and control your screen display. As you saw, viewports may be set so that one viewport shows your entire drawing while another viewport shows a zoomed view. With the availability of up to four user-defined viewports, zooms, and pans, your viewing and drafting screen display combinations are virtually unlimited.

You have seen how to develop highly accurate geometry in AutoCAD's World Coordinate System (WCS) by combining drawing and editing tools. We hope we have convinced you that editing tools are far more than erasers and entity movers. When editing tools are applied, drafting accuracy, efficiency, and productivity will increase.

Very few technical drawings are complete without dimensions. One of the goals of this chapter was to demonstrate how AutoCAD provides orderly and accurate size descriptions of mechanical parts. The BRACKET drawing was developed using some of AutoCAD's built-in dimensioning tools, at the same time introducing you to ANSI Y14.5M-1982 dimensioning standards.

The next two chapters continue and build on the 2D drafting, editing, and ANSI Y14.5 dimensioning practices. Chapters 5 and 6 will guide you through the development of five detailed parts of a robotic arm. Each of the five parts will be saved as a block and then re-used to develop a final multi-detail working drawing.

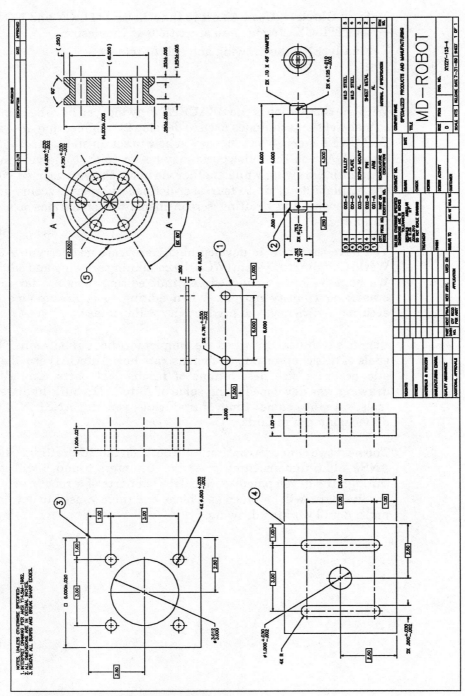

The Robot Arm Multi-Detail Drawing

CHAPTER 5

Building a Multi-Detail Working Drawing (Phase 1)

DEVELOPING THE PARTS

Our next project will be to draft and dimension a robot arm. In this and the next chapter, we will use separate exercises to develop the arm, pin, mount, plate, and pulley as individual parts. We will save each part as a separate drawing that can be inserted into another drawing, creating a multi-detail drawing. This practice is referred to as developing and using a parts library.

As we draw the parts, we will introduce several new drawing and editing commands. These include ARRAY, BASE, BLOCK, CHAMFER, COPY, FILLET, INSERT, MINSERT, MOVE, STRETCH, and WBLOCK. We will also use several more dimensioning features, including the automatically updating associative dimensioning.

There are three types of exercises: drawing the parts, dimensioning the parts, and wblocking them for later insertion. If you have the SIA DISK, you can do all three types of exercise for each part, or you can skip the drawing exercise and go directly to the dimensioning or wblocking exercises. If you don't have the disk, you'll need to do each exercise in sequence. Each part is developed in a new drawing named TEMP. The new TEMP drawing will replace any previous TEMP drawing.

There are several optional drawing completion sequences, to complete a view or finish dimensioning a part for instance. If you don't complete them and you aren't working from the SIA DISK, that's okay, but your parts won't quite match ours in some of the illustrations that follow.

A Word About Parts and Parts Libraries

You can develop your own library of the parts commonly used in your industrial or institutional drafting operations. These may include components like fastening devices, shafts, pulleys, gears, mounting brackets, and springs. The library may be developed in 2D, 3D, or a combination of both, depending on your requirements.

Parts are groups of entities that can be inserted into any number of drawings, saving the effort of redrawing them. AutoCAD uses BLOCK to group and store entity parts. *Blocks* can be real-world objects (parts), or symbols like section markers or bubbles. When you insert a block, you can scale, rotate, or mirror it. You can also insert a block exploded into its constituent entities, so that they can be edited.

You can store any number of blocks in a library drawing or in your prototype drawing. They can be stored visibly or invisibly. Then when you start a new drawing with that prototype, or insert that library drawing into the current drawing, all of its blocks will be available for individual insertion and use.

You can also store parts as individual drawing files on disk. This is the approach we will use in Chapters 5 and 6. In this case, they are not stored as blocks, but as separate drawings containing the individual entities making up each part or symbol. We'll keep all three of the parts we will create in this chapter in a single temporary file, saving each part as an individual drawing file on disk as we go. Such drawings can then be individually inserted into other drawings as blocks or as their individual constituent entities. In fact, any AutoCAD drawing can be inserted into any other AutoCAD drawing as a block.

The five parts in this parts library provide you with examples and techniques that can save you valuable drafting time when you need to make changes because of engineering change orders (ECO's) or when you want to use modified parts in other designs. Instead of drafting new parts, you can simply draft stock parts once, save them as blocks or files, and then modify or reuse the stock part from your library when you need a similar part or when you receive an ECO. If stored as a separate file, each part drawing can either be inserted into a new drawing or used as a prototype to be modified.

This chapter's exercises use the PROTO-C drawing which we configured as the default drawing in Chapter 3. Initially, only the prototype's border and main title block will be visible, with the optional title blocks, text, and notes frozen. Let's start with the arm.

Part One: The Arm

This exercise will concentrate on the FILLET command, on associative and radius dimensioning, and on blocks. We'll develop the arm drawing with two orthographic views: the front and the top.

In AutoCAD, there are always several ways to do most things. We are going to use PLINE, COPY, and STRETCH to draw the arm's profile and top view. After we develop the object lines for the two views, we'll draw one circle and copy it. We'll complete the fillets on each corner of the arm's front view and then dimension the arm. The final step will be to save the part as a drawing file for later insertion into the multi-detail subassembly drawing.

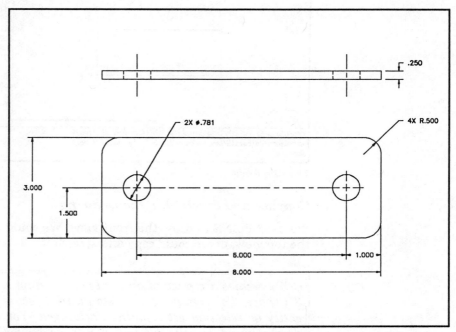

The Arm

To start the arm, use the PLINE command to draw the front view profile.

Drawing the Arm's Profile

Enter Selection: **1.**	Begin a NEW drawing named **TEMP**.
Command: **ZOOM**	Center, point 10,9 with height 13.
Command: **SNAP**	Set to 0.25.
Command: **<F8>**	Or <^O> to toggle ortho on.
Command: **PLINE**	Draw an 8 x 3 rectangle with lower left corner point at 6,6.

Create last segment with the Close option:
Arc/Close/Halfwidth/Length/Undo/Width/<Endpoint of line>: **C**

Your drawing should match the following illustration.

```
Layer OBJECT Ortho Snap            2.2500, 14.7500        AutoCAD
                                                          * * * *
                                                          Setup

                                                          BLOCKS
                                                          DIM:
                                                          DISPLAY
                                                          DRAW
                                                          EDIT
                                                          INQUIRY
                                                          LAYER:
                                                          SETTINGS
                                                          PLOT
                                                          UCS:
                                                          UTILITY

                                                          3D
                                                          ASHADE

                                                          SAVE:


Arc/Close/Halfwidth/Length/Undo/Width/<Endpoint of line>:
Arc/Close/Halfwidth/Length/Undo/Width/<Endpoint of line>: C
Command:
```

The Arm Profile

Copying and Stretching the Drawing

We used PLINE to draw the front view. We could do the same to create
the top view, or we could copy and stretch it.

COPY

> *COPY creates a replica of an entity or selection set anywhere in 2D or*
> *3D space. The command uses standard object selection. The original*
> *entity or selection set remains unchanged. You can show and drag*
> *displacement by picking two points or by using an absolute X,Y*
> *displacement value.*
> `<Base point or displacement>/Multiple:`
> `Second point of displacement:`

➡ *TIP: When picking points, make your reference (base) point a logical point*
on the object(s) you are copying.

To do a multiple copy, enter an **M** at the base point prompt. COPY then
reprompts for base point (absolute displacements don't apply here) and
repeatedly prompts for second points. You can make as many copies as
you like by picking repeated second points. Enter a <RETURN> to exit the
command when you are done.

Another way to enter a displacement is to pick the first point (anywhere
will do) and enter the second point as a relative or polar point, such as

@2,3 or @6<90. To use an absolute displacement, enter an X,Y value at the base point or displacement prompt and then <RETURN> at the second point of displacement prompt.

➥ *NOTE: Be careful that you don't <RETURN> accidentally at the second point prompt. If you do, your first point will be erroneously interpreted as a displacement, sending the copy into outer space where you can't see it.*

While we're discussing COPY, we should also mention the MOVE command. MOVE is identical to COPY in its interaction, except it moves the original entity instead of creating a new one. MOVE has no Multiple option.

MOVE

> *MOVE moves an entity or selection set to a new drawing location anywhere in 2D or 3D space. See COPY.*
> ```
> Base point or displacement:
> Second point of displacement:
> ```

Once we have copied the front profile, we will stretch it into the shape of the top view.

STRETCH

> *STRETCH lets you extend (or shrink) certain entities by selecting them with a crossing window and picking a base and new point of displacement. You can stretch lines, arcs, traces, solids, polylines, and 3D faces. Entity endpoints that lie inside the crossing window are moved, those outside the crossing window remain fixed, and the lines or arcs crossing the window are stretched. Entities which are defined entirely within the crossing window (all endpoints, vertices, and definition points) are simply moved. The definition point for a block or shape is its insertion base point; for a circle, the center point; for text, the lower left corner.*
> ```
> Select objects to stretch by window... Base point:
> New point:
> ```

With the STRETCH command, you can change the shape of geometry while still preserving connections. STRETCH can either make objects larger or it can shrink them. When associatively dimensioned geometry is stretched with DIMASO on, dimensions will be updated to reflect the size change.

When stretching arcs, the arc's center point and its starting and ending angles are adjusted so that the distance from the midpoint of the chord to the arc is held constant. Traces and solids are handled like lines, while polylines are handled segment by segment. Polyline width, tangent, and curve fitting information is not modified by the STRETCH command.

Let's use COPY and STRETCH to create the top view, then CIRCLE and COPY to add the holes.

Copying and Stretching the Top View

Continue in the previous TEMP drawing.

```
Command: COPY
Select objects: L
Select objects: <RETURN>
<Base point or displacement>/Multiple: 6,9
Second point of displacement: 6,11          Or pick polar point @2<90.

Command: STRETCH
Select objects to stretch by window...
Select objects: C
First corner:              Pick point ①.
Other corner:             Pick point ②.
Select objects: <RETURN>
Base point:               Pick any point, such as a corner.
New point:                Pick polar point @2.75<90.

Command: CIRCLE
3P/2P/TTR/<Center point>: 7,7.5
Diameter/<Radius>: D
Diameter: .781

Command: COPY
Select objects: L
Select objects: <RETURN>
<Base point or displacement>/Multiple: 6,0    The displacement.
Second point of displacement: <RETURN>    Default to use first value as absolute displacement.
```

When you have completed these steps, your drawing should look like the illustration below.

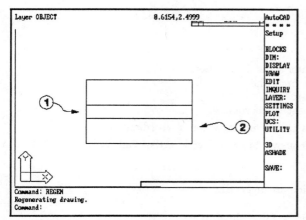
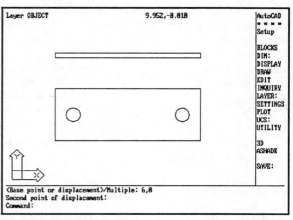

STRETCH Pick Points   *Arm Front and Top Views*

We need to add hidden lines to the top view, but the circle diameters don't fall on snap increments. We could osnap long lines to the circles' quadrant points, then trim them at the top view polyline, but there's a better way — point filters.

Constructions With Point Filters

Point filters (sometimes called XYZ point filters) were invented for 3D, but they make valuable electronic construction lines in 2D work. For now, we'll ignore the Z coordinate until we get to the 3D chapters.

In manual drafting, you use construction lines by scribing a temporary line from a known point to the area where you want to establish a new point. Then you establish the new point at some desired distance or aligned to another known point. Point filters work for orthographic points in the same manner. Pick one coordinate on an object, and AutoCAD reprompts for the other(s). To invoke point filters, enter a period and the letter(s) of the coordinate(s) you want to pick first, at any prompt that accepts a point. Point filters can be combined with osnaps. When combined, you will need to re-enter the point filter and osnap modes before repicking if you pick an invalid point.

Let's use point filters, OSNAP, LINE, and CHPROP to create the top view's hidden lines and center lines.

Aligning With Point Filters

Continue in the previous TEMP drawing.
Make sure SNAP and ORTHO are on. Zoom in if needed.

Command: **LINE**	See Left Hole Center Line illustration.
From point: **.X**	Take X coordinate from the next point.
of **CEN**	Osnap it to CENter.
of	Pick left circle to set X coordinate.
(need YZ):	Pick ① 0.5 inches below top view for Y coordinate.
To point:	Pick ② 0.5 inches above top view, with ortho control.
To point: **<RETURN>**	
Command: **CHPROP**	Change the last line to layer CL.
Command: **LINE**	See Left Hole Hidden Line illustration.
From point: **.X**	X coordinate from next point.
of **QUA**	QUAdrant.
of	Pick left circle.
(need YZ):	Pick ③ on bottom line of top view for Y coordinate.
To point:	Pick ④ on top line of top view, with ortho control.
To point: **<RETURN>**	
Command: **CHPROP**	Change the last line to layer HL.
Command: **COPY**	See Copy Hidden Line With QUA illustration.
Select objects: **L**	Select last line.
<Base point or displacement>/Multiple: **QUA**	
of	Pick same side of left circle.
Second point of displacement: **QUA**	
of	Pick other side of left circle.
Command: **<RETURN>**	
COPY Select objects: **<F9>**	Copy all three lines from left hole to right hole with CEN osnaps.
Command: **SAVE**	

The resulting top view should look like the Finished Top View illustration below.

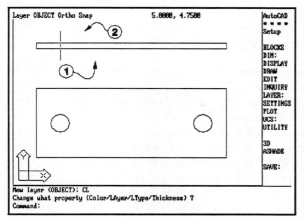

Left Hole Center Line

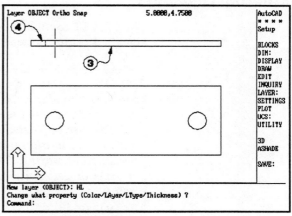

Left Hole Hidden Line

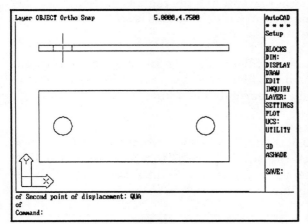

Copy Hidden line With QUA

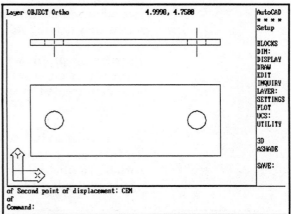

Finished Top View

To finish the front view, we need to fillet the corners.

Filleting Geometry

The FILLET command is most commonly used for generating an arc of a specified radius between two entities.

FILLET

> *FILLET creates an arc with a predefined radius between any combination of lines, circles, and arcs. FILLET extends or trims entities as needed to draw the specified arc, if geometrically possible. A **single** polyline can be filleted at selected vertices, or globally at all vertices, but not in combination with other entities. An arc entity is inserted at the preset fillet radius. The default fillet radius is 0, which causes the entities or segments to be extended or trimmed to their intersection point.*
> ```
> Polyline/Radius/<Select two lines>:
> ```

Before FILLET can be used, you often need to first define the radius. The radius may be specified either by entering the radius value or by picking two points on the drawing screen. Once the radius is set, it is maintained as the new default value until changed.

Because the profile we want to fillet is a single polyline, we can fillet one corner at a time or we can do all four corners at once. Filleting one corner at a time treats the entity as four individual lines instead of as a single polyline.

Set the fillet radius to 0.5, then fillet the four corners of the front view. To fillet one corner, pick the two lines close to what will be the fillet corner. To fillet all corners at once, use the FILLET command's Polyline option and select the polyline.

Filleting the Arm's Corners

Continue in the previous TEMP drawing.

```
Command: FILLET                              Set the radius.
Polyline/Radius/<Select two lines>: R        R for Radius.
Enter fillet radius <0.0000>: .5             Enter the radius value.

Command: <RETURN>                            Or use the space bar to repeat.
FILLET                                       Fillet lower left corner.
Polyline/Radius/<Select two lines>:          Pick two points, both at ①.
                                             The lower left corner fillets.

Command: <RETURN>
FILLET                                       Fillet all corners at once.
```

```
Polyline/Radius/<Select two lines>: P      Polyline option.
Select 2D polyline:                        Select the polyline.
4 lines were filleted

Command: SAVE                              And continue.
                                           or
Command: END                               Take a break.
```

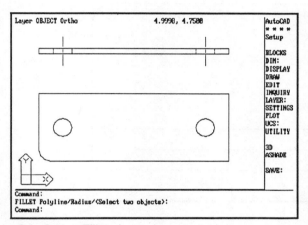

One Corner Filleted

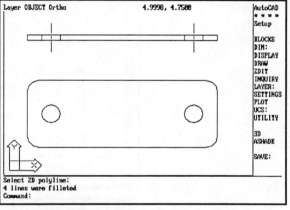

Completely Filleted Arm

Additional Features of the FILLET Command

When you fillet circles and arcs, the result may not be what you expect. If this happens, use U or UNDO and try the fillet again, picking different endpoints or picking in a different order.

A useful trick with FILLET is to connect, extend, or trim two entities to their common geometric intersection by setting the fillet radius to zero. This is a great tool for trimming or extending lines to clean up corners.

To finish this first part, we need some dimensions.

Dimensioning the Arm

The dimensioning exercise which follows concentrates on the RADIUS dimensioning command and on the AutoCAD program's associative dimensioning capability. This exercise assumes that the associative dimension variable, DIMASO, is on (the default).

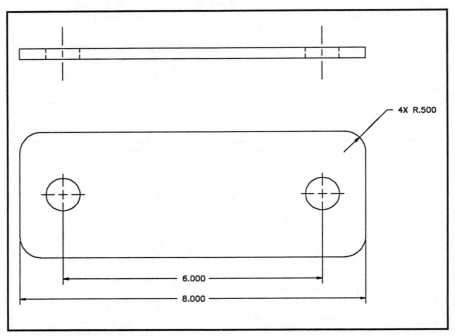

The Dimensioned Arm

If you have the SIA DISK, you can dimension either the TEMP drawing you just created, or the ready-to-dimension ARM-D drawing from the disk. If you don't have the disk, you'll need to use the TEMP drawing.

Radius Dimensioning

The fillets need a radius dimension, which is done with the dimensioning mode's RADIUS subcommand. RADIUS is virtually identical in operation to the DIAMETER subcommand (see Chapter 4). The default radius dimension text begins with the letter R, the standard way of designating a radius dimension, although the prompt doesn't show the R. Let's try it, using a text override. Also, add the two hole center marks and lines, and the two horizontal dimensions shown, so we can use them in the following associative dimensioning exercise.

Dimensioning the Fillet Radius

 Continue in TEMP, or begin a NEW drawing named TEMP=ARM-D.

 Continue in or edit an EXISTING drawing named TEMP.

```
Command: SETVAR                Set LUPREC to 3.
Command: ZOOM                  Center point 10,7.5 with height 8.

Command: DIM
Dim: DIMCEN                    Set center marks to 0 (off).

Dim: RAD                       RADius, the upper right fillet.
Select arc or circle: NEA
to                             Put cursor on snap point at 45 degrees from arc to pick point ①.
Dimension text <0.500>: 4X <>        Enter override text with < > imbedded.
Text does not fit. Enter leader length for text: <F8>    Ortho off and pick point ②.

Dim: DIMCEN                    Set center marks to -.1.
Dim: CEN                       Pick one circle, repeat for other.

Dim: HOR                       Toggle ortho back on, enter 6-inch dimension shown.
Dim: HOR                       Repeat for 8-inch dimension.

Command: SAVE
```

We used a little trick with OSNAP's NEArest option to get the leader line to intersect the arc at exactly 45 degrees. It should look like the Radius and Horizontal Dimensions illustration that follows. To get a proper gap between the horizontal dimensions and the object, we held the pick points of the extension lines back 0.125 inches from the end/intersection of the line and arc. If you need to osnap the extension lines to such a point for accuracy, you can accomplish the same thing by resetting DIMEXO (EXtension line Offset).

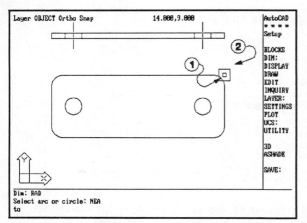

Pick Points for Radius Dimension

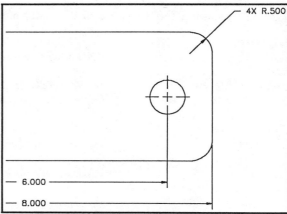

Radius and Horizontal Dimensions

Now, let's watch these associative dimensions adjust along with the geometry when stretched and scaled.

Associative Dimensioning

AutoCAD's default dimensioning is associative. Associative dimensioning automatically updates dimensions when you edit a drawing. If you change the geometry of an object using an editing command such as STRETCH, associative dimensioning will automatically update the dimension text to reflect the change. When associative dimensioning is turned on, the dimension lines act as if they are linked to the object. Actually, they are not linked, but are controlled by point entities on a special layer called DEFPOINTS. These points are visible, but never plotted. They are part of the dimension entities and are located where they are likely to be stretched and scaled along with the objects associated with the dimensions. When the defpoints are stretched or scaled, the dimension is recalculated.

Associative Dimensioning Variables

There are two variables that control associative dimensioning:

DIMASO — Dimensions that are generated with DIMASO on (1) are associative. DIMASO off (0) causes dimension text, arrows, dimension lines, and extension lines to be generated as separate entities. The default value is on.

DIMSHO — Controls the screen updating of dimensions as they are dragged. If DIMSHO is on (1), associative dimensions will be constantly recomputed as they are dragged. We recommend that you turn DIMSHO off if you are using a computer with a slow processing speed. With DIMSHO off, the original dimension image can be dragged until the final size is determined, then the resulting dimension is calculated and displayed.

Associative Dimensioning Subcommands

The associative dimensioning subcommands let you make changes to dimension entities. They use normal object selection, but if any entities other than dimension entities are in the selection set, they will be ignored. This makes it easy to make global changes to all of a drawing's dimensioning entities by specifying a selection set window that encompasses the entire drawing.

UPDate — Updates existing dimension entities to use the current settings of the dimension variables, the current text style, and the current UNITS settings, such as LUPREC.

HOMetext — Repositions the text of an existing dimension entity to its "home" default position.

NEWtext — Respecifies the dimension text for existing dimension entities. If you enter nothing for the new text string, the default calculated dimension measurement will be used as the text.

These commands give associative dimensions a lot of flexibility, but sometimes it isn't enough. If you need to edit them in other ways, such as breaking an extension line, you'll have to explode them.

Exploding Associative Dimensions

Exploding a dimensioning entity into its component parts lets you selectively edit the dimension's individual entities.

EXPLODE

> *EXPLODE converts the selected block, polyline, dimension, or hatch into individual entities.*

Stretching and Scaling Geometry

Let's see STRETCH and SCALE in action with associative dimensions. We've already generally described the STRETCH command. SCALE is even simpler.

SCALE

> *SCALE changes the size of existing entities. The entities are scaled relative to the base point selected. The same scale factor is applied to the X and Y axes. Enter a numerical scale factor or use the Reference option to pick a reference and new length. A numerical scale factor is the default.*
> `Base point: <Scale factor>/Reference:`

We'll scale the front view by 1.5, then stretch it one inch longer. This is a good place to use an UNDO mark in case we decide to undo several steps at once.

Scaling and Stretching the Arm

Continue in the previous TEMP drawing.

```
Command: UNDO
Auto/Back/Control/End/Group/Mark/<number>: M          Set a mark.

Command: ZOOM                 Center point 13,7 with height 9.

Command: SCALE
Select objects:               Select the arm and dimensions with a Crossing window.
Base point:                   Pick center of right hole.
<Scale factor>/Reference: 1.5

                              The object is rescaled and the dimensions are recalculated.
                              (You may have to zoom in a bit to see.)

Command: STRETCH
Select objects to stretch by window...
Select objects: C             Crossing window of right end including hole and dimensions.
Base point:                   Pick point ①.
New point:                    Pick point ②.
```

The drawing is now altered to reflect the scaling and stretching. Note that the horizontal and radius dimensions have updated to reflect the editing of the object.

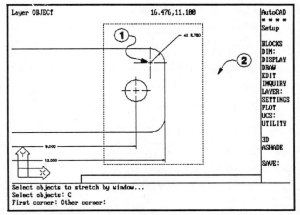

Stretch Window

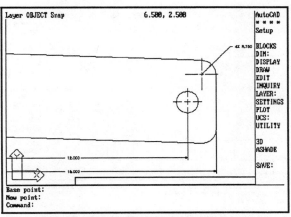

Results of SCALE and STRETCH

Notice that the *scale* of the dimension entity itself doesn't change, although the text changes to show the new dimension. If you want larger dimension text, arrows and so on, you need to change DIMSCALE, the overall dimensioning scale factor, and update the dimensions. Also notice that the radius dimension now sports a center mark because STRETCH updates all stretched dimensions to the *current* dimensioning variable settings. To restore it with no center mark, reset DIMCEN and update it.

Let's adjust DIMSCALE and DIMCEN, update the dimensions, then UNDO back to restore the previous drawing conditions.

Updating Dimensions

```
Command: DIM
Dim: DIMSCALE            Set to 2.
Dim: UPD                 UPDate.
Select objects:          Select the center marks and horizontal dimensions.

Dim: DIMCEN              Set to 0.
Dim: UPD                 Update the radius dimension.

Command: UNDO
Auto/Back/Control/End/Group/Mark/<number>: B       For Back.
DIM STRETCH SCALE ZOOM
Mark encountered         The mark stops UNDO.
```

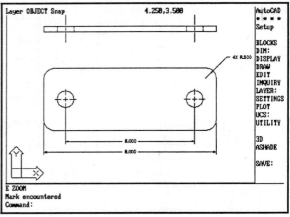

Updated Dimensions　　　　　　　　Restored Arm

OPTIONAL: Completing the Arm's Dimensions

If you wish to practice the techniques covered in Chapter 4 by completing the arm's dimensions, use the following illustration and instructions.

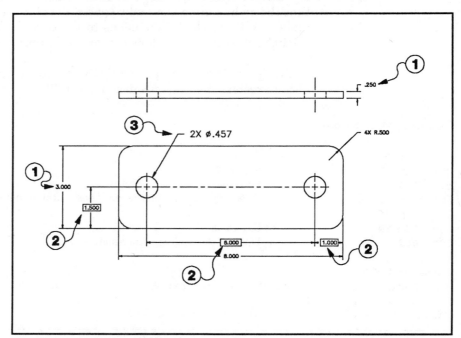

OPTIONAL: The Completely Dimensioned Arm

① **Vertical Dimensions** — Use the VERTICAL dimensioning command to complete the normal dimensions, picking the .25 dimension from bottom to top.

② **Basic Dimensions** — Use the HORIZONTAL and VERTICAL dimensioning commands to generate the dimensions, then zoom in and add the box with a polyline. You can create just one box, then use COPY to replicate it.

③ **Diameter With Limits** — Set DIMLIM, DIMTP, and DIMTM. Use the DIAMETER dimensioning command with DIMCEN off (0). Enter the text as 2X < >.

Finally, save or end the drawing.

In Chapter 6, we'll insert this completed and dimensioned part into a larger multi-view drawing. To prepare for this, we'll save it (without title block) as a separate file which can be used as a block.

Blocking Entities Into Groups

In this part of the exercise, we will block the arm drawing so that it can be inserted into the multi-detail drawing. A *block* is a set or group of entities which forms a compound object. A block is defined and manipulated by AutoCAD as a single entity. This makes editing (such as moving, copying, rotating, or scaling) blocks very simple. For example, moving a complex part can be as simple as moving a line.

A block is not an entity. It is a definition in the drawing's database. The block definition contains other entities (even other nested blocks). A block can be defined in a drawing without being in use or visible.

To use a block, you have to insert it with the INSERT command. An inserted block definition is often casually called a block, but it is more accurately called an *insert* entity. Actually, any drawing file can be inserted into any other by the INSERT command. Inserting another file into the current drawing as a block creates a new block definition in the current drawing. The block definition gets the name used in the insertion and contains all of the entities in the inserted drawing file.

The following list describes BLOCK and its related commands.

BLOCK

The BLOCK command defines a group of entities as a block within the current drawing. (Use the INSERT command to insert blocks into your drawing.) You define a block by choosing an entity selection set which is deleted from the current drawing and stored as a block definition in the drawing. (OOPS will restore the entities.) You are prompted for a block name and insertion base point. The base point is a reference point relative to which the block will be inserted and scaled. Such blocks may only be inserted in the drawing within which they are defined.
Block name (or ?): Insertion base point:

INSERT

*INSERT inserts an image of a block definition into the current drawing. You pick the insertion point, X,Y,Z scale values, and the rotation angle. The insertion point is relative to the block's base point. The default X scale factor is 1, and the Y scale defaults to equal the X scale. Rotation angle defaults to 0. If you preface the block name with an asterisk, like *FRONT, then an actual copy of each individual entity in the block's definition is inserted instead of an insert entity image. This is often referred to as insert* (insert-star) or a *block (star-block).*
Insertion point: X scale factor <1> / Corner / XYZ:
Y scale factor (default=X): Rotation angle <0>:

WBLOCK

WBLOCK (Write BLOCK) writes a drawing, a selection set, or a block definition to disk as a new drawing file (not a block definition). A "wblock" is not an entity; it is a command that creates an ordinary drawing file which can be inserted into other drawings, or can be recalled from the main menu option Number 2 – Edit an existing drawing. When wblocking, you are prompted to enter a file name, a block name, an insertion base point, and to select the wblock entities. An equal sign as a block name makes it look for a block in the drawing that matches the file name. It then writes the block to disk as individual entities in a new drawing file. A <RETURN> or space as a block name requires you to enter a base point and use normal object selection to select entities which are deleted and wblocked. No new block is created in the current drawing.
File name: Block name: Insertion base point:

MINSERT	*MINSERT (Multiple INSERT) is a combination of the commands INSERT and (rectangular) ARRAY. MINSERT lets you insert a multiple copy of a block in a rectangular array pattern. The command has the same prompts as the INSERT command for insertion point, X,Y scaling, and rotation angle, plus ARRAY-like prompts for rows and columns.* `Number of rows (---) <1>: Number of columns (|||) <1>:`
BASE	*Any drawing can be inserted into another drawing. By default, every drawing file has a base point of 0,0,0, relative to which it is inserted into other drawings. The BASE command establishes an alternative insertion base point.*

When you create a drawing file with WBLOCK, only layer information, text styles, nested block definitions, and linetypes pertinent to (actually used by) the entities being wblocked are written to the file. UCS's, views, and viewports are never written.

When you need to make repetitive parts, use blocks. Blocks increase efficiency and reduce drawing file size. Each entity adds to a drawing file's byte count. When you create and block an entity once and insert the block definition many times, the entity only exists once in the drawing file, in a block definition. Each time the image is replicated by the INSERT command, only one additional entity is created, an *insert* entity. Insert entities are very efficient, only containing reference to the block definition name, X, Y and Z scale values, and a rotation (and attributes, if any, which will be covered later). Because all the individual entities of the block definition are not duplicated, the savings in storage space that results from inserting a block as a single primitive entity is significant. (Inserting a *block duplicates the entities and yields no savings.)

Block definitions may contain other blocks. These are called nested blocks. Nested blocks are an efficient space saver within a drawing file.

Wblocking the Arm

We are going to use WBLOCK to create a drawing file containing only the dimensioned arm, without border, title block or extraneous information. Block names can be up to 31 characters long, but drawing files are limited to the operating system's capacity — eight characters for DOS. The characters used may include letters, numbers, the dollar sign ($), the hyphen (-), and the underline (_) characters. The file name is automatically assigned the extension .DWG. It is written to the current directory unless a path is specified.

You can code the file names. For example, designate a file intended to be inserted as a block by prefacing the name with a leading letter **B**, like B-ARM. Or you can organize them by subdirectory location and have all eight characters available for the name.

When you are prompted for the block name, you have these four options:

Name — Writes the entities which comprise the definition of the specified block.

= — Is shorthand for the above when the block and the output file have the same name.

* — Causes the entire drawing to be written to the file. This is similar to the SAVE command, except that only pertinent information is written.

<RETURN> — Or a space prompts you to select objects and the insertion base point.

Let's use the WBLOCK command twice. First, to write the entire ARM drawing (including title block) as a separate file from our TEMP file. This will have the effect of purging all unused data to save disk space. Then we'll use WBLOCK again to write out only the dimensioned arm for later insertion.

Wblocking the Arm Drawing

 Continue in TEMP, or begin a NEW drawing named TEMP=ARM-W.

 Continue in or edit an EXISTING drawing named TEMP.

```
Command: WBLOCK
File name: ARM
Block name: *                        For entire drawing. It writes the file.

Command: WBLOCK                      Write the arm.
File name: B-ARM
Block name: <RETURN>                 Use entity selection.

Insertion base point:                Pick lower left corner at ①.
Select objects: W                    Window dimensioned arm, omitting title block.
Select objects: <RETURN>             Selection set is complete.
                                     It writes the file and deletes the entities.
```

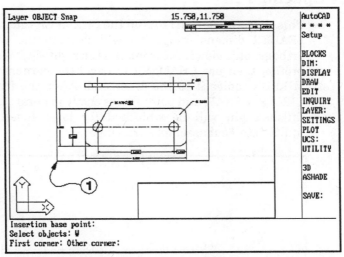

WBLOCK Insertion Base Point and Window

Like the ERASE command, wblocking deletes the entities. If you need to retain them as individual entities, use OOPS to restore the drawing after wblocking it. If you want them in the drawing as a group (a block insert), then use the INSERT command, like this.

Reinserting the Arm

Continue in the previous TEMP drawing.

```
Command: INSERT
Block name (or ?): B-ARM
 Insertion point: @                     The last point.
 X scale factor <1> / Corner / XYZ: <RETURN>
 Y scale factor (default=X): <RETURN>
 Rotation angle <0>: <RETURN>

Command: U          Undo the INSERT to clear the TEMP drawing for the next part.

Command: SAVE       Or END to take a break.
```

The arm came back as a single entity, an insert. Let's move on to the next part, the spacing pin.

Part Two: The Spacing Pin

This exercise concentrates on the CHAMFER command and on LIMIT and LEADER dimensioning. We will develop the pin drawing with two orthographic views: the front and the right side. We'll draw the front view profile, then use CHAMFER to bevel the corners of one end of the pin. MIRROR copies it to the other end. After the front view is completed, CIRCLE, OSNAP, and point filters easily generate the right side view. The finished pin will be wblocked for later insertion into Chapter 6's multi-detail subassembly drawing.

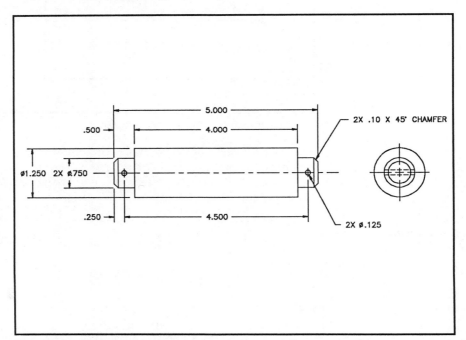

The Spacing Pin Drawing

To start the pin, use PLINE to draw the front view profile and CIRCLE for the drill hole.

Drawing the Pin's Front View Profile

Enter Selection: **1.**	Begin a NEW drawing named **TEMP**.
Command: **ZOOM**	Center, point 10,9 with height 5.
Command: **<F8>**	Or <^O> to toggle ortho on.
Command: **LINE**	Draw a 6-inch horizontal center line, centered in display.
Command: **CHPROP**	Change it to layer CL.
Command: **PLINE**	Draw shaft — a 4 x 1.25 rectangle, centered.
Command: **<RETURN>** PLINE	Draw 0.75 x 0.5 left end.
Command: **CIRCLE**	Draw 0.0625 radius circle at middle of left end.

When you have completed this step, your drawing should look like the illustration below.

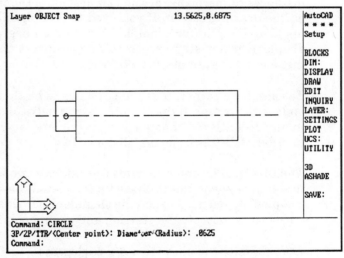

Pin's Front View Profile

Now we're ready to use CHAMFER.

Chamfering Geometry

CHAMFER creates a new line segment at a specified inset relative to the intersection of two lines. CHAMFER is similar to the FILLET command, except it only works on lines and straight polyline segments.

CHAMFER

> *CHAMFER creates a beveled edge for intersecting lines and contiguous segments of a 2D Polyline. CHAMFER trims or extends two lines or polyline segments at specified distances from their intersection or vertex point, and creates a new line to connect the trimmed ends. Alternatively, you can chamfer an entire polyline at once with the Polyline option. CHAMFER requires two distance values. The first distance value is applied to the first selected line, the second distance to the second line. The default for distances is 0.*
> `Polyline/Distances/<Select first line>:`

Before the CHAMFER command can be put into effect, you need to specify the first and second chamfer distances. You can enter the chamfer distances numerically, or you can designate them by picking two points on the drawing screen. If you need to describe the chamfer in terms of angle and depth (for example, .1 deep x 60 degrees) you'll have to use simple trigonometry or geometry to convert the information to two distances (for example, 0.1 x 0.1732).

To chamfer a corner, pick the two lines to be chamfered at their closest ends to the corner. If the chamfer is symmetrical, the picks may be made in any order. If the chamfer is nonsymmetrical, you must pick the lines in order of distance one and distance two.

The CHAMFER command trims the existing two lines and generates the new line segment, but this is not a completed chamfer representation. To complete it, you need to add the shoulder line. This is easy to do if you use object snap to locate the starting and ending points.

Let's chamfer the pin with a .1 x 45 degree (0.1 x 0.1) chamfer. Then add the shoulder line with OSNAP INT, and mirror it all to create the right end.

Chamfering and Mirroring the Pin

Continue in the previous TEMP drawing.

```
Command: CHAMFER
Polyline/Distance/<Select first line>: D          Enter D for Distance.
Enter first chamfer distance <0.000>: .1          Enter value.
Enter second chamfer distance <0.100>: <RETURN>

Command: <RETURN>
CHAMFER Polyline/Distance/<Select first line>: P  Polyline.
Select 2D polyline: L                             Pick the left end polyline.
2 lines were chamfered

Command: LINE                                     Draw the shoulder line.
From point: INT                                   Use osnap INT from ① to ②.

Command: MIRROR                                   Create the right end.
Select objects:                                   Select line, chamfered polyline, and circle.
First point of mirror line: MID
of                                                Pick shaft at ③.
Second point:                                     Pick any point above with ortho on, like ④.
Delete old objects? <N> <RETURN>

Command: SAVE
```

Before MIRROR, your drawing should look like the Chamfered Left Side of Pin illustration below; afterwards, it should look like Mirrored Right Side.

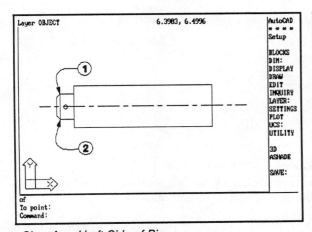

Chamfered Left Side of Pin

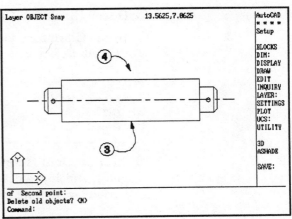

Mirrored Right Side

If you wish, you can complete the pin by drawing the right side view.

OPTIONAL: The Pin's Right Side View

Osnaps and point filters make drawing the circles of the right end easy. Remember that the innermost concentric circle is created by the .1 x 45 degree chamfer. After you have generated the circles, develop the hidden lines which represent the .125 diameter drill holes and the center lines in both the front and side views.

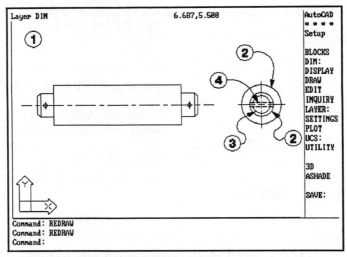

OPTIONAL: Completed Right Side View

① **PAN** — Pan or zoom to the view shown above.

② **Outer Circles** — Draw the two outer circles with SNAP.

③ **Inner Chamfered Circle** — Use a **.Y** point filter and OSNAP INT for the radius, like this:

```
Diameter/<Radius>: .Y
of INT
of (need XZ):    Pick a point above the center point.
```

---

④ **Hidden Drill Hole Lines** — The hidden lines representing the drill holes, which are developed in the right side view, may be drafted in various ways. The following is just one such way.

LINE — OSNAP QUAdrant with ortho on from top of right drill hole through the three circles. Repeat for bottom of drill hole.

TRIM — Select the second (middle) circle as cutting edge and trim both ends of both lines.

CHPROP — Change both lines to layer HL.

Finally, save the drawing.

Now we're ready to dimension the pin.

Dimensioning the Pin

This exercise concentrates on limits dimensioning and on the LEADER dimensioning subcommand. These dimensions are shown in the following illustration.

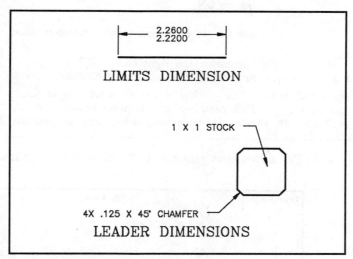

Limits and Leader Dimensions

Dimensioning in Limit Form

To generate dimensions in limit form, set the DIMTP plus and DIMTM minus tolerance values and set the DIMLIM variable on. We'll also turn DIMTIX (Text Inside eXtension) on to force the text inside the lines. It would otherwise go above or below the extension lines due to limited space.

Let's set up limits dimensioning and dimension the diameter with vertical dimensions as shown in the illustration below.

Setting Limits

Continue in TEMP, or begin a NEW drawing named TEMP=PIN-D.

Continue in or edit an EXISTING drawing named TEMP.

Command: **PAN**	Pan to the view shown below.
Command: **LAYER**	Set DIM current.
Command: **SETVAR**	Set LUPREC to 3.
Command: **DIM**	Set up for limits dimensioning.
Dim: **DIMTP**	Set to 0.003.
Dim: **DIMTM**	Set to 0.003.
Dim: **DIMLIM**	Set to ON.
Dim: **DIMTIX**	Set ON to force text inside extension lines.
Dim: **VER**	Dimension the right end.

First extension line origin or RETURN to select: **<RETURN>**
Select line, arc, or circle: Select the shoulder line at ①.
Dimension line location: Pick center of text location shown.
Dimension text <.750>: **2X %%c<>** Override text, using %%c to generate diameter symbol.

The dimension generated should match the following illustration.

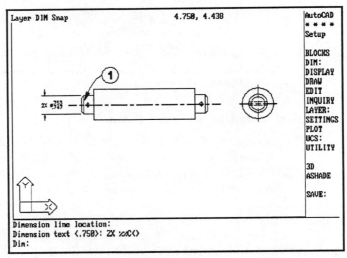

Diameter Dimension in Limits Form

Next, let's use some leaders.

Leaders — Pointing to Specific Drawing Locations

Although the DIAMETER and RADIUS dimensioning commands provide automatic leaders when they are developed, there are many occasions when you will want to develop leaders to point to specific locations or parts on your drawings. When this is the case, the LEADER dimensioning command provides the tool for the job.

LEADER creates both simple (one- or two-segment) and complex (multi-segment) leaders. Complex leaders are developed by picking a leader starting point and then several subsequent endpoints of the leader body. After you have completed the leader line(s), a <RETURN> causes a horizontal leader shoulder to be generated. AutoCAD then prompts you for the dimension text. The text will be justified according to the direction of the shoulder.

The leader shoulder is always horizontal, with a default direction in the same direction as the previous segment. You can override that, as shown below, by making the last segment a short horizontal. When the last segment is horizontal, the shoulder is omitted.

Use the following instructions to draw the leader for the chamfer dimension on the front view.

Developing a Leader and Text

Continue in dimensioning mode from the previous exercise.

```
Dim: 'PAN                        Transparently pan to the view shown below.

Dim: LEA                         LEAder.
Leader start point: MID
of                               Pick point on chamfer.
To point:                        Pick next endpoint of leader line.
To point:                        Pick second endpoint to override the shoulder.
To point: <RETURN>               Exit point picking.
Dimension text <.750>: 2X .10 X 45%%D CHAMFER    Enter text.

Dim: EXIT
Command: SAVE
```

Your leader should match ours below.

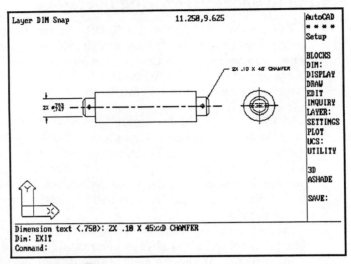

Leader With Text

Controlling Leader Text

Notice that the previous 0.750 value of the vertical dimension was presented as the default leader text. You can use this as the leader text or imbed it with a < > in the text string. A good trick is to use another dimension mode to measure something, then cancel or enter a space when prompted for text. The measured dimension will then be the default text for a following leader.

OPTIONAL: Completing the Pin's Dimensions

If you wish to complete the pin's dimensions, use the following illustration and instructions.

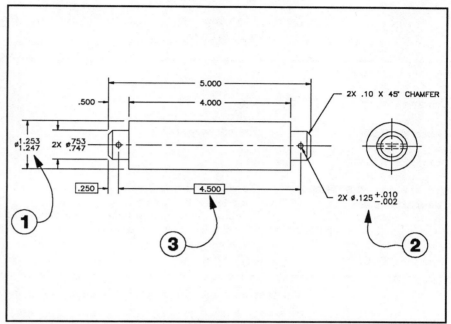

OPTIONAL: The Completely Dimensioned Pin

① **Outer Diameter Limits** — Use the VERTICAL dimensioning command and enter the text as %%c<>.

② **Hole Diameter With Tolerances** — Set DIMTOL, DIMTP, and DIMTM, and use the DIAMETER dimensioning command with DIMCEN on (1). Enter the text as 2X %%c<>.

③ **Horizontal and Basic Dimensions** — Set DIMTOL off and use the HORIZONTAL dimensioning command to generate the dimensions, then add one box with a polyline and use COPY to replicate it where shown.

Finally, save or end the drawing.

Wblocking the Pin

We need to wblock the pin to disk so it can be inserted into Chapter 6's multi-detail drawing.

Wblocking the Pin

Continue in the previous TEMP drawing.

Command: **VIEW**	Restore view BDR.
Command: **WBLOCK**	
File name: **B-PIN**	
Block name: **<RETURN>**	To select entities.
Insertion base point: **6,7**	Pick lower left point.
Select objects: **W**	Window entire pin including dimensions, excluding title blocks.
Select objects: **<RETURN>**	When selection set is complete.
Command: **QUIT**	

The last part we will create in this chapter is the servo motor mount.

Part Three: The Servo Motor Mount

This exercise focuses on the rectangular ARRAY command and on diameter dimensioning large circles to ANSI standards. We'll draw the mount in a front and a right side orthographic view. After drawing the front and side profiles, we'll draw one circle with center marks and then array it to create four other circles. After the geometry is completed, we'll dimension the mount and wblock it for later insertion into the multi-detail subassembly drawing.

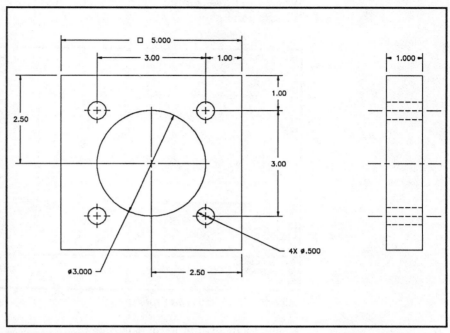

The Servo Motor Mount

To start the mount, use PLINE to draw the profiles and CIRCLE for the hole.

Drawing the Mount's Front and Side Profiles

Enter Selection: **1.**	Begin a NEW drawing named **TEMP**.
Command: **SNAP**	Set to 0.25
Command: **ZOOM**	Center, point 10,8 with height 9.
Command: **<F8>**	Or <^O> to toggle ortho on.
Command: **PLINE**	Draw front 5 x 5 with lower left corner at 5,6.
Command: **PLINE**	Draw side 1 x 5 with lower left corner at 14,6.
Command: **CIRCLE**	1.5 radius centered on square.

When you have completed these steps, your drawing should look like the illustration below.

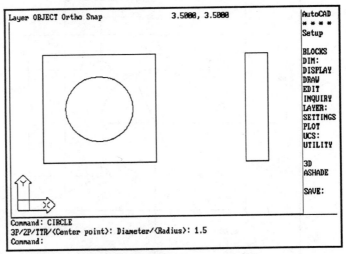

Mount's Front and Side Profiles

Now let's draw and array the holes.

Rectangular Arrays

The ARRAY command makes multiple copies of objects in rectangular or polar (circular) patterns. It can be a valuable time-saving drafting tool for spacing entities in patterns.

ARRAY

> *ARRAY copies selected entities in rectangular or polar patterns. A rectangular array prompts for the number and spacing of rows and columns. A polar array prompts for center point, number of copies to make, the angle to fill with the copies, and whether to rotate each copy.*
> Rectangular or Polar array (R/P):

When you array objects, the objects maintain their individual entity properties such as layer, linetype, and color information.

The following exercise concentrates on the rectangular ARRAY command. Polar ARRAY will be covered when we draft the pulley in Chapter 6.

When you select rectangular, you are prompted for the number of horizontal rows and vertical columns to be arrayed. Usually, you will set up the array so that the rows and columns are constructed in the positive X and Y directions. This assumes that the lower left object is selected as the object to array and the row and column distances are both positive values. However, when you enter a negative value for the row or column distance, the objects are constructed to the left (negative X for row) or down (negative Y for column).

Let's draw the hole circle and circle center line, then array them.

Using a Rectangular Array

Continue in the previous TEMP drawing.

```
Command: CIRCLE          0.25 radius circle at 1 x 1 inch from lower left corner.
Command: LAYER           Set DIM current.
Command: DIM1            Dimensions one and exits automatically.
Dim: CEN                 Select the circle.

Command: ARRAY
Select objects: W        Window the small circle and circle center line.
Rectangular or Polar array (R/P): R
Number of rows (---) <1>: 2
Number of columns (|||) <1>: 2
Unit cell or distance between rows (---): 3
Distance between columns (|||): 3

Command: SAVE            To file name TEMP.
                         Unless you have the SIA DISK, also save to file name MENUTEST for use in
                         Chapter 12.
```

And the holes are arrayed as illustrated.

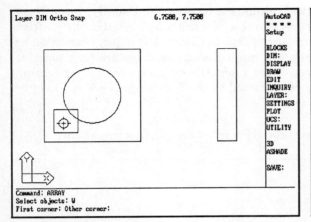

Windowing Entities for Array

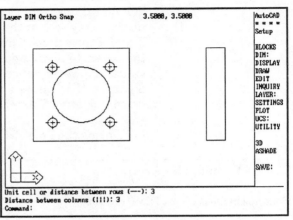

Entities are Rectangularly Arrayed

If you prefer, you may designate the distance between rows and columns by defining a *unit cell*. When you are prompted for the unit cell, or distance between rows, pick two points on the drawing screen which represent opposite corners of a rectangle. These picks provide AutoCAD with the row and column spacing. When you enter row and column spacing in this way, the Distance between columns (| | |) : prompt is skipped.

OPTIONAL: *Completing the Two Views*

If you wish, you may complete the side view of the mount, adding center and hidden lines. Note that center lines for the small holes and the hidden lines for the large hole are located in the same position on the right side view. To avoid superimposing linetypes and yet properly describe the geometry, draw four short lines representative of the ends of the center lines, with gaps between them and the object profile.

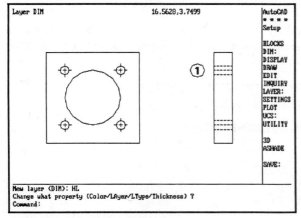 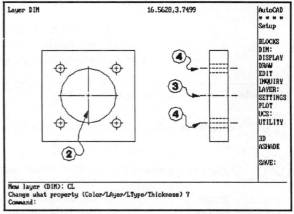

OPTIONAL: Hidden Lines   *Center Lines*

① **Hidden Lines** — Set the layer to HL and draw the top three hidden lines shown above.

② **Large Center Line** — Set the layer to CL and draw the large circle's center line.

③ **Small Center Lines** — Draw two short line segments aligned with the center top hidden line, but not touching object profile.

④ **Bottom Hidden and Center Lines** — Use MIRROR or COPY to copy the top hidden and center lines to the bottom.

Save or end the drawing. Unless you have the SIA DISK, also save the drawing to the file name, MENUTEST. You will use the drawing later, in Chapter 12, to try out the ANSI Y14.5 Menu System.

Dimensioning Larger Circles to ANSI Standards

We want to use the mount to demonstrate how to draw diameter dimensions for large circles according to ANSI standards. The rest of the dimensioning is optional.

If it can fit the diameter dimension text inside the circle, AutoCAD automatically places it at the center. To avoid this, you can override the default dimension text and pad it with spaces. This will make the dimension text too long to fit in the circle, forcing it to be placed outside with a leader. If you wish the resulting diameter dimension leader to project from the right side of the circle, enter the dimension text first and then the spaces. If you want the leader to project to the left, enter spaces first and then the dimension text. The number of spaces needed will depend on the diameter of the circle, but a few too many won't hurt.

Let's dimension the three-inch diameter circle on the mount's front view. Before you begin dimensioning, set the DIM layer current and set the limits dimensioning variables.

Diameter Dimensioning Large Circles

 Continue in TEMP, or begin a NEW drawing named TEMP=MOUNT-D.

 Continue in or edit an EXISTING drawing named TEMP.

```
Command: ZOOM                      Center point 6,7 height 6.
Command: LAYER                     Set DIM current.
Command: SETVAR                    Set LUPREC to 3.

Command: DIM
Dim: DIMLIM                        Set ON.
Dim: DIMTP                         Set to 0.012.

Dim: DIA
Select arc or circle:              Pick the 3" circle at point ①.
                                   This will become the leader point.
Dimension text <3.000>: <20 spaces> <>    Enter 20 leading spaces and <>.
Text does not fit.
Enter leader length for text: <F8>    Ortho off and pick leader endpoint ②.
Command: EXIT
Command: ZOOM                      Zoom Previous.
Command: SAVE
```

If you did not enter enough spaces, use the UNDO command and try again. The mount drawing should now contain the diameter dimension located outside the circle, as shown below.

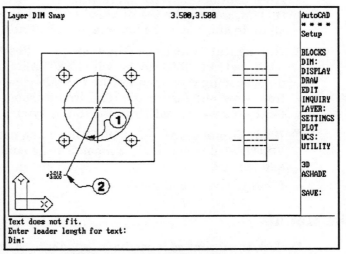

The Leadered Diameter Dimension

OPTIONAL: *Completing the Mount's Dimensions*

If you wish to complete the mount's dimensions, use the following illustration and instructions.

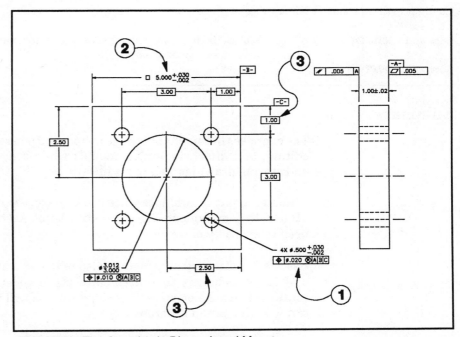

OPTIONAL: The Completely Dimensioned Mount

① **Hole Diameter With Tolerances** — Set DIMTOL, DIMTP, and DIMTM, and use the DIAMETER dimensioning command with DIMCEN off (0) to dimension the lower right hole. Enter the text as 4X %%c< >.

② **Horizontal Tolerance Dimensions** — Reset DIMTP and DIMTM to 0.02. Set LUPREC to 2 with 'SETVAR. Use the HORIZONTAL dimensioning command for the top side view dimension. For the top front view, enter the text as four leading spaces and < > to make room for the *square* symbol. Draw the square symbol with lines or a polyline.

③ **Basic Dimensions** — Set DIMTOL off and use the HORIZONTAL and VERTICAL dimensioning commands to generate the dimensions, then add the box.

Finally, save or end the drawing.

Wblocking the Mount

Wblock the mount so it can be inserted into the multi-detail drawing in the next chapter. Use the same WBLOCK procedure you used on the arm and the pin drawings.

Wblocking the Mount Drawing

Continue in the previous TEMP drawing.

Command: **WBLOCK**   Wblock both views with dimensions to file name B-MOUNT, with insertion base point 4,4.

Command: **QUIT**

Summary

The exercises in this chapter have introduced you to several new drawing, editing, and dimensioning commands while concentrating on creating and storing drawings as a parts library.

Although point filters, introduced in the arm exercise, were created for 3D use, they are among those versatile AutoCAD commands that can be used in a variety of ways.

Associative dimensioning, shown also in the arm exercise, automatically updates dimensions to reflect edits made to existing parts. As you continue to use associative dimensioning, you will find that this tool, too, can work for you in different ways.

In order to store the exercise drawings in your parts library, you saved them with the WBLOCK command as individual drawing files. In Chapter 6, these parts will be combined into one multi-detail drawing.

When you begin Chapter 6, you will make the final two pieces of the robot arm: the plate and the pulley. Both of these exercises will introduce you to additional drawing, editing, and dimensioning tools. The final exercise in Chapter 6 will show you how to insert and manipulate the five parts of the robot arm to create the subassembly multi-detail working drawing.

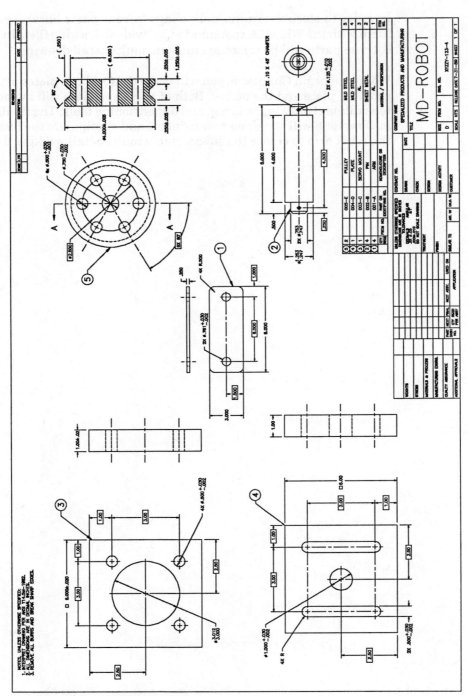

The Robot Arm Multi-Detail Drawing

Building a Multi-Detail Working Drawing (Phase 2)

ASSEMBLING THE PARTS

In this chapter, we will continue to develop parts for the robot arm. Then we'll insert the parts drafted in Chapter 5 and this chapter into another drawing to create a multi-detail working drawing.

We will be using several new commands: ARC, CHANGE, HATCH, PLOT, and PRPLOT. We will also discuss some additional features of the previously introduced ARRAY (polar), COPY, INSERT, MOVE, and WBLOCK commands. And we will learn to use several more dimensioning features, such as techniques for rescaling associative dimensioning (DIMLFAC, DIMSCALE, and UPDate), suppressing extension lines (DIMSE1 and DIMSE2), and angular dimensioning.

The first half of the chapter creates two more parts in three main steps for each: drawing the part; dimensioning the part; and wblocking it. If you have the SIA DISK, you can do or skip any of these main steps. If you don't have the disk, you'll need to do each in sequence. Each part is developed in a new drawing named TEMP which will replace any previous TEMP drawing. Start the drawings in this chapter with the PROTO-C that you configured in Chapter 3.

In the second half of the chapter, we'll create a D-size prototype, insert all the parts of the robot arm into it, adjust some dimensions, and then plot it.

As in Chapter 5, there are several optional drawing completion sequences available. If you don't complete them, and you are not working from the SIA DISK, your parts won't quite match our illustrations.

Part Four: The Adjustment Plate

In the adjustment plate exercises, we draft and dimension a two-view orthographic drawing of an adjustment plate, concentrating on the INSERT, ARC, CHANGE, STRETCH, COPY, MOVE, and TRIM commands.

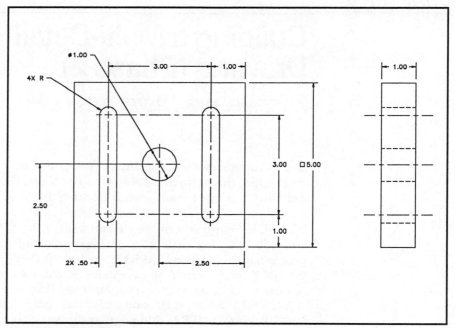

The Adjustment Plate

You may notice that the PLATE drawing is similar to last chapter's mount drawing, which we wblocked as B-MOUNT. Let's take advantage of that by inserting and editing the previous part.

First we'll set up a new drawing. We'll insert B-MOUNT with an asterisk to load its entities individually, not as a block. (This does *not* create a B-MOUNT block definition in the current drawing.) Then, we'll erase all the extraneous dimensions. We'll also erase the right-hand holes so we can show two different ways to create the slots: by trimming circles and by stringing lines and arcs together.

Drawing the Plate's Front and Side Profiles

Enter Selection: **1.**	Begin a NEW drawing named TEMP=PROTO-C.
Command: **SNAP**	Set to 0.25
Command: **ZOOM**	Center, point 10,9 with height 9.
Command: **<F8>**	Or <^O> to toggle ortho on.
Command: **INSERT**	Insert the mount.
Block name (or ?): ***B-MOUNT**	Asterisk inserts it as individual entities.

```
Insertion point: 4,4
Scale factor <1>: <RETURN>
Rotation angle <0>: <RETURN>
```

Command: **ERASE**   Erase all dimensions, hidden, and center lines not shown below.
                                       Erase the right-hand pair of holes.

At this point the mount remnants look a little irregular.

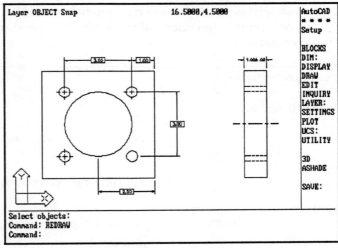

Mount Remnants for the Plate

Let's edit it into the proper form.

Changing Existing Entities

The CHANGE command modifies the geometry or options of existing
entities like lines, circles, text, attribute definitions, and block inserts.

CHANGE

> *CHANGE lets you modify existing entities. You can change the endpoints
> of lines (the nearest endpoint is pulled to the change point). You can
> respecify the center and radius of circles. You can enter new text or you
> can enter new values for any text or attdef option. You can enter a new
> origin or rotation angle for a block insert. If you select multiple entities,
> you will be prompted appropriately for each. Once you have completed
> the CHANGE command, you may have to regenerate the screen to see the
> revisions.*
> ```
> Properties/<Change point>:
> ```

➥ *NOTE: CHANGE is also capable of modifying properties like color and linetype, but use CHPROP instead. This capability of CHANGE will be dropped in future versions of AutoCAD.*

After changing the radius of the large circle, we'll use STRETCH to adjust the dimension extension lines to the new quadrant points. Then we'll use lines and TRIM to make the left-hand slot. We can rework the side view hidden and center lines with COPY and MOVE. When you use Multiple at the COPY base point prompt, it reprompts for the base point. After you pick a base point, you are continuously prompted for the second point of displacement (positions of the multiple copies) until you terminate the command.

Editing the Mount to Make a Plate

Continue in the previous TEMP drawing.

```
Command: ZOOM                                Center 11,9 with height 8.

Command: CHANGE
Select objects:                              Select the large center circle.
1 selected, 1 found.
Select objects: <RETURN>
Properties/<Change point>: <RETURN>          Leaves center point unchanged.
Enter circle radius: .5

Command: SETVAR                              Set LUPREC to 2.
Command: STRETCH                             Adjust the existing dimensions.
Select objects to stretch by window...
Select objects: C                            Select end of dimension line at ①.
Base point: NOD                              Node.
of                                           Osnap to node controlling assoc. dimension at ①.
New point: QUA                               Quadrant.
of                                           Left side of center circle.

Command: LAYER                               Set DIM current.
Command: DIM
Dim: CEN                                     Pick the center circle.
Dim: UPD                                     UPDate the side view top dimension to 1.00.
Dim: EXIT                                    Or <^C>.
Command: LAYER                               Set OBJECT current.
Command: SETVAR                              Set LUPREC back to 4.

Command: LINE                                Draw left side of slot.
From point: TAN
to                                           Pick left side of top hole.
To point: TAN
```

```
to                                              Pick left side of bottom hole.
To point: <RETURN>
Command: <RETURN>
LINE From point: TAN                            Repeat for right side.

Command: TRIM                                   Trim the two circles to make a slot.
Select cutting edge(s)...
Select objects:                                 Select the two new tangent lines.
Select objects: <RETURN>
Select object to trim: <Snap off>               Toggle snap off. Pick each circle in the slot.
Command: <Snap on>                              Back on.

Command: MOVE                                   Move hidden line from ② to ③.
Command: MOVE                                   Move hidden line from ④ to ⑤.

Command: COPY                                   Copy the side view's center line.
Select objects:                                 Select center line of side view.
<Base point or displacement/Multiple: M         Multiple.
Base point:                                     Pick snap point on line.
Second point of displacement:                   Copy to ⑥.
Second point of displacement:                   Copy to ⑦.
Second point of displacement: <RETURN>

Command: SAVE
```

The plate is nearly done. It needs only one more slot.

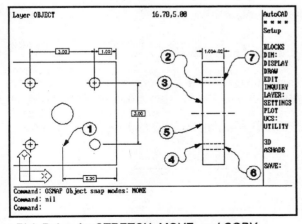

Pick Points for STRETCH, MOVE, and COPY

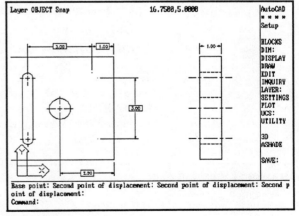

Plate With One Slot

Obviously we could copy the slot we have, but we'd rather demonstrate how lines and arcs can be strung together.

Drawing Arcs

The ARC command draws a circle segment in nearly any possible way.

ARC

> *The ARC command draws any segment of a circle greater than one degree and less than 360 degrees. Except for the three-point option, arcs are constructed in a counterclockwise direction. An arc or line can be drawn immediately tangent to the last arc or line by defaulting its* Start point: *or* From point: *prompts. The default is three-point arc construction, but you can use several other methods.*
> Center/<Start point>:

AutoCAD provides eleven different methods for drawing arcs. Start the ARC command by entering the first letter(s) of the option and AutoCAD prompts you for the next input.

Pick points — three points on the arc.
SCE — start point, center, end point.
SCA — start point, center, included angle.
SCL — start point, center, length of chord.
SEA — start point, end point, included angle.
SER — start point, end point, radius.
SED — start point, end point, starting direction.
CSE — center point, start point, end point.
CSA — center point, start point, angle.
CSL — center point, start point, length of chord.
<RETURN> — continuation of previous line or arc.

Let's draw the arcs for this exercise with *line-arc continuation*. After invoking the ARC command, respond to the first prompt with a <RETURN> or by pressing the space bar. The arc's starting point and direction will be assigned from the end point and ending direction of the last line or arc.

Drawing Lines and Arcs

Continue in the previous TEMP drawing.

```
Command: ARC
Center/<Start point>: C            Center point.
Center:                            Pick upper center point of right slot.
```

```
Start point:                                Pick .25 to the right of center at ①.
Angle/Length of chord/<End point>:          Pick opposite side at ②.

Command: LINE
From point: <RETURN>                         Starts tangent to last arc.
To point:                                   Drag and pick point ③. Notice it's forced tangent.
To point: <RETURN>

Command: ARC
Center/<Start point>: <RETURN>               Starts tangent to last line.
End point:                                   Pick point at ④.

Command: LINE
LINE from point: <RETURN>                     Starts tangent to last line.
To point:                                   Pick end point at ① again.
To point: <RETURN>

Command: LAYER                               Set DIM current.
Command: DIM                                 Use CENter dimensioning on both arcs.
Dim: EXIT

Command: LAYER                               Set CL current.
Command: OSNAP                               Set running mode ENDpoint.
Command: LINE                 Use four LINE commands to connect the arc center lines.
Command: OSNAP                               Set running mode to NONe.
```

Except for optional dimensions, the plate is complete. It should match the last of the following four illustrations.

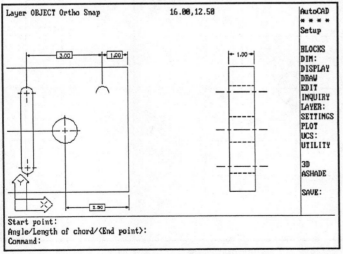

Top Arc of the Slot

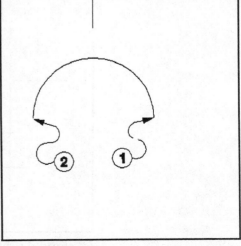

Detail of Slot Arc

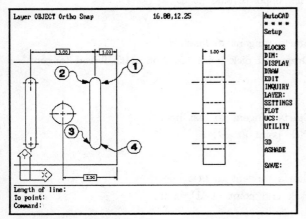

Slot Completed

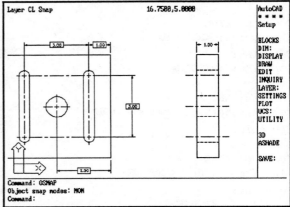

Slot and Arc Center Lines

OPTIONAL: *Completing the Plate's Dimensions*

If you wish, you can complete the plate's dimensions to match the following illustration. We have already used the required techniques several times in the last chapter.

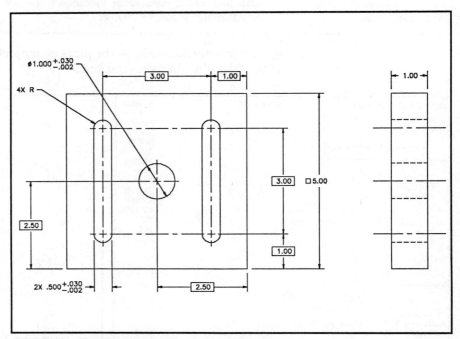

OPTIONAL: The Completely Dimensioned Plate

Wblocking the Plate

Our final step will be to wblock the plate for later insertion into the multi-detail working drawing.

Wblocking the Plate Drawing

Continue in the previous TEMP drawing.

Command: **VIEW**   Restore view BDR.

 You already have the B-PLATE file.

 Wblock both views with dimensions to file name B-PLATE with insertion base point 4,4.

Command: **QUIT**

The last part to be drafted is the pulley.

Part Five: The Pulley

This exercise shows how to draft and dimension a two-view orthographic drawing of a pulley. It concentrates on the polar ARRAY and HATCH commands, on angular dimensioning, and on suppressing dimensioning extension lines.

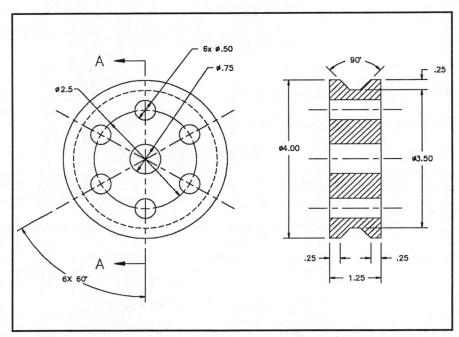

The Pulley

We will develop the front view profile with concentric circles by drawing one circle and center line, and then arraying it in a polar fashion. The section view will be drawn with the crosshairs aligned with the front view.

Drawing the Pulley's Front and Section Profiles

Enter Selection: **1.**	Begin a NEW drawing named **TEMP**.
Command: **SNAP** Command: **ZOOM**	Set to 0.25 Center, point 10,8 with height 7.
Command: **CIRCLE**	Draw four circles at 8,8 with radii of 2, 1.75, 1.25, and 0.375.
Command: **LINE**	Draw a vertical line through the centers of the circles.
Command: **CHPROP**	Change line and 1.25 radius circle to layer CL, and 1.75 radius circle to HL.
Command: **LINE**	Draw section view profile as shown below. All points are on snap.

The basic layout of the pulley should match the following illustration.

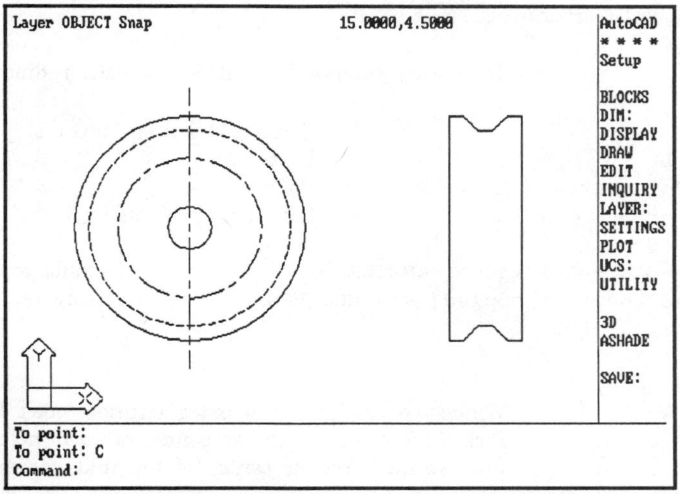

Basic Layout of Pully Front

Now we need to array the holes and trim the center lines.

Polar Arrays

In Chapter 5, we used the ARRAY command to copy an object in a rectangular pattern. ARRAY can also be used to copy and space objects in polar, or circular, patterns.

When you select the polar option, you are prompted for the number of items in the array, the angle to fill, and whether or not the objects are to be rotated as they are arrayed. The polar angle between items is the angle to fill divided by the number of items. Include the original object when you count the number of items in the array. The Angle to fill: prompt determines the direction around the center point for the array. A positive value indicates a counterclockwise (CCW) array and a negative value indicates a clockwise (CW) array. For a full circular array, accept the default <360> degrees.

We need to do a bit of trickery with temporary circles and TRIM to get our center lines right. The dimensioning CENTER command puts in straight lines, not curved like we need. So we'll temporarily use smaller circles for the holes and trim our vertical and circular center lines. When we replace the holes with the right size circles, the center lines will extend into the circles.

Using Polar Array

Continue in the previous TEMP drawing.

```
Command: CIRCLE                        Temporary bottom hole at 8,6.75 with radius 0.1875 (not .25).

Command: ARRAY                         Array the bottom hole.
Select objects: L                      Last.
Rectangular or Polar array (R/P): P    Polar.
Center point of array:                 Pick center of pulley.
Number of items: 6
Angle to fill (+=CCW,-=CW) <360>: <RETURN>          Default to 360 degrees.
Rotate objects as they are copied? <Y> <RETURN>     Irrelevant.

Command: TRIM
Select cutting edge(s)...
Select objects: W                      Window everything (the extra entities won't hurt).
Select object to trim:                 Pick 1.25 radius circle at center of each hole.
Select object to trim:                 Pick vertical line at center of top and bottom holes.
Select object to trim: <RETURN>
                                       The newly trimmed arcs may look straight until you regenerate.

Command: LAYER                         Set DIM current.
Command: DIM
Dim: CEN                               Add center marks to both top and bottom holes, then EXIT.
Command: LAYER                         Set layer OBJECT current.
Command: ERASE                         Erase the six temporary holes.
Command: CIRCLE                        Draw two real holes: top at 8,9.25 and
                                       bottom at 8,6.75 with radii 0.25.

Command: ARRAY                         Polar, the vertical lines, center marks, and both holes
                                       three times 360 degrees rotated as copied.

Command: SAVE
```

The following illustrations show the pulley before and after the trim and final array steps.

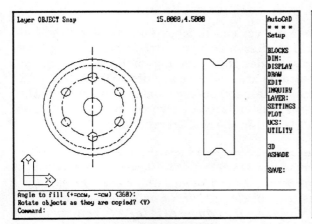

Before Trimming With Temporary Holes

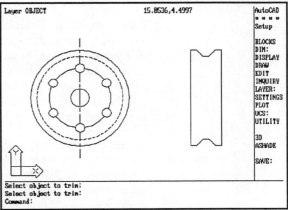

After Trimming With Tempory Holes

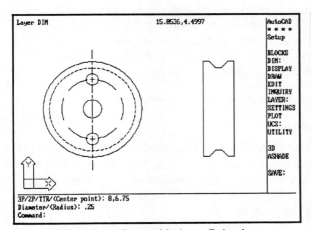

Real Holes, Lines, Center Marks to Polar Array

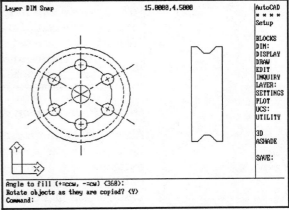

Completed Array

Next, we'll hatch the section view.

Sectional Views

The right view of the pulley drawing will be a full section view, and will therefore have section lines representing a full cutting plane. The hypothetically cut surface is represented by *cross hatching* (parallel lines which run at a 45-degree angle across the part) on the part surfaces where an imaginary cutting plane intersects the object. These section lines and many other more complex patterns can be generated with the HATCH command.

Hatch and Pattern Filling

Many drafting disciplines use various hatches and pattern fills. For example, an architectural drafter may use hatch patterns to create different surface textures to designate roofing material, siding, or excavated earth. Many patterns are available in AutoCAD's ACAD.PAT library of standard hatch patterns. You may hatch with any of the available standard patterns, customize your own complex patterns, or define a simple pattern style within the HATCH command.

HATCH

> *The HATCH command cross-hatches or pattern-fills an area defined by a boundary. The boundary must be continuous and closed, formed by any combination of lines, arcs, circles, polylines, or 3Dfaces. The hatch patterns available are defined in a file named ACAD.PAT. You can also specify the spacing and angle for parallel or cross-hatched continuous lines. The HATCH command's default creates a block with a hidden name and inserts it. If you precede the pattern name with an asterisk, like *name, the hatch will instead be drawn with individual line entities. You can also choose a style of hatching for nested boundaries: Normal, Outermost, or Ignore. Hatching is always defined and generated relative to the X,Y axes and plane of the current UCS.*
> `Pattern (? or name/U,style):`

Hatch Pattern Icon Menus

AutoCAD contains over 40 different hatch patterns in the ACAD.PAT library. If your system supports the AUI, you may view and select patterns from a three-page hatch pattern icon menu. Pull down [Draw] and select [Hatch...] to display these menus. The first two pages of the pattern icon menus are displayed below.

Many of AutoCAD's pre-defined hatch patterns represent ANSI standard material descriptions. By selecting a specific pattern or naming convention, you will be able to easily represent materials from aluminum to zinc in technically accurate sectional form.

Since the default patterns are internally generated blocks, they may be controlled as single entities. If it is necessary to edit a single line of a pattern, specify it with a leading asterisk, or use the EXPLODE command to convert the pattern into individual entities.

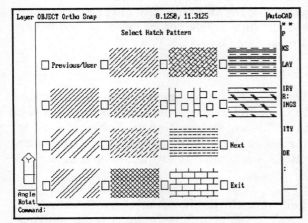

Hatch Pattern Icon Menus

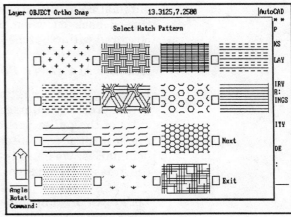

More Hatch Patterns

Hatch Options

When the HATCH command is invoked, you are presented with four major options for generating or querying patterns. They are:

? — Provides a list of pattern names.

Name — Inputs the name of the hatch pattern.

U (User) Defined Hatching — Presents a series of hatch definition prompts, from which you define a hatch pattern.

Style — Provides for the style boundary codes as described below. You specify a style with a comma after the name, like *name,I*.

Hatch Styles

AutoCAD offers three different styles of hatching to accommodate the hatching of nested boundaries, such as several concentric circles. The hatching affects only the boundary objects selected.

N (Normal) — The default style hatches from the outermost selected boundary inward until it encounters an internal boundary. As each internal boundary is encountered, hatching turns off or on until the next internal boundary is encountered.

O (Outermost) — Hatches from the outermost selected boundary inward until it is turned off by an internal boundary. It does not turn back on.

I (Ignore Style) — Hatches everything within the outer boundary, ignoring all internal geometry without turning off.

Except for the Ignore style, *selected* text, attributes, shapes, traces, and solids are treated differently from other entities. Hatching is automatically turned off whenever any of these entities are contacted and turned back on when passed. This avoids the problem of text being obscured within hatched areas.

Hatch and Pattern Boundaries

Hatching boundaries must be carefully defined by separate entities which precisely intersect but do not overlap (no overhangs). Since the sides of the pulley section profile are two continuous lines, we need to break them at each interior line so the individual areas have continuous boundaries. We'll use the BREAK command to divide the lines at each of the areas to be hatched.

Let's draw dividing lines and break the profile at each line's intersection. Since AutoCAD's object selection tends to find the more recent entities first, you can't select the first line at its intersection with the interior line even if you want it to break there. If you do, AutoCAD will try to select the more recently drawn interior line. You'll have to select the outer line in a clear space and then use the F option to reselect the break point at the intersection. However, the first break will make the polylines the most recent entities, so subsequent breaks can be done without the F option.

Defining Individual Hatch Boundaries

Continue in the previous TEMP drawing.

Command: **SNAP**   Set to 0.125.

Command: **LINE**   Aligning the crosshairs with the top, center, and bottom holes, draw the six visible lines shown below in the section view.

Command: **OSNAP**   Set running mode to INT.
Command: **BREAK**
Select object: Select profile line at point ①.
Enter second point (or F for first point): **F**   Respecify first point.
Enter first point: Pick line intersection ②.
Enter second point: Pick same point.

Command: **<RETURN>**
BREAK Select object: Select another line intersection twice to break.
                                                          Repeat for other ten intersections.
Command: **OSNAP**   Set running mode to NONe.

Each side of the pulley in the section view now consists of seven short lines.

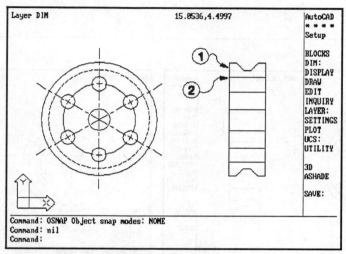

Lines and Points of First Break

Use the following instructions to hatch the first area, then use a similar technique to create and hatch the three remaining hatch areas. You can hatch the remaining areas at the same time by selecting the HATCH command and treating all three as one selection set. This procedure provides an efficient means for simultaneously hatching (with the same pattern) various areas on a drawing.

The following steps will show you how to generate a user-defined 45-degree hatch pattern. This user-defined pattern represents section lines for the full section drawing of the pulley. This technique is usually referred to as creating hatches *on the fly*.

Creating User-Defined (U) Hatching

Continue in the previous TEMP drawing.

```
Command: LAYER              Set current layer to HATCH.

Command: HATCH
Pattern (? or name/U,style): U
Angle for crosshatch lines <0>: 45
Spacing between lines <1.0000>: .1
Double hatch area? <N> <RETURN>
Select objects: W           Window the top as shown below.
Select objects: <RETURN>    Finish selection and hatch.
```

```
Command: <RETURN>              When repeated, hatch assumes the same pattern and skips prompts.
HATCH Select objects:          Select three windows, one for each shown below.

Command: SAVE
```

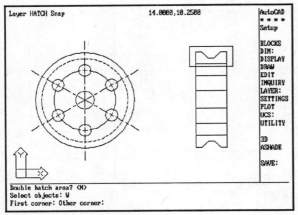

Window for First Hatch   **Three Windows for Repeated Hatch**

That completes the two views, without dimensions. The illustrations above show the windows to select the boundaries and the results. We demonstrated a user-defined pattern, but the ANSI31 hatch pattern at 0.8 scale and 0 degrees creates an identical effect.

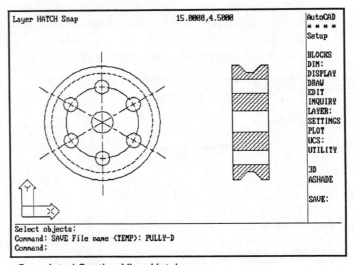

Completed Section View Hatches

➡ *TIP: It is often best to define boundaries with new entities traced over existing geometry. Put these entities on a unique layer so they can be easily turned off or erased. This ensures proper boundaries while leaving the original geometry intact.*

Hatching and Drawing Size

One side effect of using hatches is the impact on disk space. Unlike normal blocks, which can be very efficient due to repetition, each use of the HATCH command creates a unique block that actually takes up slightly more space than if it were individual lines. Closely spaced or broken line patterns can use large amounts of disk space and memory, and can slow drawing regeneration to a crawl. Therefore, use intricate patterns sparingly, add hatching only before creating the final output, or freeze the hatch pattern's layer to avoid slow regenerations.

Dimensioning the Pulley

This section concentrates on developing angular dimensions and on suppressing redundant extension lines.

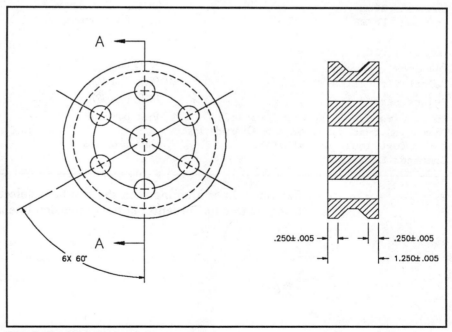

The Pulley With Dimensions

Angular Dimensioning

The dimension arc created by angular dimensioning spans the angle between two nonparallel straight lines. The lines to be dimensioned do not have to intersect. When you select ANGULAR, you are prompted for the two lines the angular dimension will span. After the two lines are selected, you are prompted for the dimension arc location point. Extension lines will generate automatically if the dimension arc does not intersect the line(s) being dimensioned. There is also a prompt for dimension text location. You can either pick a text location or <RETURN> to default and center the text on the dimension arc.

Let's dimension the angle between the polar-arrayed holes.

Creating Angular Dimensions

 Continue in TEMP, or begin a NEW drawing named TEMP=PULLEY-D.

 Continue in or edit an EXISTING drawing named TEMP.

```
Command: ZOOM                              To the view shown.
Command: LAYER                             Set DIM current.

Command: DIM
Dim: ANG                                   ANGular.
Select first line:                         Pick line ①.
Select second line:                        Pick line ②.
Enter dimension line arc location:         Pick point ③.
Dimension text <60>: 6X < > Override text.
Enter text location: <RETURN>              Center of arc.
Command: EXIT
```

Extension lines aligning with the two lines selected are drawn, and the text is placed at the center of the dimension line arc.

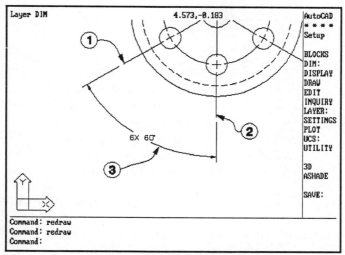

The Angle Between Holes Is Dimensioned

Suppressing Extension Lines

In manual drafting, you only draw an extension line when you need it. Naturally, you omit an extension line that would overlap or duplicate an existing line. AutoCAD doesn't always know when to omit an extension line. The next exercise concentrates on two techniques for suppressing extension lines: setting the DIMSE1 and DIMSE2 dimension variables, and a trick where you pick your points.

There are occasions when extension lines are superimposed on top of each other. You can avoid having them overlap by turning one, or both, of the following variables off. You will want to suppress (turn off) extension lines for most BASELINE and CONTINUE dimensions, and for many other horizontal or vertical dimensions where BASELINE or CONTINUE don't work well. For an example, see the section view dimensions below. You may also want to suppress the first or second extension line of a dimension when the object itself acts as an extension line.

The first technique controls extension lines by setting dimension variables.

DIMSE1 — When on, suppresses the first extension line. The first extension line is determined by your first extension line location pick.

DIMSE2 — When on, suppresses the second extension line, your second extension line location pick.

Let's see how CONTINUE works with the default settings.

Overlapped Extension Lines

Continue in the previous TEMP drawing.

```
Command: ZOOM                          To the view shown.
Command: SETVAR                        Set LUPREC to 3.

Command: DIM
Dim: DIMTOL                            Set to ON.
Dim: DIMTP                             Set to 0.005.
Dim: DIMTM                             Set to 0.005.

Dim: HOR                               Dimension bottom left shoulder, right to left.
Dim: CON
Second extension line origin:          Pick outside bottom right shoulder.
Dimension text <1.250>: <RETURN>

Dim: U          Undo, and both left extension lines disappear.
Dim: REDRAW     The first dimension's first extension line reappears.
Dim: U          Undo two times to delete the first dimension.
Dim: EXIT       To save the settings.
```

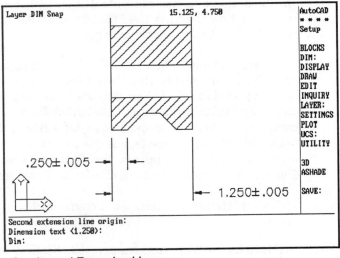

Overlapped Extension Lines

The purpose of that exercise was to show that the HORIZONTAL and CONTINUE first extension lines were overlapping. BASELINE works the same way. That may not seem a big problem on screen, but when plotting, extensions that overlap may plot poorly.

To deal with this, turn DIMSE1 off for the initial HORIZONTAL dimension, leave it off for all but the last in the series of BASELINE or CONTINUE dimensions, and turn it back on for the last BASELINE or CONTINUE dimension. Then only the last dimension will draw an extension line, which will serve all the preceding dimensions.

Let's repeat the previous dimensions with DIMSE1 on to suppress the first extension line.

Controlling DIMSE1 for Baseline Dimensions

Continue in the previous TEMP drawing.

```
Dim: DIMSE2
Current value <Off> New value: ON

Dim: HOR               Dimension bottom left shoulder, right to left.
Dim: CON               Pick outside bottom right shoulder.

Dim: DIMSE2
Current value <On> New value: OFF
Dim: EXIT
```

It may look the same as before, but this one is guaranteed to plot perfectly.

The other technique uses a different method to pick the extension line location points. AutoCAD does *not* draw an extension line if the point for an extension line origin is aligned with the dimension line location point. You can use this to suppress extension lines simply by where you pick them, without bothering to reset DIMSE1 or DIMSE2. The disadvantage to this is that your extension line origin points will not necessarily be *on* the object where they will be sure to be moved, stretched, or scaled with it.

Try this technique for dimensioning the right shoulder.

Controlling Extension Lines by Picking

Continue in the previous TEMP drawing.

```
Command: DIM1
Dim: HOR
First extension line origin or RETURN to select:        Pick inside of right shoulder.
Second extension line origin:              Pick on existing right extension line, in line
                                      with existing left shoulder dimension line at ①.
Dimension line location: @             Same point.
Dimension text <.250>: <RETURN>

Command: SAVE
```

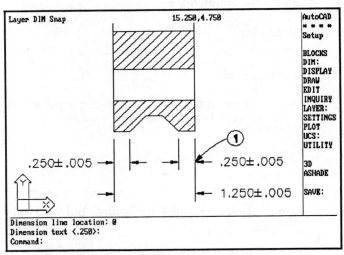

Dimensions With Suppressed Extension Lines

The section view needs to be located in the front view by a cutting plane.

Cutting Planes

Since the right side view is drawn as a sectional view, it needs a *cutting plane* arrow to show where the section was cut. The cutting plane is shown in the following illustration as two large arrows, a bold dashed line, and large key letters.

We can get dimensioning's LEADER to do most of the work for us, using layer OBJECT for bold lines and an explicit PHANTOM linetype.

Cutting Plane Lines and Arrows

Continue in the previous TEMP drawing.

Command: **ZOOM**	Center 10,7.5 height 8.
Command: **LAYER**	Set layer OBJECT current (for bold lines).
Command: **ERASE**	Erase vertical center lines through front view.
Command: **LINETYPE**	Set to PHANTOM (overriding layer linetype default).
Command: **DIM**	
Dim: **DIMSCALE**	Set to 2 (double everything's size).
Dim: **LEA**	LEAder.
Leader start:	Pick ①.
To point:	Pick ②.
To point:	Pick ③.
To point:	Pick ④.
To point: **<RETURN>**	
Dimension text <.250>: **A**	
Dim: **DIMSCALE**	Set back to 1.
Dim: **<^C>**	
Command: **COPY**	Copy the A from the bottom to the top of the section line.
	Copy the arrow head from the top to the bottom of the section line.
Command: **LINETYPE**	Set back to BYLAYER.
Command: **SAVE**	

The resulting section line is illustrated below.

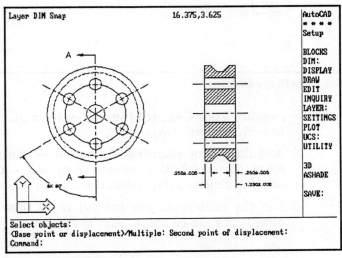

Section Line and Arrows

OPTIONAL: *Finishing the Pulley*

If you wish to finish up the pulley, you need to add more center lines and additional dimensions.

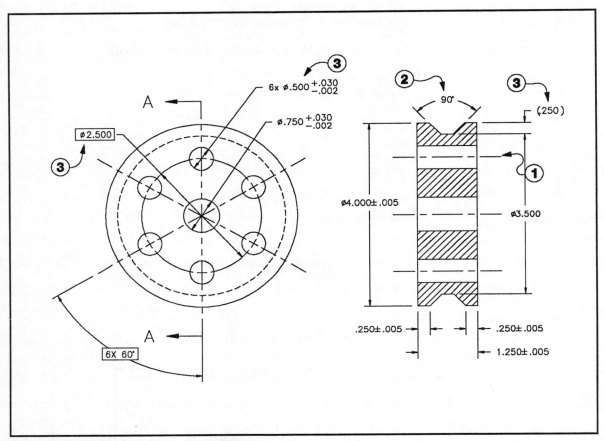

OPTIONAL: Completing the Pulley Drawing

① **Section View Center Lines** — Set layer CL current and draw center lines through the three holes.

② **Angular Dimensioning V-Groove** — Turn layer HATCH off (to avoid object selection interference) and set DIM current. Using angular dimensioning, select the top two sloping lines.

③ Use the techniques you learned in Chapter 5 for the rest of the dimensions shown above. Save the file.

Wblocking the Pulley

Next, we will wblock the pulley so it can be inserted into the multi-detail drawing in the next section.

Wblocking the Pulley Drawing

Continue in the previous TEMP drawing.

Command: **VIEW**   Restore view BDR.

    You already have the B-PULLEY file.

    Wblock both views with dimensions to file name B-PULLEY with insertion base point 5,4.

Command: **QUIT**

That completes all of the parts needed for our multi-detail working drawing.

Multi-Detail Working Drawings

Working drawings convey the information necessary to manufacture, construct, assemble, or install a mechanical device. Working drawings are divided into drawing types, such as multi-detail, assembly, or exploded assembly, according to their use in manufacturing. The most common multi-view drawings are assembly or exploded assembly drawings, but we'll use our existing parts to build a multi-detail drawing.

A multi-detail drawing places two or more unique parts on the same drawing sheet(s). Each item is identified by its assigned *bubble* number (like ①). Its relative manufacturing information is provided in a parts listing.

If you have the SIA DISK, you can jump right into this exercise. Otherwise, you need each of the robot arm parts that were developed and dimensioned in Chapters 5 and 6, and wblocked to separate disk drawing files.

The following exercise inserts the five parts of the robot arm into the multi-detail drawing, as shown in the following illustration. (This same illustration at a larger scale is on the facing page of this chapter.) The exercise concentrates on inserting and scaling blocks, and on adjusting associative dimensions.

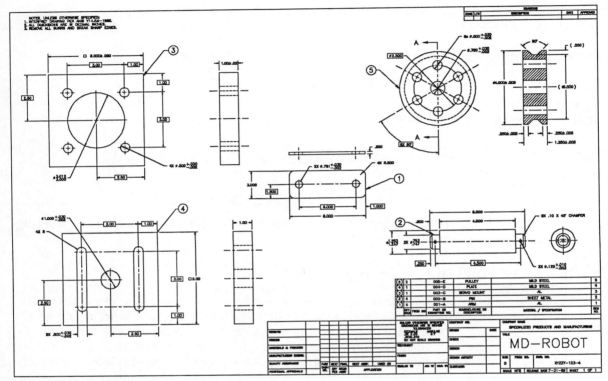

The Robot Arm Multi-Detail Drawing

Drawing Setup

These parts won't fit on a C-size prototype drawing, so we'll adapt
PROTO-C to make a D-size sheet. We need to STRETCH it and adjust its
location, UCS's, and limits. Since we don't know what sort of plotter you
have, we made our border clearances generous enough to accommodate
any D-size plotter. PROTO-C has a 21 x 16 inch border centered with 0.5
inch borders in a 22 x 17 inch sheet. We'll stretch the border by 11 and 4
in the X and Y directions to make it 32 x 20 inches with 1 inch borders in
a 34 x 22 inch sheet.

Making a D-Size Sheet

 You can skip this. You have the PROTO-D file.

 Begin a NEW drawing named PROTO-D=PROTO-C.

```
Command: SNAP                              Set to 0.125.
Command: LAYER                             Thaw and turn ON all layers, using the * wildcard.
Command: LIMITS                            Reset to 0,0 and 34,22.
Command: ZOOM                              Zoom .8

Command: STRETCH                           Stretch to the right, as illustrated below.
Select objects to stretch by window...
Select objects: C                          Enclose all but general notes and left end of border in Crossing
                                             window.
Base point:                                Pick any point.
New point: <Ortho on>                      Toggle ortho on and pick polar point @10<0.

Command: <RETURN>                          Stretch the top border edge, general notes,
STRETCH                                     and revision block up 4 inches.

Command: MOVE                              Select everything and move 0.5,0.5 to recenter in new limits.

Command: UCS                               Osnap the Origin to lower left corner of border.
                                            Save UCS to name BDR.

Command: VIEW                              Save current view to name ALL.
                                            Window 0,0 to 32,20 and save to view name BDR.
                                            Restore view SCRATCH.

Command: UCS                               Restore UCS SCRATCH.
                                            Reset the Origin to 0.5,0.5.
                                            Save UCS to name SCRATCH.

Command: VIEW                              Window -1.5,-1.5 to 36,24 and save to view name SCRATCH.
                                            Restore view BDR.

Command: UCS                               Restore BDR.

Command: LAYER                             Freeze NOTES,????-?? then thaw TITL-OT.

Command: END
```

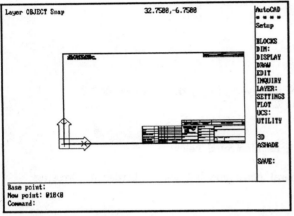

Stretched to the Right

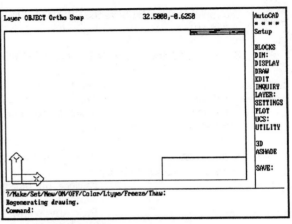

Finished PROTO-D

We'll use the new prototype to create the MD-ROBOT drawing.

The parts list currently has only one line. We need to array it upward to make five lines, then extend the vertical dividing lines to the new top line.

Starting the MD-ROBOT Drawing

Enter Selection: **1.**	Begin a NEW drawing named **MD-ROBOT=PROTO-D.**
Command: **LAYER**	Thaw NOTES,????-OT.
Command: **ZOOM**	Window 20,0 to 33,8 for the parts list.
Command: **ARRAY**	
Select objects:	Select the top line of parts list.
Rectangular or Polar array (R/P): **R**	Rectangular.
Number of rows (---) <1>: **5**	
Number of columns (|||) <1>: **<RETURN>**	
Unit cell or distance between rows (---): **INT**	Osnap INT to pick distance from
Other corner: **INT**	bottom to top of first line's space.
Command: **EXTEND**	Select new top line as boundary edge and select all seven vertical dividing lines as objects to extend.
Command: **VIEW**	Restore view BDR.
Command: **SNAP**	Set to 0.5.

Now that we're ready to start inserting parts, your drawing should look like the illustration below.

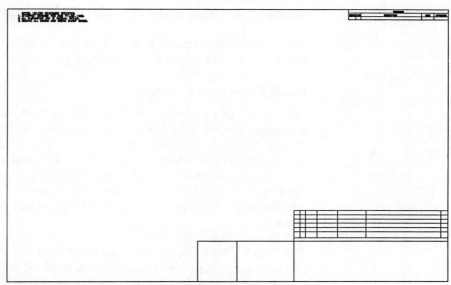

Title Blocks, Expanded Parts List, and Notes

Inserting Blocks

The INSERT command inserts drawings or blocks into a current drawing. After selecting INSERT, you are prompted for the block name to insert. If the block is already defined in the current drawing, its existing definition is used. If not, AutoCAD searches its library path on disk for a drawing that matches the block name and, if found, inserts it. When inserted, a drawing file creates a block definition (unless inserted with a leading asterisk). You can override and redefine an existing block in the current drawing with a drawing from disk by specifying the name with an equal sign in the same way we start a new drawing from a prototype. For example, BLOCKNAME=DWGNAME would redefine the existing block named BLOCKNAME with the contents of the drawing file DWGNAME. The same equal sign technique can be used to insert a new block with a name differing from the drawing file name.

Editable Block Inserts

When a block is inserted, it is treated as a single entity. You can access its individual entities by preceding the name of the block with an asterisk, like *B-ARM, when you insert it. This performs the same function as inserting a block normally and then using the EXPLODE command. In either case, the *inserted or exploded block can be edited.

After the name, INSERT prompts for the insertion point, which you can specify while dragging the block. Next you set the scale.

Block Scale and Rotation

After you have provided the block name and insertion point, you are prompted for the scale factors with the X scale factor <1> / Corner / XYZ: prompt. By default, it prompts for X and Y and sets Z equal to X, but if you enter the key letters XYZ, it will also prompt for the Z scale factor for 3D blocks. AutoCAD multiplies the X and Y dimensions of all entities in the block by the X and Y scale factor you enter. You can even specify negative values so AutoCAD will insert *mirrored* images of the block.

The X and Y scale factors can also be defined by picking a corner point on the screen in response to the scale prompt. The X,Y distances from the insertion point to this corner point become the X and Y scales. (This is identical to the Corner option, which makes it sort of redundant.) If the picked corner point is below or to the left of the insertion point, you get a negative scale. Another convenient way to specify scale with a corner point is to use a point such as **@3,7** relative to the insertion point, where 3 becomes the X scale and 7 the Y scale. Using a corner point works best for blocks that are designed to be one unit square, so the lower left corner of the block is at the insertion point and the upper right corner of the block drags to the corner point picked. For example, a simple 1 x 1 square block can be inserted with various X,Y scales to represent *any* rectangular or square hole.

The final prompt is for the rotation angle relative to the insertion point. The block may then be rotated to any angle. A counterclockwise rotation will be a positive angle and a clockwise rotation will be a negative one.

Let's insert the B-PIN, B-PLATE, B-MOUNT, and B-PULLEY blocks into the drawing.

Inserting Blocks Into the Current Drawing

Continue in the previous MD-ROBOT drawing.

```
Command: INSERT
Block name (or ?): B-PLATE
Insertion point: 0.5,1.5                        Lower left corner of border.
X scale factor <1>/corner/XYZ: <RETURN>         Default to 1:1.
Y scale factor (default=X): <RETURN>            Default to equal X.
Rotation angle <0>: <RETURN>                    Default to horizontal.

Command: <RETURN>
INSERT Block name (or ?) <B-PLATE>:             Repeat for: B-MOUNT at 1,9.5; B-PIN at 20.5,5; and
                                                B-PULLEY at 19.5,11.5.

Command: SAVE
```

If you need to adjust the location of these blocks due to conflicts, use the MOVE command. Remember that AutoCAD recognizes the block as a single entity. Pick any point on the block and AutoCAD will select the entire block. Then simply drag it and pick a new point.

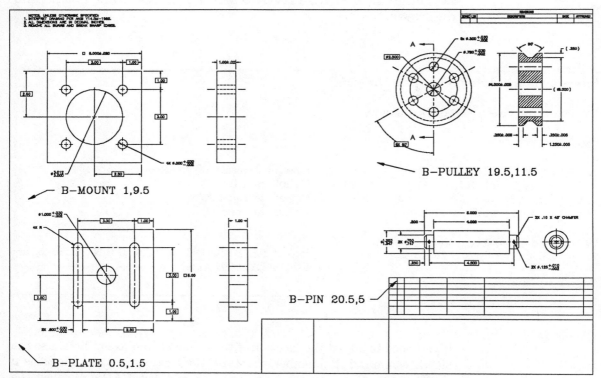

Suggested Block Insertion Points

The remaining B-ARM block won't fit at full scale. To give you an exercise in block redefinition and dimension updating, we will insert it at half scale. Because this makes the dimensions half as big, they will need updating and the block will require editing.

OPTIONAL: Editing the B-ARM Dimensions

There are two optional methods for inserting and editing these dimensions: *insertion and DIMLFAC updating; or normal insertion and block redefinition in the SCRATCH UCS. Whichever you choose, make sure LUPREC and all dimension variables are set as they were when the dimension was created before updating each dimension.

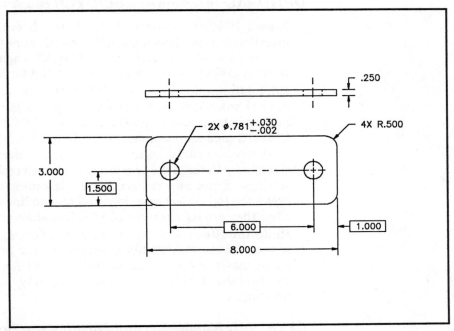

OPTIONAL: Editing the B-ARM Dimensions

OPTIONAL: *Insertion and DIMLFAC*

Insert Block — Insert *B-ARM at 0.5 scale, using a leading asterisk on the name to insert it as individual, editable entities.

Edit Dimensions — Set DIMLFAC (dimension linear factor) to 2. A DIMLFAC of 2 will make the half-size objects measure twice as big to generate the right size text. Use STRETCH, MOVE, SCALE, and the dimension UPDATE command to update each dimension. Make sure LUPREC and all dimension variables are set as needed before updating, scaling, or stretching dimensions. Refer to the arm dimensioning exercise in Chapter 5 for the settings. Erase and replace the circle center marks. Use BREAK to break the top view center lines and hidden lines to create visible gaps, since they are too short for LTSCALE to show gaps. Save the drawing. The other method uses normal insertion and block redefinition.

OPTIONAL: Insertion and SCRATCH Block Redefinition

Insert Blocks — Insert B-ARM at 0.5 scale as a normal block insertion into the drawing's BDR view. Change the UCS to SCRATCH, restore view SCRATCH, and insert *B-ARM again at full scale to allow editing, taking note of your insertion point for later reference.

Edit Dimensions — Set DIMSCALE to 2 before updating the dimensions, which makes them all twice as big to compensate for the half scale insertion. Use STRETCH, MOVE, SCALE, and the dimension UPDATE command to update each dimension. Make sure LUPREC and all dimension variables are set as needed before updating, scaling, or stretching. Refer to the arm dimensioning exercise in Chapter 5 for the settings. Erase and replace the circle center marks. Use BREAK to break the top view center lines and hidden lines to create visible gaps, since they are too short for LTSCALE to show gaps.

Redefine Block — After all the dimensions are updated, use BLOCK to redefine the B-ARM block, employing the previous insertion point as the insertion base point. Restore view BDR and UCS BDR, and you will find the B-ARM block insertion already updated. Now save your drawing.

OPTIONAL: Numbering and Labeling the Parts and Title Block

Each part in a multi-detail drawing is assigned an identifying part number or letter. In this example, the parts are identified by a number enclosed in a circle (referred to as a bubble). Each bubble is linked to the part it represents by a leader which points from the bubble to the part. Refer to the following illustration for the bubble number/part matchups. (A larger scale of this same illustration is on the facing page of this chapter.) You can also enter the part description text in the parts list, and any additional title block text you desire before plotting.

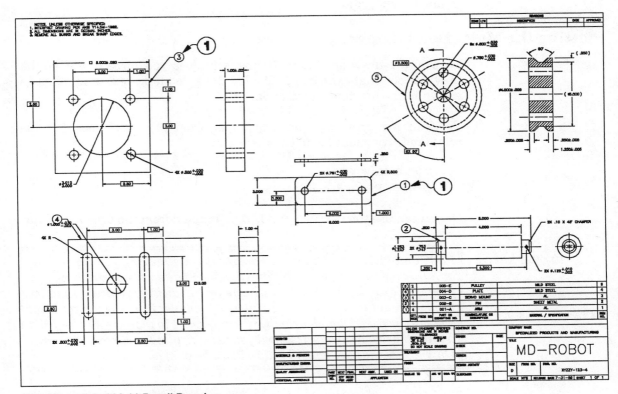

The Completed Multi-Detail Drawing

① **Part Bubbles**

Draw the circles first, with 0.25 radius.

Use STYLE (or the [Options] pull-down [Fonts...] icon menu) to define the new text style ROMAND with font file ROMAND, defaulting all other settings. Use 0.25 high DTEXT with middle justification to enter the key numbers.

Set DIMSCALE to 2 and use the LEADER dimensioning command to draw the leaders. Osnap the first To point: to the circle with NEArest, then cancel the rest of the leader with <^C>.

Set DIMSCALE back to 1 and the text style back to ROMANS.

Thaw all layers and set PART-CX current. Set snap to 0.03125 and zoom in to the parts list to add 0.125 text with DTEXT.

Add any other desired title text or notes, adjusting height to 0.1 as needed and setting the appropriate xxxx-CX layer current.

End the drawing (to plot it from the main menu) or save it (to plot from the drawing editor).

Plotting the Multi-Detail Drawing

To plot the drawing, thaw all layers (unless you already did in the previous optional exercise) to display the title block, text, and notes as shown in the previous illustration.

You can plot from the main menu or from the PLOT (or PRPLOT) command. The main menu choices are:

3. Plot a drawing

4. Printer Plot a drawing

Or you can use the PLOT (or PRPLOT) command from the drawing editor.

PLOT/PRPLOT

> *PLOT and PRPLOT (printer plot) are the two methods for getting output, or hard copies, from your drawing file. PLOT directs your drawing to a plotter or to a plot file. PRPLOT directs your drawing to a printer plotter (such as a dot matrix or laser printer.) If you plot from the main menu, you will be asked which drawing file you want to plot. If you plot from within the drawing, it's assumed you want to plot the current drawing. Only layers that are on and thawed will be plotted.*

For a check plot, scale isn't critical and either plotting or printer plotting is okay (we'll refer generically to either one as *plotting*). If your plotter can't handle D-size, just plot it to FIT (the largest that will fit) instead of 1:1 scale.

Whether you plot from the main menu or from the drawing editor, the plot dialogue as shown in the following exercise is the same.

For both plotters and printers, you may "Write the plot to a file." This will write a file of your current drawing in the output format of your plotter (or printer) configuration. It prompts for file name, and adds the extension .PLT for plotter file or .LST for printer plot file. The file contains data that would have been sent directly to the plotter. Because all circles, curves, and text are converted to lots of little vectors, a .PLT or .LST file may be up to five times larger than a .DWG file.

Plotting to files is useful with RAM-resident plot spooling programs that can plot or print in the background as you draw. Plotting to file may also be necessary for plotting in a network environment or plotting to a port that AutoCAD's configuration doesn't support. For example, if your plotter configures only as a serial device in AutoCAD, but in your system as a network device or parallel port, you can plot to file and then send it to the device or port using network commands, the DOS PRINT command, or the DOS COPY/B command and option.

Assuming you are configured for and connected to a plotter (or printer plotter), let's try plotting.

Plotting the MD-ROBOT Drawing

Enter selection: **3** (or **4** to PRPLOT) from the main menu, and enter drawing name MD-ROBOT.

. . . OR . . .

Continue in the previous MD-ROBOT drawing and enter the PLOT command.

And you get the plot dialogue:

```
What to plot -- Display, Extents, Limits, View or Window <D>: V        View.
View name: BDR                                                         Our border view.

Plot will NOT be written to a selected file
Sizes are in Inches
Plot origin is at (0.00,0.00)
Plotting area is 32.00 wide by 20.00 high (MAX size)
Plot is NOT rotated 90 degrees
Pen width is 0.010
Area fill will NOT be adjusted for pen width
Hidden lines will NOT be removed
Plot will be scaled to fit available area

Do you want to change anything? <N> Y       We'll change pen assignments and scale.
```

Entity Color	Pen No.	Line Type	Pen Speed	Entity Color	Pen No.	Line Type	Pen Speed
1 (red)	1	0	16	9	1	0	16
2 (yellow)	1	0	16	10	1	0	16
3 (green)	1	0	16	11	1	0	16
4 (cyan)	1	0	16	12	1	0	16
5 (blue)	1	0	16	13	1	0	16
6 (magenta)	1	0	16	14	1	0	16
7 (white)	1	0	16	15	1	0	16
8	1	0	16				

```
Line types: 0 = continuous line        Pen speed codes:
            1 = ..................
            2 = .   .   .   .   .   .   .   .   Inches/Second:
            3 = --------------------        1, 2,  4,  8, 16
            4 = - - - - - - - - - -
            5 = -- -- -- -- -- -- -      Cm/Second:
            6 = --- --- --- --- ---         3, 5, 10, 20, 40
            7 = -- - -- - -- - -- -
            8 = __ -- __ -- __ -- __ -

Enter line types, pen speed codes
blank=go to next, Cn=go to Color n, S=Show current choices, X=Exit
Do you want to change any of the above parameters? <N> Y
```

When we set up layers, we decided color 2 (yellow) would be bold, colors 1 (red) and 4 (cyan) would be thin, and the rest would be a medium pen. Now is the time to set these pen/color relationships. The color assignment menu also allows you to set plotter linetypes. Plotter linetypes can be useful for topographic maps and other applications where individual line or arc segments are too short for AutoCAD's software linetypes. We will leave them set to the default 0 (continuous) and rely on software linetypes.

By trial and error, you will learn how fast each type and width of pen can go. Set your pen speed in the color setup below. You have a limited number of speed increments to choose from (see the above exercise) with 1, 2, 4, 8, and 16 denoting inches per second, while 3, 5, 10, 20, and 40 indicate centimeters per second.

The color setup rotates through each color, prompting for pen number, linetype, and pen speed for each. You can shortcut it and jump to any color number at any prompt by entering *Cn*, where *n* is the color number. We show an individual line for each entry below, but the screen doesn't actually scroll during color setup.

Setting Pen/Color and Speed

```
Enter values, blank=Next value, Cn=Color n, S=Show current values, X=Exit

Layer        Pen  Line  Pen
Color        No.  Type  Speed

1 (red)       1    0     16     Pen number <1>: C2        Jump to 2 (yellow).

2 (yellow)    1    0     16     Pen number <1>: 3         Pen 3 will be bold.

2 (yellow)    3    0     16     Line type <0>: <RETURN>   Default.
8
2 (yellow)    3    0     16     Line type <0>: 12         Or the speed that works for you.
```

Continue setting colors 1 (red) and 4 (cyan) to pen 2 (maybe 8 for speed) for thin. The rest can default to pen 1 for medium, but you may need to set speed.

```
4 (cyan)      2    0      8     Pen number <1>: E         Exit.
```

You will now be prompted for plotting to file, units, and several other factors. The plot origin is the lower left extreme of the available plot area. The plotting size is the available plot area for the currently set sheet size. You can enter a standard size, such as A or D, or you can enter X,Y width and height to specify other sizes. Plots can be rotated for landscape or portrait orientation. The plotter pen width should be set to the smallest pen width; it controls the line spacing for area fills and wide polylines. You can adjust area fill boundaries to compensate for pen width, or let the pen center line scribe the boundary. Hidden line removal applies to 3D. Our plotting scale will be 1:1 in this case, but if your plotter doesn't handle D-size, use a smaller scale or enter F for fit.

After you have stepped through all the settings and the plotter and paper is properly set up and positioned, <RETURN> to start the plot.

Units, Origin, and Scale

```
Write the plot to a file? <N> N
Size units (Inches or Millimeters) <I>: <RETURN>
Plot origin in Inches <0.00,0.00>: <RETURN>

Standard values for plotting size
```

Size	Width	Height	
A	10.50	8.00	Your plotter may offer more or fewer sizes.
B	16.00	10.00	
C	21.00	16.00	
MAX	32.00	20.00	

```
Enter the Size or Width,Height (in Inches) <MAX>: <RETURN>    Or D for D-size.

Rotate 2D plots 90 degrees clockwise? <N> <RETURN>
Pen width <0.010>: <RETURN>
Adjust area fill boundaries for pen width? <N> <RETURN>
Remove hidden lines? <N> <RETURN>

Specify scale by entering:
Plotted Inches=Drawing Units or Fit or ? <F>: 1=1
Effective plotting area:  32.00 wide by 20.00 high
Position paper in plotter.
Press RETURN to continue or S to Stop for hardware setup <RETURN>
```

```
Processing vector: 160              It displays a vector count as it plots.
Plot complete.
Press RETURN to continue: <RETURN>  Returns to the main menu or drawing editor.
Command: QUIT                       If you plotted from the drawing.
```

And our robot project is complete.

Summary

This chapter had continued to expand your tool kit of drawing, editing, and dimensioning commands. Its exercises have concentrated on developing new parts for your parts library, calling up and editing a part from your parts library, and using your parts library to assist you in creating the D-size multi-detail drawing from five separate drawings.

The plate and pulley exercises introduced you to many new drafting and editing commands, including the versatile HATCH, and several more of AutoCAd's built-in dimensioning tools. By controlling the dimension linear factor (DIMLFAC) and UPDATE commands, you were able to insert parts from your library at reduced or enlarged scales and yet vary the dimension text height and other dimensioning features to reflect the current drawing requirements.

As you proceed through STEPPING INTO AutoCAD, you will find that blocks are used for many purposes. In our multi-detail drawing, blocks were inserted in various ways, but they were all inserted and scaled in two dimensions. Later exercises will guide you through the development and manipulation of 3D blocks.

Just about all drawings eventually wind up as hard copies. To insure that your parts can be plotted at virtually any scale within your plotter's paper size capabilities, it is essential to begin your drawings from prototype drawings. Whether you plot or printer plot, the dialogue is virtually the same. As the multi-detail exercise shows, plotting may be performed in multiple colors, linetypes, speeds, and thicknesses. Although color and linetypes are useful features, assigning varying pen speeds and thicknesses may prove even more useful. Varying a plot's linetype thickness will certainly enhance a hard copy's readability.

Although AutoCAD makes extensive plotting features available, you should remember that the primary function of hard copies is to convey information from one person to another. Therefore, use the information presented in this chapter to help you keep your plots as readable as possible.

As you continue with Chapter 7, you will be introduced to the procedures for creating and storing a symbols library. The library symbols will then be used to generate ANSI Y14.5 level dimensioning. To make the ANSI Y14.5 symbols more efficient, we will show you how to attach attribute information to them. Chapter 7 also shows you how attributes can automate the generation of parts lists and the extraction of information for bills of materials.

Let's proceed to Chapter 7 and begin building our new symbols library.

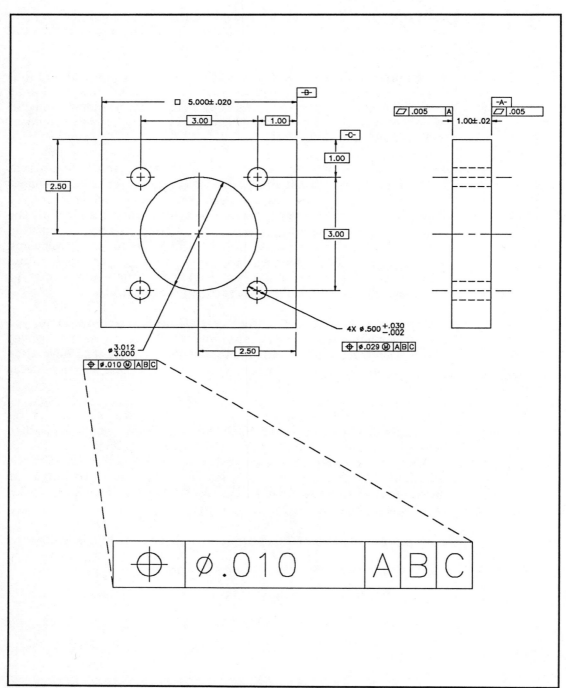

MOUNT Dimensioned With ANSI Y14.5 Symbols

Creating Symbol Libraries and Attributes

Smart Blocks

AutoCAD's *attributes* are special text values (strings of characters) which are part of an inserted block. Attributes allow you to preset text style, height, layer, color, location, and rotation relative to the block. You could preset all of this with ordinary text entities, but you would also have to preset the text value. Once blocked, text entities cannot usually be edited without redefining or exploding the block. With attributes, you can enter the text value at the time of block insertion, and edit the text value or the style, height, layer, color, location, and rotation at any time without exploding or redefining the block. Unlike text, attributes have a prompt to tell the user what sort of value is expected upon insertion.

Attributes were designed for attaching data, such as model numbers, sizes, quantities, and brand names to blocks. We call these data-laden parts. This data can be accessed or extracted for use in bills of materials or external database programs. And attributes have a second, equally valuable, use. You can use them to preset, control, and prompt for text such as title block text or symbol identifiers. We call these *smart symbols* or *intelligent text*.

You need numerous standard symbols to do full ANSI Y14.5 drafting and dimensioning. Creating a library of symbol blocks saves you the trouble of having to draw these symbols repeatedly. Symbol libraries can consist of virtually any drafting symbol. If you find yourself repeatedly drafting or copying a geometric object, it should probably be made into a symbol. Making a symbol library, or buying a commercially developed library, will increase your productivity regardless of your drafting application.

Typical drafting symbol libraries include ANSI Y14.5M GDT (geometric dimensioning and tolerancing) symbols, and welding, fastening, piping, electronic, fluid power, and architectural symbols. Many of these symbols have associated text. The productivity of a GDT symbols library can be greatly enhanced by incorporating text in the form of attributes into the blocks. Such attributes can prompt upon block insertion for values (like form tolerance) and then automatically insert the values as text with the style, scale, and position controlled.

This chapter steps you through using attributes to create a library of GDT symbols for dimensioning by ANSI Y14.5M-1982 standards, to attach data to parts, and to extract that data for bills of materials. After completing the exercises in this chapter, you will be able to create your own custom symbols and data-laden parts for any drafting application.

The symbols we create in this chapter will be used in the next chapter for geometric dimensioning and tolerancing. If you have the SIA DISK, you already have these symbols, so you can pick and choose which chapter exercises you want to do. If you don't thoroughly understand attributes, or if you don't have the SIA DISK, you should do it all.

The ANSI Y14.5 Menu System

The exercises in this chapter develop several of the ANSI Y14.5 symbols used in the SIA DISK's Y14.5 Menu System. This custom menu system with its AutoLISP, macros, and standardized symbols provides a good example of how symbol libraries can make your drafting more productive. If you would like to develop a complete ANSI symbols library on your own, we recommend the document entitled *American National Standard Engineering Drawings and Related Document Practices, Dimensioning and Tolerancing: ANSI Y14.5M-1982.*

Building Smart Symbols With Attributes

Symbols may be created in any shape and size that AutoCAD can draw. Our first, a feature control frame, is two simple boxes with an attribute for the tolerance. We'll get to the creation of the attribute in a moment, but first let's plan how it will be scaled and inserted.

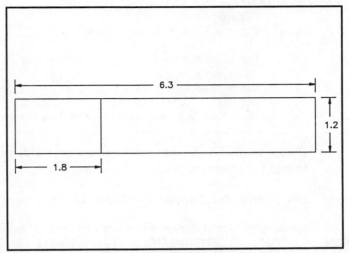

Feature Control Frame Sized for 1-Inch Text

The scaling method used for our Y14.5 symbols is the same as that used by AutoCAD for dimensioning and dimension text. Set DIMTXT to the height that you want the text to appear in the plotted output, 0.125 in our case. Set DIMSCALE to the drawing plot scale, such as 4 for a quarter-scale drawing. When AutoCAD draws a dimension, it scales the text to DIMSCALE x DIMTXT, or 0.125 x 4 = 0.5 inch text in this example. Then when the drawing is plotted at quarter scale, the text ends up 0.5 divided by 4, or 0.125 again.

We could make our attribute symbol text 0.125 and scale the rest of the symbol geometry proportionately, but that would lock us into a 0.125 text standard. Instead, we'll make the attribute symbol text one inch high and insert it at DIMSCALE x DIMTXT. That allows us to change the DIMTXT to any standard we like, change DIMSCALE to any drawing plot scale needed, and still be sure the symbols are inserted at the right scale. This is the method used by the Y14.5 Menu System for scaling dimensions, text, and symbols.

Let's draw the frame, sized proportionately to one-inch text.

Drawing a Feature Control Frame

Enter Selection: **1.**	Begin a NEW drawing named TEMP.
Command: **LAYER**	Freeze TITL-* and set layer DIM current.
Command: **ZOOM**	To a height of 10.
Command: **SNAP**	Set to 0.25.
Command: **LINE**	Draw 10.5 x 2 box, with dividing line illustrated above.

Before we make a block of the feature control frame, we'll use attributes to add the tolerance text.

Attributes: Intelligent Symbol Text

ATTDEF	*ATTDEF (ATTribute DEFinition) defines how attribute text will be prompted for and stored. Attributes are saved in blocks which can contain additional entities.* *(See prompts in exercise below.)*

Three other commands and two entities make up the world of attributes. We'll define the commands in more detail when we use them later in the chapter. They are:

> **ATTDISP** — Controls the display mode of the attribute after the block is inserted.

> **ATTEDIT** — Allows editing of the attribute text after it has been inserted into a drawing.

> **ATTEXT** — Extracts attribute text and formats it in report form.

The ATTDEF command creates an entity called an *attdef*. An attdef contains all the text style, height, layer, color, location, and rotation information for the attribute, as well as a *tag* name (used to extract its data), a default text value, and a prompt. To use an attribute, you make it part of a block. The block usually contains other entities, but can be nothing but an attdef. You can make it a block with the BLOCK command, or by inserting a drawing file that contains attdefs into the current drawing. Such a drawing file can be created by wblocking attdefs (and other entities) to disk. The CHANGE command can be used to change the attribute definition before it is blocked.

When you insert an attribute-laden block, it creates an entity called an *attrib*. Attrib entities are subentities of insert entities (inserted blocks) and are accessible only by AutoLISP, LIST, ATTDISP, ATTEDIT, or

ATTEXT. You can't select them independently of the block insert. If you explode the block insert, it destroys the attribs and reverts them to attdefs.

Defining an Attribute

The following exercise creates an attribute definition which, when inserted in the Y14.5 feature control frame block, prompts the user for a form tolerance value and then inserts the value (text) into the frame. An attribute definition has Invisible, Constant, Verify, and Preset modes which are on (Y) or off (N). These will be explained later. For now, we'll use the normal defaults (all off) which make visible, variable attributes.

Let's attach a variable attribute to the feature control frame.

Creating a Tolerance Value Attdef

Continue in the previous TEMP drawing.

```
Command: ATTDEF
Attribute modes — Invisible:N  Constant:N  Verify:N  Preset:N
Enter (ICVP) to change, RETURN when done: <RETURN>        Leave all at default N.
Attribute tag: TOLERANCE                                  The identifying label.
Attribute prompt: Enter form tolerance
Default attribute value: <RETURN>                         Blank default.
Start point or Align/Center/Fit/Middle/Right/Style:       Pick 0.5 right and up
                                                          from corner of tolerance frame ①.
Height <0.1250>: 1                                        Set for 1" text height.
Rotation angle <0>: <RETURN>
```

Now you have an attdef entity, which displays its tag name at its start point. To make this usable as an attribute, you must make it a block.

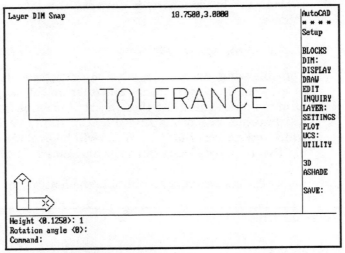

Tolerance Attdef

Including Attributes in Blocks

Attributes may be stored with any block, or may even be the only entities in a block. The BLOCK command only defines a block in the current drawing, so we'll use WBLOCK to write a drawing file that can be used as a block in any drawing. Let's store the form tolerance attribute with the feature control frame as a drawing named S-FRAME.

Wblocking the Frame and Tolerance Attribute

```
Command: WBLOCK
File name: S-FRAME
Block name (or ?): <RETURN>
Insertion base point:              Pick lower left corner of left frame.
Select objects: W                  Select both frames and the attdef.
6 found.
Select objects: <RETURN>
```

The frames and attribute disappear and are written to the S-FRAME.DWG file. But what if you decide to change some of the data in the attdef entity?

Editing Attribute Definitions

If you haven't yet created the block with WBLOCK or the BLOCK command, you can use the CHANGE command to edit attdef entities. It works much like the CHANGE command for editing text entities, with additional tag and attribute prompts.

To change the attribute definition after making the block definition, you can either use INSERT to insert *blockname*, or you can use EXPLODE to explode a previously inserted attribute-laden block. Either command will separate the block into its individual entities, including the original attdef. EXPLODE will destroy any existing attrib entities in the exploded block. In either case, CHANGE can modify the attdef and then redefine the block. If you redefine the block in the current drawing with BLOCK, it won't be available in other drawings unless wblocked to disk. If you write it to a drawing file with WBLOCK, it isn't automatically redefined in the current drawing. To redefine such a block in the current drawing, use INSERT with an equal sign to reinsert and redefine the block, like INSERT *blockname=filename*.

Be careful when redefining attribute-laden blocks, because all existing insertions of the block will be affected. Existing constant attributes will be lost and replaced by new constant attributes. Existing variable attributes will be retained in previous block insertions, but new variable attributes will not be added. To use new variable attributes, erase the block inserts and reinsert them.

Fortunately, you can also edit individual attrib entities (not attdefs) *after* insertion. We'll see how after we insert a couple of blocks.

Inserting Attribute-Laden Blocks

When you insert a block with an attribute, you are prompted for standard block information like insertion point, scale, and rotation. If it is a normal variable attribute, you are prompted for the value. Let's insert the feature control frame (S-FRAME) block with its attribute.

Inserting a Block With Attributes

```
Command: INSERT
Block name (or ?): S-FRAME
Insertion point:                          Pick a point.
X scale factor <1> / Corner / XYZ: .5     Scale as a quarter scale drawing with 0.125 text
                                          (0.125 x 4).
Y scale factor (default=X): <RETURN>
Rotation angle <0>: <RETURN>
Enter attribute values
Enter form tolerance: .003                Enter up to four-digit tolerance value.
```

When the feature control frame block is inserted, you will see the `Enter form tolerance:` prompt. Entering this value automatically inserts it into the feature control frame at the appropriate scale and location.

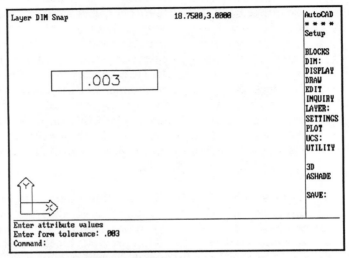

Inserted S-FRAME With Tolerance

We created an insert entity with an attrib subentity attached. Invoking the LIST command and selecting the block insert will display data for both the insert and attrib entities.

Notice that the block dragged at full scale before insertion. It would be nice if you could drag the block into place at the insert scale rather than the defined scale.

Presetting Block Scale and Rotation

Because you have to give an insertion point first, then specify scale and angle, you can't see the angle or the final size of the block until after it has been placed. This makes it hard to visually drag blocks into place. You have the option of presetting the scale and rotation, thereby establishing the scale or angle, *before* the insertion. With presets, you can drag the block at the right scale and angle as you pick the insertion point.

The preset options are not shown in the insert prompt:

> **Scale** and **PScale** will prompt for scale factor which will be preset to X, Y, and Z axes.
>
> **Xscale** and **PXscale** only preset an X scale factor.
>
> **Yscale** and **PYscale** only preset a Y scale factor.

Zscale and **PZscale** only preset a Z scale factor.

Rotate and **PRotate** preset rotation angle, which you can enter from the keyboard or by picking two points.

Type the first one or two characters of the preset option at the insertion point prompt. Options prefixed with a P establish a preliminary scale and rotation value to aid in insertion. Then, after the insertion point is selected, the normal prompts are displayed so you can change the preset values. You cannot mix fixed presets, like Xscale, with preliminary presets, like PYscale. If you try to mix them, the preliminary presets become fixed, and you will not be reprompted for their values after the insertion.

Let's reinsert the S-FRAME block with a preset scale.

Block Inserts With Presets

Continue in the previous TEMP drawing.

```
Command: INSERT
Block name (or ?) <S-FRAME>: <RETURN>
 Insertion point: S                    Scale.
 Scale factor: .625
 Insertion point:                      Drag it and pick a point.
 Rotation angle <0>: <RETURN>
Enter attribute values
Enter form tolerance: %%c.005          Try a diameter symbol.
```

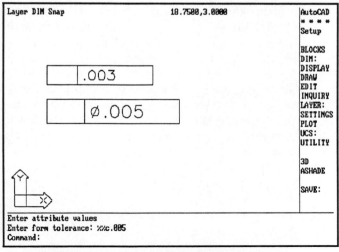

S-FRAME With Diameter, Inserted With Preset Scale

Preset options are great in menu macros which transparently apply preset options, making dragging while in the INSERT command natural and easy. This is how the Y14.5 Menu System inserts the GDT symbols.

Editing Attributes

Inserted blocks containing attributes may be copied, moved, scaled, rotated, and arrayed as a whole. You can also edit any value or parameter of existing attrib entities after insertion. The ATTEDIT command allows you to edit attributes without exploding their block insert.

ATTEDIT

> *ATTEDIT (ATTribute EDIT) lets you edit attributes, individually or globally. The default setting edits attributes one at a time, allowing you to change value, position, height, angle, style, layer, or color. Global edits are confined to changing value. You can control your selection set by block name, tag name, or attribute value.*
> `Edit attributes one at a time? <Y>`

To globally edit attributes, respond to the ATTEDIT command's `Edit attributes one at a time? <Y>` prompt with **N**. Global editing is limited to changing the attrib text value itself, not any of the other parameters.

To edit attributes individually, respond with a **Y** or `<RETURN>` to the `Edit attributes one at a time? <Y>` prompt. Use normal object selection to select the attribs (not the blocks), and you will see the `Value/Position/Height/Angle/Style/Layer/Color/Next <N>:` prompt for each. When it prompts, it marks each attribute with an "X" so you can keep track of which one you are editing. The "X" stays on the current attrib until you tell it to move on with a `<RETURN>` or **N** (for Next), so you can edit any or all parameters. When editing the text value, you are prompted to `Change or Replace <R>` it.

Global editing or individually changing the text value works like a word processor's global search and replace, prompting you for the `String to change:` and the `New string:` to substitute in the old string's place. If the string to change occurs more than once in a single attribute, only the first occurrence is changed.

Whether editing text one occurrence at a time or globally, you can filter the attributes to be edited. AutoCAD allows you to use wildcard characters (* or ?) to restrict block names, attribute tags, or attribute text values, like AL*A or R??ROO. The default * specifies all attributes.

Let's edit the attributes in our feature control frame block.

Editing Attributes

```
Command: ATTEDIT                                   Try a global edit.
Edit attributes one at a time? <Y> N
Global edit of attribute values.
Edit only attributes visible on screen? <Y> <RETURN>
Block name specification <*>: S-FRAME             Our block name.
Attribute tag specification <*>: TOL*             Our tag was TOLERANCE.
Attribute value specification <*>: <RETURN>
Select Attributes: C                              Select both with crossing window.
2 attributes selected.
String to change: %%c                             Search for all diameter symbols.
New string: <RETURN>                              Replace with nothing, deleting them.

Command: <RETURN>                                 Try individually changing position and layer.
ATTEDIT
Edit attributes one at a time? <Y> <RETURN>
Block name specification <*>: <RETURN>
Attribute tag specification <*>: <RETURN>
Attribute value specification <*>: <RETURN>
Select Attributes: C                              Select them all.
2 attributes selected.
Value/Position/Height/Angle/Style/Layer/Color/Next <N>: P        Position.
Enter text insertion point:          Drag it and pick a new point.
Value/Position/Height/Angle/Style/Layer/Color/Next <N>: <RETURN>  Next.
Value/Position/Height/Angle/Style/Layer/Color/Next <N>: L         Layer.
New layer : TEXT
Value/Position/Height/Angle/Style/Layer/Color/Next <N>: <RETURN>  Next.

Command: ERASE                                    Clean the screen. Erase both.
```

The attributes were updated to reflect the editing, as shown below.

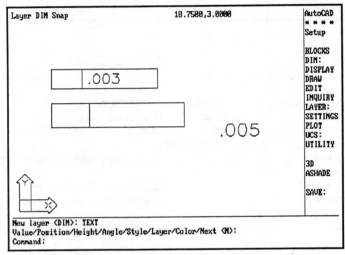

Edited Attributes

When you have both normal text information to present and the need for variable attributes in blocks, it is better to use attributes for both. Text entities within blocks cannot be changed without redefining the block, which would destroy the attributes.

There is another convenient tool for editing attributes.

Attribute Editing and Insertion By Dialogue Box

If your system supports dialogue boxes (which require the AUI), you may edit attributes with the DDATTE command.

DDATTE
> DDATTE (Dynamic Dialogue ATTribute Edit) edits attribute string values with a dialogue box. You can only edit one block at a time. It presents the current value and lets you specify a new value.

DDATTE provides a nice visual interface but is limited to selecting a single block and editing all the attribute text values that it contains. It cannot edit other parameters, such as position.

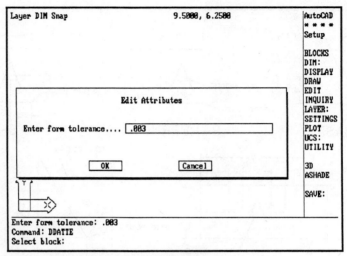

DDATTE Attribute Edit Dialogue Box

Attribute Entry by Dialogue Box

Attribute information is normally prompted for on the command line during the INSERT command. However, if your system supports AUI and the system variable ATTDIA (attribute dialogue) is set to a non-zero value, the same attribute dialogue box that DDATTE uses (shown above) is instead used to enter attribute values during block insertions.

Finishing the Y14.5 GDT Symbol Library

Unless you have the SIA DISK, you need to use the techniques presented above to create and wblock the remaining symbols to be used for the dimensioning exercises in the next chapter. The SIA DISK's Y14.5 Menu System includes all of the following symbols and more.

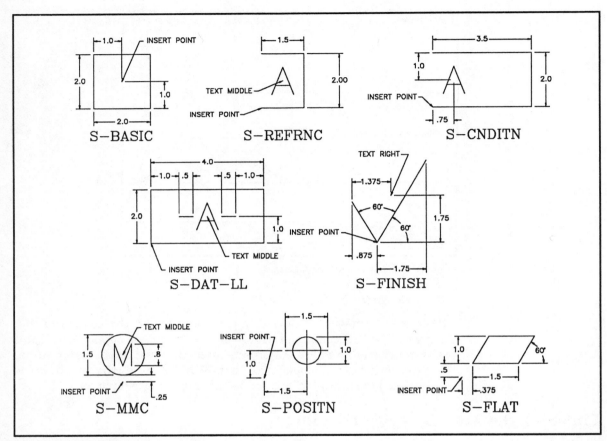

The Y14.5 GDT Symbols Library

Use the following table to help you define the attributes in the above symbols. All use the default modes (N for each of the invisible, constant, verify, and preset modes) and text style ROMANS. For the sake of completeness, information for the S-FRAME symbol you already made is included.

Block Name	Attribute Tag	Attribute Prompt	Default	Justification
S-BASIC	(none)			
S-CNDITN	DATUM	Datum	A	Middle
S-DAT-LL	DATUM	Datum	A	Middle
S-FINISH	FINISH	Finish value	(none)	Right
S-FLAT	(none)			
S-FRAME	TOLERANCE	Enter form tolerance	(none)	Left (start point)
S-MMC	(none — letter M is just text)			
S-POSITN	(none)			
S-REFRNC	DATUM	Datum	A	Middle

Y14.5 GDT Symbols and Attributes

The insertion points for the above symbols are shown in the illustration. Now, let's make the symbols.

Making the Symbols

 You have the symbol drawing files. Skip this exercise.

 Continue to create the symbols shown above.

Continue in the previous TEMP drawing or start a new drawing named TEMP.

Command: **LAYER**	Freeze TITL-* and set layer DIM current.
Command: **ZOOM**	To a height of 10.
Command: **SNAP**	Set to 0.25.

Command: **LINE**	Draw the three sides of the S-CNDITN box.
Command: **ATTDEF**	Define S-CNDITN's DATUM attribute as shown above.
Command: **WBLOCK**	Wblock the attribute and lines to filename S-CNDITN with the illustrated base point.

Repeat the process for *each* of the symbols in the above table and illustration.

Command: **INSERT**	Test *each* symbol by inserting it.
Command: **QUIT**	The wblocking saved the symbols.

We'll use these symbols for Chapter 8's geometric dimensioning and tolerancing exercises. Meanwhile, let's proceed to the next section on creating data-laden parts and extracting their attribute information.

Creating Parts and Extracting Their Data

Attributes can automate the creation and extraction of information like part numbers, part descriptions, material, specification numbers, and cost. This is the type of information on a drawing's parts list. Let's extract a simple parts list from the attribute tags and values attached to a .25-20UNC 2A hexagonal head cap screw (hex bolt). Here is a typical parts list:

QTY-REQD	CODE	LENGTH	EST-COST
4	HX01	1.50	.78

Example of Extracted Parts List Attribute Information

Adding attributes can be time consuming, but being able to extract the information for parts lists and estimates makes it worth the time spent. To keep our exercise simple, we'll use just the **QTY-REQD**, **CODE**, **LENGTH**, and **EST-COST** attributes to demonstrate a variety of modes.

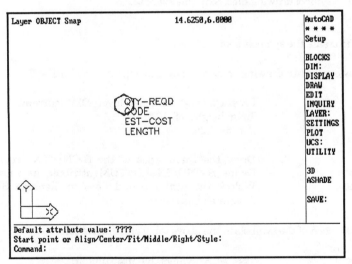

Bolt Head With Attribute Tags

First we'll draw a .25-20UNC 2A X 1.50 hex bolt and block it with attribute information defining a typical parts list description. Then we'll insert it several times and extract the attribute information needed to generate a parts list.

You can easily draw the hex bolt head with the POLYGON and ROTATE commands.

POLYGON

> *The POLYGON command draws 2D regular (all sides equal) polygons from 3 to 1024 sides. The size of the polygon is determined by specifying the radius of a circle in which the polygon is inscribed (inside), or circumscribed (outside), or by specifying the length of one of the polygon's sides. Polygons are closed polylines. Use PEDIT to edit polygons.*
> `Number of sides:   Edge/<Center of Polygon>:`
> `Inscribed in circle/Circumscribed about circle (I/C):`

ROTATE

> *ROTATE lets you rotate entities around a designated base or pivot point. The rotation angle can be entered as a numeric angle, by picking a point relative to the base point, or by a reference angle option. The reference option lets you specify the rotation angle relative to a base angle, usually on an existing entity.*
> `<Rotation angle>/Reference:`

If you have the SIA DISK, you can skip to the insertion and data extraction portion of this sequence, but if you aren't familiar with the invisible, constant, verify, and preset attribute modes, you should follow the entire exercise.

Drawing the Bolt

 You have the HX25-20 file. Start a new TEMP drawing and continue, or you may skip this exercise.

 Begin a NEW drawing named TEMP and continue.

`Command: ZOOM`	Zoom to a height of 4 in a clear area.
`Command: POLYGON`	Create the head view of the bolt.
`Number of sides: 6`	
`Edge/<Center of Polygon>:`	Pick any point.
`Inscribed in circle/Circumscribed about circle (I/C): C`	Circumscribed.
`Radius of circle: .1875`	Half distance across flats for .25 bolt's head.
`Command: ROTATE`	It draws it at the wrong angle.
`Select objects: L`	Select last.
`Base point: @`	Last point.
`<Rotation angle>/Reference: 90`	
`Command: CIRCLE`	Draw a .1875 radius circle at the same lastpoint. (The circle may not look round until regenerated.)
`Command: SAVE`	

We need to set the attribute modes and define the attribute tags to be attached to the bolt. These won't be the default visible variable attributes.

Attribute Modes

Remember that an attribute definition has invisible, constant, verify, and preset modes, which can be on (Y) or off (N). Here is a more complete explanation:

Invisible — When off (the default), the attribute value will be displayed on the screen and plotted normally; when on, the inserted attribute is invisible.

Constant — The default, off, creates a *variable* attribute, prompting for value each time the block is inserted into the drawing. If on, it assigns the attribute a fixed (constant) value for all insertions. A constant attribute cannot be edited after insertion.

Verify — Off, the default, inserts the attributes without user verification; if on, you are prompted to verify each value upon insertion.

Preset — If off, variable attribute values are prompted for during block insertion. If on, prompts are suppressed and the default value will be assigned. This inserts variable attributes as if they were constant attributes, except it allows the values to be edited after insertion. The system variable ATTREQ has the same effect when applied globally to all attributes. If ATTREQ is 1 (on, the default) non-preset variable attributes are prompted for during insertion. If ATTREQ is 0 (off) the default values are used.

These modes have been at their N (or off) defaults for everything so far. We'll use examples of all four modes in the HX25-20 block. The attributes and modes are shown in the following table.

Tag	I	C	V	P	Attribute Prompt	Default	Constant
QTY-REQD	Y	N	Y	N	Quantity required	1	
CODE	Y	Y	N	N	(none)	(none)	HX01
EST-COST	Y	N	N	Y	Estimated Cost	.78	
LENGTH	Y	N	N	N	Length	????	

HX25-20 Bolt Block Attributes

All of these will be left justified, the default. We'll set the modes listed as we define each attdef. All are invisible, so they won't clutter up the finished drawing. They could be placed on a separate layer to provide even more control over the visibility and colors.

QTY-REQD is variable, like all previous attdefs in this chapter, but it is also in verify mode, so it will prompt for an extra confirmation of value upon insertion. CODE shouldn't change from one insertion to another, so it has a constant value. EST-COST might change, but we think it will be .78, so we preset it. Like a constant, it inserts without prompting but can be changed later by ATTEDIT. LENGTH is a simple variable attribute. Its ???? default is a good place holder for values that you may not know upon initial insertion. You can <RETURN> to skip them, then later replace then with ATTEDIT. It's easy to search on ???? for a global update.

Let's set modes and define attdefs. To set modes, keep entering the I, C, V, or P letter key at the attribute modes prompt until the prompt shows the right combination. Then enter a <RETURN> to continue. Each time you enter one of the key letters I, C, V, or P, it toggles the current state of that mode.

Setting Attribute Modes

Continue in the previous TEMP drawing.

```
Command: ATTDEF
Attribute modes — Invisible:N  Constant:N  Verify:N  Preset:N
Enter (ICVP) to change, RETURN when done: I          Sets Invisible: Y.
Attribute modes — Invisible:Y  Constant:N  Verify:N  Preset:N
Enter (ICVP) to change, RETURN when done: V          Sets Verify: Y.
Attribute modes — Invisible:Y  Constant:N  Verify:Y  Preset:N
Enter (ICVP) to change, RETURN when done: <RETURN>

Attribute tag: QTY-REQD
Attribute prompt: Quantity required
Default attribute value: 1
Start point or Align/Center/Fit/Middle/Right/Style:      Pick center of head.
Height <0.1250>: <RETURN>
Rotation angle <0>: <RETURN>
```

```
Command: <RETURN>                    Repeat for CODE attdef.
ATTDEF                               Toggle C and V to set Invisible:Y Constant:Y Verify:N Preset:N.
Attribute tag: CODE
Attribute value: HX01
Start point or Align/Center/Fit/Middle/Right/Style: <RETURN>    Defaults below previous.

Command: <RETURN>                    Repeat for EST-COST attdef.
ATTDEF                               Toggle C and P to set Invisible:Y Constant:N Verify:N Preset:Y.
Attribute tag: EST-COST
Attribute prompt: Estimated cost
Default attribute value: .78         Value will be entered by preset insertion.
Start point or Align/Center/Fit/Middle/Right/Style: <RETURN>

Command: <RETURN>                    Repeat for LENGTH attdef.
ATTDEF                               Toggle P to set Invisible:Y Constant:N Verify:N Preset:N.
Attribute tag: LENGTH
Attribute prompt: Length
Default attribute value: ????
Start point or Align/Center/Fit/Middle/Right/Style: <RETURN>

Command: SAVE
```

After you repeat the ATTDEF command and are prompted for the text
"Start point or...," the previous attribute tag highlights. If you
<RETURN> at this point, it places the new tag directly below the previous,
just like repeated TEXT commands.

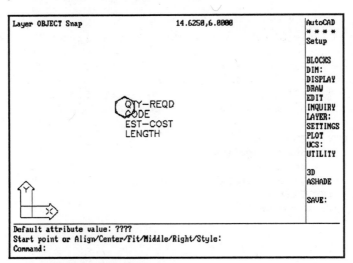

Bolt Head With Attribute Tags

When you select multiple attributes to block, you need to pay attention
to the order of selection.

Attribute Selection Order

With no or only one attribute, you don't have to worry about selection order when wblocking or blocking. But with multiple attributes, you should control the order of the prompts upon insertion. You can do this by the order of selection when blocking or wblocking. If you just select all by a window or crossing, they will come back in the reverse order of creation, because AutoCAD finds most recent entities before older ones. You can plan for this when you create them, or you can select the attdef entities one at a time in the order you choose.

Blocking the Bolt and its Attributes

Continue in the previous TEMP drawing.

```
Command: BLOCK
Block name (or ?): HX25-20
Insertion base point:             Pick the center of the head.
Select objects:                   Select the circle and polygon.
Select objects:                   Pick each attdef in order created, top to bottom.
Select objects: <RETURN>          The bolt head and attdefs disappear.
```

Now the block is defined in the current drawing. We're going to discard this TEMP drawing after we've explored attributes, so wblock it if you want to save it permanently.

OPTIONAL: Wblocking an Existing Block

```
Command: WBLOCK
File name: HX25-20
Block name: =     Writes the block definition equal to the file name.
```

When you insert the HX25-20 block, its attributes will be controlled by the modes that were set when you defined it.

Invisible, Constant, Verify, and Preset Inserts

Recall that QTY-REQD is variable with verify mode, CODE is constant, EST-COST is preset to .78, and LENGTH is a simple variable attribute with a ???? place holder default. Let's observe the action of these as we insert the block with attributes back into the current drawing.

Inserting the HX25-20 Block Attributes

 Continue in the previous TEMP drawing or begin a NEW drawing named TEMP.

 Continue in the previous TEMP drawing.

```
Command: ZOOM                  Zoom to a height of 2.

Command: INSERT
Block name (or ?): HX25-20
Insertion point:               Pick point at top left, then <RETURN> to default scale and rotation.

Enter attribute values
Quantity required <1>: 4
Length <????>: <RETURN>        Default and change it later.
                               The constant CODE and preset EST-COST are inserted without prompting.
Verify attribute values
Quantity required <4>: <RETURN>  Reprompts for verification with entered value as default.

Command: <RETURN>
INSERT                         Insert another at middle left with quantity 2 and length 3.

Command: SAVE
```

When the block is inserted, the attribute values are invisible. You may, however, want to control attribute visibility for verification and editing.

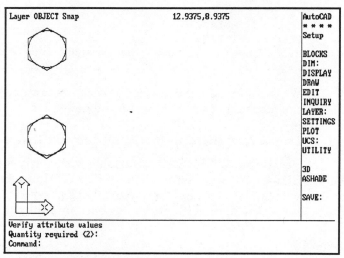

Inserted Bolt With Invisible Attributes

Controlling Attribute Visibility

When you use invisible attributes, you may need to override the invisibility to check or modify values. The command ATTDISP globally sets attribute display mode after insertion.

ATTDISP

> *ATTDISP (ATTtribute DISPlay) controls attribute visibility after insertion. ATTDISP overrides the ATTDEF invisible/visible settings. The default is Normal, which lets the modes set by ATTDEF control visibility individually.*
> `Normal/ON/OFF <Off>:`

Let's make the HX25-20 block's attributes visible so we can check and edit them. The ATTDISP command toggles the attribute display normal, on, and off. Notice that the values are displayed, not the tags.

Editing Invisible Attributes

Continue in the previous TEMP drawing.

```
Command: ATTDISP
Normal/ON/OFF <Normal>: ON                  And the attribute values are displayed.

Command: ATTEDIT                            Or use the DDATTE command.
Edit attributes one at a time? <Y> <RETURN>
Block name specification <*>: <RETURN>
Attribute tag specification <*>: <RETURN>
Attribute value specification <*>: <RETURN>
Select Attributes:          Pick .78 and ???? values in top left insertion, then <RETURN>.
Value/Position/Height/Angle/Style/Layer/Color/Next <N>: V    Value.
                            Change .78 to .63 and ???? to 2.5 using the Replace option.

Command: ATTDISP
Normal/ON/OFF <On>: N       Now set the attribute display to normal.
                            After regeneration, the values disappear from the screen.
Command: SAVE
```

The following illustration shows the edited values before we set ATTEDIT back to normal.

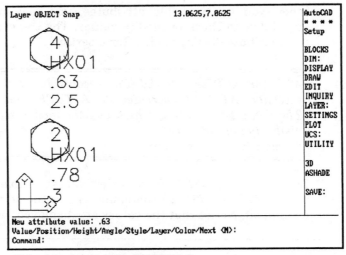

Edited Attributes With ATTEDIT On

Setting ATTEDIT to off makes all attributes, even normally visible ones, invisible. ATTEDIT resets the ATTMODE system variable, which can also be used by SETVAR to control visibility. ATTMODE 0 is off, 1 is normal, and 2 is on.

Now that we've created and inserted data-laden blocks, let's see how to extract the data.

Extracting Attribute Information

The ATTEXT command extracts attributes and writes a file. Databases or spreadsheet programs can then process the extracted file for analysis and report generation.

ATTEXT

> *Use ATTEXT (ATTribute EXTract) to extract attribute data from your drawing. This information is formatted into an ASCII text file in one of three possible formats: CDF, SDF, or DXF. (See below.) CDF is the default format. You can extract all attributes, or select certain entities to extract attributes from.*
>
> CDF, SDF, or DXF Attribute extract (or Entities) <C>:

In order to make sense of extracted attribute information, you need a way to format the *fields* (items) of data. When you use ATTEXT, you are prompted for one of the following output formats:

CDF (Comma Delimited File) — Produces a format which contains one record for each block reference. The data fields are separated by commas, and their width varies with the width of the extracted data. CDF is easy to use with BASIC programs. Additionally, some database packages, like dBASE III, can read this format directly with an APPEND FROM...DELIMITED operation.

SDF (Standard Data File) — Is considered the standard for input to microcomputer databases. SDF files use spaces to separate and standardize the data fields, usually aligning the data into columns. If the extracted data width exceeds the space allocated in the SDF template, the data will be truncated. SDF is used mostly for FORTRAN programs, for dBASE COPY...SDF files, or for dBASE APPEND FROM...SDF operations.

DXF (Drawing Interchange File) — Is AutoCAD's format, and is most commonly used by third-party programs. ATTEXT uses a subset of the DXF file format.

```
'HX25-20', 4,'HX01', 0.63, 2.500
'HX25-20', 2,'HX01', 0.78, 3.000
```

PART-CDF.TXT — Sample CDF Output

```
HX25-20          4HX01        0.63   2.500
HX25-20          2HX01        0.78   3.000
```

PART-SDF.TXT — Sample SDF Output

To create a CDF or SDF file, you need to provide a *template* file for ATTEXT to use. (The DXF format is a fixed format, and needs no template.) The following exercise goes through the process of creating a template and extracting the data, but does not process the data further. You need a program such as dBASE III or IV, Lotus 123, or even a word processor to process the data. Processed data can then be imported back into AutoCAD. For example, Lotus might tabulate quantities and generate a bill of materials that would be imported into AutoCAD as text. Using Lotus and dBASE to import and process data is covered in the book, INSIDE AutoLISP, also from New Riders Publishing.

The first step is to create a template.

Template Files

The template file is a format instruction list which tells AutoCAD where to put the information in the extracted data file. If you have the SIA DISK, you already have the BOLT.TXT template file. Otherwise, you will need to create the following file in an ASCII text format. You can do so with DOS's EDLIN program editor, or with most other text editors or word processors in programming (nondocument) mode. See Appendix A for more information on text files and text editors.

```
BL:NAME      C011000
QTY-REQD     N004000
CODE         C008000
EST-COST     N008002
LENGTH       N008003
```

BOLT.TXT Template File

Each line of the template file has two items. The first is the attribute tag name, like QTY-REQD, which must match exactly. The second defines the output format for that field, for example N004000. The format specification has three parts. The first is the character **N** or **C** which determines if the data is to be treated as a number or a character (alphanumeric). The next three digits define the total field width in characters. The last three digits define the number of characters following the decimal of floating point (real) numbers. If the last three digits are zeros, the number is treated as an integer and any decimal portion is rounded off.

In addition to tag names, we can also extract information about the block itself, like BL:NAME for the block's name. Using BL:X, BL:Y, or BL:Z could give us additional information about the block's coordinate position. Other extractable block information includes nesting level, counter number, entity handle, layer, rotation angle, X, Y, and Z scale, and 3D extrusion components. See your AutoCAD Reference Manual for details.

Let's create the above template and extract both a CDF and an SDF file using the BOLT.TXT template.

Extracting Attributes

 You have the BOLT.TXT file. Continue in the previous TEMP drawing.

 Create the above BOLT.TXT file. Then continue in the previous TEMP drawing.

```
Command: ATTEXT
CDF, SDF, or DXF Attribute extract (or Entities) <C>: C          CDF.
Template file: BOLT
Extract file name <TEMP>: PART-CDF
2 records in extract file.

Command: ATTEXT
CDF, SDF, or DXF Attribute extract (or Entities) <C>: S          SDF.
Template file <BOLT>: <RETURN>
Extract file name <TEMP>: PART-SDF
2 records in extract file.

Command: QUIT
```

That produced the two extract files, PART-CDF.TXT and PART-SDF.TXT shown earlier. The PART-SDF file is repeated below so we can look at one problem.

```
HX25-20        4HX01        0.63    2.500
HX25-20        2HX01        0.78    3.000
```

PART-SDF.TXT — Sample SDF Format

Notice how the 4 in the first numeric field runs into the HX01 of the CODE field. That's because numbers are right justified and character fields are left justified. That doesn't hurt if you are using the extract file as food for a spreadsheet, database, or other program that knows where to start reading each field, but it's a nuisance if you simply want to export a list, format it in your word processor, and print it out. There is a way to add blank columns between fields in the extract file. Just use a *dummy* tag name in the template. Since ATTEXT won't find any attributes for it, it will output as a blank.

Our BOLT.TXT template with an added dummy tag would be:

```
BL:NAME      C011000
QTY-REQD     N004000
DUMMY        C002000
CODE         C008000
EST-COST     N008002
LENGTH       N008003
```

BOLT.TXT Template File With Dummy Tag

An SDF extract using this file would add two blanks between the QTY-REQD and CODE fields, producing:

```
HX25-20      4   HX01      0.63   2.500
HX25-20      2   HX01      0.78   3.000
```

PART-SDF.TXT With Added Spaces

➡ *NOTE: Be careful not to use the same (or default) name for both the template and the extract file, or the extract file will overwrite the template.*

Summary

This chapter has given you a foundation, in the form of an efficient and productive symbols library, upon which your ANSI Y14.5 dimensioning system may be built. Developing the Y14.5 symbols has not only shown you how to create *standard* symbols, but also how to increase your drafting efficiency with *smart* symbols which can be accurately generated and plotted at virtually any drawing scale.

The feature control frame exercise showed you how to add attributes to your symbols to create intelligent text that prompts the user for a feature control tolerance value whenever the feature control frame symbol is inserted. You will find this technique useful for defining attributes whenever you need additional symbols or symbols libraries.

This chapter also showed you how to use attributes to automate the creation and extraction of information like parts lists and bills of materials. When you added attributes to the hex bolt, you saw how productive it was to export information for analysis and report generation.

Attributes provide tremendous power for annotating your drawings. They add a versatile tool to your drafting tool kit. But remember, good data management is necessary for efficient and productive drafting. This holds true for non-graphic data, like attributes, as well.

When you proceed to Chapter 8, you will be introduced to a list of ANSI Y14.5 dimensioning rules and a suggested practical sequence for dimensioning to ANSI standards. You will be shown how to use your new Y14.5 symbols to assist you in adding datums, feature control references, and Y14.5 symbols to parts drawings. Chapter 8 also expands upon the drafting techniques you have already learned and shows you how to build an assembly drawing from multi-detail subassembly components.

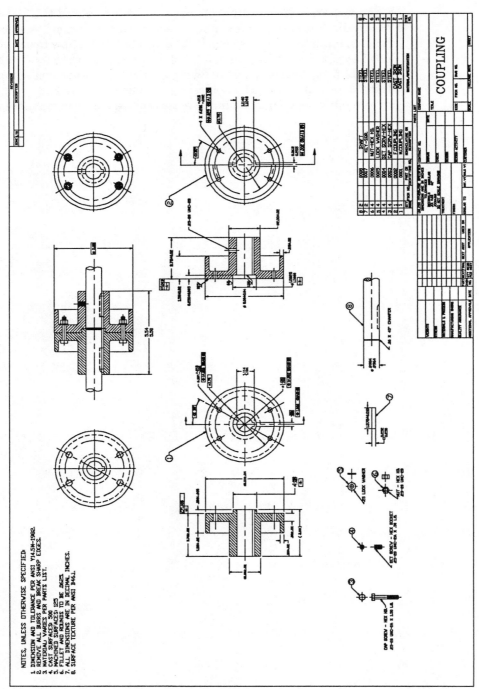

ANSI Y14.5 Geometric Dimensioning and Tolerancing

Geometric Dimensioning and Tolerancing

MAINTAINING THE DESIGN INTENT

The purpose of most mechanical drawings is to convey accurate geometric and textual information to those responsible for an object's production and marketing. The purpose of the ANSI Y14.5M-1982 geometric dimensioning and tolerancing standards, upon which this chapter is based, is to insure that a drawing has a single interpretation. We will use the symbols developed in Chapter 7 to guide you through the geometric dimensioning and tolerancing process in AutoCAD that is necessary to maintain the design intent of your drawings. Our example exercise takes you through the drawing and dimensioning of a two-view orthographic part drawing according to ANSI Y14.5M-1982 standards.

Although we only draw the two views (shown below) of the complete coupling, the facing page drawing shows how they fit the purpose of geometric dimensioning and tolerancing by clearly depicting the interrelationship of mating parts in an assembly drawing.

Drawing the M-Coupling in Two Views

Before we can start dimensioning, we need to draw the M-coupling shown below. If you have the SIA DISK, you already have the drawing and can either skip to the dimensioning section or draw it for practice. First, we'll use the MULTIPLE command to draw the six concentric circles.

MULTIPLE

> *MULTIPLE is a command modifier. To automatically repeat any command in a loop, enter MULTIPLE before that command. To end the command loop, cancel with <^C>. No prompt is issued when you enter the MULTIPLE command.*

MULTIPLE is primarily intended for menus, and is used in many pull-down menu items.

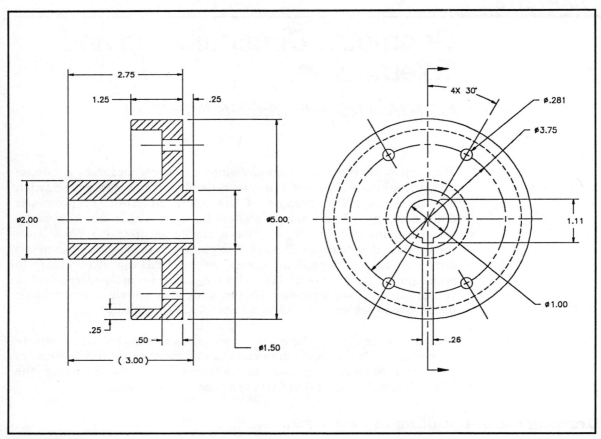

The M-Couple

Let's draw the basic front view.

Drawing the M-Couple

```
Enter selection: 1
```
Begin a NEW drawing named M-COUPLE.

```
Command: ZOOM
```
Window 5,6 to 16,12.
```
Command: SNAP <F8>
```
Set to 0.125 and toggle ortho on.

```
Command: MULTIPLE
Command: CIRCLE
3P/2P/TTR/<Center point>:
Diameter/<Radius>: D
Diameter: 5
```
Pick 13,9.

Diameter.

```
CIRCLE 3P/2P/TTR/<Center point>: @          Same center point.
Diameter/<Radius>:                          Continue with diameters 4.5, 3.75, 2, 1.499, and 1.
CIRCLE 3P/2P/TTR/<Center point>: @1.875,0   The temporary bolt hole at the right.
Diameter/<Radius>: .1405                     Diameter 0.281.
CIRCLE 3P/2P/TTR/<Center point>: <^C>       Then cancel to exit.
```

Command: **DIM**	Set DIMCEN to 0.0625, use CEN on the hole and restore DIMCEN to -0.1.
Command: **LINE**	Draw a center line through the temporary hole.
Command: **CHPROP**	Change the 4.5 and 2 diameter circles to layer HL, the 3.75 diameter circle to layer CL, and the center line and marks to DIM.
	See the following illustration captioned Before Arraying Holes.
Command: **ARRAY**	Array the hole, center line, and marks. Polar, six times, rotated.
Command: **ERASE**	Erase the right and left holes, center marks and lines.
Command: **LAYER**	Turn layer DIM off, and toggle snap off.
Command: **TRIM**	Trim the center line circle and lines from within the four holes.
Command: **LAYER**	Turn layer DIM back on and toggle snap back on.
Command: **PLINE**	Rough in the keyway.
From point:	Pick center of 1.0 diameter circle.
	Continue with @.13,0 @0,-.61 @-.26,0 and @0,1.
Command: **SAVE**	

That completes the basic front view of the coupling.

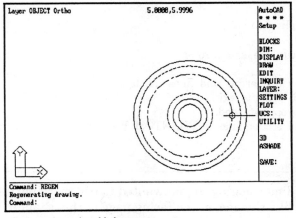

Before Arraying Holes

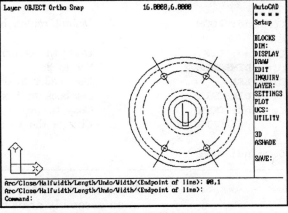

After Array, Trim and Rough Keyway

Let's trim the keyway and draw the section view.

Drawing the Section View

Continue in the previous M-COUPLE drawing.

Command: **TRIM**	Trim both ends of the polyline from within the circle, and the circle from within the polyline.
Command: **ARRAY**	The upper right and lower left circles: polar; center 13,9; angle to fill 30; rotate objects.
Command: **PLINE**	Rough out the section cuts as shown below. Align the vertical dimensions with the front view. Align with the 1.499 diameter circle's top and bottom using a .Y point filter with QUA osnap. Remember the top line in the bottom half of the section represents the keyway.
Command: **MULTIPLE FILLET**	Set R to 0.0625 and do ten fillets shown below. Hint: when filleting, position pickbox *on* each intersection and pick twice.
Command: **HATCH**	Pattern ANSI31 at scale 1, rotation 0, pick all four polylines.
Command: **CHPROP**	Change the hatches to layer HATCH.
Command: **LINE**	Add rest of object lines to section view. Align the keyway top edge using a .Y point filter with INT osnap.
Command: **ERASE**	Erase the two construction circles.
Command: **LAYER**	Set layer CL current.
Command: **LINE**	Add the center lines shown below. Osnap END for the diagonal.
Command: **LAYER**	Set layer OBJECT current.
Command: **ZOOM**	Default center, height 8.5.
Command: **DIM**	Draw the section cut line and arrows.
Dim: **DIMSCALE**	Set to 2.
Dim: **LEA**	Use leader to draw one arrow and lines (no text).
Dim: **DIMSCALE**	Set back to 1 and <^C> to exit.
Command: **COPY**	Copy the arrow to opposite end.
Command: **CHPROP**	Change the vertical section line to PHANTOM linetype.
Command: **SAVE**	

The views are ready for dimensioning. If you wanted to use these parts in an assembly drawing like the one on the facing page of this chapter, you would wblock them now before adding the dimensions.

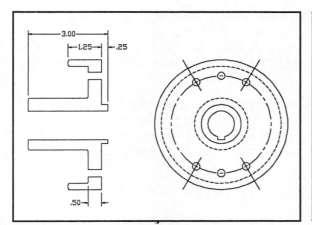

After Trim, Rough Section and Fillets   Completed Front and Section Views .

Steps and Rules for Production Dimensioning

The following information, while based on the ANSI Y14.5M-1982 geometric dimensioning and tolerancing standards, is not intended to be complete or a substitute for the standard.

Size Description Standards

Size descriptions of engineering drawings should be drawn according to acceptable GDT standards. In the United States, the two most commonly used standards are the American National Standards Institute (ANSI Y14.5M-1982) and the Department of Defense (DOD MIL-STD-8).

The ANSI Y14.5M standards were written for the metric system of measurement. Most U.S. industries using the ANSI Y14.5 adhere to the standards, but substitute the customary U.S. linear unit of decimal inches for metric units. This book uses decimal inch units for size descriptions.

It is important to note that geometrics (ANSI Y14.5) do not replace *plus and minus dimensioning.* Instead, they act together as a joint size description to insure that a drawing carries with it a single interpretation of production requirements.

ANSI Y14.5M-1982 Dimensioning Rules

Geometric dimensioning and tolerancing is intended to accurately define the engineering intent of a mechanical drawing by describing part function and mating part relationships. In order to communicate this information, drawings should conform to standard rules of dimensioning. Here are some of those rules:

■ All dimensions should have a tolerance, except for those dimensions specified as reference, maximum, minimum, or commercial stock size. You may apply a tolerance directly to the dimension, indicate it by a general note, or locate it in a supplementary block (title block) of a drawing.

■ Dimensions for size, form, and location of features should be as complete as possible.

■ Each dimension required to produce an end product should be shown. Reference dimensions should be kept to a minimum.

■ Dimensions are selected and arranged to suit the function and mating relationship of a part. They should not be subject to more than one interpretation.

■ The drawing should define the part without specifying manufacturing methods. For example, give only the diameter of a hole without indicating whether it is to be drilled, reamed, punched, etc.

■ Dimensions should be arranged to give optimum readability. Dimensions should be shown in true profile views with reference to visible (continuous) lines.

■ Where an overall dimension is specified, one intermediate dimension is omitted or identified as a reference dimension.

■ Dimensions are usually placed outside the envelope (outline) of a view. Place dimensions within the outline of a view only if it aids in clarifying the size description.

Let's practice some standard dimensioning steps on the two views of the M-coupling.

Geometric Dimensioning and Tolerancing Steps

The following seven steps to GDT are a practical sequence for dimensioning AutoCAD drawings according to ANSI standards.

- Establish dimensioning datum locations

- Locate holes and slots

- Locate and size features

- Give overall sizes

- Size holes

- Add feature control references and symbols

- List notes

The following sections practice these dimensioning steps, building on the dimensioning techniques covered in earlier chapters. You will now find dimensioning more complete and less tedious than in earlier chapters, thanks to the use of the Y14.5 symbols we made in Chapter 7.

Pan or zoom as needed throughout the rest of this chapter, using 'PAN or 'ZOOM transparently if you are in the middle of a command. Liberally using osnaps in dimensioning helps you keep extension line origins accurate while allowing snap to control the dimension line and text locations for consistency.

If you have the SIA DISK, you have a clean drawing of the coupling to use for dimensioning. Otherwise, you need the drawing from the previous exercises.

Establish Dimensioning Datum Locations

Dimensioning datum locations are selected on the basis of the toleranced features, geometric relationship, and the requirements of the design (design intent). Datums are defined as the theoretically perfect surface, or center lines, from which dimensions emanate. These perfect surfaces or center lines are required to insure manufacturing repeatability. Datums are identified by a datum feature symbol like the one shown below. Each datum is designated by a letter of the alphabet, identified by a dash on each side of the datum letter. All letters of the alphabet may be used to identify a datum except I, O, and Q because these might be mistaken for numerals.

You do not necessarily need to draw datum boxes and lines at the time you determine the datum locations, but we will do so in the following exercise. The illustration below shows where the datum surfaces are located on the M-coupling.

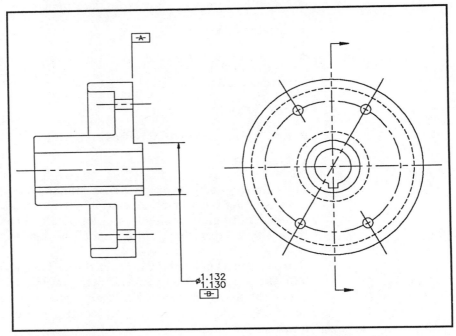

Locating Datums

These features were selected to represent the datum surfaces because of the fit requirements between this and its mating coupling.

Let's add the datum lines and symbols. The B datum is associated with a vertical dimension, which we will also add.

Datum Locations

  Begin a NEW drawing named M-COUPLE=D-M-COUP.

  Continue in the previous M-COUPLE drawing.

Command: **LAYER**	Set DIM current and freeze HATCH.
Command: **SETVAR**	Set LUPREC to 3.
Command: **SNAP**	Set to 0.0625.

```
Command: DIM
Dim: DIMLIM                        Turn on, set DIMTP to 0 and DIMTM to 0.002.
Dim: VER                           Use osnap INT, with %%c<> as text, then <^C> to exit.
Command: LINE                      Draw leaders shown above for the A and B datums.
Command: STRETCH                   Select text only with small Crossing window.
                                   Toggle ortho off and stretch text to end of leader.

Command: INSERT                    Insert the A datum where shown.
Block name (or ?): S-DAT-LL
Insertion point: S                 Preset scale.
Scale factor: .125
Insertion point:                   Drag and pick.
Rotation angle <0>: <RETURN>
Enter attribute values
Datum <A>: <RETURN>

Command: <RETURN>
INSERT                             Repeat for B datum below dimension text.
Command: SAVE
```

The resulting dimension and datums are shown above. Next, we locate holes.

Locating Holes and Slots

Locate holes and slots in relationship to each other, in chain (CONTINUE), baseline (BASELINE), or polar (ANGULAR) dimensioning form, or from a datum or an origin.

We'll locate the four holes in the front view using a basic polar angular dimension and a diameter dimension on the circular center line. These dimensions are designated as *basic* dimensions by the placement of basic dimension rectangles around them, using our S-BASIC block. Basic dimensions mean that a size or location is theoretically perfect. No plus or minus tolerance will be attached to these dimensions. But since it is impossible to repeatedly manufacture any part to absolute perfection, it is necessary to control the location by adding feature control dimensions. We will add feature control dimensions later in this chapter.

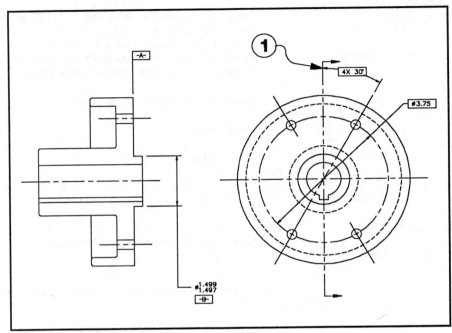

Locating the Four Holes With Basic Dimensions

Locating Holes

Continue in the previous M-COUPLE drawing.

Command: **SETVAR**	Set LUPREC to 2.
Command: **DIM**	
Dim: **DIMLIM**	Turn off.
Dim: **DIMCEN**	Set to 0.
Dim: **DIA**	Dimension circular center line, enter <> followed by 28 spaces to force text outside.
Dim: **ANG**	Dimension upper right hole.
Select first line:	Pick cutting plane line.
Second line:	Pick center line protruding from hole.
Enter dimension line arc location:	Pick point ① on cutting plane line, with pick box slightly to right of line.
Dimension text <30>: **4X <>**	Also pad text with extra leading and trailing space to make room for box.
Enter text location: **<RETURN>**	Default to middle.

```
Command: INSERT
Block name (or ?): S-BASIC
Insertion point: NOD
of
X scale factor <1> / Corner / XYZ: .X


Rotation angle <0>: <RETURN>
Command: <RETURN>
INSERT
```

Insert basic dimension box on angular dimension.
Osnap to node of angular dimension entity (center of text).
Pick middle of text.
Use .X point filter and osnap ENDpoint to left dimension line
to set X scale factor. Use @0,.125 for Y.

Repeat for diameter dimension. (You can't osnap node because of extra spaces.)

```
Command: SAVE
```

Locating and dimensioning features is the next step.

Locating and Sizing Features

Locate features such as angles, notches (cutouts), rounds, and curves of parts from a datum or from the features' points of origin. Size and dimension the features to clearly describe their characteristics.

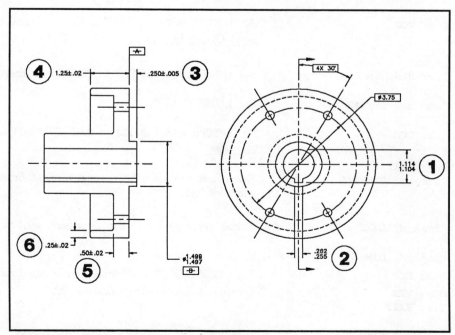

Locating and Sizing the M-Coupling's Features

➡ *TIP: When dimensioning curves and rounds, hold the first extension line origin back a bit from the tangent point to give clearance. This is easier than temporarily resetting DIMEXO. Use .X or .Y point filters and osnaps if needed.*

To locate and size the features of the M-coupling, add the dimensions shown above. Remember to suppress extension lines when picking their origins at existing datum or extension lines. To do so, toggle DIMSE1 or DIMSE2 on, or pick the origin at the dimension line's intersection with the datum or existing extension line.

Locating and Sizing Features

Continue in the previous M-COUPLE drawing.

Command: **SETVAR** Command: **DIM**	Set LUPREC to 3.
Dim: **VER**	Set DIMLIM on, DIMTP to 0.004, DIMTM to 0.006, and dimension the keyway height ①. Osnap INT at the bottom.
Dim: **HOR**	Set DIMTP to 0.002, DIMTM to 0.005, and dimension the keyway width ② with INT osnaps.
Dim: **HOR**	Set DIMTOL on, DIMTP to 0.005, and dimension the face setback ③.
Command: **SETVAR**	Set LUPREC to 2.
Dim: **HOR**	Set DIMTP and DIMTM to 0.02, DIMTAD on, and dimension flange depth ④.
Dim: **EXIT** Command: **STRETCH**	Select text with small Crossing window. Stretch to left of extension line.
Command: **LINE**	Add a short leader to the dimension ④.
Command: **DIM** Dim: **HOR** Dim: **VER** Dim: **EXIT**	Turn DIMTAD off and dimension flange face thickness ⑤. Dimension flange edge thickness ⑥.
Command: **SAVE**	

After features come overall dimensions.

Giving Overall Sizes

Dimension overall width, height, and depth to clearly describe the size of the part. If possible, place overall sizes between views that share similar dimensions. For example, when overall width or diameter is shared by the front and top views, attach the width dimension to the view which describes the shape in true profile.

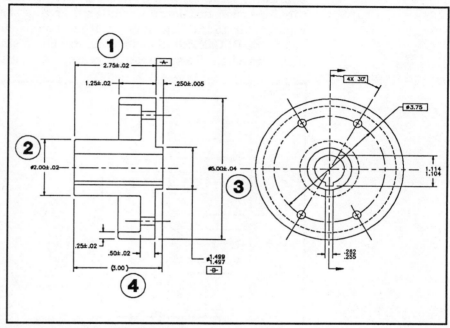

Adding Overall Size Dimensions

Add the overall dimensions shown above to the coupling.

Adding Overall Dimensions

Continue in the previous M-COUPLE drawing.

```
Command: DIM
```

Dim: **HOR**	Dimension depth at ①.
Dim: **VER**	Dimension diameter at ② with %%c<> as text.
Dim: **VER**	Set DIMTP and DIMTM to 0.04 and use %%C<> for overall diameter ③.
Dim: **HOR**	Turn DIMTOL off and use (<>) for reference dimension text ④.

The last bit of dimensioning involves sizing the holes.

Sizing Holes

Generally, you size holes, counterbores, countersinks, and spotfaces with the DIAMETER dimensioning command. Pad the text with leading or trailing spaces if you need to force the text outside, and extend the leaders to drawing locations that do not interfere with other dimensions. Locate the dimension text in an uncluttered area of the drawing, keeping its relationship to the hole obvious. If the hole is small, like our four bolt holes, the DIAMETER dimensioning command omits the dimension line inside the circle. To suppress the center mark, set DIMCEN to 0.

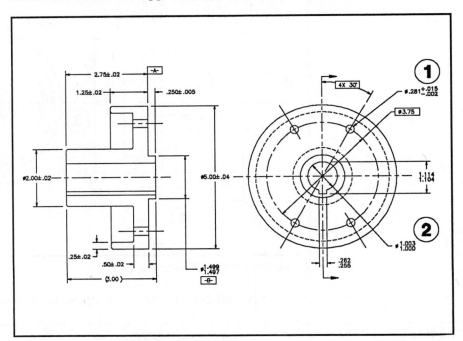

Adding Hole Sizes to the Coupling

Let's add the hole sizes shown above to the drawing.

Sizing Holes

Continue in the previous M-COUPLE drawing.

Command: **SETVAR**	Set LUPREC to 3.
Command: **DIM**	
Dim: **DIMCEN**	Set to 0 to turn off, and toggle ortho off.
Dim: **DIMTOL**	Turn on, and set DIMTP to 0.015 and DIMTM to 0.002.
Dim: **DIA**	Dimension upper right hole with text 4X ⬦ at ①.
	You may have to zoom in close and toggle snap off to pick it, since the pick point controls the text location.
Dim: **DIMLIM**	Turn on, set DIMTP to 0.003, and DIMTM to 0.
Dim: **DIA**	Dimension circle of keyway hole at ②, then <^C> to exit.
Command: **<^B>**	Or <F9> to toggle snap back on.
Command: **SAVE**	

Adding Feature Control References and Symbols

Feature control references and symbols insure that quality control is maintained in manufacturing. Feature control references specify each tolerance zone by a value and by its geometric relationship to the feature. As shown in the keyway example below, the form tolerance of a hole may be controlled by stating that it maintains *position* within a form tolerance zone of [.002] at *maximum material condition* to datum [-A-] and to datum [-B-].

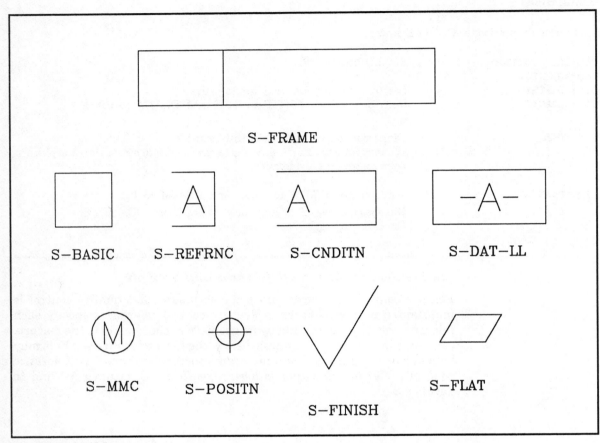

Y14.5 Symbol Library

Let's use the symbols shown above (which you need from Chapter 7 or from the SIA DISK) to add the necessary feature control references and symbols. Use the following instructions to insert the feature control frame and other symbols at the keyway hole dimension.

Inserting Your Y14.5 Symbols

Continue in the previous M-COUPLE drawing.

```
Command: ZOOM                    Zoom in close on the keyway hole's dimension.

Command: INSERT                  Add feature control frame to keyway hole.
Block name (or ?): S-FRAME
Insertion point: S               Preset scale.
Scale factor: .125               DIMTXT 0.125 times DIMSCALE 1.
Insertion point:                 Insert at ①.
Rotation angle <0>: <RETURN>

Enter attribute values
Enter form tolerance: %%c.002    Enter a diameter symbol and the tolerance value.

Command: <RETURN>                Add the position symbol.
INSERT                           Insert S-POSITN at the same insertion point and 0.125 scale.

Command: <RETURN>                Add the MMC symbol.
INSERT                           Insert S-MMC at ② and 0.125 scale.

Command: <RETURN>                Add the A datum reference symbol.
INSERT                           Insert S-REFRNC at ③ and 0.125 scale.
Enter attribute values
Datum <A>: <RETURN>              Default to A.

Command: <RETURN>                Add the B datum condition symbol.
INSERT                           Insert S-CNDITN at ④ and 0.125 scale.

Command: <RETURN>                Add another MMC symbol.
INSERT                           Insert S-MMC in the condition box.

Command: SAVE
```

The completed feature control frame reference symbol set should look like the following illustration.

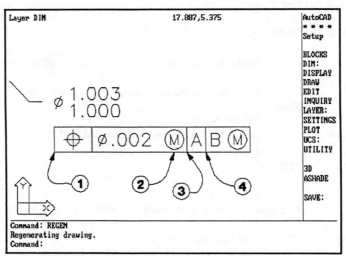

Y14.5 Feature Control Reference With Insertion Points

➡ *NOTE: Our snap setting and scales worked out for the insertion points, but often they won't align so well. In such cases, use INT osnaps for the insertions (except S-MMC, which uses NEA).*

Use the illustration below and your Y14.5 symbol library to complete the remaining references.

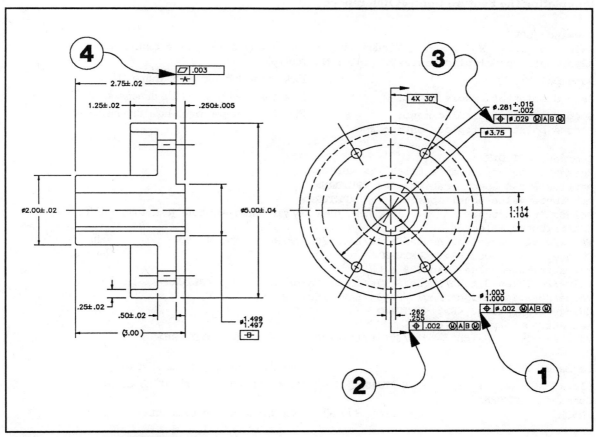

All Feature Control Symbols Are Added

For the upper right hole and keyway width, you could insert S-FRAME (with text %%c.029 and .002 respectively), and insert S-POSITN, S-REFRNC, S-CNDITN, and 2 S-MMC symbols for each. But since the text of the S-FRAME's TOLERANCE attribute is the only difference, you can copy and ATTEDIT the keyway hole's feature control frame reference.

Completing the Feature Control References

```
Command: COPY
Select objects: W              Window all parts of keyway hole's feature control frame.
<Base point or displacement>/Multiple: M   Multiple.
Base point:                    Pick lower left corner of frame ①.
Second point of displacement:  Pick below keyway width dimension at ②.
Second point of displacement:  Pick below upper right hole dimension at ③.
Second point of displacement: *Cancel*
```

```
Command: ATTEDIT
Edit attributes one at a time? <Y> <RETURN>
Attribute tag specification <*>: <RETURN>
Attribute value specification <*>: <RETURN>
Select Attributes:             Pick hole, then keyway width attribute text, then <RETURN>.
2 attributes selected.
Value/Position/Height/Angle/Style/Layer/Color/Next <N>: V      Value.
Change or Replace? <R>: <RETURN>                               Replace.
New attribute value: %%c.029
Value/Position/Height/Angle/Style/Layer/Color/Next <N>: <RETURN>   Next.
Value/Position/Height/Angle/Style/Layer/Color/Next <N>: V
Change or Replace? <R>: <RETURN>
New attribute value: .002
Value/Position/Height/Angle/Style/Layer/Color/Next <N>: <RETURN>
```

```
Command: INSERT                Add the tolerance to the A datum.
Block name (or ?) <S-MMC>: S-FRAME   With text .003 at scale 0.125 at ④.
Command: <RETURN>
INSERT                         Insert S-FLAT in the frame at the same insertion point.
```

```
Command: SAVE
```

Now, all that's needed to complete the drawing are the general notes.

List Notes

Add general notes to convey information pertinent to the part. Use notes when part description lends itself to written, rather than graphic, form. For example, the section profile has ten radii, all of which are 0.0625. This lends itself to specification by a general note rather than by dimensioning and tolerancing symbols.

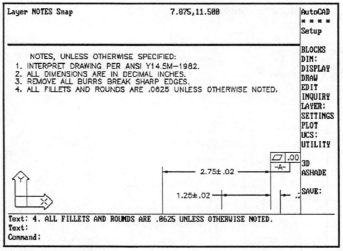

The General Notes

We'll use an osnap trick to align our new text and match the interline spacing of the existing general notes. We osnap the text start point to the insertion point of the previous text, then enter a blank line to space down one line and begin our real text. After entering the text, use VIEW to zoom out to see the entire finished drawing.

Adding to the General Notes

Command: **LAYER**   Thaw layer NOTES and set it current.
Command: **ZOOM**   Zoom to upper left to see existing notes.

Command: **DTEXT**
Start point or Align/Center/Fit/Middle/Right/Style: **INS** Osnap INSertion point.
of   Pick last existing line of text.
Height <0.125>: **<RETURN>**
Rotation angle <0>: **<RETURN>**
Text: **<SPACE><RETURN>**   Continues to next line.
Text: **4. ALL FILLETS AND ROUNDS ARE 0.0625 UNLESS OTHERWISE NOTED.**
Text: **<RETURN>**

Command: **VIEW**   Restore view BDR.
Command: **LAYER**   Thaw TITL*, HATCH, and set TITL-CX current.

Command: **DTEXT**   Add the 0.5 high title, and any other title block text you desire.

Command: **END**

The finished M-COUPLE drawing should match the following illustration.

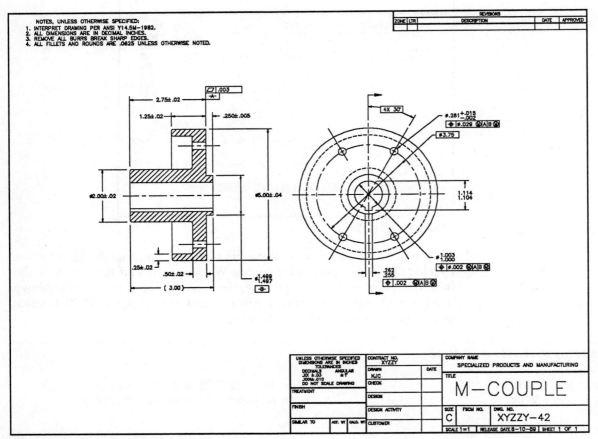

The Completed M-COUPLE Drawing

Summary

The exercises in Chapter 8 introduced you to the MULTIPLE command and numerous useful techniques for drafting with AutoCAD. We provided you with a suggested set of steps and rules for production dimensioning. By following the sequence of the seven dimensioning steps, you will increase your drawings' dimensioning integrity, and your own efficiency and productivity.

Plan and perform your dimensioning so that the original intent of the design is maintained throughout the production process. Dimensioning should convey a single interpretation of the size and shape of a part.

Misinterpretation of dimensions may result in the manufacture of unusable parts, which can cost a company time, money, and lowered productivity. You can avoid these types of problems by simply dimensioning your part drawings according to a standard such as ANSI Y14.5.

When you proceed to Chapter 9, you will be introduced to 3D extrusion drafting. Chapter 9 shows you how to specify an object's geometry in the X, Y plane, and its thickness in the Z plane. You will find that many parts lend themselves nicely to the technique of extrusion drafting.

Let's go on to Chapter 9 and step into the third dimension with extrusion drafting.

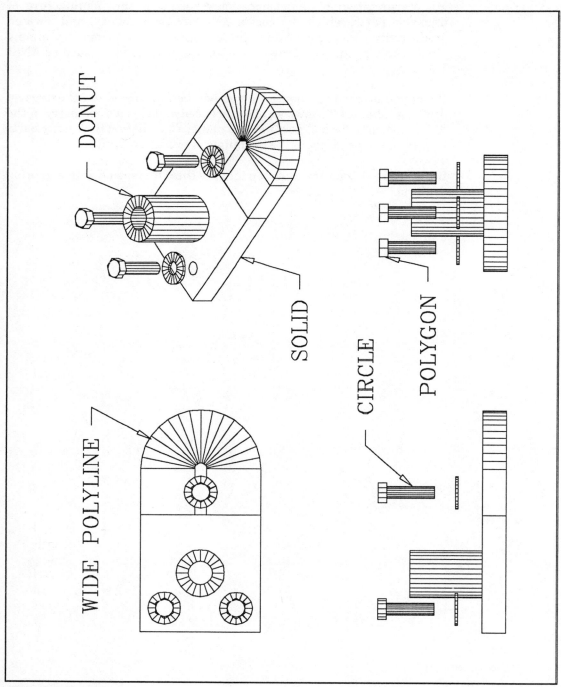

Extruded 3D Part

CHAPTER 9

3D Extrusion Drafting

QUICK AND EASY 3D IMAGES

This chapter will show you how to use AutoCAD's extrusion techniques and commands to create three-dimensional drawings with what we have, up until now, considered to be two-dimensional entities.

Two-dimensional entities, like circles and arcs, are constrained to a single X,Y plane. Extrusion (sometimes called 2-1/2D) adds thickness to these entities by extruding them in the Z axis. However, they are still essentially two dimensional, because their bases and tops are still constrained to the X,Y plane and all points in the Z axis are perpendicular to their base points. In other words, you can't create 3D curves or angles by extrusion. AutoCAD Release 10 has more complete 3D capabilities which we will explore in the following chapters. But for now, we will ease our way into 3D with the extrusion method.

This chapter introduces the THICKNESS system variable, and the DONUT, FILL, HIDE, SELECT, SOLID, PEDIT, and VPOINT commands. We will also revisit the UCS, VPORTS, CHPROP, OFFSET, and POLYGON commands. All of these commands and settings can be applied to most of the familiar entity types to create extruded 3D images.

Extrusions are easy to work with and very useful in 3D drafting, enabling you to quickly rough out 3D images. You draw just like in 2D, but by manipulating the entity thickness and base elevation, you change 2D entities into 3D. Many parts and objects have geometric characteristics that lend themselves nicely to extrusion drafting. Parts with geometric shapes such as cylinders and rectangular solids may be extruded into realistic looking 3D geometry. Examples of extrudable entities are shown below.

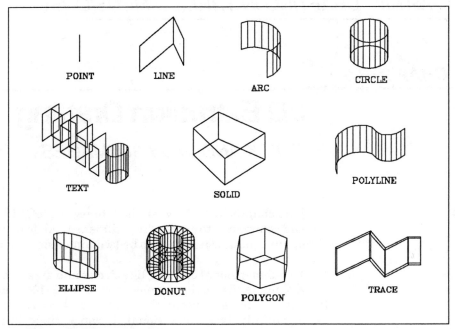

Extruded 3D Entities

In the following exercises, we will create a new 3D prototype drawing with viewports and viewpoints set up to show simultaneous 2D and 3D views. We will draw a 3D part with a one inch thick bullet-shaped base plate, two holes, a slot, and a hub. We'll add bolts and washers.

This chapter's exercises use some AutoCAD Release 10 commands which are unavailable in Release 9. If you are working with AutoCAD Release 9, watch for the notes that tell you how to perform the equivalent steps, and ignore references to the UCS, VPORTS, and CHPROP commands.

If you are using the SIA DISK, you already have the PROTO-3D drawing file. You can skip the following exercise to create it, or you can go ahead and explore the exercise in a temporary drawing.

Setting Up a Prototype for 3D

We want to retain text styles and most of the settings of our prototype drawing, but the title block material isn't relevant to a 3D drawing. If viewed or plotted in 3D, the title block and border would be skewed to an odd angle and would probably obstruct the drawing image. We'll erase it.

Without a border, our BDR UCS is irrelevant, so we'll reset the default to World. We'll also realign the SCRATCH UCS to match, rotated 180 degrees about 0,0. The old SCRATCH view will still align us with the new SCRATCH UCS, but we need to save a new WORLD view to match the default World UCS.

Viewports, which were introduced in Chapter 4, offer a drafter the unique advantage of being able to view objects in 2D and 3D at the same time. We want to simultaneously see the top (plan), front, and right side views as well as a 3D view of our drawing, so we'll set up four viewports.

Modifying the Prototype for 3D

 Begin a NEW drawing named TEMP, or skip this exercise.

 Begin a NEW drawing named PROTO-3D.

```
Command: LAYER              Thaw all layers with a * wildcard for name.
Command: ERASE              Choose everything with Crossing.
Command: UCS                Reset to World.
Origin/ZAxis/3point/Entity/View/X/Y/Z/Prev/Restore/Save/Del/?/<World>: <RETURN>

Command: VIEW               Name and save the current view as WORLD.

Command: UCS                Realign the SCRATCH UCS.
Origin/ZAxis/3point/Entity/View/X/Y/Z/Prev/Restore/Save/Del/?/<World>: Z
Rotation angle about Z axis <0.0>: 180
                            Save the UCS to name SCRATCH, replacing the existing SCRATCH.
                            Reset the UCS to World.

Command: VPORTS
Save/Restore/Delete/Join/SIngle/?/2/<3>/4: 4
```

Now we have four identical views, as shown below. Notice that the limited grid area indicates that we are in the World UCS.

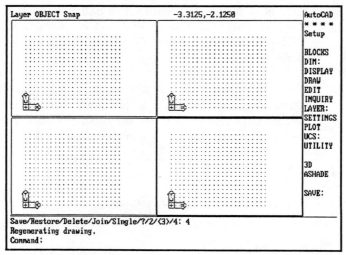

Four Views of Our World

To get differing top, front, side, and 3D views, we alter our viewpoint.

Viewpoints for Simultaneous 2D and 3D Views

Use the VPOINT command to view the current viewport from any point in 3D space.

VPOINT

> VPOINT (ViewPOINT) lets you determine the direction and angle for viewing a drawing by selecting a 3D viewpoint. Issuing the command regenerates the drawing with a parallel projection from the 3D point that you specify. The original default is the plan view, looking from 0,0,1. The current default is the current viewpoint. You have three ways to define a viewpoint: by entering X,Y,Z values; by supplying an angle in the X,Y plane and from the X,Y plane; or by picking a point on the compass icon, using the axes tripod for reference.
> ```
> Rotate/<View point> <0.0000,0.0000,1.0000>:
> Enter angle in X-Y plane from X axis <270>:
> Enter angle from X-Y plane <90>:
> ```

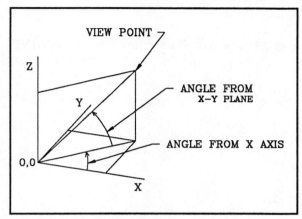

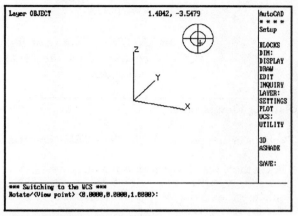

Viewpoint Rotate Angles   *Viewpoint Compass and Axes*

Any point you specify determines only the angle of view, not a viewing
distance from the objects. The resulting view is always looking towards
0,0,0 at the *entire* drawing from the specified angle. The objects don't
move; only your point of view changes.

When specifying the angle with a point, VPOINT thinks and displays
defaults relative to 1.0, like 0.5000,-0.5000,0.6000, but you will find it
easier to enter whole numbers, like 5,-5,6. Either method specifies the
same angle. The point for the angle can also be specified by relative
points, osnaps, or point filters if desired.

If you use the interactive method of selecting a viewpoint with a
<RETURN> at the initial prompt, the compass and axes tripod are
displayed. Then you pick a point on the compass to select a good
viewpoint. This method works well for some users but may be confusing
to others. The compass represents a flattened *globe*, with its center being
the *north pole* (straight down, plan view, viewpoint 0,0,1). The small
inner circle represents the *equator* and the outer circle represents the
south pole (straight up, 0,0,-1). With the compass and tripod, a small cross
(+) represents your cursor. As you move the cursor to the desired location
on the compass, the tripod will dynamically show the current orientation
position. When you have the orientation you want, pick the point to exit
and AutoCAD will regenerate that viewpoint.

The instructions below provide absolute X,Y,Z points for viewpoints in
the right and bottom viewports. If you would rather use one of the other
two methods (rotation or compass and tripod) feel free to do so. Any of

these methods will achieve the same result. The instructions set front, side, and 3D viewpoints in the bottom left, bottom right, and upper right viewports.

➡ *NOTE: If you are an AutoCAD Release 9 user, execute the VPOINT command for the 3D view, then save it with the VIEW command to the name 3D.*

Setting Viewpoints

Continue in the previous PROTO-3D or TEMP drawing.

Click in the lower left viewport to make it active.
```
Command: VPOINT
Rotate/<View point> <0.0000,0.0000,1.0000>: 0,-1,0          Front view.
Regenerating drawing.
```

Click in the lower right viewport to make it active.
```
Command: <RETURN>
VPOINT Rotate/<View point> <0.0000,0.0000,1.0000>: 1,0,0          Side view.
```

Click in the upper right viewport to make it active.
```
Command: <RETURN>
VPOINT Rotate/<View point> <0.0000,0.0000,1.0000>: 5,-5,6          3D view.
```

```
Command: ZOOM            Zoom the upper right as illustrated.
                         Zoom Window in each of the other viewports from -1,-1,-1 to 22,17.
```

Click in the upper left (plan) viewport to leave it active.
```
Command: VPORTS          Save to name 3D.
Command: END
```

The display should look like the illustration below.

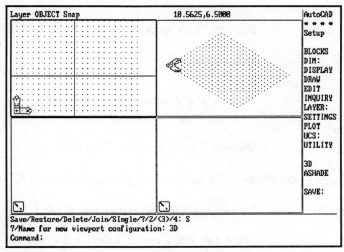

Right Viewport With 3D Viewpoint

In the bottom two viewports, the UCS icon is replaced by a *broken pencil* icon to indicate that point selection will be unpredictable at these angles. Osnaps and point filtering will be useful in these viewports, but we will use them primarily for observation.

This saved PROTO-3D drawing will be our basic 3D prototype. Now we can begin extruding our 3D part.

Drawing With 3D Extrusions

Since 3D extrusions are an extension of 2D, we'll start out in two dimensions and extend into three. Before we draw our part in earnest, we'll rough it out to see how lines, arcs, and circles act in 3D extrusions.

➡ *NOTE: If you are an AutoCAD Release 9 user, restore the new 3D view at the end of this exercise.*

Roughing Out in 2D

`Enter selection: ` **1**	Begin a NEW drawing named PART3D=PROTO-3D.
`Command: ` **ZOOM**	Left corner -1,-1 with height 8.
`Command: ` **SNAP**	Set to 0.25.
`Command: ` **LINE**	Draw a 5 x 5 square with lower left corner at 0,0.
`Command: ` **<RETURN>**	
`LINE`	Draw a 2 inch line from ① to ②.
`Command: ` **ARC**	
`Center/<Start point>: ` **<RETURN>**	To continue tangent to the line to ③.
`Command: ` **LINE**	
`From point: ` **<RETURN>**	To continue tangent to the arc to ④.
`Command: ` **CIRCLE**	Draw two 0.275 radius holes at 1,1 and 1,4.
`Command: ` **ZOOM**	Click in the 3D viewport and zoom in closer.

Click in the upper left viewport to leave it active.

As you can see, our part is rather flat.

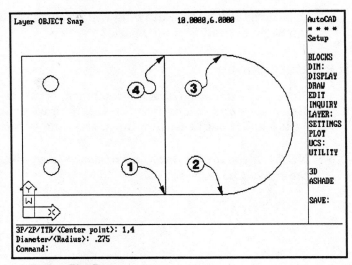

A Rather Flat Part

To give it some depth, we need to manipulate its thickness.

Thickness Makes the Extrusion

To make our base plate one inch thick, we'll use the THICKNESS entity property. Just as every entity has a color, linetype, and layer, it also has a thickness. The default thickness is 0, which is why our part looks flat. The CHPROP command can change this.

Changing Entity Thickness

Continue in the previous PART3D drawing.

```
Command: CHPROP
Select objects:                Select all entities.
Change what property (Color/LAyer/LType/Thickness) ? T
New thickness <0.0000>: 1
Change what property (Color/LAyer/LType/Thickness) ? <RETURN>
```

Now we have four views of a wireframe 3D part drawing.

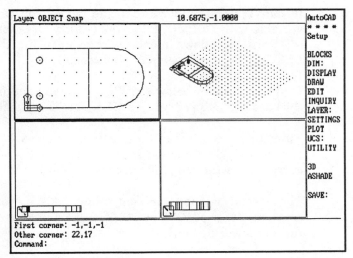

3D Part in Wireframe

Using CHPROP after the fact is often most efficient, particularly when dealing with many different thicknesses. But as with most things in AutoCAD, thickness can also be controlled in other ways. If you use SETVAR to set the THICKNESS system variable, all subsequent entities will be created with the new default thickness.

Elevation, Thickness, UCS's and Construction Planes

The X,Y plane of the current UCS is known as the current construction plane. Thickness is always relative to the current construction plane, which has a default Z elevation of zero. When you designate a thickness, either positive or negative, it will be from the current construction plane.

➡ *NOTE: The ELEV command and the ELEVATION system variable can be used to create a current construction plane with a non-zero Z relative to the current UCS, but this is not recommended in Release 10. The combination of non-zero elevations and elevated UCS's just gets too confusing. Also, the CHANGE command can change existing entity thicknesses and elevations, and the ELEV command can reset the THICKNESS system variable. If you have Release 10, don't get used to using CHANGE and ELEV for these purposes because they will be dropped in future releases of AutoCAD. However, if you have Release 9, you will have to use CHANGE and ELEV (as well as SETVAR) to control entity base elevations and thicknesses.*

If your system supports dialogue boxes, you can set the THICKNESS variable with DDEMODES or the [Entity Creation...] selection from the [Settings] pull-down menu. (But avoid using the dialogue box to set ELEVATION unless you have Release 9.)

To draw above or below the WCS construction plane, you need to raise the base elevation of entities. There are three methods.

First, prior to drawing an entity, base elevation can be controlled by setting a UCS with a non-zero Z relative to the WCS. This relocates the current construction plane above or below the WCS X,Y plane.

The second method for controlling base elevation after an entity's creation is to use MOVE or COPY with a non-zero Z coordinate or offset to raise or lower the entity.

The third method is to simply specify a non-zero Z coordinate for an entity's first point to establish its base elevation. This works for drawing most types of new entities, and AutoCAD reprompts with an error message when it can't accept the Z coordinate.

We'll use the first method with the DONUT command to add an extruded hub to our part. We want to draw an extruded entity with a base at the WCS Z axis elevation of one inch, so we'll reset the UCS origin to 0,0,1 relative to the WCS. That will establish the current elevation and construction plane one inch above the WCS. We'll also set a thickness of three inches, which will have its base at this new plane. Remember, if you are in the user coordinate system (UCS) instead of the world coordinate system (WCS), the "W" on the Y axis of the icon disappears. Similarly, the "+" at the icon's center means you are looking down (positive Z) at the icon. The plus disappears when your viewpoint looks at the UCS from below (negative Z). The user coordinate system was introduced in Chapter 3 and will be used extensively in Chapter 10.

DONUT

> *The DONUT (or DOUGHNUT, if you prefer) command draws solid filled rings and circles. The donut entities are closed wide polylines. You give an inside diameter value (or two points) and an outside diameter (or two points). DONUT repeats its* Center of doughnut: *prompt until you cancel or <RETURN> to exit.*
> Inside diameter :   Outside diameter :
> Center of doughnut:

Let's elevate our UCS, set THICKNESS using the SETVAR command, and draw a donut.

➡ *NOTE: If you are an AutoCAD Release 9 user, use the ELEV command to set the new elevation to 1.0 and the thickness to 3.0.*

Drawing a Thick Donut in an Elevated UCS

```
Command: UCS            Set Origin to 0,0,1.
Command: SETVAR         Set THICKNESS to 3.

Command: DONUT
Inside diameter <0.5000>: 1
Outside diameter <1.0000>: 2
Center of doughnut:              Pick point at center of square.
Center of doughnut: <RETURN>     To exit.
```

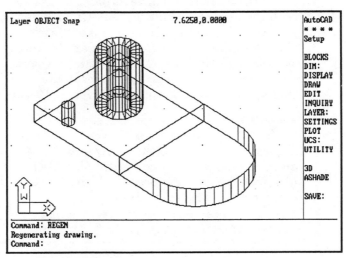

The Extruded Donut

That looks pretty good for a wireframe, but how will it look with hidden lines removed?

Hidden Line Removal

Extruded drawings like the PART3D drawing are drawn in a 3D mode called *wireframe*. In wireframe, all the lines which make up the drawing are displayed. As the drawing becomes more complex, these lines may confuse, more than explain, an object's shape. To make drawings look realistic and solid, you can use the HIDE command to suppress the lines that would normally be hidden from the current viewpoint.

HIDE

> *When you work in 3D, you see the edges of all entities. The HIDE command calculates solid areas defined by those edges and determines what would be hidden or suppressed from your viewpoint. HIDE only evaluates circles, polylines (assigned a width), solids, traces, 3Dfaces, meshes, and extruded edges of entities assigned a thickness as opaque surfaces. In addition, extruded circles, polylines (assigned a width), solids, and traces are considered solid entities, having top and bottom faces.*

Only the current viewport will show the hidden lines removed. Let's set the 3D viewport current and run HIDE.

Removing the Hidden Lines

Click in the upper right viewport to make it active.

```
Command: HIDE
Regenerating drawing.
Removing hidden lines: nnn
```
Number *nnn* counts vectors processed.

Now the 3D image in the upper right viewport is decidedly clearer.

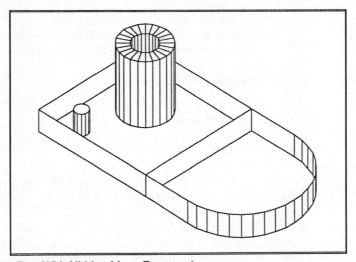

Part With Hidden Lines Removed

➡ *NOTE: We'll use HIDE frequently in the following exercises. If you're working on a slow machine, you may omit some of the hides to save time.*

The cylindrical hub, a polyline created by the DONUT command, looks quite solid, but the base created with lines and arcs is open, with no top or bottom. We'll make our part more solid in a moment, but first let's explore a couple more HIDE issues.

Hidden Line Removal Speed

As a drawing becomes more complex, HIDE takes geometrically more time, because it must compare every line to every other line in the drawing.

You can increase the speed of hidden line removal by displaying only the part of your drawing you wish to hide. AutoCAD hides only the entities displayed in the current viewport, so you can save time by zooming in to what you want to see. Turning layers off doesn't help; they are still considered as if visible. But entities on frozen layers are ignored by HIDE. A fast computer will also help.

Hiding and Plotting

Using HIDE in the drawing editor doesn't affect the plot. At the beginning of the plot dialogue, you are informed of the current plot-hide setting: whether hidden lines will or will not be removed. You can change the setting by responding affirmatively to the Do you want to change anything? <N> prompt. Then you will be asked if you want to Remove hidden lines? near the end of the plot dialogue. If you plot with hidden lines removed, AutoCAD uses the same process as it does on screen, and it takes about the same amount of time, plus the normal plot time.

Where Do Hidden Lines Go?

The HIDE command does not actually *remove* lines from a drawing. It only suppresses their display.

You also have the option of displaying hidden lines as if on another layer. This allows you to control their color and linetype. To do so, create a layer (or layers) with a name that corresponds to the layer name of the entities to be hidden. Such layers are named with the prefix HIDDEN attached to the original layer name, like HIDDENOBJECT for the OBJECT layer. Then when you execute a HIDE, the hidden lines that would otherwise be suppressed are temporarily drawn on the HIDDEN-prefixed layer. This does not create new entities, just temporary lines that can be displayed or suppressed by turning the HIDDEN-prefixed layer on and off. If such a layer exists and is on during plotting, those lines will be plotted according to the settings for its layer. Although you cannot edit these temporary lines, you can use the layer settings to control the on/off, color, and linetype properties. This allows you to view or plot drawings with hidden lines in the colors and linetypes of your choosing.

Solidifying Extrusions

As we saw earlier, lines and arcs extrude like fences, not like solid objects fully enclosing a 3D space. They are suitable for some images, but generally we need to use entities that will have a top and bottom enclosure when extruded. These *solid* entities include circles, traces, wide polylines (including those generated by DONUT), and the solid entity itself.

SOLID

> *SOLID draws solid filled areas or extruded volumes. If the FILL command (or system variable FILLMODE) is set to on (1), the solid is displayed filled. These areas can be triangular or quadrilateral (four sided). You enter points in a triangular or bow tie order to get a triangle or quadrilateral. The first two points are the endpoints of a starting edge; the next point defines the cornerpoint of a triangle; at the fourth point prompt, you can <RETURN> to close the triangle or enter a fourth point to define a quadrilateral. The command repeats the third and fourth point prompts, adding on new solids with the previous third and fourth points as new first and second points, until you <RETURN> at the third point prompt or cancel it.*
> `First point: Second point: Third point: Fourth point:`

FILL

> *FILL, an on/off toggle command, controls whether polylines, solids, and traces are displayed and plotted as filled, or if just the outline is displayed and plotted. In either case, they will still hide as usual. The default setting is on.*

If you drew a solid over the square's lines, it would be hard to select the lines to later erase them. You could just erase them first, but when drawing complex 3D objects, you often need construction lines to draw to. The SELECT command provides an easy way to erase construction lines.

SELECT

> *SELECT lets you pick entities to retain as a selection set. At the next entity selection prompt, use the Previous option to reselect the retained set. You can create the selection set with standard object selection. SELECT is often used in menu macros.*

Let's select the square of lines, replace them with a solid, erase them, and turn FILL off. Then we'll do another HIDE to see the difference in solidity.

➡ *NOTE: If you are an AutoCAD Release 9 user, restore the view WORLD, set elevation to 0, and set thickness to 1. Before issuing the HIDE command below, restore the view 3D.*

Using SELECT, SOLID, and FILL

Continue in the previous PART3D drawing.

Click in the upper left viewport to make it active.

```
Command: UCS                       Reset to World.
Command: SETVAR                    Set THICKNESS to 1.

Command: SELECT
Select objects:                    Select all four lines of the square.

Command: SOLID
First point:                       Pick lower left corner of square.
Second point:                      Pick lower right corner of square.
Third point:                       Pick upper left corner of square.
Fourth point:                      Pick upper right corner of square.
Third point: <RETURN>

Command: ERASE                     Erase the lines.
Select objects: P                  Previous.
Select objects: <RETURN>

Command: FILL
ON/OFF <On>: OFF

Command: REGEN
```

Click in the upper right viewport to make it active.

```
Command: HIDE
Command: SAVE
```

Your drawing should now look like the illustration below.

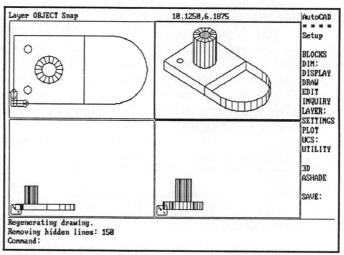

Part With Solid Base

Before the regeneration, the part looked a bit too solid, obscuring the donut and circles. New entities are drawn with the current fill setting, but a regeneration is required before it affects existing entities. As you saw when you turned FILL off, HIDE doesn't care if FILL is on or off.

➥ *NOTE: There is a conflict between having FILL off for drawing solids and polylines in 3D work and having FILL on for drawing wide polyline borders in 2D work. You may resolve this by plotting 2D and 3D portions separately, on the same sheet, with FILL set appropriately for each. In later chapters, we will explore AutoCAD's full 3D entities, which can represent solid volumes without being affected by FILL.*

Now we need to complete the curved portion of the base, which is supposed to have a slot in it. We can salvage our existing geometry by turning it into a wide polyline.

Editing Polylines With PEDIT

The PEDIT command allows you to make various changes to existing polylines, to convert lines and arcs into polylines, and to add lines, arcs, and polylines to other existing polylines.

PEDIT

> *PEDIT edits 2D polylines, 3D polylines, and 3D polygon meshes. Editing 3D polylines and meshes is a subset of 2D polyline editing with its own set of prompts. There are two basic sets of editing functions. The first set operates on the entire polyline; the second set lets you edit individual vertices. The default response is X to exit the command. The default for the vertex editing option is N for next vertex.*
> ```
> Close/Join/Width/Edit vertex/Fit curve/Spline curve/
> Decurve/Undo/eXit <X>:
> Next/Previous/Break/Insert/Move/Regen/Straighten/
> Tangent/Width/eXit <N>:
> ```

Here are the main level PEDIT options.

PEDIT Options

Close/Open — Close adds a segment (if needed) and joins the first and last vertices to create a continuous polyline. PEDIT toggles between open and closed. When the polyline is open, the prompt shows close; when closed, the prompt shows open.

Join — Adds arcs, lines, and other polylines to an existing polyline.

Width — Sets a single width for all segments of a polyline, overriding any individual widths already stored.

Edit vertex — Presents a set of options for editing vertices.

Fit curve — Creates a smooth curve through the polyline vertices.

Spline curve — Creates a curve using polyline vertices as control points. The curve usually will not pass through the polyline vertex points.

Decurve — Undoes a Fit or Spline curve back to its original definition.

Undo — Undoes the most recent editing function.

eXit — The default, <X>, gets you out of PEDIT and returns you to the command prompt.

To edit individual segments or vertices within a polyline, select the edit vertex option to get into the edit vertex subcommands. The first vertex of the polyline will be marked with an "X," which shows you what vertex you are editing. Move the "X" with <RETURN>'s (or "N's" for next) until you get the vertex you want to edit. Editing options include moving the vertex, inserting a new vertex, or straightening the segment. Here are those options.

PEDIT Edit Vertex Options

Next/Previous — Next/Previous gets you from one vertex to another by moving the "X" marker to a new current vertex. Next is the default.

Break — Splits or removes segments of a polyline. The first break point is the vertex where you invoke the Break option. Use Next/Previous to get to another break point. Go performs the break. (Using the BREAK command is usually more efficient than using a PEDIT Break unless curve or spline fitting is involved.)

Insert — Adds a vertex at a point you specify after the vertex currently marked with an "X." This can be combined with Break to break between existing vertices.

Move — Changes the location of the current vertex to a point you specify.

Regen — Forces a regeneration of the polyline so you can see the effects (like width changes) of your vertex editing.

Straighten — Removes all intervening vertices from between the two vertices you select, replacing them with one straight segment. It also uses the Next/Previous and Go options.

Tangent — Lets you specify a tangent direction at each vertex to control curve fitting. The tangent is shown at the vertex with an arrow, and can be dragged or entered from the keyboard.

Width — Controls the starting and ending width of an individual polyline segment.

eXit — Gets you out of vertex editing and back to the main PEDIT command.

We'll use PEDIT to convert the lines and arc into a polyline. Then we'll use OFFSET to offset the polyline to the inside. The offset distance will be half of the polyline width that we will use when we widen the polyline with PEDIT to form the slot.

➡ NOTE: If you are an AutoCAD Release 9 user, restore the view WORLD. Before issuing the HIDE command, restore the view 3D.

Forming the Slot With PEDIT

Continue in the previous PART3D drawing.

```
Command: PEDIT                                  Create the polyline.
Select polyline:                                Pick one of the two straight lines, in any viewport.
Entity selected is not a polyline
Do you want to turn it into one? <Y> <RETURN>        Convert it.
Close/Join/Width/Edit vertex/Fit curve/Spline curve/Decurve/Undo/eXit <X>: J
                                                Join others to it.
Select objects:                                 Select the arc and the other line.
2 segments added to polyline
Close/Join/Width/Edit vertex/Fit curve/Spline curve/Decurve/Undo/eXit <X>: <RETURN>
                                                Exit.


Command: OFFSET
View is not plan to UCS. Command results may not be obvious.
                                                You get this message if not in plan view.
                                                It's OK. It will be obvious enough in this case.
Offset distance or Through <Through>: 1.125
Select object to offset:                        Pick any point on the polyline.
Side to offset?                                 Pick any point inside the polyline.
Select object to offset: <RETURN>               Exits.

Command: ERASE                                  Erase the original polyline.

Command: PEDIT                                  Widen the new polyline.
Select polyline: L
Close/Join/Width/Edit vertex/Fit curve/Spline curve/Decurve/Undo/eXit <X>: W
Enter new width for all segments: 2.25
Close/Join/Width/Edit vertex/Fit curve/Spline curve/Decurve/Undo/eXit <X>: <RETURN>

Command: HIDE
Command: SAVE
```

The resulting polyline slot is illustrated below.

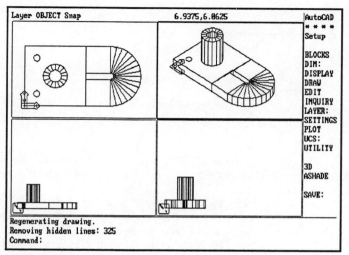

Slot Formed by Polyline

That completes the basic volume of our part. We'll ignore the square end of the slot, which should be round. The two round holes, represented by circles, are also inadequately shown. An extruded circle appears as a solid cylinder, not as an empty hole. And no matter what entity we use for the holes, it won't open up a hole in the face of the solid base. There are better tools for dealing with these in the following chapters. However these better tools are more complex to use. This chapter's simple extrusions are good for quick and rough part development.

Let's add bolts to the part as we look more closely at extruding circles.

Extruding a Hexagon Bolt

The bolts in this exercise are drafted in a simplified style. Leaving the threads off the bolts will help keep the exercise as brief as possible. To create the extruded bolt shank with CIRCLE, change the THICKNESS variable and use point filters to set the base elevation. The POLYGON-generated bolt head's base is positioned by establishing a new UCS origin at the top of the shank.

➡ *NOTE: If you are an AutoCAD Release 9 user, restore the view WORLD, set elevation to 3.0, and set thickness to 2.0. Before issuing the POLYGON command, set elevation to 5.0 and set thickness to 0.34375. Before issuing the HIDE command, restore the view 3D.*

Extruding a Bolt

Click in the upper left viewport to make it active.

Command: **SETVAR**   Set THICKNESS to 2.

Command: **CIRCLE**   Draw the bolt.
3P/2P/TTR/<Center point>: **.XY**
of   Pick center of lower left hole.
(need Z): **3**
Diameter/<Radius>: **.25**

Command: **UCS**   Relocate UCS to top center of extruded circle.
Origin/ZAxis/3point/Entity/View/X/Y/Z/Prev/Restore/Save/Del/?/<World>: **O**   Origin.
Origin point <0,0,0>: **CEN**
of   Pick top of bolt shaft extruded circle in 3D viewport.

Command: **ZOOM**   Zoom in on bolt in upper right 3D viewport.
Command: **SETVAR**   Set THICKNESS to 0.34375 (11/32, the head thickness).

Command: **POLYGON**
Number of sides: **6**
Edge/<Center of polygon>: **@**   Lastpoint was new UCS origin.
Inscribed in circle/Circumscribed about circle (I/C): **C**
Radius of circle: **.375**

Command: **HIDE**

As you can see when you do a HIDE, the top of the bolt head is not closed.

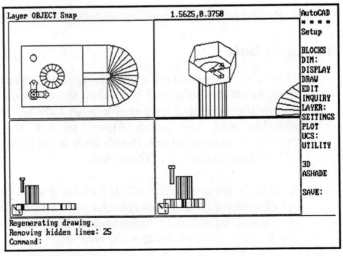

The Open Bolt Head

Since POLYGON creates a zero-width polyline, you could close it by drawing the polygon with half the desired radius (0.1875), using PEDIT to make its width equal to the real desired radius (0.375). This is similar to the technique you used to create the earlier slot.

Another technique, which we show below, is to use an extruded circle to effectively close the top. Then we'll copy the bolt to the other hole and slot.

➡ *NOTE: If you are an AutoCAD Release 9 user, restore the view WORLD. Before issuing the DONUT command, set the view elevation to 2.0 and the thickness to 0.109. Call up the view 3D to make object selection easier, and use the SELECT command to pick the bolt and washer entities. Restore the view WORLD and use COPY Previous to copy the bolt and washer to the other hole and slot. Then invoke the view 3D to check your work.*

Closing the Bolt Top

```
Command: CIRCLE              Fill the head.
3P/2P/TTR/<Center point>: @
Diameter/<Radius>: .375

Command: UCS                 Reset Origin to 0,0,-3.
Command: SETVAR              Set THICKNESS to 0.109.

Command: DONUT              Make a washer at lastpoint @ with I.D. 0.562 and O.D. 1.375.

Command: COPY               Copy the bolt and washer to the other hole and slot.
                            Select entities in front, side, or 3D viewports and pick base and displacement
                            points in plan view.

Command: HIDE
Command: SAVE
```

That completes our 3D part which, when hidden, should look like the following illustration.

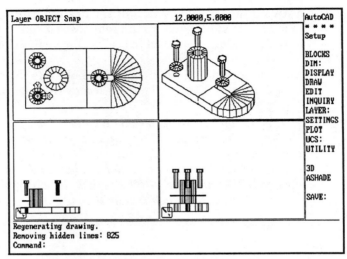

Completed Part With Hidden Lines Removed

As we have noted, there are several limitations to extrusion techniques. In the next chapters, we will explore AutoCAD's full 3D methods.

Summary

In this chapter, you set up and used a 3D prototype drawing, which you will use again in Chapter 10. As you developed PROTO-3D, you set AutoCAD's viewports, UCS's, and viewpoints so that you could simultaneously view your part drawing in two dimensions and in three. We also introduced you to AutoCAD's tools for extrusion drafting which, although limited to "2-1/2 dimensions," provide an easy method for roughing out many 3D parts.

When first extruded, the PART3D entities were displayed in wireframe mode. 3D wireframe drawings are useful when describing relatively simple parts. But as a part's 3D geometry becomes complex, hidden lines should be removed to display a more realistic-looking 3D image. Although processing hidden lines may be time-consuming, you can control layers and views to efficiently hide selected parts of the drawing.

Some entities lend themselves quite well to extrusion drafting, appearing in a solid-looking form. For example, when circles, traces, and wide polylines are extruded, they show a top and a bottom. These two-and-a-half dimension extrusions are useful in a drafter's tool kit. You will find that they nicely complement AutoCAD's full 3D capabilities, which we'll explore in the following chapter.

Chapter 10 will show you how to use 3D surfacing tools to develop comprehensive 3D drawings in the user coordinate system (UCS). You will be guided through the development of a part in full 3D, and then you will be shown how to capture and display 2D orthographic and auxiliary views, and 3D perspective or parallel projection views, from your 3D drawings.

Let's explore full 3D.

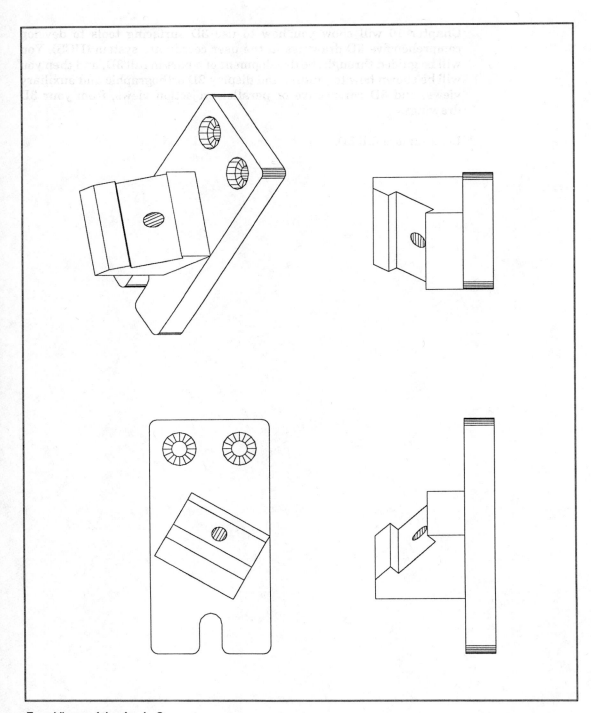

Four Views of the Angle Support

3D Drafting in the User Coordinate System

3D DRAFTING AND DESIGN

3D drafting is often the most effective way to describe a shape. Isometric, oblique, axonometric, and perspective drawings are often used to communicate designs to individuals with little or no technical drafting experience. Traditionally, 3D drafting has been an addition to the standard engineering drawings necessary for manufacturing. But with AutoCAD, you can reverse the process and efficiently draft parts in three dimensions, then capture engineering drawing views from the 3D database. In this chapter, we will create a 3D surface model, which we will then use to create the next chapter's two-dimensional drawings.

AutoCAD's full 3D goes well beyond 2-1/2D extrusions. It depends on two main elements: a group of commands that creates full 3D entities; and manipulation of the User Coordinate System (UCS). The UCS offers an efficient way to develop geometry in 3D space. Unlike the traditional, fixed World Coordinate System (WCS), the UCS is specifically designed to be re-oriented to allow drafting in any position or angle. This allows so-called 2D (or 2-1/2D) entities to be placed anywhere in space.

Full 3D means that any of an entity's coordinate points can exist anywhere in space. Points, lines, and 3D polylines are full 3D entities. 3D polylines are just like 2D polylines except they cannot have width or arc segments. They cannot be curve fit, but they can be spline fit. See the book INSIDE AutoCAD, also from New Riders Publishing, for more detailed information on 3D polylines and spline fitting. Points, lines, and 3D polylines are useful for construction lines and wireframe drawings, but you need surfaces to represent real objects.

The concept behind surface modeling is to create drawings of virtually any shape which, when viewed with hidden lines removed, display as realistic looking models. This chapter introduces you to the useful surface modeling techniques available through AutoCAD's two 3D surface entities: the 3Dmesh and the 3Dface. The 3Dface is simply a three- or four-cornered surface created by the 3DFACE command. Meshes are more complex. At its simplest, a mesh resembles a face, a single surface with three or four corner points. But a mesh is actually a special form of polyline, called a *3D polygon mesh*. A mesh is an array of faces with up to 256 x 256 vertices. This allows you to define multi-faceted surfaces like tabulated surfaces, ruled surfaces, surfaces of revolution, and edge-defined surfaces as single entities.

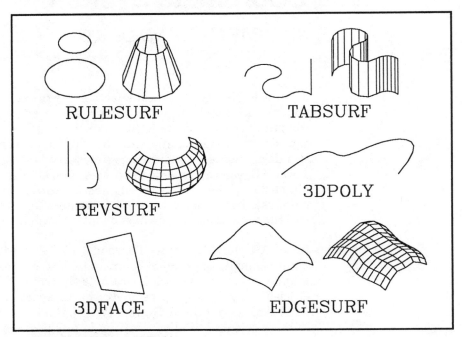

Typical 3D Surfaces and Entities

AutoCAD's 3D polygon mesh tools can surface model virtually any part. In this chapter, we will draw a realistic 3D image of an angle support, using lines and polylines to rough it out and RULESURF, TABSURF, REVSURF, and 3DFACE to surface it.

The User Coordinate System

The key to getting around in 3D is the UCS. You can set the UCS to an unlimited number of positions or orientations, each of which can be saved and restored.

Thus far, we have only used the UCS as a means of shifting our coordinate system for ease of coordinate entry in 2D. The current UCS position determines where points are entered. You can relocate the UCS more dramatically than we have so far, shifting its origin and rotating its axes by any distance or angle about any of the X, Y, or Z axes. The UCS may be positioned in several ways. These include origin, 3point and X,Y,Z rotation. Use whichever method you prefer. We often use 3point together with object snap for accurate positioning.

You can enter points within the UCS as if you were working in the WCS Cartesian coordinate system, creating 3D drawings from 2D entities at any point or angle in space. This is because 2D entities are always created in the current construction plane, which is the X,Y plane of the current UCS (unless modified by ELEVATION). Although the full 3D entities and commands can be used regardless of the current UCS, setting specific UCS's can make coordinate entry seem easier and more logical.

The [Settings] pull-down menu has two items to make setting UCS's easier. [UCS Options...] calls an icon menu of preset UCS orientations, and [UCS Dialogue...] calls the DDUCS dialogue command.

DDUCS | *DDUCS (Dynamic Dialogue User Coordinate System) displays dialogue boxes that control the User Coordinate System. You can also use it to create or rename a UCS.*

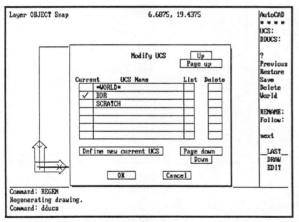

Modify UCS Dialogue Box

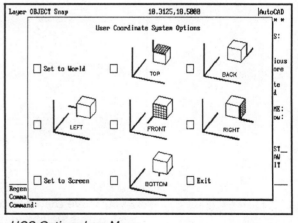

UCS Options Icon Menu

Working in 3D can be confusing at times, so the UCS icon is an on-screen indicator of your current UCS orientation. The UCS icon may be set to move to the new origin or it may remain in the lower left corner of the viewport. For most 3D drafting, there is an advantage to having the UCS icon located at the origin.

A "+" character on the icon, as shown in the illustration above, means that the UCS icon is located at the origin of the current UCS. You can set it to display at the origin by setting the UCSICON command, but when that would cause it to fall off the screen, it omits the "+" and shifts to the screen's lower left corner.

There may be occasions when you are not sure from which angle you are viewing your drawing. When you view your drawing from above (positive Z), the UCS icon displays a box at its base. When you view your drawing from below (negative Z), the box is removed.

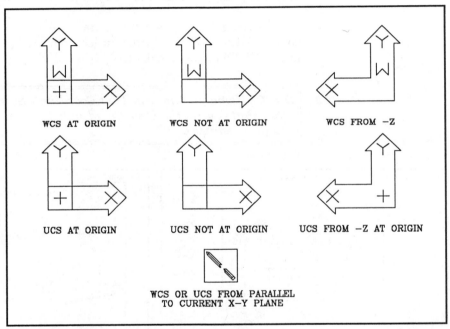

UCS Icon Displays

As you move the UCS to establish new drafting planes, you will need to develop an efficient method for managing your 3D drawings. As we take you through 3D construction drafting techniques, we will show you how to manipulate, save, and restore UCS's.

3D Techniques for the Angle Support

We will use three main techniques to draw the angle support shown on this chapter's facing page. First, we will rough it out by drawing a temporary 3D construction envelope on the CONST layer. The construction envelope is the rough perimeter form of the part. It gives us points and lines to orient and snap to as we draw the detailed part.

Second, we will use UCS's liberally, reorienting our current UCS (and its construction plane) to various points, lines, and planes of the construction envelope.

Third, we will draw portions of the part in the SCRATCH UCS. Although the angle support isn't a very complex part, 3D images often get so dense you can't see points to osnap to. By drawing simple portions in a SCRATCH UCS and then moving them into their real locations in the WCS, we sidestep this complexity. You will find this *building block* drafting technique increasingly useful as you continue with the 3D modeling and design techniques.

Drawing the Construction Envelope

The purpose of construction drafting is to develop a framework to guide you in drawing the part and to assist you in setting UCS positions. Using the uncluttered envelope framework to position UCS's is easier than trying to position them on the geometry of the developing part, and more flexible than trying to set up and recall named UCS's for every possible case encountered.

We will need two envelopes, one for the angle base and one for the angle bracket. We'll draw the envelopes with lines rather than with extruded entities so we can avoid obscuring other entities to come, and keep our osnaps straightforward. Lines also provide the right type of entities to guide some of the 3D commands we will use later.

If you have SIA DISK, you have the completed envelope in a drawing named ENVELOPE.DWG. If you are comfortably familiar with using the LINE, COPY, UCS, ROTATE, and VPOINT commands in 3D, with setting up viewports, and with osnapping in 3D, then you can skip to the section on TABSURF and drafting with polylines, where we begin developing the angle base profile.

Dimensioned Construction Envelope

We'll begin the ANGLE drawing with the PROTO-3D prototype from Chapter 9 or the SIA DISK. We'll set the current layer to CONST, and draw a 4" x 8" rectangle for the part's base. After we draw the rectangle, we'll copy it one inch up, in the positive Z axis direction, to make the top. Then we'll draw lines connecting the two rectangles to form the sides. To locate the starting points and endpoints of these lines, we'll set a running OSNAP INTersect.

Drawing the Envelope With 3D Lines

```
Enter Selection: 1            Begin a NEW drawing named ANGLE=PROTO-3D.
```

Click in the upper left (plan) viewport to make it active.
```
Command: LAYER               Set CONST current.
Command: SNAP                Set to 0.25.
```

```
Command: LINE                Draw a 4" x 8" rectangle with lower left corner at 3,3,0.
Command: COPY
Select objects:              Select all four lines.
<Base point or displacement>/Multiple: 0,0,1        One inch up.
Second point of displacement: <RETURN>    Use first point as displacement.
```

Click in the upper right (3D) viewport to make it active.

Command:	**ZOOM**	Zoom in close in upper right viewport.
Command:	**OSNAP**	Set to ENDP.
Command:	**LINE**	Draw a vertical line at each of the four corners.
Command:	**OSNAP**	Set to NONe.
Command:	**ZOOM**	Zoom each of the viewports to match the illustration below.
Command:	**VPORTS**	Save to name 3D.
Command:	**UCS**	Set Origin to lower left corner of base (3,3,0).

You probably noticed that the last four lines we drew were vertical. In Release 10, line entities are full 3D, with their endpoints anywhere in space, so the old 3DLINE command is no longer needed. Lines and coordinates default to the current UCS Z elevation of zero, but we used osnap to force the upper endpoints to the copied rectangle.

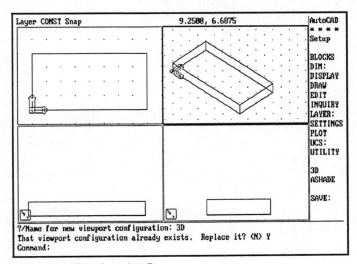

The Base Envelope in 3D

Next, draw a 2.5" x 3" rectangle to represent the overall form of the angle bracket which sits on top of the base. We will draw this rectangle in its finished location by setting an elevated and skewed UCS, but you could alternatively draw the rectangle in the current UCS and move and rotate it into position. After we draw the rectangle, copy it three inches up and draw lines connecting the two rectangles as before.

But first, we have to set the UCS in two steps: offsetting the origin and rotating it about the Z axis.

Completing the Envelope

```
Command: UCS                          Set the Origin to 4,0,1.
Command: <RETURN>
UCS                                   Rotate UCS to angle of the bracket.
Origin/ZAxis/3point/Entity/View/X/Y/Z/Prev/Restore/Save/Del/?/<World>: Z
Rotation angle about Z axis <0.0>: 60

Command: LINE                         Draw a 2.5" x 3" rectangle with lower left corner at the UCS origin.
Command: COPY                         Copy it up with displacement 0,0,3.

Command: OSNAP                        Set to INT.
Command: LINE                         Draw the four verticals, in the 3D viewport.
Command: OSNAP                        Set to NONe.
```

That completes the envelope.

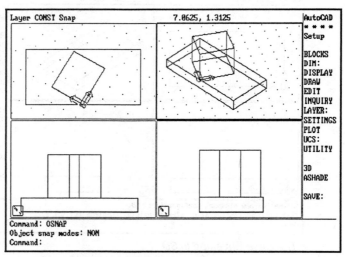

Completed Base and Top Envelope

Now let's move our construction framework to the SCRATCH UCS, where we'll do most of the work. This keeps the current "real" area of the drawing clear for assembling the parts as we create them.

Setting Up the SCRATCH UCS

We have a SCRATCH UCS set up in our prototype. Let's move the envelope to it, using the ROTATE command. This will demonstrate why we earlier set up SCRATCH 180 degrees opposite of the WCS. We can work equally well in the normal 3D viewports or in the SCRATCH UCS and viewports, and transport our handiwork back and forth with a simple ROTATE command.

Moving the Envelope to the SCRATCH UCS

Click in the upper left viewport to make it active.
```
Command: UCS                    Set to World.

Command: ROTATE
Select objects:                 Select everything.
24 found.
Select objects: <RETURN>
Base point: 0,0
<Rotation angle>/Reference: 180
Command: REDRAWALL
```

The image has disappeared into the void. We need to set up duplicates of our viewports, oriented to the SCRATCH UCS, to view it.

Viewpoints in the UCS

To set up SCRATCH, you might think we can simply set the SCRATCH UCS current and duplicate the same viewpoint settings used in Chapter 9 (to set up our 3D viewports). But first we need to make one little adjustment. Generally, you think about your viewpoints in the context of the WCS, regardless of your current UCS. Therefore, the VPOINT command temporarily switches into WCS point entry when used in a UCS. However in this case, we *do* want to input the viewpoints in the current UCS so they will have the same relationship to the current UCS as their counterparts did to the WCS in the 3D viewports.

AutoCAD's WORLDVIEW system variable controls this. When WORLDVIEW is set to its default 1 (on), VPOINT always returns to the WCS, with the message *** Switching to the WCS ***. But when set to 0, VPOINT interprets input relative to the *current* UCS.

Setting Up Viewpoints in the SCRATCH Viewports

Command: **SETVAR**	Set WORLDVIEW to 0.
Command: **UCS**	Set to SCRATCH.
Command: **VPOINT**	Set to 0,0,1 in the upper left viewport.
Command: **ZOOM**	Zoom in on right side of upper left viewport.

Repeat VPOINT and ZOOM for each viewport, with viewpoint 0,-1,0 in the bottom left, 1,0,0 in the bottom right, and 5,-5,6 in the top right.

Command: **VPORTS**	Save as name SCRATCH.
Command: **SETVAR**	Set WORLDVIEW back to 1.
Command: **SAVE**	

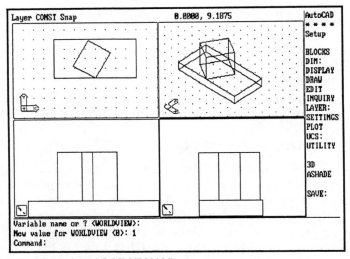

The Completed SCRATCH Viewports

Drafting With Polylines and TABSURF

We'll draw the profile of the base with AutoCAD's PLINE and PEDIT commands.

Polyline entities can be 2D or 3D, or even 3D meshes, created by the PLINE, 3DPOLY, and mesh family of commands. All are polyline entities if you list them. The main difference between the 2D and 3D polylines is that 3D polylines consist only of zero-width straight line segments anywhere in space, while 2D polylines are a connected sequence of line and arc segments with any widths, but restricted to a single plane.

Because all of their segments may be treated and manipulated as one entity, both types are commonly used to define profiles from which to generate surface meshes. The following exercise uses 2D polylines to generate the base profile, from which a surface is projected with TABSURF.

Developing the Angle Base Profile

We'll draw the inside radius for the base's notch with the Arc mode of the PLINE command, which lets you generate a single continuous polyline made up of straight and arc segments. In Arc mode, you can drag a polyline arc by its endpoint. To continue the polyline with straight segments, use the Line option. Arc mode always draws each arc tangent to the previous arc or line segment, unless you specify a different starting direction with the Direction option. Here are the Arc mode options:

```
Arc/Close/Halfwidth/Length/Undo/Width/<Endpoint of line>:
```

Once we draw the polyline, we can use the FILLET command to radius all of the outside corners in one operation. You can draft the base in either of the top viewports, although you will find it easier to draw in the upper left 2D plan viewport.

Drawing the Angle Base Profile

 Continue in the previous ANGLE drawing, or begin a NEW drawing named ANGLE=ENVELOPE.

 Continue in the previous ANGLE drawing.

```
Command: LAYER              Set current layer to OBJECT.
Command: SNAP               Set to 0.125.

Command: PLINE
From point:                 Pick lower left corner of base ①.
Current line-width is 0.00
Arc/Close/Halfwidth/Length/Undo/Width/<Endpoint of line>:    Polar point @1.625<90.
Arc/Close/Halfwidth/Length/Undo/Width/<Endpoint of line>:    Polar point @1<0 ②.
Arc/Close/Halfwidth/Length/Undo/Width/<Endpoint of line>: A  Arc.

Angle/CEnter/CLose/Direction/Halfwidth/Line/Radius/Second pt/Undo/Width/<Endpoint of
arc>:                       Drag and pick polar point @0.75<90 ③.
Angle/CEnter/CLose/Direction/Halfwidth/Line/Radius/Second pt/Undo/Width/<Endpoint of
arc>: L                     Line.
Angle/CEnter/CLose/Direction/Halfwidth/Line/Radius/Second pt/Undo/Width/<Endpoint of
arc>:                       Finish tracing the base and close the last segment.
```

```
Command: FILLET                          Set Radius to 0.25.
Command: <RETURN>
FILLET Polyline/Radius/<Select two objects>: P        Polyline.
Select 2D polyline:                      Pick base profile.

Command: SAVE
```

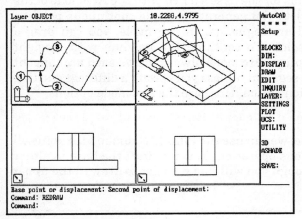

Drawing the Polyline Arc Notch

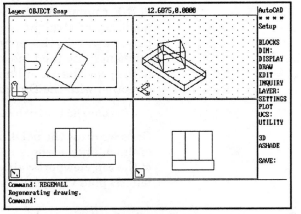

The Completed Polyline Base

All of the angled vertices of the base profile were filleted in one operation. To fillet individual corners, just select two segments instead of using the Polyline option, but they must both be segments of the same polyline.

Now that we have a profile curve, we can generate a surface.

Drawing With Surfaces

AutoCAD's primary surface entity is the 3D polygon mesh. Mesh vertices are designated by *M* (column) and *N* (row) indices. You can create a mesh with the 3DMESH command by inputting each vertex coordinate by row and column. That gets tedious, however, for all but the simplest surfaces.

3DMESH

> *3DMESH creates three-dimensional polygon meshes. Give the mesh size and specify the vertices as 2D or 3D points, starting with vertex (0,0) and ending with vertex (M,N). 3D meshes act like 3Dfaces fused together, and are treated as one entity. The meshes are created open. Close the mesh by editing it with the PEDIT command.*
> Mesh M size: N size: Vertex (0, 0):

PEDIT can be used to close or open meshes, move vertices, and to smooth meshes in a manner similar to spline or curve fitting.

3DMESH is intended primarily for automated use by AutoLISP programs. For manual use, AutoCAD has concentrated the power of 3D meshes into four efficient 3D polygon mesh commands. These are:

■ RULESURF (Ruled Surfaces) — Generates a ruled surface between two *defining curves* such as polylines, arcs, or circles.

■ TABSURF (Tabulated Surfaces) — Projects a defining curve at some distance and angle in space. The top and bottom remain open and parallel.

■ REVSURF (Revolution Surface) — Revolves a defining curve about some axis. REVSURF is most often used to create holes, cylinders, cones, domes, and spheres.

■ EDGESURF (Edge-Defined Coons Surface Patch) — Surfaces an area bounded by four adjoining edges.

All of these surfacing commands operate in the same general manner, using existing entities to define their edges, profiles, axes, and directions. The surfaces are generated between or project from existing entities, leaving them unchanged.

The mesh density is controlled by the SURFTAB1 and SURFTAB2 system variables. The higher the SURFTAB setting, the denser and more accurate the mesh, and the longer it takes to regenerate and hide. If you are not concerned about generating extremely realistic 3D polygon meshes or if you wish to keep your workstation's performance as fast as possible, keep the SURFTAB values reasonably small.

■ SURFTAB1 — sets the distance for the development of "tabulation" lines in the direction of revolution.

■ SURFTAB2 — sets the distance for the development of "tabulation" lines if the selected path curve is a line, arc, circle or spline-fit polyline.

Let's take a closer look at the TABSURF command (not to be confused with the SURFTAB system variables).

Tabulated Surfaces

Tabulated surfaces generate a 3D polygon mesh which is defined by a path curve and a direction vector. The path curve (also known as the directrix) may be a selected line, arc, circle, 2D polyline, or 3D polyline.

The direction vector (also known as the generatrix) may be a selected line, 2D polyline, or 3D polyline. The direction vector defines the direction and length along which the path curve is projected. If a polyline is selected as direction vector, it is interpreted as if it were a single segment from its first to its last vertex.

TABSURF

> *TABSURF, or tabulated surface, generates a 3D polygon mesh by projecting an entity (path curve) through space along a direction vector.*
> `Select path curve:  Select direction vector:`

Tabulated surfaces have no intermediate vertices along the direction vector. One half of the mesh vertices are placed along the curve path and the other half are offset along parallel curve paths the length and direction of the direction vector. In other words, there are two vertices in the M direction, along the direction vector, by N vertices along the path curve. The system variable SURFTAB1 defines the 3D mesh density of the tabulated surface in the N direction. (Note that SURFTAB1 and 2 *do not* correspond to M and N as you might assume.) The tabulation lines are omitted in straight segments, so the SURFTAB1 setting only affects curves.

Extending the Base With TABSURF

We'll leave SURFTAB1 set to 6, its default, and select the polyline profile as our path curve. For the direction vector, we'll use one of the corner lines of the envelope. Select the corner line near its bottom end, because it is interpreted from the endpoint nearest its pick point to the opposite endpoint.

Generating the Base With TABSURF

Continue in the previous ANGLE drawing.

```
Command: TABSURF
Select path curve:            Pick the polyline base.
Select direction vector:      Pick one of the one-inch verticals, near its bottom.
```

The results of TABSURF look much like an extruded entity, with parallel top and bottom, but the "extrusion" need not be perpendicular to the base entity.

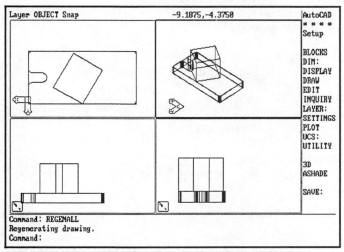

Envelope With TABSURF Base

After the tabulated surface has been generated, take a close look and see what you think. If the polygon mesh needs fewer or more tabulations, you can simply erase (or U) the tabulated surface, reset the variable SURFTAB1, and try it again.

As we create our surfaces, we will move them into place in the 3D viewports.

Moving the Parts to Their Final Destination

To keep the construction site clean, periodically move completed geometry to the assembly location. This location could be anywhere in 3D space, but we like to keep it an easy rotation away, about the WCS 0,0,0 because it is simple to use and remember. When you do this rotation, make sure your UCS is set to SCRATCH or to the WCS.

After we rotate the part into place, we'll look at it with our saved 3D viewports. Then we'll save the UCS 3D view for future use. Once saved, views may be restored into any current viewport. Whenever you wish to display or work on the drawing in the saved view, simply restore it. (Notice that the UCS is independent of saved views and viewports.)

Moving Completed Geometry With ROTATE

Continue in the previous ANGLE drawing.

```
Command: ROTATE
Select objects:                Select Last, the TABSURF mesh.
Base point: 0,0,0
<Rotation angle>/Reference: 180

Command: VPORTS              Restore 3D.
```

Click in the 3D viewport to make it active.
```
Command: VIEW                Save to name 3D for later use.

Command: SAVE
```

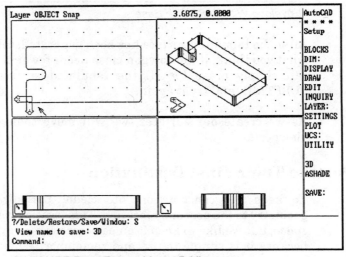

TABSURF Base Rotated Into 3D Viewports

Even more important than keeping a construction site uncluttered, moving completed geometry allows for multiple use of single construction entities. It also avoids interference by the newly created mesh entities, which object selection would tend to find before the earlier envelope entities.

Next in the base construction is a pair of holes.

Surfacing the Drill Holes and Spotfaces

The angle base contains two drill holes and spotfaces. We'll create them with REVSURF, defining the wall profile and revolving it about a center axis. First we need to draw the axis and profile with a line and a polyline. We'll use a temporary UCS, and the TRIM and PEDIT commands to accurately define the profile polyline.

Setting Up for REVSURF

Command: **VPORTS**	Restore SCRATCH.
Command: **LINE**	Draw a center line from 10,4,-1 to 10,4,2.
Command: **COPY**	Copy the center line twice, with displacements of @.2625,0 and @.5625,0.
Command: **LINE**	Draw a line through the three lines, from 10,4,.625 to 11,4,.625.
Command: **CHPROP**	Change the center line to layer CL.

Click in the bottom left viewport to make it active.

Command: **ZOOM**	Zoom in on the lines.

```
Command: UCS                          Set the UCS shown in the below left illustration.
Origin/ZAxis/3point/Entity/View/X/Y/Z/Prev/Restore/Save/Del/?/<World>: 3
Origin point <0,0,0>: ENDP
of                                    Pick bottom of center line.
Point on positive portion of the X-axis <11.0000,4.0000,-1.0000>: ENDP
of                                    Pick bottom of right line.
Point on positive-Y portion of the UCS X-Y plane <10.0000,5.0000,-1.0000>: END
of                                    Pick top of center line.
```

```
Command: TRIM
Select cutting edge(s)...
Select objects:                       Select all lines in lower left viewport.
Select object to trim:                First pick all four ends above and below base envelope lines.
Select object to trim:                Next pick four ends to remove inside envelope.
Select object to trim: <RETURN>
```

Command: **PEDIT**	Select one trimmed line and use the Join option to join all three.
Command: **SAVE**	

The ready-to-surface hole setup should look like the illustration, below right.

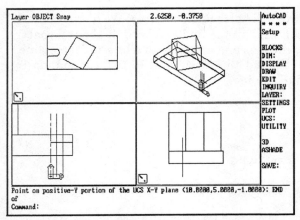

3Point UCS Set for REVSURF

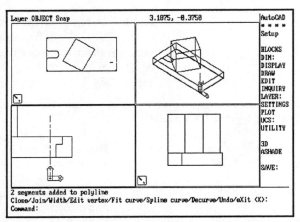

Trimmed Lines to Generate REVSURF

Now we can use REVSURF to generate a hole.

Surfaces of Revolution

REVSURF generates a 3D polygon mesh by revolving an entity or curved path profile around a selected axis.

REVSURF

> *REVSURF (REVolution SURFace) generates a 3D polygon mesh by revolving a profile "path curve" around a selected axis.*
> `Select path curve:  Select axis of revolution:`
> `Start angle <0>:  Included angle (+=ccw, -=cw)`
> `<Full circle>:`

For a full-circle surface, the direction of rotation is unimportant, but for partial circular surfaces, you need to know how to visualize it. The direction of rotation or revolution may be visualized by using the *right hand rule*, as follows:

RIGHT HAND RULE — Using your right hand, extend your thumb along the axis of revolution. With the thumb pointing toward the end of the axis line which is furthest from the pick point, curl your fingers. Your fingers will point in the direction of the rotation.

The axis of rotation defines the M direction (controlled by SURFTAB1) and the path curve defines the N direction (controlled by SURFTAB2). The SURFTAB2 setting is ignored by straight segments, but controls the density of tabulation lines for curved segments.

Let's try two SURFTAB1 settings as we revolve the hole profile about its center line.

Drawing Holes With REVSURF

```
Command: REVSURF
Select path curve:                          Pick the polyline profile.
Select axis of revolution:                  Pick the center line.
Start angle <0>: <RETURN>
Included angle (+=ccw, -=cw) <Full circle>: <RETURN>

Command: U                                  Undo the REVSURF to try a finer mesh.

Command: SETVAR                             Set SURFTAB1 to 16.
Command: REVSURF                            Repeat it, as above.

Command: ZOOM                               Zoom Previous in lower left viewport.

Command: UCS                                Restore SCRATCH.
Command: COPY                               Copy Last with displacement 0,2.

Command: ROTATE                             Select Last and Previous, rotate 180 degrees about 0,0.
```

Click in the lower right viewport to make it active.
```
Command: VIEW                               Restore the view named 3D.
Command: VPORTS                             Save again to name SCRATCH.

Command: SAVE
```

The trade-off between speed and precision, as demonstrated by the two SURFTAB1 settings, is a constant factor in 3D drafting.

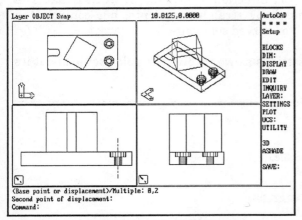

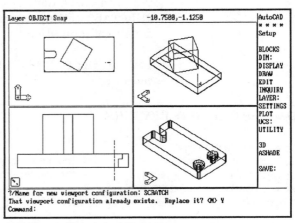

REVSURF and Holes in SCRATCH Viewports   3D View of Base and Hole

Let's move up to the angle bracket.

Drawing the Angle Bracket Profile With TABSURF

We can use much the same technique to generate the angle bracket as we used for the angle base, although in this case we need to work in a UCS that is perpendicular to the WCS. The UCS 3point option can set our UCS on the left front face of the angle bracket profile. But it would be easier to work if our view was perpendicular to this UCS, as if the left front of the bracket was our plan view. It can be tricky to calculate the viewpoint needed for this view. Fortunately, AutoCAD can help with the PLAN command.

PLAN

> *A PLAN view is defined as a view point of 0,0,1 in the selected UCS. It can be applied to the current UCS, a previously saved UCS, or to the WCS.*
> `<Current UCS>/Ucs/World:`

Let's orient our UCS to the bracket's left front and set our plan view to it.

Setting Up the UCS and Plan View for TABSURF

Continue in the previous ANGLE drawing.

Click in the bottom left viewport to make it active.
Command: **UCS**   Use ENDP osnaps to set a 3point UCS:
                                              origin ①, point on X axis ②, and point on Y axis ③.

Click in the top left viewport to make it active.
Command: **PLAN**
`<Current UCS>/Ucs/World:` **<RETURN>**   Current UCS.
`Regenerating drawing.`

Command: **ZOOM**   Zoom in close, as shown below.

Command: **UCS**   Save to name LSIDE.
Command: **VIEW**   Save to name LSIDE.

Your top left viewport should match ours, below. (You'll notice some interference from the real objects at the left side.)

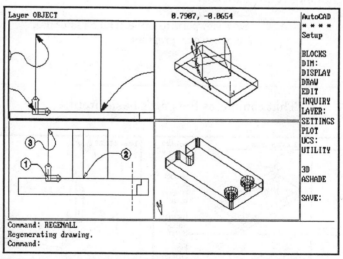

UCS Plan to Left Side for TABSURF

Now it is a simple matter to draw a polyline for the end profile. We'll overlap the ends, then use TRIM and PEDIT to close it accurately.

Projecting the End Profile Polyline With TABSURF

Click in the top left viewport to make it active.
```
Command: PLINE
From point:                        Osnap INT to top left corner of angle envelope.
Current line-width is 0.0000
Arc/Close/Halfwidth/Length/Undo/Width/<Endpoint of line>:
                                   Continue with points: @0,-3 @2.5,0 @0,1.25 @0.375<-135 @1.75<135
                                   @0.375<45 and @1<135.


Command: TRIM                      Trim off part of polyline above angle envelope.


Command: PEDIT                     Close the polyline with the Close option.


Command: TABSURF                   Project it to the opposite side of the envelope.
Select path curve:                 Pick the polyline.
Select direction vector:           Pick the top right front edge of the envelope at ①.


Command: UCS                       Restore SCRATCH.
Command: ROTATE                    Rotate Last 180 degrees about 0,0.
```

Click in the lower right viewport to make it active.
```
Command: VPORTS                    Set to SIngle.
                                   Save viewports to name 3DSI for later use.
Command: HIDE                      To view our progress.


Command: SAVE
```

That completes the part's basic profile.

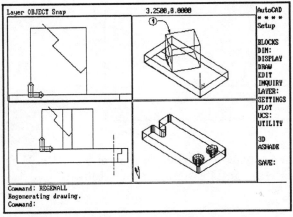

Polyline Before TRIM and PEDIT Close

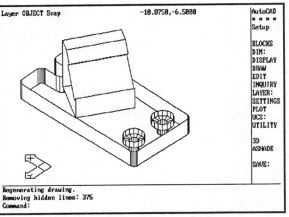

TABSURF With HIDE in Single Viewport

We need to close up some surfaces. The top of the base and the ends of the angle bracket are still open. Also, we need to put a hole through the angled and back faces of the angle bracket, which are now completely closed. First, the hole.

RULESURF for Surfaces Between Two Curves

We can't use TABSURF or REVSURF for the angle bracket's hole because the two ends are inclined toward each other. This is a job for RULESURF, which will generate a straight-line ruled surface between two path curves anywhere in space.

To define the path curves, draw a circle on the back face of the angle bracket and a corresponding ellipse on the inclined front face. We will use these and RULESURF to generate the hole. The ellipse is a polyline.

ELLIPSE

> *The ELLIPSE command gives you several methods for constructing ellipses. The default setting assumes a first axis defined by an* `Axis endpoint 1` *and an* `Axis endpoint 2`*; the other axis distance is defined as half the length of the other axis.*
> `<Axis endpoint 1>/Center:`

Rather than draw in the middle of the faces, it's easier to draw centered on the previous polyline at the left edge, using it as an axis line. An ellipse is a polyline and it's hard to control twist between circles and polylines with TABSURF, so we'll also make the circle as a polyline. First we'll draw the circular ellipse, then we'll use two lines to project the polyline circle center and top quadrant points from the back onto the inclined plane to define the top and center of the ellipse. We'll work in our previous LSIDE UCS.

Projecting Circles to Ellipses

Continue in the previous ANGLE drawing.

```
Command: VPORTS          Restore SCRATCH.
```

Click in the top left viewport to make it active.
```
Command: UCS             Restore LSIDE.
Command: VIEW            Restore LSIDE.
```

```
Command: ELLIPSE                    Draw a 0.5 diameter circle.
<Axis endpoint 1>/Center: C
Center of ellipse:                  Pick midpoint of left vertical of polyline.
Axis endpoint: @0,.25
<Other axis distance>/Rotation: .25


Command: LINE                       Draw horizontal lines intersecting right side inclined face,
                                    from top and quadrant and center of ellipse.


Command: ELLIPSE
<Axis endpoint 1>/Center: C
Center of ellipse: INT
of                                  Pick center line at inclined face.
Axis endpoint: INT
of                                  Pick top line at inclined face.
<Other axis distance>/Rotation: .25


Command: ERASE                      Erase horizontal lines.
Command: SAVE
```

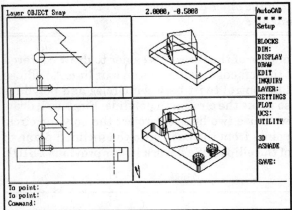

Circular Ellipse With Projected Lines

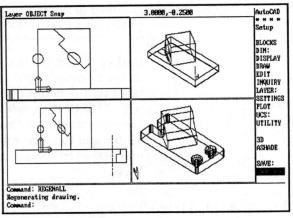

Completed Ellipses

➡ *NOTE: Our circle center and quadrant points were on our snap increment, but if they weren't, you would have problems aligning the line start points. You can't osnap to the center or quadrant of an ellipse, but you can duplicate the ellipse with a temporary circle entity for osnapping.*

Now we need to rotate our ellipses into the planes of the back and inclined front faces. The ROTATE command can rotate any entity about any axis in space, as long as it is the Z axis. But since UCS can orient the Z axis anywhere, this gives unlimited freedom of rotation. The WCS (or SCRATCH UCS) will suffice for the circular ellipse, but we need to use the UCS ZAxis option to set up for the inclined face ellipse rotation.

Rotations in Space

```
Command: ZOOM                              Zoom in top right viewport.
Command: UCS                               Reset to World.

Command: ROTATE                            Rotate circle into plane of back face.
Select objects:                            Pick circular ellipse.
Base point: INT
of                                         Pick top corner of envelope above ellipse, in top right viewport ①.
<Rotation angle>/Reference: 90

Command: UCS                               Try the ZAxis option, picking in top left viewport.
Origin/ZAxis/3point/Entity/View/X/Y/Z/Prev/Restore/Save/Del/?/<World>: ZA
Origin point <0,0,0>: END
of                                         Pick one end of polyline segment through ellipse ②.
Point on positive portion of Z-axis <1.7500,-0.0000,-2.0490>: END
of                                         Pick other end ③.

Command: ROTATE                            Rotate ellipse 90 degrees about 0,0.

Command: SAVE
```

The viewports should display the ellipses in their proper orientations, ready to move to the bracket's center for use with RULESURF.

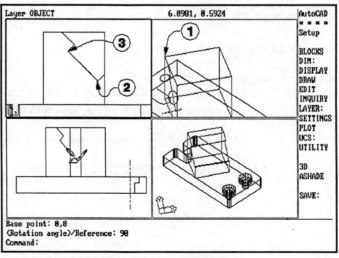

Pick Points for ZAxis, and Rotated Ellipses

Ruled Surfaces

The RULESURF command generates a polygon mesh which approximates a ruled surface between two entities.

RULESURF

> *RULESURF (RULEd SURFace) generates a 3D polyline mesh depicting the ruled surface between two entities. The two entities can be points, lines, arcs, circles, 2D polylines, or 3D polylines. If one boundary, such as a circle or closed polyline, is closed, then the other boundary must be a point or be closed. A point can be used with any another entity.*
> Select first defining curve:
> Select second defining curve:

Since AutoCAD starts ruled surfaces from the endpoint closest to the point of selection, you need to select appropriately matched locations on the two entities. If you select non-matching locations, the ruled surface lines may intersect. Because it is hard to get circles aligned with polylines, substitute polylines generated by DONUT or ELLIPSE for circles.

A ruled surface is generated as a 2 x N polygon mesh. The number (not spacing) of the ruled surface faces is controlled by the SURFTAB1 system variable. Unlike TABSURF and REVSURF, RULESURF makes no attempt to align lines with vertices. Any alignment other than at endpoints is coincidental.

Let's move our ellipses into place and rule the surface for the hole.

Connecting Ellipses With RULESURF

Continue in the previous ANGLE drawing.

Click in the top left viewport to make it active.

Command: **UCS**   Use 3point with INT osnaps to set to top of bracket envelope: origin at front right corner ①, X point back right ② and Y point back left ③.

Command: **MOVE**   Move both ellipses with displacement 1.5,0.

Command: **SETVAR**   Check to see if SURFTAB1 is still 16.

```
Command: RULESURF
Select first defining curve:          Pick circular ellipse.
Select second defining curve:         Pick inclined ellipse.

Command: UCS                          Restore SCRATCH.
Command: ROTATE                       Rotate Last 180 degrees about 0,0.

Command: VPORTS                       Restore viewport 3DSI.
Command: HIDE                         And the hole loses its depth.

Command: SAVE
```

The hole is there, but the solid face of the bracket created by the earlier TABSURF obscures it.

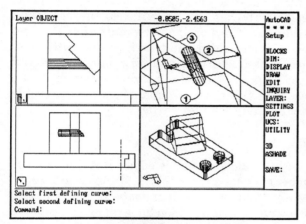

Ellipses and RULESURF at Center of Envelope

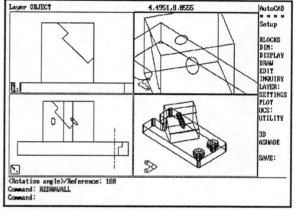

RULESURF Rotated Into Part Before HIDE

We need to replace the obscuring front and back faces of the mesh with a series of smaller facets surrounding the hole. You might think RULESURF would offer an easy way to fill in around a hole, but it won't work well. Avoiding twist is a nuisance; the corners and rule lines won't align and the radiating array of rule lines will be too visible. A better tool for this is 3DFACE.

Surface Modeling With 3DFaces

3DFACE defines individual three- or four-cornered 3Dface entities, similar to solid entities or individual facets of polygon meshes.

3DFACE

> *3Dfaces are shapes defined by either three or four corner points. You can define nonplanar faces by varying the Z coordinates for the corner points, however only faces with coplanar Z coordinates will hide other entities. You can construct 3dfaces with visible or invisible edges.*
> First point: Second point: Third point: Fourth point:

Unlike SOLID, which needs points entered in a criss-cross fashion, you enter 3Dface points in a natural clockwise or counterclockwise fashion. To draw a three-sided face, enter a <RETURN> at the fourth point prompt. For convenience in entering groups of faces, the command repeatedly prompts for additional third and fourth points after the first set of prompts. It uses the previous third and fourth points as the first and second points of each subsequent face and terminates when you <RETURN> at the third point prompt. When entering groups of faces, enter the points two by two, in an S pattern. Groups of faces with invisible common edges are good for defining complex surfaces.

Invisible Edges on 3Dfaces

3Dfaces may be created with visible or invisible edges. AutoCAD allows you to designate any number of edges as invisible. A 3Dface whose edges are all invisible is called a *phantom* because it cannot be seen or selected, but will hide lines behind it when you do a hidden lines removal. To define an invisible edge, enter an **I** *before picking the first vertex* of that edge.

Sometimes you need to display invisible edges to determine where the 3Dfaces are positioned or to edit them. The SPLFRAME variable controls the display of invisible edges. When SPLFRAME is set to zero (the default), invisible edges are not displayed. When set to a non-zero value such as 1, all invisible edges are displayed.

Let's close up the left side of the angle bracket with 3Dfaces.

Closing Irregular Shapes with 3DFACE

Command: **VPORTS**   Restore SCRATCH.

Click in the top left viewport to make it active.
Command: **UCS**   Restore LSIDE.
Command: **VIEW**   Restore LSIDE.

Command: **LAYER**   Freeze layer CONST to suppress clutter.

Command: **OSNAP**   Set to INT.

Command: **3DFACE**
First point: Pick ①.
Second point: Pick ②.
Third point: **I**   Pick ③.
Fourth point: Pick ④.
Third point: **I**   Pick ⑤.
Fourth point: Pick ⑥.
Third point: **I**   Pick ⑦.
Fourth point: Pick ⑧.
Third point: **<RETURN>**

Command: **SETVAR**   Set SPLFRAME to 1 (on).
Command: **REGEN**   To see the invisible edges.

Command: **UNDO**   Undo the SPLFRAME setting.
Auto/Back/Control/End/Group/Mark/<number>: **2**
REGEN SETVAR Regenerating drawing.

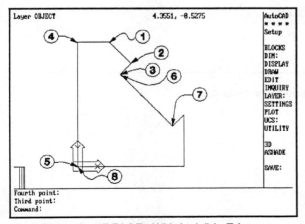

Pick Points for 3DFACEs With Invisible Edges

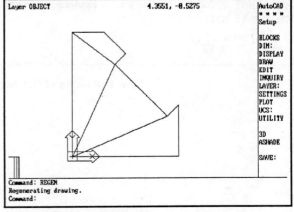

3DFACEs With SPLFRAME On

Now we can complete the left side and copy it to create the right side. We'll use SELECT to preselect the polyline perimeter before it gets obscured by the faces.

Completing the Left Side 3DFaces

Command: **SELECT**	Select the polyline at ③ for later erasure.
Command: **3DFACE**	
First point: **I**	Pick ①.
Second point: I	Pick ②.
Third point:	Pick ③.
Fourth point: **\<RETURN\>**	
Third point:	Pick ④.
Fourth point:	Pick ⑤.
Third point: **\<RETURN\>**	
Command: **ERASE**	Previous (the polyline).
Command: **OSNAP**	Set to NONe.
Command: **SETVAR**	Set SPLFRAME to 1.
Command: **REGEN**	
Command: **COPY**	All faces (taking care to avoid ellipses), displacement 0,0,-3.
Command: **SETVAR**	Set SPLFRAME to 0.
Command: **UCS**	Restore World.
Command: **ROTATE**	All faces 180 degrees about 0,0.
Command: **VPORTS**	Restore viewport 3DSI.
Command: **HIDE**	
Command: **SAVE**	

Now the sides of the bracket are closed.

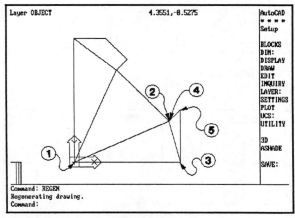

Pick Points for 3DFACEs

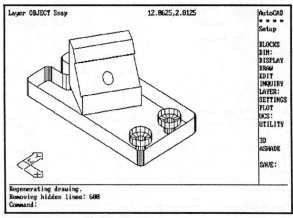

Bracket Faces With HIDE

To close the back and inclined front around the holes, we need to get rid of the existing mesh faces that obscure them.

Exploding Meshes Into Faces

When you explode a polygon mesh, it turns into individual 3Dfaces. (There is no reverse command to combine faces into meshes.) We can explode the body of the angle bracket into faces, then rotate the obscuring faces back into our SCRATCH view where they can serve as the framework to construct sets of 3Dfaces about the holes.

Exploding Meshes

Continue in the previous ANGLE drawing.

Command: **EXPLODE**	Explode the TABSURF body of the bracket into faces.
Command: **ROTATE**	Rotate back and inclined front faces 180 degrees about 0,0.
Command: **VPORTS**	Restore SCRATCH.
Command: **UCS**	Use Entity option, pick inclined front face.
Command: **PLAN**	Set to current UCS.
Command: **ZOOM**	Zoom way in, as shown below.
Command: **CHPROP**	Change polyline base, circular ellipse, and back face to frozen layer CONST.

Command: **LINE**	Draw from approximate center of ellipse to @2,0.
Command: **ARRAY**	Polar, center of ellipse, 10 items, 180 degrees.
Command: **TRIM**	Trim all lines from inside of ellipse.
Command: **ERASE**	Erase ellipse.

Now we are set up to draw a group of faces.

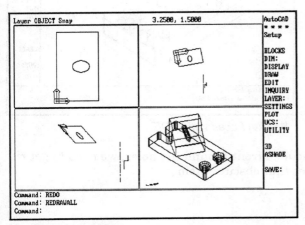

Inclined Face in Plan

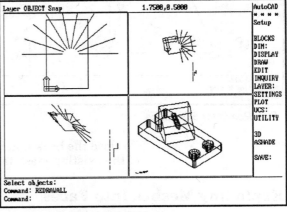

Arrayed Lines for 3DFACEs

When possible, 3Dfaces should be copied, mirrored, or rotated to provide identical 3Dfaces in symmetrical locations. We only need to draw the top half, then we can use MIRROR to duplicate it. Remember to enter an **I** before every first and third (odd) point prompt to make the edge invisible. Enter the points in an S pattern.

Weaving a Hole With 3DFaces

Command: **OSNAP**	Set to INT,END.
Command: <Snap off>	Toggle snap off.
Command: **3DFACE**	
First point: **I**	Pick ①.
Second point:	
Third point: **I**	
Fourth point:	
Third point: **I**	

```
Fourth point:
```
                              Continue picking third and fourth points, with an **I** before each third.
                              At corners, pick corner points — not intersection of lines near corners.

```
Third point: <RETURN>
```
                              When done.

```
Command: OSNAP
```
                              Set to NONe.
```
Command: <Snap on>
```
                              Toggle snap on.

```
Command: ERASE
```
                              Erase arrayed lines and original inclined face.
```
Command: REDRAW
```

```
Command: MIRROR
```
                              Mirror all faces down across their horizontal center line.

```
Command: UCS
```
                              Reset to World.
```
Command: ROTATE
```
                              All faces 180 degrees about 0,0.

```
Command: VPORTS
```
                              Restore viewport 3DSI.
```
Command: HIDE
```
                              And the inclined face of the bracket is closed, with a hole.

```
Command: VPORTS
```
                              Restore viewport 3D and look at the four views.
```
Command: SAVE
```

If you got it right, the drawing with faces before mirroring should look
like it did *before* drawing the faces, because all edges in open space are
invisible.

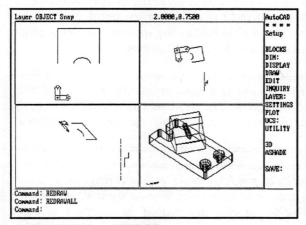

3DFACEs Before MIRROR   3DFACEs in 3D View

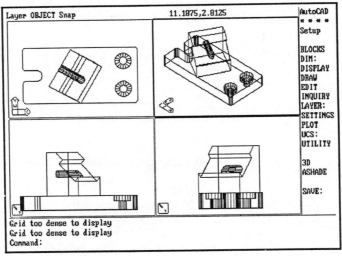

Nearly Finished, in Four Views

You can use a similar process to generate the back faces and the top and bottom of the base. But first let's discuss some alternative ways of setting up your 3Dfaces.

Points for Positioning in Space

We used the intersections and endpoints of an array of lines to osnap our faces. Another good technique is to use temporary point entities and osnap Node to them. AutoCAD makes it easy to generate a series of points along entities with the DIVIDE and MEASURE commands.

DIVIDE

> *DIVIDE marks an entity into equal length segments. You can divide lines, circles, arcs, and polylines. The divided entity isn't physically separated; point entities (or optionally, blocks) are placed as markers at each division point.*

MEASURE

> *MEASURE marks an entity at predetermined segment lengths. You can measure lines, circles, arcs, and polylines. The entity isn't physically separated; point entities (or blocks) are placed as markers at each segment point.*

Points inserted by DIVIDE and MEASURE are commonly used as temporary Node osnap points. To make it easy to later erase them or change them to another layer, they become the Previous selection set.

You can make them more visible with the PDMODE and PDSIZE system variables.

PDMODE and PDSIZE Point Display Variables

The system variables which control point appearance and size are PDMODE (Point Display MODE) and PDSIZE (Point Display SIZE).

PDMODE controls the style of a point. These are the point values and descriptions:

0 — A point "dot," the default.

1 — A non-appearing point.

2 — A "tick mark," displayed as a cross (+).

3 — An "X."

4 — A vertical line projecting up from the point (|).

32 — A circle.

64 — A square.

These values can be combined. For example, 98 (2 + 32 + 64) consists of a cross, a circle, and a square. The AutoCAD program includes a slide named POINTS that shows all the combinations. You can display it with the SLIDE command, as shown below.

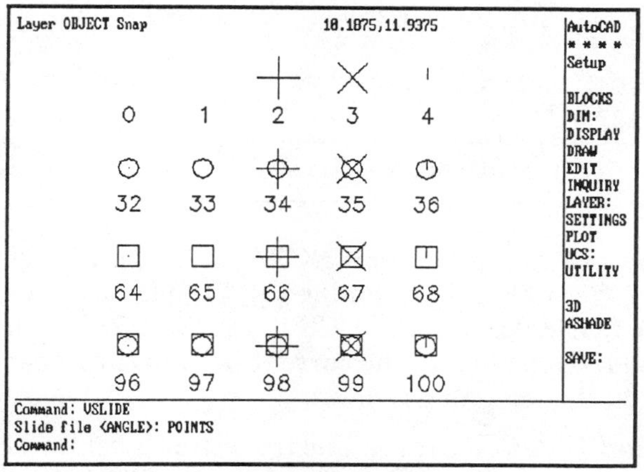

PDMODE Complex Points Example

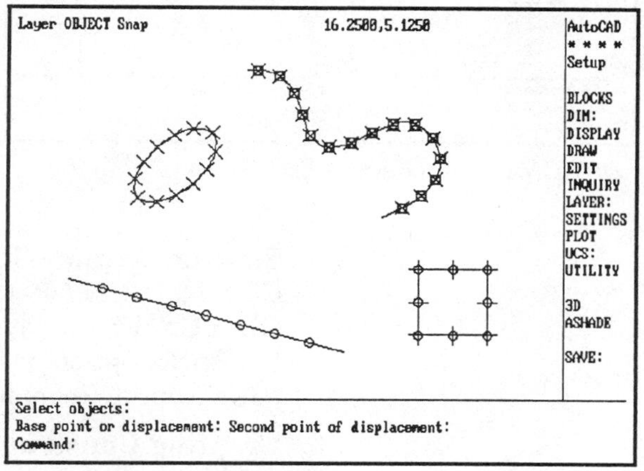

Entities Divided With Points

PDSIZE controls the size of point styles. A positive value designates the absolute size of the point figure in drawing units. A negative value sizes it as a percentage of the current viewport or screen height, making points appear to be a consistent size regardless of drawing scale or zoom.

Generating temporary points with DIVIDE or MEASURE and making them easy to see with PDMODE and PDSIZE sets up a good framework to hang surfaces on. There is no *best* way to model most surfaces; many different methods can accomplish the same task. Remember to keep modeling as neat and efficient as possible. If the model is to be shaded in AutoShade, it becomes even more important to develop the faces in a well-organized geometric pattern. See INSIDE AutoCAD for more on shading.

OPTIONAL: Closing the Back Face

Close the back face in much the same manner as the front inclined face. Since the circular ellipse is centered in the 3 x 3 square, create one-eighth of the surface and then mirror and array it.

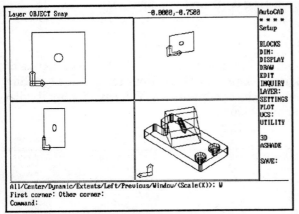

OPTIONAL: Back Face in Plan —See ①

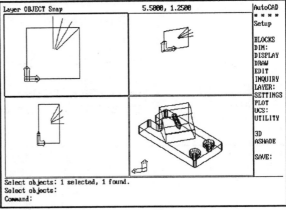

Ready for 3DFACEs —See ②

① **Setting Up the View** — Restore viewport SCRATCH. Thaw layer CONST. CHPROP the circular ellipse and back 3Dface to layer OBJECT. Freeze layer CONST again. Set UCS to the back face with the Entity option. Use PLAN to align to the current UCS in the upper left viewport. Zoom in on the top half as shown.

② **Creating Construction Lines** — Draw a line from circle's center to face's corner. Polar array it four times about circle's center 45 degrees. Trim the lines from within the circle. (If you have trouble using the circular ellipse as a cutting edge, replace it with a real circle.) Erase the circular ellipse.

③ **Drawing 3Dfaces** — Set osnap to INT,END. Turn snap off. Zoom in closer on the corner. Use 3DFACE to draw the three faces, entering an

I (invisible edge) before *each* first and third point pick. Set osnap to NONe and toggle snap on. Erase the four lines.

④ **Arraying Faces** — Zoom Previous. Mirror the three faces horizontally to the left. Polar array all six faces four times to fill 360 degrees.

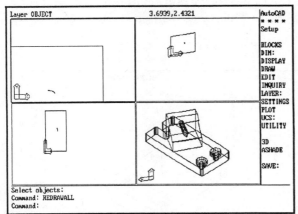

OPTIONAL: The Three 3DFaces —See ③

Mirrored and Arrayed Faces —See ④

⑤ **Rotating Faces Into Part** — Set UCS to World. Rotate all the faces 180 degrees about 0,0. Restore viewport 3DSI. Set a viewpoint of -5,5,6 and zoom in close to view or hide it. Save your results.

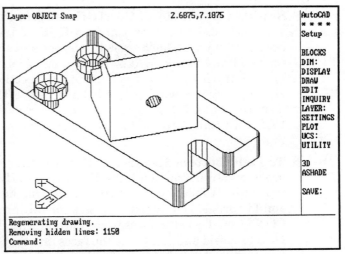

OPTIONAL: Back Face With HIDE —See ⑤

All we need to do now is close the top and bottom of the base.

OPTIONAL: *Closing the Base's Top and Bottom*

Closing the base's top and bottom will be a little complicated due to the more complex edge and the two holes. Divide the surface to define a square around the holes that can be filled. You can also create a quarter-pie set of faces for the typical large and small radiuses, and copy and mirror them to the rest. Then you will just have easy-to-fill rectangular areas left.

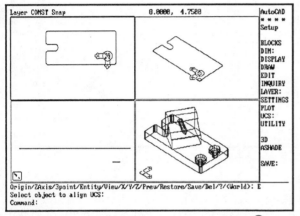

OPTIONAL: Polyline Base and Circles —See ①

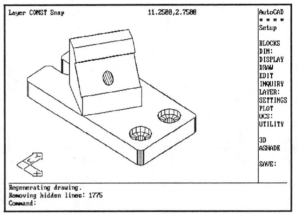

Finished 3D View With HIDE —See ②

① **Setting Up** — Restore SCRATCH viewports. Thaw layer CONST and set it active. Erase everything on CONST layer except the polyline base with notch. (Don't erase the center and ziz-zag polyline from the countersink.) REDRAWALL. Draw a circle, using INT osnaps in the lower left viewport, osnapping to intersections of center line and zig-zag polyline with polyline base. Move the polyline base with displacement 0,0,1. Draw a second, larger circle in the same way. Set UCS with Entity option to larger circle. Erase the center and zig-zag lines.

② **Top and Bottom 3DFaces** — Divide the top of the base into regular areas with construction lines. Set layer OBJECT current and fill the top with 3Dfaces, using COPY, MIRROR, and ARRAY to duplicate similar areas. Use invisible edges for all interior edges. Turn layer CONST off. Copy the faces to the bottom with displacement 0,0,-1. Set UCS to World and rotate the top faces into the 3D view. Erase and redo faces around the holes to fit the smaller bottom holes. Rotate the bottom faces into the 3D view. Restore viewport 3DSI and look at it with HIDE.

③ **Finished Views** — Restore viewports 3D and look at the four views.

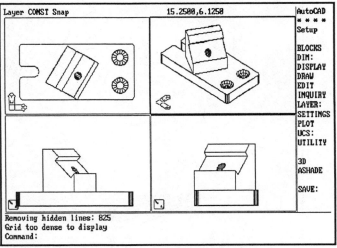

OPTIONAL: Finished, in Four Views —See ③

EDGESURF: Coons Patch Surfaces

The last of the surface generating commands is EDGESURF, a command that is not often used in mechanical drafting.

EDGESURF

> *EDGESURF generates a 3D polygon mesh by approximating a Coons surface patch from four adjoining edge entities. Each edge can be a line, arc, or open polyline, anywhere in 3D space. The endpoints of the edge entities must touch, combining to form a closed path. You can pick the edges in any order. The first edge or entity selected defines the M direction (controlled by SURFTAB1) of the mesh. The two edges that touch the M edge define the N direction (controlled by SURFTAB1).*

EDGESURF fills the area inside its boundaries with an interpolated bicubic surface patch, mathematically correct but probably not the actual contour you would program a machine tool to cut. Examples of boundary sets and their generated surfaces are shown below.

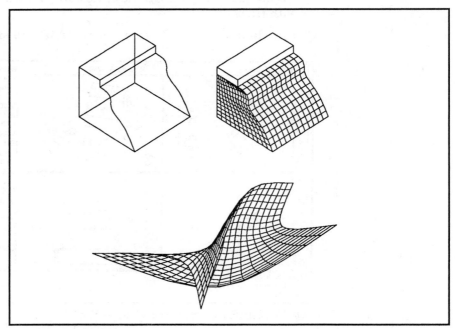

EDGESURF Examples

Experiment with EDGESURF. You may find it useful for approximating surfaces that fill irregular areas.

Summary

This chapter has introduced you to the tools you need for full 3D drafting and design. You can see how being able to quickly and accurately manipulate the User Coordinate System (UCS) is the most important feature for efficient 3D performance.

The angle support exercise showed you three fundamental techniques for 3D drafting: developing and using a construction envelope; orienting, saving, and restoring a UCS; and using a scratch UCS and a building-block approach to drawing. These three techniques work together to provide you with an efficient and productive method for developing virtually any part in full 3D.

This chapter also expanded on the 3D wireframe techniques which were presented in Chapter 9, and introduced AutoCAD's three-dimensional polygon mesh tools. These tools include 3D meshes, ruled surfaces, tabulated surfaces, surfaces of revolution, and edge-defined coons surface patches. As you saw in the exercises, 3D meshes may be used to surface model virtually any 3D shape or part.

Some parts may require surface modeling with 3D faces. 3D faces are a versatile tool, convenient for closing those hard-to-model surfaces.

You may want to create and surface model specific shapes, and then save them in a 3D modeling library. Geometry such as the drill and spotface, developed in this chapter, provide you with a good example of a useful 3D library drawing. Try expanding the 1 x 1 block technique presented in Chapter 7 to a 1 x 1 x 1 technique.

In the next chapter, we will view a 3D part, capture the views, insert them into an engineering drawing, and dimension them with geometric dimensioning and tolerancing techniques.

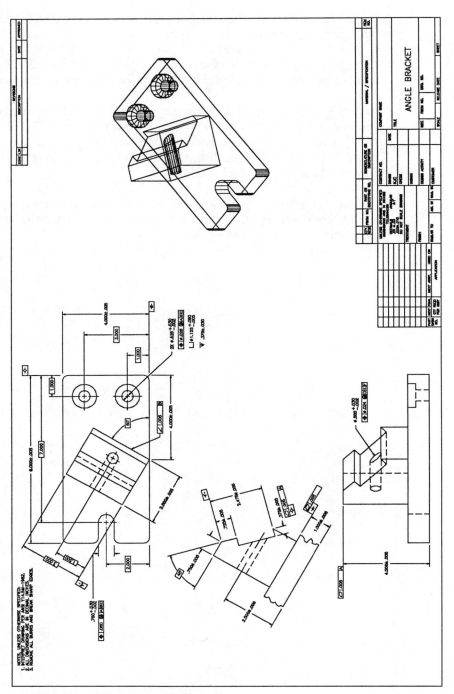

The Multi-View Angle Support Drawing

CHAPTER 11

3D Manipulations

DYNAMIC VIEWS, BLOCKS, MULTI-VIEW DRAWINGS, AND ADVANCED SURFACING

In this chapter, we will create a multi-view drawing from last chapter's surface model. This procedure is based upon the process of developing the model first in 3D, then creating drawings to accurately communicate the design concept. This chapter also includes an optional exercise for modeling a universal joint and yoke assembly with AutoCAD's 3D surfacing tools.

The multi-view drawing is created by inserting several blocks from Chapter 9's angle support drawing into a drawing which can then be annotated and dimensioned. Each block views the original 3D drawing from one of the orientations needed for the multi-view drawing. These are the plan, front, and 3D (parallel projection) views in Chapter 9's viewports, and an auxiliary view which is the same as Chapter 9's LSIDE orientation.

A combination of the WBLOCK (or BLOCK), UCS, and INSERT commands make it possible to combine multiple views in a single drawing. Wblocking (or blocking) and inserting blocks is relative to the UCS that is current when the commands are executed. To create blocks for multiple views, you simply orient the UCS to each desired view and block the object in that orientation. Multiple blocks from differing orientations can be inserted into a single UCS, maintaining the orientations that they were blocked with. In this chapter, we will insert four such blocks into a D-size drawing.

Capturing Orthographic and Parallel Projection Views

There are several ways to achieve the orientations needed for the blocks. You can set the UCS first and then use PLAN to orient the view, but that requires zooming in after the PLAN command. You can use the VPOINT command to orient the view and then set the UCS to match, but VPOINT is sometimes awkward for odd angles. The approach we like is to orient the view with the DVIEW command, then set the UCS to match. DVIEW is a fast, powerful, interactive command for controlling views. You can use it to try out several different views without a screen regeneration; to view the drawing from different angles, directions, and distances; to put your drawing in perspective view; to do hides; to work with subsets of the whole drawing's entities; and to clip foreground or background portions of the drawing. We'll use wblocking and various orientations to explore the features of DVIEW.

Dynamically Viewing 3D Drawings With DVIEW

The DVIEW command allows you to view a drawing in much the same way a cameraman moves around a set, taking shots from different distances, angles, and magnifications. DVIEW is much more flexible than the VPOINT command. VPOINT offers only a few ways to set the viewing angle, and insists on viewing the entire drawing through 0,0,0, which usually requires a subsequent pan or zoom. DVIEW offers a rich set of options to achieve any angle or magnification in a single step.

DVIEW

> *DVIEW (Dynamic VIEW) is a tool for viewing 3D models in space. DVIEW is similar to the VPOINT command. However, in DVIEW you can dynamically drag and rotate the 3D model with the aid of slide bars. You can display a perspective view of the model and toggle back and forth between parallel and perspective views. The DVIEW command is similar to the concept of using a camera to view a target. You can set a camera point, target point, lens length, and position front and back clipping planes. The default is parallel (not perspective) projection.*
> ```
> CAmera/TArget/Distance/POints/PAn/Zoom/TWist/CLip/
> Hide/Off/Undo/<eXit>:
> ```

DVIEW uses the same names and terms used in cinematography, so use your imagination when we refer to panning and zooming the camera. For example, you can establish the line of sight used to view your drawing by setting a camera or a target option, or by two points. The camera comes equipped with zoom lenses. Unlike real cameras, this one has no distortion and only goes into perspective mode when the Distance option is used. Clipping may be used to show cut-away or sectional views. And the camera may be twisted to any angle, even turned upside down — something the VPOINT command cannot do.

Most of the DVIEW options accept input from the DVIEW *slider bars* in addition to typed input.

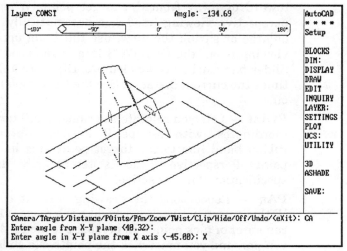

A DVIEW Slider Bar

The slider bars provide a way to interactively drag and pick numeric values like scale, distance, or magnification. The slider bar looks like a ruler with a moving diamond anchored at the current setting. As you move your cursor along the bar, the indicator diamond slides with it, the coords display is replaced by a dynamic display of the equivalent input value, and the DVIEW image updates as quickly as it can keep up. In some options, the bar displays other values to guide you. The values shown on the slider bar are not in the same terms as the input values. For example, the Distance option accepts typed input in drawing units, but shows 1X, 4X, and 16X as guide values (relative to the current view) along the slider bar. Picking with the slider bar is quick and intuitive, but not precise. When you want precise values, use the slider to get it looking about right, then use the keyboard to input the precise number. The values on the slider bar vary with the DVIEW options.

DVIEW Command Options

CAmera — Rotates the camera angle around the target point by entering angles or using the slider bars. Rotation is like the VPOINT Rotate option: you enter the angle *up* from the current X,Y plane, then the angle from the X axis *in* the X,Y plane. This rotates the camera around the existing target point.

TArget — Rotates the target angle relative to the existing camera point. This is the opposite of the CAmera option.

Distance — Moves the camera along the existing line-of-sight angle, toward or away from the target point. When you select distance, perspective viewing (mode) is automatically turned on. To simply enlarge or shrink the view, use the Zoom option. When perspective viewing is on, the UCS/WCS icon is replaced by a perspective icon. Slider bar marks are labeled 0X, 1X, up to 16X, meaning that value times the current distance. See the Off option for turning perspective off.

POint — Lets you relocate the camera and target points using X,Y,Z coordinates, with osnaps if needed. No slider applies, but a rubber-band line to the target point aids in specifying the camera point. Perspective mode is temporarily disabled during point specification if it was active.

PAn — Repositions the drawing without changing magnification. Without perspective, it works like the normal PAN command and you can enter or pick points. In perspective mode, the perspective shifts as you pan and you must pick the points. No slider applies, but you can drag the image as you pick the second point.

Zoom — With perspective on, Zoom lets you set the camera's lens length in millimeters by entering a value or using the slider bar. With perspective off, it works like the ZOOM command's Center option except that magnification is by scale factor instead of view height, and the value by input or slider is in terms of the nX-type scale factor.

TWist — Allows you to twist the view around the current line of sight. You can enter a value in degrees counterclockwise, or drag it with a rubber-band line from the view center to the crosshairs. When dragging, the angle displays on the status line.

CLip — Sets front and back clipping planes, such as you would use to see a section through an object. The cutting planes are placed perpendicular to the line of sight at the designated position between the camera and target (or beyond the target if a negative back clip is specified). Clip options include Back, Front, and Off. Perspective automatically turns the front clip on, with the plane at the camera's position unless you place it in front of the camera. This default prevents objects behind the camera from appearing in perspective.

Hide — Removes hidden lines on the current DVIEW selection set. This allows you to examine the effects of hide on selected portions of the drawing.

Off — Turns perspective mode off.

Undo — Undoes the last DVIEW command. You can repeatedly undo, back to the beginning of the command.

eXit — Ends and exits the DVIEW command. After exiting, the current drawing is regenerated in the new DVIEW. Cancel instead if you want to redisplay the drawing as it was before you entered DVIEW.

Spend time experimenting with DVIEW's features. If your drawing seems to disappear, it's probably off screen, or zoomed so far in or out that it appears as blank space or a dot.

DVIEW uses normal object selection, but if you have no objects selected, it uses a house-shaped icon to indicate orientation during DVIEW option settings. You can also create your own icon by making a one-unit-sized 3D block named DVIEWBLOCK.

The [Display] pull-down menu [Dview Options] item calls the DVIEW Options icon menu, with the frequently used Camera, Pan and Zoom options.

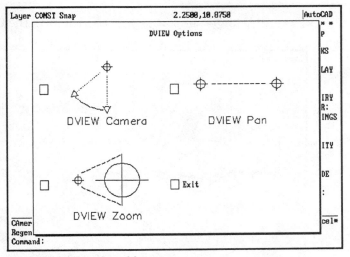

DVIEW Options Icon Menu

Using the DVIEW Camera

We'll use DVIEW to view the back side of the angle support and to establish the views needed for our multi-view drawing's blocks. When you select DVIEW's selection set, you can speed up performance by selecting only as many entities as you need to represent the objects you wish to manipulate. Avoid selecting curves, text, and meshes because they slow things down considerably. For example, we'll exclude the holes of the angle support by using the object selection Remove mode after windowing the whole thing.

To get started, set up the ANGLE drawing from Chapter 10, unless you have the SIA DISK.

Setting Up

 You are already set up. Skip to the exercise called Applying DVIEW Camera and Hide.

 Edit an EXISTING drawing named ANGLE.

Command: **UCS**	Reset to World.
Command: **VPORTS**	Restore 3DSI.
Command: **CHPROP**	Change everything on OBJECT layer to CONST.
Command: **LAYER**	Thaw and turn all layers on.
Command: **ZOOM**	Zoom All.
Command: **ERASE**	Erase the construction envelope.
Command: **ZOOM**	Zoom Previous.

The entire angle support should be visible on the CONST layer.

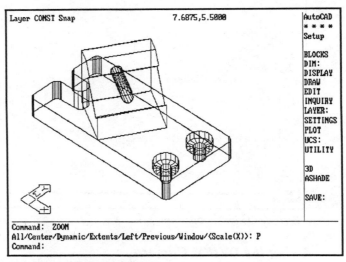

Prepared 3D Angle Support

Now let's use the Camera option sliders to rotate the camera around the target and view the back of the angle support from a bird's-eye view, with a Hide option. Then use Camera again to set a top view and wblock it to file name T-TOP. The T- prefix will designate temporary blocks.

Applying DVIEW Camera and Hide

 Begin a NEW drawing named ANGLE=DV-ANGLE.

 Continue in the above ANGLE drawing.

```
Command: DVIEW
Select objects:                 Select all but the three holes.
CAmera/TArget/Distance/POints/PAn/Zoom/TWist/CLip/Hide/Off/Undo/<eXit>: CA        Camera.
Enter angle from X-Y plane <40.32>:    Drag angle to about 35 degrees on the coords display.
Enter angle in X-Y plane from X axis <-45>:    Drag angle to about 135 degrees.
                                The camera angle should look like the illustration below.

CAmera/TArget/Distance/POints/PAn/Zoom/TWist/CLip/Hide/Off/Undo/<eXit>: H         Hide.
Removing hidden lines: 325

CAmera/TArget/Distance/POints/PAn/Zoom/TWist/CLip/Hide/Off/Undo/<eXit>: CA
Enter angle from X-Y plane <35.02>: 90
Enter angle in X-Y plane from X axis <135.00>: 0
CAmera/TArget/Distance/POints/PAn/Zoom/TWist/CLip/Hide/Off/Undo/<eXit>: <RETURN>

Command: WBLOCK             To file T-TOP, base point 3,3 and select everything.

Command: OOPS              OOPS the drawing back.
Command: SAVE
```

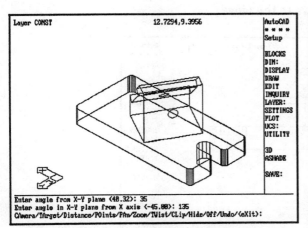

The Back Dynamically Viewed With HIDE

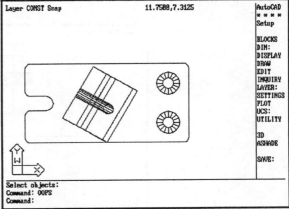

Top View for T-TOP

The Target option is used in exactly the same manner as Camera, except the angles are opposite.

Using the DVIEW Points Option

The Points option works like VPOINT, except you can set the target point instead of being forced to look at 0,0,0. Let's use Points to set new target and camera points to get a front view for wblocking.

Setting Points for the Front View

Continue in the previous ANGLE drawing.

```
Command: DVIEW
Select objects:                 Select a representative sampling.
CAmera/TArget/Distance/POints/PAn/Zoom/TWist/CLip/Hide/Off/Undo/<eXit>: PO
Enter target point <7.0284, 5.7917, 1.1358>: 7,3,0   Center of the base.
Enter camera point <7.0284, 5.7917, 10.4094>: 7,0,0   Straight in front.
CAmera/TArget/Distance/POints/PAn/Zoom/TWist/CLip/Hide/Off/Undo/<eXit>: <RETURN>
```

```
Command: UCS                    Set with the View option.
```

```
Command: WBLOCK                 To file T-FRONT, base point 3,0 and select everything.
```

```
Command: OOPS                   OOPS the drawing back.
```

After setting the view, we used the UCS View option to align the UCS so we could wblock it relative to the view.

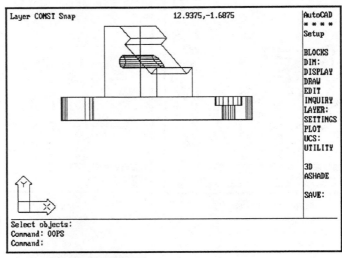

Front View for T-FRONT

The auxiliary view needed to show the profile of the angle bracket is nearly the same, but aligned to the left face. We can use the Points option by osnapping the points to points at opposite sides of the inclined front face.

Osnapping Points for the Auxiliary View

Continue in the previous ANGLE drawing.

```
Command: DVIEW
Select objects:              Select a representative sampling.
*** Switching to the WCS ***
CAmera/TArget/Distance/POints/PAn/Zoom/TWist/CLip/Hide/Off/Undo/<eXit>: PO
Enter target point <7.0000, 3.0000, 0.0000>: INT
of                           Pick a point on right side of angle bracket ①.
Enter camera point <7.0000, 0.0000, 0.0000>: INT
of                           Pick corresponding point on left side of bracket ②.
CAmera/TArget/Distance/POints/PAn/Zoom/TWist/CLip/Hide/Off/Undo/<eXit>: <RETURN>
*** Returning to the UCS ***
Regenerating drawing.
Grid too dense to display
```

```
Command: UCS                 Set with the View option.
```

```
Command: WBLOCK              To file T-AUX, osnap base point INT at ①, select everything.
```

```
Command: OOPS                OOPS the drawing back.
Command: SAVE
```

Since the current UCS was not the WCS, DVIEW temporarily switched into the WCS during input. You normally think of views in terms of the WCS, so it is used during input unless the WORLDVIEW system variable is set to a non-zero value.

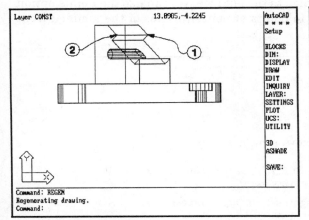

Pick Points for DVIEW Points

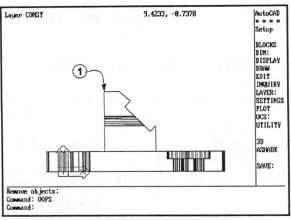

Auxiliary View for T-AUX

The last view we need to wblock is the 3D view, so let's play around with perspective on the way there.

Using DVIEW Distance, Pan, and Zoom

The Distance option puts DVIEW and your drawing into perspective mode until you return to normal with the Off option. When you exit DVIEW in perspective mode, you are limited. PAN, ZOOM, and SKETCH are prohibited. Other commands can be used, but you can't pick points or osnap in a perspective viewport. The solution is simple. Just enter points from the keyboard or use multiple viewports and pick in a non-perspective viewport. Object selection works okay in perspective.

Set perspective with an initial distance of 24 and pan as shown in the two illustrations below. Then, still in perspective, adjust the camera angle and zoom in on it.

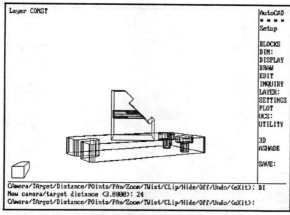

Perspective Distance at

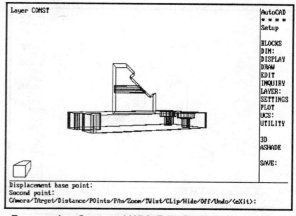

Perspective Centered With Pan Option

3D Perspective Viewing

Continue in the previous ANGLE drawing.

```
Command: DVIEW
Select objects:                                    Select a representative sampling.
*** Switching to the WCS ***
CAmera/TArget/Distance/POints/PAn/Zoom/TWist/CLip/Hide/Off/Undo/<eXit>: DI
New camera/target distance <3.0000>: 24            Or pick 8X with slider.

CAmera/TArget/Distance/POints/PAn/Zoom/TWist/CLip/Hide/Off/Undo/<eXit>: PA
Displacement base point:                           Pick point on object.
Second point:                                      Drag to center and pick.

CAmera/TArget/Distance/POints/PAn/Zoom/TWist/CLip/Hide/Off/Undo/<eXit>: CA
Enter angle from X-Y plane <0.00>:                 Drag to about 41 and pick.
Enter angle in X-Y plane from X axis <-0.00>:      Drag to about -132 and pick.

CAmera/TArget/Distance/POints/PAn/Zoom/TWist/CLip/Hide/Off/Undo/<eXit>: Z
Adjust lenslength <50.000mm>:                      Drag to about 60 to fill screen and pick.
CAmera/TArget/Distance/POints/PAn/Zoom/TWist/CLip/Hide/Off/Undo/<eXit>: <RETURN>
Command: SAVE
```

The perspective is still active after exiting the DVIEW command. If you
pan to re-center it after getting the perspective just right, the pan will
alter the vanishing point.

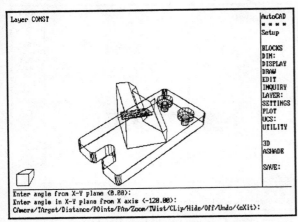

Perspective Improved With Camera Option

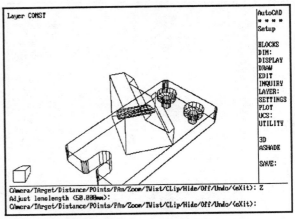

Perspective Zoomed

We don't really want a perspective for our multi-view drawing, so let's turn it off and adjust our 3D view with the Pan and Camera options. With perspective off, we can pan freely.

Adjusting and Wblocking a 3D Dview

Command: **DVIEW**
Use the Off option to exit perspective mode.
Pan slightly to re-center it.
Use CAmera to adjust the angle; we used 52 and -135 degrees.
Exit DVIEW.

Command: **SETVAR**
Set SPLFRAME to 1. We want to get all the 3Dfaces.

Command: **UCS**
Set with the View option.

Command: **WBLOCK**
To file T-3D, base point -3,3 (below and to left), select everything.

Command: **QUIT**

Since we now have all our needed views for the multi-view drawing wblocked to individual drawing files, we can quit the ANGLE drawing and turn to inserting the blocks into a title sheet.

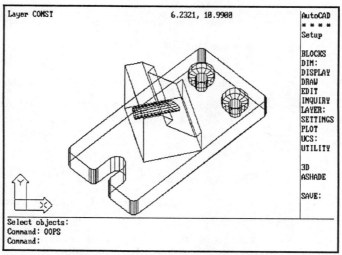

```
Layer CONST                    6.2321, 10.9900         AutoCAD
                                                       * * * *
                                                       Setup

                                                       BLOCKS
                                                       DIM:
                                                       DISPLAY
                                                       DRAW
                                                       EDIT
                                                       INQUIRY
                                                       LAYER:
                                                       SETTINGS
                                                       PLOT
                                                       UCS:
                                                       UTILITY

                                                       3D
                                                       ASHADE

                                                       SAVE:



Select objects:
Command: OOPS
Command:
```

3D View for T-3D

Inserting Captured Blocks

In this part of the exercise, we will create a multiple view engineering drawing of the angle support. This drawing will be made up of the front and top orthographic views, one auxiliary view, and the 3D parallel projection view. We'll insert these previously wblocked views of the angle support into a D-sized title sheet and use them as tracing templates to create a proper set of 2D views. We'll complete the drawing by adding geometric dimensioning and tolerancing.

Allow plenty of room for dimensioning between each view when you place the blocks onto the D-sized sheet. CAD drafting often requires substantial amounts of dimensioning space. The exact spacing between the blocks is not critical, but the alignment is. When developing an orthographic drawing, the views must align. You can use snap, osnap, and point filters to align them during or after insertion so that shared dimensions, such as width, height, and depth, are common in each view. In this exercise, snap will be sufficient.

Use the PROTO-D drawing from the SIA DISK or from Chapter 6, and the T-TOP, T-FRONT, T-AUX, and T-3D files you wblocked in this chapter. Except for T-AUX, we'll insert the blocks at their default 1:1 scale and 0 rotation angle. T-AUX must be aligned with the skewed bracket in the top view. To align it, set a temporary UCS before inserting.

Inserting the Views

Enter selection: **1**	Begin a NEW drawing named M-ANGLE=PROTO-D.
Command: **VIEW**	Restore view BDR.
Command: **SNAP**	Set to 0.5.
Command: **INSERT**	Insert T-TOP, using default scale and angle.
Command: **UCS**	Align 3point UCS to bracket in top view, using osnap INT.
Command: **INSERT**	Insert T-AUX aligned with bracket.
Command: **UCS**	Previous.
Command: **INSERT**	T-FRONT aligned with top, and T-3D.
Command: **INSERT**	T-3D in the space to the right.
Command: **MOVE**	To adjust positions if needed, carefully maintaining alignment.

When you have inserted the four blocks and are satisfied with their positions, you should see the following.

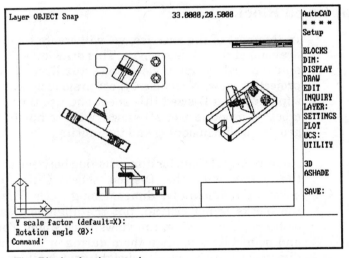

The Blocks Are Inserted

Now we need to turn the orthogonal views into proper 2D drawings.

Editing the Views Into 2D

Before dimensioning, we need to trace the angle support views to create 2D drawings. Because the angle support was developed in 3D, it includes detail (such as the curves and holes) that becomes confusing in 2D. It is generally easiest to trace over such images than to try to edit them into an acceptable 2D form.

Tracing the blocks is actually very quick and easy because the geometry is already there. You don't have to enter coordinates or calculate distances; you just osnap everything. And, if you need to, you can use point filters to align the adjacent views.

We want the new entities we create to all be in the X,Y plane of the WCS (or our BDR UCS), with Z coordinate values of zero. But osnap will normally snap many of these points to non-zero Z coordinates. They would *look* right, but it wouldn't really be a proper drawing and might complicate dimensioning and the appearance of linetypes. We could override the Z coordinates with point filters, but there is an easier way. The FLATLAND system variable makes AutoCAD act like it did before it became full 3D, locking all so-called 2D entities (including lines) to the WCS X,Y plane. We'll turn FLATLAND on before we begin to draw.

➡ *NOTE: FLATLAND is scheduled to disappear in future releases of AutoCAD. When it does, you'll have to resort to the point filter technique. It's a good candidate for a menu macro.*

Let's edit the top view.

Editing the Top View

Continue in the previous M-ANGLE drawing.

Command: **ZOOM**	Zoom in close on the top view.
Command: **SNAP**	Set to 0.0625.
Command: **SETVAR**	Set FLATLAND to 1 (on).
Command: **PLINE**	Trace base perimeter with square corners, an arc at the notch, and close it.
Command: **FILLET**	Set radius to 0.25 and use Polyline option on perimeter.
Command: **OSNAP**	Set to END,INT.
Command: **CIRCLE**	Use the 2P option to osnap five circles to the three holes. Zoom in close and turn off snap for the hole in the bracket (which *is* a circle at this angle), then Zoom P and turn snap on.
Command: **LINE**	Draw perimeter and inclined face lines of bracket.

Command: **LINE**	Use onsnap PERP and TAN for the hole's hidden lines.
From point: PER	
to	
To point: TAN	Pick any point on line of back face of bracket.
to	
To point: **‹RETURN›**	Pick point on top of circle (hole).
Command: **‹RETURN›**	
LINE From point:	Repeat for bottom hidden line of hole.
Command: **OSNAP**	Set to NONe.
Command: **CHPROP**	Change three hidden lines to layer HL, as shown below.
Command: **ERASE**	Erase the T-TOP block.
Command: **REDRAW**	
Command: **END**	

When you have edited the view to your satisfaction, remove the 3D block drawing. Remember, you can save the temporary T-TOP drawing on the disk if you want. Your drawing should now look similar to the illustration below.

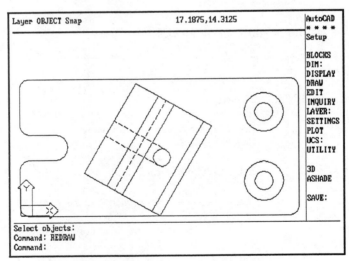

The Edited Top View

➡ *TIP: The T-TOP block is no longer in use in the M-ANGLE drawing, but it is still in the drawing database. To save file space and increase drawing loading speed, unused blocks, layers, linetypes, shapes, and styles can be removed with the PURGE command.*

> *PURGE* | *PURGE removes unused blocks, layers, linetypes, shapes, and styles from the drawing database. It must be executed at the start of a drawing editor session, before any drawing or editing commands are given. PURGE prompts you for confirmation before it removes each item.*

Let's purge the T-TOP block.

Purging Blocks

```
Enter selection: 2              Edit an EXISTING drawing named M-ANGLE.

Command: PURGE
Purge unused Blocks/LAyers/LTypes/SHapes/STyles/All: B    Blocks.
Purge block T-TOP? <N> Y
Command: SAVE
```

You have several choices for cleaning up the 3D view.

OPTIONAL: Cleaning Up the 3D View

The 3D view is acceptable as a wireframe, although the 3D polygon mesh holes are a bit densely detailed. You can accept it as-is (we did), or use one of the following alternatives.

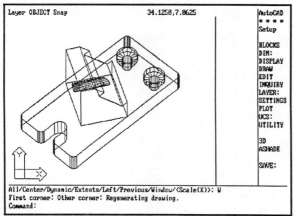

3D Wireframe View As-Is

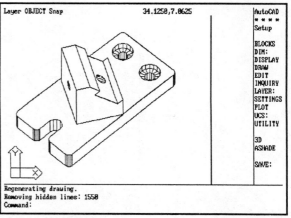

3D View With HIDE

Wireframe Option — If you want to edit the view into a better wireframe, you can trace over it in a similar manner to the top view. Instead of tracing over it completely, you can salvage part of it by exploding the block. Then, for example, you can redraw the holes with ellipses and lines and erase the meshes of the holes. You may need to turn FLATLAND back on and work in various UCS's for the best effect.

HIDE Option — You can do a HIDE or plot the drawing with hidden lines removed, but it isn't very practical. The hide will take a very long time to consider all the irrelevant lines in the border, 2D views, and dimensioning. There are two alternatives: the DXB method or plotting the 3D view separately from the rest of the drawing, but on the same sheet. Briefly, the DXB method involves configuring AutoCAD for an ADI plotter with the DXB option, then plotting the view to a file with hidden lines removed. The DXB file is then imported into the drawing with the DXBIN command. Both of these alternatives are covered in detail in the book, INSIDE AutoCAD.

OPTIONAL: Completing the 2D Front and Auxiliary Views

If you want to fully complete the M-ANGLE drawing, trace over the front and auxiliary views in the same manner as the top view.

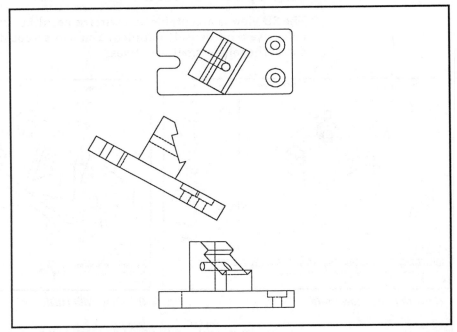

OPTIONAL: Completed Front and Auxiliary Views

Front View — Zoom in, make sure FLATLAND is on (1), set osnap to INT,END, turn snap off, and use LINE to draw everything but the bracket hole. You may have to zoom in closer in some areas. After the lines are drawn, zoom in on the bracket hole and draw two ellipses, connected by two lines. To get the ellipse on the inclined face correct, you'll have to trace it with 16 polyline segments and do a PEDIT Fit curve on it. Then erase the block. REDRAW. Use CHPROP to move hidden lines to layer HL. Save it.

Auxiliary View — Zoom to see the view and align the UCS with the Entity option. Use DVIEW TWist, zoom to align it to the screen (30 degrees), and zoom in close. Use lines with FLATLAND on and osnap INT,END to trace it all. Zoom in closer, or zoom out and align with other osnaps and point filters on the top view if needed. Erase the T-AUX block and redraw it. Restore view BDR and UCS BDR. End the drawing and reload to purge the now unused blocks. Save it.

Dimensioning 2D Views

There's nothing special about completing a drawing constructed in this manner. The views are now ordinary two-dimensional drawings. You can add geometric tolerancing and dimensioning using the same techniques covered in Chapters 4, 5, 6, and 8. Or you might want to do it with the Y14.5 Menu System, as explained in the next chapter. The completed dimensioning is shown below, and at a larger scale on the facing page of this chapter.

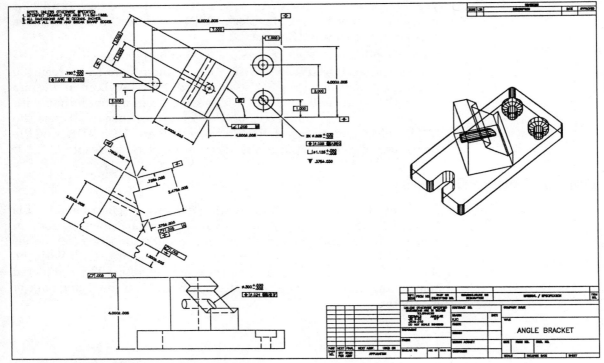

The Dimensioned Multi-View Angle Support

You can also turn on and fill in the title block, weight block, application block, parts list, revision list, and general notes as shown above, if you want the practice.

Dimensioning a 3D View

Dimensioning a 3D view is sometimes required for assembly instructions and exploded parts drawings. We'll apply angular, diameter, and horizontal dimensions to the 3D view of the angle support. The actual dimensioning commands work exactly as you are used to, but a little preparation is required before you can use them. There are two problems to consider.

First, some dimensioning commands expect to find certain kinds of entities. For instance, the ANGular dimensioning command expects you to select two lines, and DIAmeter or RADius dimensions expect you to select circles or arcs. But our 3D object is made up of 3D meshes and 3Dfaces — not lines, 2D polylines, arcs, and circles. So we sometimes have to add dimensionable entities before dimensioning. Be sure the drawing is in the appropriate UCS for each entity when added, and use osnaps to make sure the added entities align with the existing 3D geometry.

Second, you have to align UCS's to the entities being dimensioned when you dimension them. Dimensions are 2D entities and are generated in the current UCS. If the current UCS is not coplanar with the entity being dimensioned, you will actually dimension the entity's projection into the UCS, not its true size. For example, an aligned dimension in the WCS osnapped to the 2.5-inch front left baseline of the angle support would come out 2.468 in the T-3D view we wblocked earlier. In order to perform dimensioning on a 3D part, the UCS must be properly positioned to align the dimensions to the part.

Let's draw an angular dimension between the baseline of the angle bracket and the angle base. First set the UCS, then draw lines to dimension, and then dimension it. You'll need the T-3D drawing from earlier in this chapter, or the D-3D drawing from the SIA DISK.

Angular Dimensioning in 3D

Begin a NEW drawing named DIM-3D=D-3D.

Begin a NEW drawing named DIM-3D=T-3D.

Command: **SETVAR**	Set LUPREC to 3 and SPLFRAME to 0.
Command: **UCS**	Align a 3point UCS to the top of the base. Use osnap NEArest to pick two points on front top and one point on back top of base.
Command: **LINE**	Use osnap INT to trace lines along left front baseline of angle support and top front of base.
Command: **DIM1**	Dimension one and exit.
Dim: **ANG**	Angular.
Select first line:	Pick left end of new line at base of bracket.
Second line:	Pick left end of new line on top front of base.
Enter dimension line arc location:	Pick center of text shown below.
Dimension text <30>: **<RETURN>**	
Enter text location: **@**	Same point.

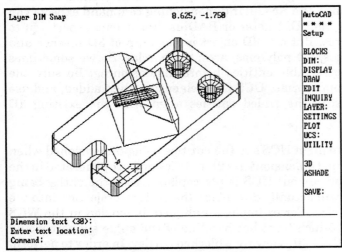

Completed Angular Dimension in 3D

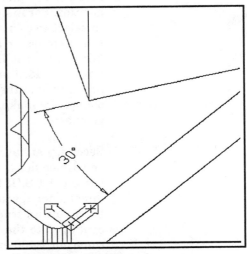

Detail of Angular Dimension

To do a diameter dimension, we first need to draw a circle over the countersunk hole, which is made of a 3D polygon mesh. The current UCS will work for this.

3D Diameter Dimensioning

Continue in the previous DIM-3D drawing.

Command: **ZOOM**	Zoom in close on the hole at the right.
Command: **CIRCLE**	Use 2P option. Osnap INT to two opposite points on top of hole.

Command: **DIM1**
Dim: **DIA**   Diameter.
Select arc or circle: Pick circle at right side.
Dimension text <1.125>: <>   Enter <> followed by 6 spaces to force text outside.
Text does not fit.
Enter leader length for text: Pick leader length shown below.

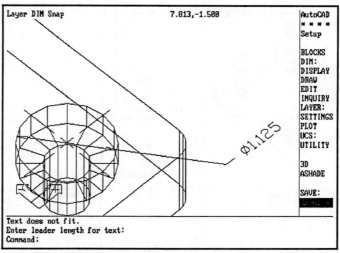

```
Layer DIM Snap                          7.813,-1.500        AutoCAD
                                                            * * * *
                                                            Setup

                                                            BLOCKS
                                                            DIM:
                                                            DISPLAY
                                                            DRAW
                                                            EDIT
                                                            INQUIRY
                                                            LAYER:
                                                            SETTINGS
                                                            PLOT
                                                            UCS:
                                                            UTILITY

                                                            3D
                                                            ASHADE

                                                            SAVE:

Text does not fit.
Enter leader length for text:
Command:
```

Completed Diameter Dimension

Horizontal and vertical dimensioning likewise requires a properly oriented UCS. But you don't need to create new entities unless you want to use the entity option. Let's dimension the height of the bracket at its back left edge.

Vertical Dimensioning in 3D

Continue in the previous DIM-3D drawing.

Command: **ZOOM**	Zoom out to see the bracket.
Command: **UCS**	Use 3point and osnaps to set to back right or back left face.

```
Command: DIM1
DIM: VER                              Vertical.
First extension line origin or RETURN to select: INT
of                                    Pick top back left corner.
Second extension line origin: INT
of                                    Pick bottom back left corner.
Dimension line location:              Pick center of text shown below.
Dimension text <3.000>: <RETURN>

Command: END                          Or QUIT if you don't want to save it.
```

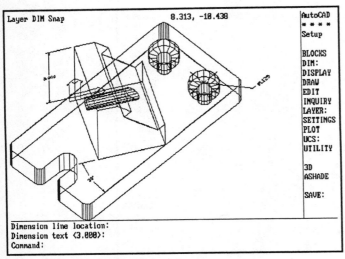

Completed 3D Vertical Dimension

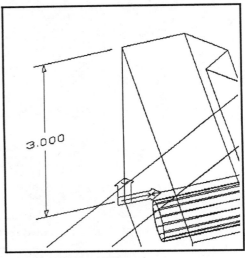

Detail of Vertical Dimension

You can use the same techniques to complete the rest of the part if you like. The process is to set your UCS, add entities if needed, and dimension normally. Take care with your osnaps because groups of 3D faces with invisible edges have lots of little unseen intersections between them. You can also add the appropriate Y14.5 symbols. The same principal applies for inserting symbols; the UCS position controls the block insertion.

Our last 3D exercise is a challenging one, for which we recommend a fast workstation.

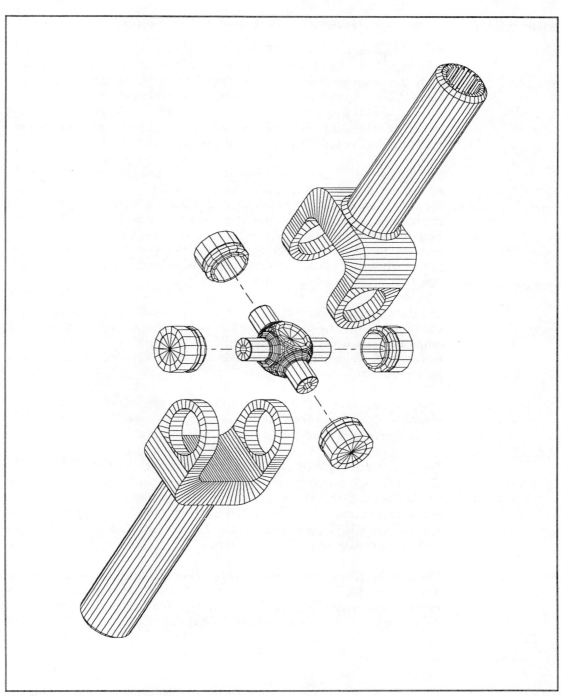

OPTIONAL: Universal Joint and Yoke Assembly

Advanced 3D Exercise — Universal Joint and Yoke Assembly

You have seen how AutoCAD can be used to make realistic looking 3D geometry, but it is capable of modeling objects much more complicated than the ones we have built so far. This optional exercise explores AutoCAD's capabilities at a more sophisticated level. By using AutoCAD's 3D polygon mesh commands to create 3D meshes, you can construct three-dimensional models of surprising complexity and realism, like the universal joint and yoke assembly we show here.

The following instructions do not provide the command sequences necessary to walk you through the construction of this model. Rather, they give you an outline to follow, and leave the details for you to work out on your own. There is no single correct way to do most of it, so you may find techniques you prefer to ours. Experiment. With these instructions, your ingenuity, and the techniques and commands we have previously introduced, you should be able to complete this exercise and test your problem-solving skills.

Build each part of the universal joint and yoke assembly separately, and then combine all the pieces into a final composite drawing. This not only helps to keep file sizes manageable, but causes displays to generate faster, and hidden line removal to complete sooner, as we work on individual parts.

The construction envelope technique introduced earlier helps you visualize the parts you are drawing. The envelope also provides convenient object snap points for the basic shape of the part being drawn.

Work in the predefined UCS and viewports, both named SCRATCH, in the PROTO-3D prototype drawing. This allows you to create 3D geometry in one portion of 3D space, within a construction envelope. Rotate finished portions of each part 180 degrees about the origin into clean space in the WCS to move them out of the way for subsequent commands, and to allow easy selection for blocking.

Use the predefined viewports, and align the UCS to aid in the steps below. Make all profiles and path curves on the CONST layer and switch when necessary to create finished meshes on the OBJECT layer. Remember to define blocks on layer 0 for future flexibility.

OPTIONAL: *The U-Joint Cap*

Begin with the REVSURF command and build one U-joint cap, wblock it, insert it into the final drawing, and array it into place for the other three caps.

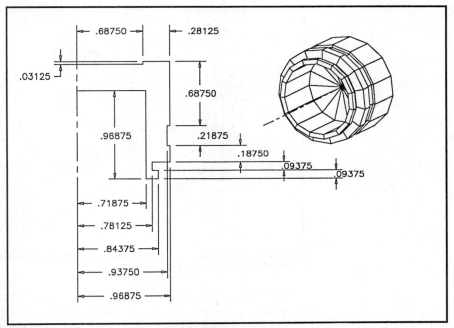

OPTIONAL: The Cap Profile and Modeled Cap

The Cap Profile — Begin a new drawing named 3D-CAP=PROTO-3D. Use the illustration above to draw the profile of the cap section as a polyline.

Build the Cap — Set the system variables SURFTAB1 to 16. Execute the REVSURF command. Select the profile polyline for the path curve, the center line for the axis of rotation, and 360 degrees of included angle. You can experiment with other SURFTAB1 and SURFTAB2 settings by erasing the mesh, changing the variables, and running REVSURF again to see the results. Your finished cap should look like the illustration above.

If necessary, mirror the completed cap so that the open end is pointing in the positive Z direction of the SCRATCH UCS, and move the center of the cap and center line to 0,0. Wblock the cap and center line to a file named B-CAP using 0,0,0 as the insertion point. When you are finished, end the drawing and continue on.

OPTIONAL: The Yoke

Next, draw the drive shaft yoke using the RULESURF, TABSURF, and EDGESURF commands and a construction envelope. Mirror and rotate the yoke later to create a second.

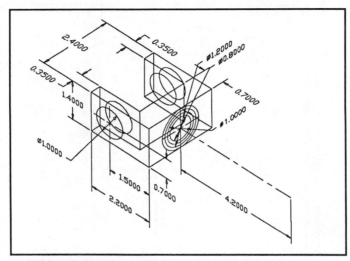

OPTIONAL: Yoke Consturction Envelope

The Envelope Please — Use the illustration above as a guide for drawing the construction envelope of the yoke. Manipulate the UCS to the three planes when necessary. When the envelope is complete, set the UCS parallel to the circles where the yoke is attached to the spline shaft.

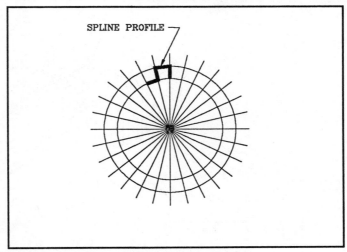

OPTIONAL: Spline to Be Arrayed

The Spline Shaft — Use the two inner circles of the construction envelope for the inner and outer boundaries of the splines, creating one complete spline profile. Draw a line from the center past the second circle and polar array it 28 times about the center. Draw a polyline with INT osnaps as shown in the above illustration. The polyline is shown wide for clarity and should be drawn with a width of zero. Array the single polyline spline 14 times about the center point. Use PEDIT to join the 14 splines into one polyline. Copy the spline polyline to the other end of the shaft center line and use TABSURF to finish the 3D spline.

Change the third construction circle to the OBJECT layer and use TABSURF to create the shaft by passing first the spline path curve along the 4.2-inch center line, then the third circle only 4.1 inches along the center line. These leave room for a 0.1-inch chamfer between the outside surface of the shaft, and the inside edge of the splines.

Build the chamfer at the end of the shaft and the weldment between the yoke and shaft with REVSURF. Use 3DFACE to close the end of one spline and array it around the shaft. The completed yoke and shaft should look similar to the one above.

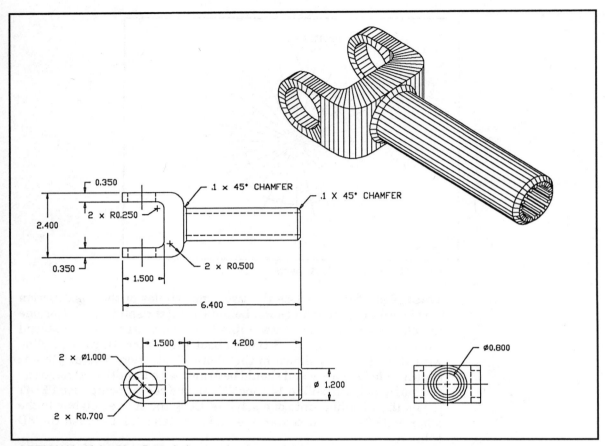

OPTIONAL: Yoke Size Description

Cut the Yoke Into Manageable Pieces — Use FILLET to radius the edges of the yoke to the dimensions shown in the illustration above. With lines, "close-off" one ear of the yoke from the body at the point where the ears intersect the arcs that the FILLET command created.

Join the arcs and lines of one side of one ear into a polyline and copy it to the other side of the same ear. With RULESURF, pick the two polylines and then the two circles, making one ear. Copy it to the other side of the yoke.

Join the arcs and lines on either the top or bottom of the yoke body into a coplanar polyline, and use TABSURF to pass this path curve along one of the 1.4-inch construction lines to model the curved surfaces of the yoke body.

Join the arcs and lines at the other side of the yoke body into two polylines and two lines on the same plane. One polyline will include two arcs and one line forming the inside curved edge of the yoke, and the other will include two short line segments, two arcs, and one longer line segment that form the outer curved edge of the yoke. The remaining two lines are the intersection of the yoke body and the two ears. With these four entities, use EDGESURF to close the yoke body top and bottom that were left open by the tabulated surfaces you made in the last step.

Wblock the yoke and shaft to a file named B-YOKE with the insertion point at the end of the shaft's center, and end this drawing.

OPTIONAL: The U-Joint

With the cap, yoke, and shaft complete, all that remains is the U-joint. This part, however, requires more analytical skills than the previous parts.

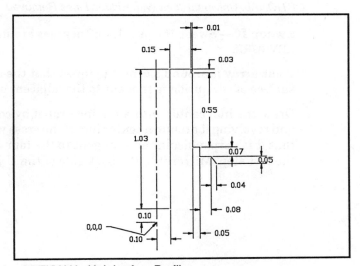

OPTIONAL: U-Joint Arm Profile

Another Profile — Begin a new drawing UJOINT=PROTO-3D. Use the above illustration to draw the U-joint's arm profile and center line.

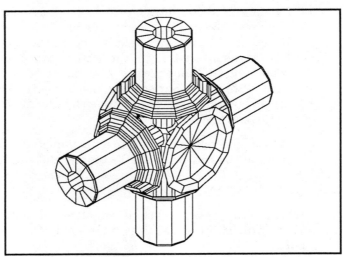

OPTIONAL: Universal Joint With Hidden Lines Removed

Sweep It — Sweep the profile 360 degrees around the center line with REVSURF.

Polar array it around a center point so that the circumference of each surface of revolution is tangent to the adjacent one.

Draw the hub center with a 0.1-inch relief by constructing a polyline and revolving it around a center line of the cross with REVSURF. Insure that it is perpendicular and tangent to the four 3D meshes created in the last step. Mirror it to the back side of the U-joint.

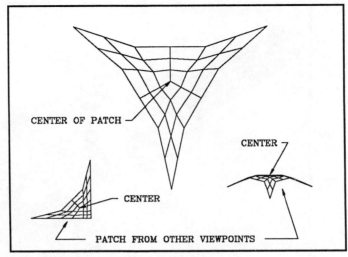

OPTIONAL: Coons Surface Patch

Fill In One Gap — Refer to the illustration above to enclose one of the remaining eight openings of the U-joint with the EDGESURF command. Notice the curve of the patch from other viewpoints. Use construction lines to divide the triangular opening into three sections, coinciding at the center of the opening. Patch one of these sections and array it about center point.

Mirror and array the resulting surface patches into position over the other openings. Your completed U-joint should look similar to the illustration above.

Wblock the U-joint to a file named B-UJOINT, with a convenient insertion point, and end the drawing.

OPTIONAL: Pulling It All Together

Now it's time to bring each of the pieces completed thus far into one exploded assembly illustration. Removing the hidden lines from this drawing will take a considerable amount of time, so plan appropriately!

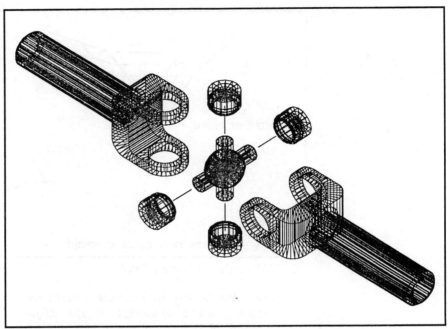

Complete Assembly in Wireframe

First the Yoke — Begin a new drawing named EXPILL=PROTO-3D. Insert the B-YOKE block first and align it as necessary to provide room for the other parts, and for mirroring the yoke 180 degrees.

Mirror the yoke to produce its counterpart on the opposing side of the U-joint and rotate the new yoke 90 degrees along its center line to accommodate the alternating U-joint arms.

Insert the CAPBLK block and align it between and below the two B-YOKE blocks.

Polar array one cap into four, using the center line of the yoke shaft as the center point.

Insert the B-UJOINT block at the center of the B-CAP array, making sure to align it carefully with the caps and yokes.

Now you can view the finished assembly from various angles with DVIEW, HIDE it, and plot it. The finished assembly is shown above in wireframe, and in the facing page illustration at the beginning of this exercise with hidden lines removed.

This completes the instructions for the optional advanced exercise. You have explored the most powerful 3D construction tools available in AutoCAD Release 10, and you have acquired skills that you can now use to draft virtually any product.

Summary

This chapter has introduced you to some new tools and some alternative methods for manipulating 3D drawings. There are several ways, for instance, to orient a 3D drawing. You can set the UCS and then use plan view; use viewpoint and then set the UCS to match; or you can use DVIEW.

DVIEW is a fast and efficient way to dynamically view your drawing without the slowdown caused by regeneration. Using camera-like terms, it allows you to drag and rotate your 3D drawing to any position and angle in full 3D space. You also saw how to view and manipulate your 3D drawing with perspective vanishing points.

This chapter showed you one of the most important 3D manipulations — 2D view extraction from 3D drawings. Once you develop a 3D part drawing, you can create blocks to extract virtually any view and trace it for engineering drawings. Dimensioning may also be performed on 3D drawings. Just as UCS control is important for generating and manipulating 3D geometry, so it is for 3D dimensioning and symbol block insertion.

The optional advanced 3D exercise was designed to test your 3D and problem-solving skills. AutoCAD may be used to construct sophisticated 3D models like the universal joint and yoke assembly. If you chose to tackle this exercise, you enhanced your 3D modeling skills beyond the general level.

Continue to explore AutoCAD's 3D commands until drawing in three dimensions becomes as familiar to you as two-dimensional drawing is to most draft persons today. Future AutoCAD releases will continue to enhance the program's 3D capabilities. Familiarity with today's 3D tools will prepare you to add tomorrow's tools to your drafting and design tool kit.

When you proceed, Chapter 12 will show you how to install the SIA DISK and configure the ANSI Y14.5 Menu System. Let's go to Chapter 12 and install and configure the SIA DISK. If you don't have the SIA DISK, Chapter 12 has some insights to help you customize AutoCAD on your own for production drafting.

SYMBOLS LIBRARY | SETTINGS | NUMERICS | VARIABLES | LAYERS

SYMBOLS LIBRARY

TOL STATUS	#DWGSC	DIM STATUS

MOVE SYM/SYMBOL INSERT | MOVE X INTERSEC | MANUAL CONSTRUCTION | MOVE | AUTO CONSTRUCTION

-A- | (M) | SQUARE Ø? | □?
-B- | (L) | (?
-C- | (S) | Ø?
-?- | (P) | BASIC DIMENSION

SETTINGS

SET TOLERANCE	PLUS
SET TOLERANCE	MINUS
TOLERANCE ON | OFF	EXIT
LIMITS ON | OFF	

PRECISION xx \| .xxx \| .xxxx
.1 | GRID | 1
.125 | SNAP | .5
.2 | AXIS | .25

NUMERICS

.01	.001	.0001
.02	.002	.0002
.03	.003	.0003
.05	.005	.0005
.07	.007	.0007
.09	.009	.0009

DIMTXT HEIGHT
.1 | .125 | .1562
.2 | .25 | USER

VARIABLES

EXTENSION 1	DRAG DIMTEXT
EXTENSION 2	HOMETEXT
SET DIMASZ	NEWTEXT
SET DIMEXO	UPDATE
SET DIMDLI	DIMASO ON | OFF
'SETVAR	DIMSHO ON | OFF

LTSCALE
.1 | .25 | .375 | USER
DIMCEN
0 | -.1 | -.2 | USER

LAYERS

0	HL
CL	NOTES
CONST	OBJECT
DIM xxx	PL
DL	TEXT
HATCH	TITL-??	????-CX

U
S
E
R
*

MAKE | NEW | SET | SET BY ENTITY | LTYPE | COLOR
? | DIALOG | FREEZE | THAW | ON | OFF

COLOR

WHITE (7)	
MAGENTA (6)	
BLUE (5)	
CYAN (4)	
GREEN (3)	
YELLOW (2)	
RED (1)	

PLOT

AUTOPLOT
AUTOPRINT

Y14MENU.DWG © NEW RIDERS PUBLISHING 1989

Chapter 12

Programming for Productivity

A MENU SYSTEM FOR Y14.5 DRAFTING

AutoCAD is written to accommodate many disciplines of drafting and design. In the field of mechanical drafting alone, drawings may be prepared by drafting trainees, detail drafters, layout drafters, design drafters, checkers, technical illustrators, or engineers. AutoCAD is used in the development of practically any product imaginable, and each industry generally has its own way of doing things. This may include using special symbol libraries and even specific *in-house* standards. These differences, and more, can be managed through AutoCAD customization.

Thus far, we have presented many of AutoCAD's commands. Although highly functional, these commands provide only a fraction of the power that is available to you. AutoCAD is designed to allow customization for your particular drafting environment. The SIA DISK's Y14.5 Menu System is an example of how AutoCAD can be customized for production drafting according to ANSI Y14.5M-1982 geometric dimensioning and tolerancing standards. If you use these standards for your normal drafting activity, or if you are interested in experiencing a customized AutoCAD environment, we recommend that you get our companion SIA DISK. A convenient order form is provided at the back of this book.

Y14.5 Menu System Features

The SIA DISK's Y14.5 Menu System allows selection by screen, pull-down and icon, icon, tablet menus, or any combination. Whichever menu or menus your system supports, the drafting functions and AutoLISP routines available on the SIA DISK will greatly increase your drafting efficiency and productivity.

The Y14.5 Menu System contains all the routines necessary for producing both decimal inch and SI metric drawings. Use the Y14.5 Menu System when you set up new drawing sheets or layers, and when you need to handle dimensioning and system variables. The drafting menus provide efficient ways to control the state, linetype, and color of any drafting layer, and come with many layers predefined and ready to use.

Grid, snap, and axis are preset in the Y14.5 Menu System. System and dimensioning variables are shown in easily recognized drafting terms and icons. You can efficiently set decimal precision, limits, and tolerances, and you can insert ANSI Y14.5M-1982 symbols from the included library.

When you dimension parts according to ANSI Y14.5 standards, the size of the feature control symbols is set according to the dimension text height and drawing plot scale. In AutoCAD, parts are commonly developed in full size (even very large parts), so the actual height of a drawing's annotation and dimension text needs to be enlarged to insure readability. The default dimension text height of the Y14.5 Menu System is 0.125. Normally, when you develop a large full-size part, you need to change the dimension text height by setting the DIMTXT variable to a larger value. The Y14.5 Menu System uses the DIMTXT value in an AutoLISP routine, and sets the size of the Y14.5 symbols accordingly. Regardless of your dimension text height setting, the Y14.5 Menu System automatically inserts the proper size symbols, and its automatic plotting and printing routines simplify getting hard copy output.

Getting Started With Y14.5

The Y14.5 Menu System has been designed to operate without conflict within your AutoCAD environment. But just to be sure, check the Y14.5 Menu System file names (after installation) with those already existing in your system. If there are any matching file names, rename or disable the existing files which may conflict with the Y14.5 Menu System files while you are using them.

The Y14.5 Menu System allows either English or metric operation. For metric unit operation, there are no special files or procedures. Simply specify the correct unit system when prompted during drawing setup, and the menu adjusts itself.

Installing the Y14.5 Menu System Files

For the Y14.5 Menu System to function properly, we must assume that it is installed in a subdirectory named \Y14. If you are not installing the system on drive C:, substitute your drive letter for C: wherever it is shown in the instructions below. Create the \Y14 subdirectory and install the menu system files in it.

Making the \Y14 Subdirectory and Installing the Files

```
C:\> MD \Y14            Make the directory.
C:\> CD \Y14            Change to the new directory.
C:\Y14>
```

```
Place the SIA disk in drive A:
C:\Y14> A:Y14-LOAD      Copy disk files into the current subdirectory.
```

Next, copy the AutoCAD configuration and overlay files into this directory as you did in Chapter 1. This will allow you to run the Y14.5 Menu System as a *stand-alone* environment, even if you should someday remove the SIA files and directory. Again, we assume your hard disk is drive C: and that ACAD is your AutoCAD subdirectory name. If not, substitute your drive letter or subdirectory name.

Creating a Y14.5 Menu System Configuration

```
C:\Y14>
C:\SI-ACAD> COPY \ACAD\ACADP?.OVL     Copy plotter and printer configuration.
C:\SI-ACAD> COPY \ACAD\ACADD?.OVL     Copy digitizer and display.
C:\SI-ACAD> COPY \ACAD\ACAD.CFG       Copy the main configuration file.
```

To integrate the Y14.5 menu with your AutoCAD menu, you will need to perform the following steps from the DOS prompt after the installation process has completed. Note the different procedures for AutoCAD Release 9 and Release 10, and just perform the procedure for the AutoCAD release you have. It will create a new menu file combining the Y14.5 files with your existing menu.

Integrating the Y14.5 and ACAD Menus

The following instructions for Release 9 and 10 assume you have AutoCAD installed in a subdirectory named \ACAD. If this is not true for your installation, substitute *your* path for \ACAD where it appears below.

Integrating Y14.5 With AutoCAD Release 9 or 10

If you have AutoCAD Release 9:
`C:\Y14\> COPY REL9.MNU+\ACAD\ACAD.MNU+Y14-2.MNU Y14.MNU`

If you have AutoCAD Release 10:
`C:\Y14\> COPY Y14-1.MNU+\ACAD\ACAD.MNU+Y14-2.MNU Y14.MNU`

➡ *NOTE: If your ACAD.MNU is not in your \ACAD directory, copy it from the \SOURCE directory which is on one of your original distribution AutoCAD diskettes. If you are using a custom menu instead of ACAD.MNU, you can substitute its name for ACAD.MNU above, but we cannot guarantee compatibility.*

Using Y14.BAT to Start Up AutoCAD

Y14.BAT is the Y14.5 Menu System's startup file. It sets up your DOS environment so AutoCAD can find the configuration files and symbols the menu system uses. The Y14.BAT file should look like the listing below. Once again, if your AutoCAD directory is not named \ACAD, then you must use a text editor or a word processor in ASCII mode to substitute your directory name everywhere \acad is shown in lower case letters in the program listing below. See Appendix A if you need help with text editors. Omit the right-hand comments; they are not part of the file.

```
SET ACAD=\Y14              Support variable.
SET ACADCFG=\Y14           Configuration variable.
SET LISPSTACK=5000         AutoLISP stack variable.
SET LISPHEAP=40000         AutoLISP heap variable.
\acad\ACAD %1 %2           Starts AutoCAD.
SET ACAD=                  Deletes variables upon exiting.
SET ACADCFG=
SET LISPSTACK=
SET LISPHEAP=
```

Y14.BAT File

The \acad\ACAD %1 %2 line runs AutoCAD from the current directory. The %1 and %2 are placekeepers that pass along any command line parameters, such as those you might use to execute an AutoCAD script file. Copy this file to your root directory or to another directory on your system's DOS path, and you can run the Y14.5 Menu System while another *working* directory is current.

Copying and Running the Y14 Batch File

```
C:\Y14> CD \                    Change to the root directory.
C:\> COPY \Y14\Y14.BAT          Copy the batch file.
C:\> Y14                        Run the Y14 batch file.
```

The Y14.BAT file will execute AutoCAD and present a screen menu. You will then be prompted to respond to three setup choices: units, scale, and sheet size. After making these choices, you will be ready to begin a new drawing with the Y14.5 Menu System. For now, QUIT this drawing.

➡ *NOTE: Release 9 users must always select either the [Release9] or [Setup] picks from the screen menu to initialize the system. It executes the same startup procedure that Release 10 executes automatically.*

Modifying the Prototype Drawing to Use the Y14.5 Menu System

You can modify the PROTO-C drawing to automatically use the new, integrated menu. To do so, edit the existing prototype drawing and load the new menu with the MENU command, then END the drawing to leave the Y14.5 menu loaded. It will then be the default menu whenever you use this prototype.

MENU

> *The MENU command loads a new menu into the current drawing. The menu that was current when the drawing was ended will be the default when the drawing is next edited. The source file for a menu is an editable ASCII text file and is named with the extension .MNU (for more on editing the .MNU file, see the ANSI Y14.5 menu anatomy section later in this chapter).*
> Menu file name or . for none <acad>:

The following exercise steps you through the process of calling up the existing PROTO-C drawing, loading the Y14.5 menu, and then ending the drawing session.

Changing the Prototype Drawing Default Menu

```
C:\> CD \Y14                    Change to the \Y14 directory.
C:\Y14\> Y14                    Start up the Y14.5 system and enter the AutoCAD main menu.
Enter Selection: 2             Edit an EXISTING drawing named PROTO-C.
Command: MENU
Menu file name or . for none <acad>: Y14   Use the Y14.5 Menu System.
Command: END
```

If you are using the Y14.5 Menu System with a digitizing tablet, the following instructions will help you configure the Y14.5 tablet menu. If you are not using a digitizing tablet, skip to the section on how the ANSI Y14.5 menu options are organized.

Installing the Y14.5 Tablet Menu

If you wish to use the Y14.5 Menu System as a tablet menu, you need to install it. The Y14.5 tablet template is shown as the facing page illustration at the beginning of this chapter. To install it, attach a copy of the template to your digitizer tablet and configure the tablet. You plot the Y14MENU.DWG file from the SIA DISK. If you don't have the SIA DISK, or if you don't have a plotter, you can photocopy the facing page illustration. It is sized to be enlarged to the correct scale by standard photocopier enlargement settings. Copy it with a 120 percent enlargement (letter-to-legal) setting.

To plot the template, see the following exercise. It uses a Y14.5 Menu System routine to set layers for either English or metric versions.

Plotting and Installing the Y14.5 Menu System Template

Enter Selection: **2**	Edit an EXISTING drawing named **Y14MENU** from the SIA DISK.
Select [Y14 Menu]	From the screen menu (Release 9 users first select [Release9]).
Select [TABLET]	From the Y14 menu.
Select [Plot Template]	From the [TABLET] menu.

Next, you will be prompted to set up either the English or metric version. Drawing layers for the unit system you select will be turned on and you will be instructed to plot a pre-defined view named PLOT.

Use AutoCAD's normal plotting procedure to plot this view on your plotter. If you are using a tablet that is larger or smaller than the standard, try plotting Y14MENU3.DWG at an appropriate scale, and continue with the configuration process.

Attaching the Template

Cut out the photocopied or plotted template along its outside lines and punch the two holes shown in its top. Affix the Y14.5 template plot to your digitizer with tape or template pins. If you are using the standard AutoCAD tablet template, place the Y14.5 template plot over tablet menu area 1, carefully lining it up with the holes in the AutoCAD template. The AutoCAD tablet menu area 1 is a grid of 25 columns by eight rows. It allows room for up to 200 special commands and macros.

Make sure that the area containing the menu boxes is inside the digitizer's effective area. If you are unsure as to where this area is, refer to your digitizer's installation manual.

Configuring the Y14.5 Tablet Menu

To use the tablet menu, you must have installed the Y14.5 Menu System files.

The configuration option of the TABLET command tells AutoCAD how many tablet menu areas you are using and specifies the number of rows and columns within each tablet area. The configuration option also enables you to respecify the screen pointing area (the tablet menu areas may not overlay the screen pointing area). AutoCAD retains the tablet configuration values as defaults until you reconfigure new tablet parameters. These tablet parameters are stored in the current configuration subdirectory, in this case, \Y14.

If you are already configured for the standard AutoCAD tablet menu, then your tablet is ready to use and you can skip to the section on how the ANSI Y14.5 menu sections are organized. If you want to configure your tablet for the integrated Y14.5 and AutoCAD menus, use the next section on configuring four tablet menu areas. If you want to configure only the Y14.5 tablet menu, skip to the following section on configuring menu area 1.

Configuring Four Tablet Menu Areas

Once inside the drawing editor, enter the TABLET command, then the [CFG] option. You may also use the Y14.5 menu to aid in your configuration by selecting [Y14 Menu], then [TABLET], and [Config 4 Areas] from the pull-down menu. You will be prompted for three corners of each tablet menu area. Use the illustration below to select your pick points. If you input the settings manually, use the following exercise as a guide.

TABLET

> *The TABLET command is used to calibrate a digitizer to input an existing paper drawing, or to configure the digitizer for up to four tablet menu areas, and define the screen pointing area.*
> Option (ON/OFF/CAL/CFG):

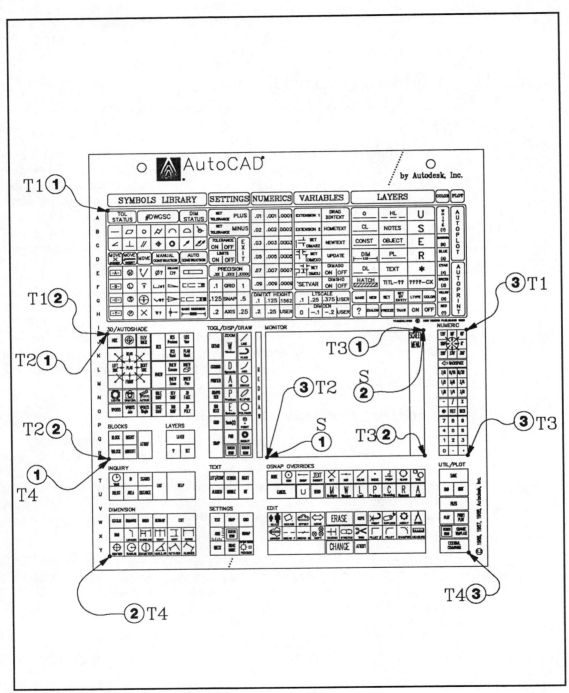

Configuring the Four Tablet Menu Areas

Manually Configuring the Four Tablet Menu Areas

```
Command: TABLET
Option (ON/OFF/CAL/CFG): CFG
Enter the number of tablet menus desired (0-4) <4>: <RETURN>
Digitize the upper left corner of menu area 1:          Pick point T1 ①.
Digitize the lower left corner of menu area 1:          Pick point T1 ②.
Digitize the lower right corner of menu area 1:         Pick point T1 ③.
Enter the number of columns for menu area 1: 25
Enter the number of rows for menu area 1: 9

Digitize the upper left corner of menu area 2:          Pick point T2 ①.
Digitize the lower left corner of menu area 2:          Pick point T2 ②.
Digitize the lower right corner of menu area 2:         Pick point T2 ③.
Enter the number of columns for menu area 2: 11
Enter the number of rows for menu area 2: 9

Digitize the upper left corner of menu area 3:          Pick point T3 ①.
Digitize the lower left corner of menu area 3:          Pick point T3 ②.
Digitize the lower right corner of menu area 3:         Pick point T3 ③.
Enter the number of columns for menu area 3: 9         That's correct — 9 columns.
Enter the number of rows for menu area 3: 13

Digitize the upper left corner of menu area 4:          Pick point T4 ①.
Digitize the lower left corner of menu area 4:          Pick point T4 ②.
Digitize the lower right corner of menu area 4:         Pick point T4 ③.
Enter the number of columns for menu area 4: 25
Enter the number of rows for menu area 4: 7

Do you want to respecify the screen pointing area? Y

Digitize lower left corner of screen pointing area:     Pick point ①.
Digitize upper right corner of screen pointing area:    Pick point ②.
```

Configuring Tablet Menu Area 1 Only

Once inside the drawing editor, select the TABLET command. You may also use the Y14.5 menu to aid your configuration by selecting [Y14 Menu], then [TABLET], and then [Config 1 Area]. You will be prompted for the three corners of the top tablet menu area. Use the following illustration as a guide. If you input the settings manually, use the exercise below to guide you. (Notice that only eight, not nine, rows are specified to maximize the screen pointing area.)

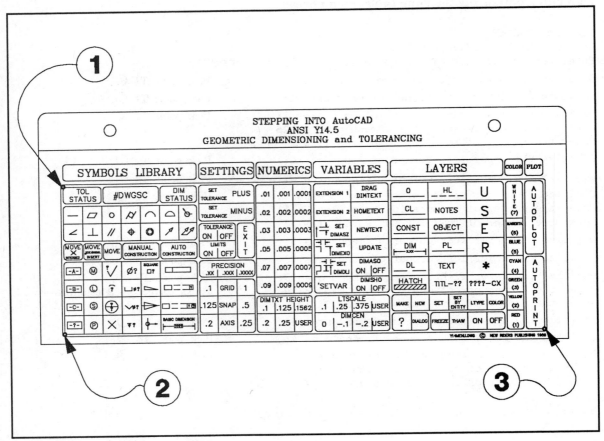

Configuring Tablet Menu Area 1 Only

Configuring Tablet Menu Area 1

```
Command: TABLET
Option (ON/OFF/CAL/CFG): CFG
Enter the number of tablet menus desired (0-4) <4>: 1

Digitize the upper left corner of menu area 1:          Pick point ①.
Digitize the lower left corner of menu area 1:          Pick point ②.
Digitize the lower right corner of menu area 1:         Pick point ③.
Enter the number of columns for menu area 1: 25
Enter the number of rows for menu area 1: 8
Do you want to respecify the screen pointing area? Y
Digitize lower left corner of screen pointing area:     Pick point.
Digitize upper right corner of screen pointing area:    Pick point.
```

This completes installation of the ANSI Y14.5 Menu System for digitizer users. Now let's look at the menu sections and what they can do.

How the ANSI Y14.5 Menu Options Are Organized

If you will be relying on the screen, pull-down, and icon menus instead of a tablet menu, you will find that the menu option descriptions presented below are similar — only the methods for invoking them are different. Digitizer users can pick commands from the tablet surface with a stylus or puck, and mouse users can select items from the screen or pull-down and icon menus. In either case, read through the descriptions given below.

Screen and Pull-Down Menus

The Y14.5 Menu System gives you a choice of methods for invoking Y14.5 commands and operations. You may select any Y14.5 Menu System operation from the screen, pull-down, icon, or tablet menus, or from any combination of these. All the menus work together. If you want to develop part of your drawing using either the screen or pull-down and icon Y14.5 Menu System menus, select [Y14 Menu] from the screen menu, as shown below.

Screen Menu With Y14.5 Menu Selection

You can then easily switch back to the standard AutoCAD menu by selecting [AutoCAD] from the screen menu. If you only configured tablet menu area 1, however, the standard AutoCAD commands will be unavailable from the tablet menu. When you want to continue using the

Y14.5 Menu System, simply reselect [Y14 Menu]. Selecting [Y14 Menu] from the screen menu automatically toggles the menu system to support the Y14.5 menu functions.

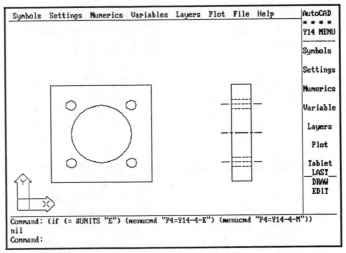

Y14.5 Screen and Pull-Down Menus

If your system supports pull-down and icon menus, all of the Y14.5 symbols can be selected from icon menus. The following illustrations show some of the Y14.5 icon menus.

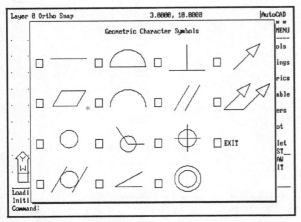

Geometric Characteristic Symbols

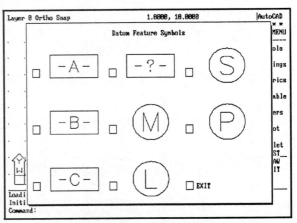

Datum Feature and Material Condition Symbols

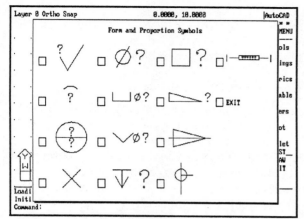

Form and Proportion Symbols

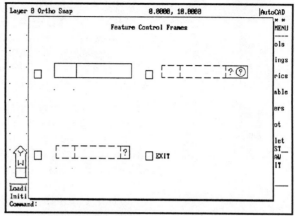

Feature Control and Datum Reference Frames

Tablet Menu Organization

The tablet menu, shown below as a guide, is divided into seven groups: Symbols Library, Settings, Numerics, Variables, Layers, Color, and Plot. The screen, pull-down, and icon menus are similarly divided.

You will find the boxes assigned to specific commands below each group. To execute a command, use your pointing device to pick the desired box. Some of the commands work together to execute a sequential operation. Each of the menu options described below may also be selected from the screen menu and, if your system supports the AUI, from the pull-down and icon menus.

The following descriptions of each Y14.5 menu group cover the English version of the menu. The metric version differs only in the numeric values used.

Symbols Library Group

The symbols library menu group includes macros to efficiently construct and control ANSI Y14.5 dimensions and symbols.

[TOL STATUS] — Displays, on the status line, the user settings of tolerance on/off, limits on/off, and tolerance plus and minus values.

[#DWGSC] — Changes the drawing scale so that user-created symbols (created at other than a one-unit scale) will be properly scaled and inserted into a Y14.5 Menu System drawing. You will not normally need to set #DWGSC because it is set by Y14.5's ACAD.LSP file when entering the drawing editor.

[DIM STATUS] — Provides a convenient location for the AutoCAD dimension status command. [DIM STATUS] displays a text screen listing status or values for all dimension variables.

ANSI Y14.5 Geometric Characteristic Symbols

The first two rows on the tablet menu contain 14 ANSI Y14.5 geometric tolerancing symbols. You can select symbols for your drawing by picking them with your pointing device. After you choose a symbol, you will be prompted for the insertion point and for either manual or automatic construction as explained below. The symbols are pre-sized to drag with your cursor at a scale relative to the current text height. Once the insertion point is picked, the symbol is automatically drawn.

Below the two symbol rows is a row containing five macros:

[MOVE INTERSEC] — Moves inserted symbols and other entities in your drawing. It uses the osnap override, INTERSection, as the first point of move displacement.

[MOVE TEXT/SYMBOL INSERT] — Moves inserted blocks and text using the osnap override, INSertion point, as the first point of move displacement.

[MOVE] is the standard AutoCAD MOVE command, and is located here for your convenience.

[MANUAL CONSTRUCTION] — Allows for the manual construction of Y14.5 symbols. After choosing a geometric characteristic symbol, select the [MANUAL CONSTRUCTION] box. When selected, the feature control frame may be inserted into the current drawing. Individual symbols, text, and datum reference frames may then be added as needed.

[AUTO CONSTRUCTION] — Allows for the automatic construction of Y14.5 symbols. After choosing a geometric characteristic symbol, select the [AUTOMATIC CONSTRUCTION] box. Once selected, the feature control frame may be inserted into the current drawing. You are then prompted for the form tolerance value, and the material condition symbol. After you respond to these prompts, you are given the option of adding datum references to the feature control frame. Each datum reference, which may include a material condition symbol, is automatically appended to the last frame or datum reference.

ANSI Y14.5 Dimensioning and Tolerancing Symbols

The next four rows of boxes on the tablet contain 24 ANSI Y14.5 geometric dimensioning and tolerancing symbols. For easy insertion, the four [DATUM] boxes have been programmed to prompt you for the corner of the datum box that will act as the insertion point. You may pick the lower left (LL), lower right (LR), upper left (UL), or upper right (UR) corner of the datum box as the symbol insertion point. Choose the insertion point by typing your choice or by selecting it from the screen menu. The two datum boxes which are "added" to the feature control frames have the osnap override, INTERSection, applied to their insertion points. This simplifies the connection (insertion) of these boxes to the feature control frames.

The datum reference frames (with or without condition references) also have the osnap override, INTERSection, applied to their insertion points to connect these symbols to feature control frames inserted in the current drawing.

Settings Group

The settings menu group provides macros for the convenient control and entry of dimensioning tolerance, precision, and general drawing variable settings.

[SET TOLERANCE PLUS] — Sets the plus value for tolerance/limit dimensioning. After picking this box, you will be prompted to input a value. Notice that the adjacent group is a numerical *pad* that you may use to input common tolerance values. When you pick one of these tolerance value boxes, the value is input.

[SET TOLERANCE MINUS] — Sets the minus value for tolerance/limit dimensioning. The operation is the same as for SET TOLERANCE PLUS.

[TOLERANCE ON|OFF] — Toggles tolerance dimensioning (DIMTOL). Toggling DIMTOL on automatically turns DIMLIM off.

[LIMITS ON|OFF] — Toggles limit dimensioning (DIMLIM). Toggling DIMLIM on automatically turns DIMTOL off.

[EXIT] — Provides a convenient exit from DIM mode.

[PRECISION .XX | .XXX | .XXXX] — Sets the number of digits past the decimal point (decimal precision). This is a transparent command and you may set it while in another AutoCAD command. If you are dimensioning an object, you can set the precision to a different value, and you will be returned to continue with your dimensioning.

Do not use this command when the default `Dimension text` `<n.nnnn>:` prompt is displayed, where *n.nnnn* represents a real number. This will cause the text, 'setvar, to replace the dimension text value. For correct tolerancing dimensions, the number of digits specified for precision should equal that set for the tolerance plus and minus digits. (For example, set precision to .XXX, and tolerance to +.003 and -.005.)

[GRID][SNAP][AXIS] — Select any of these boxes when you want to set these values. The numeric value boxes positioned to either side of the macro boxes provide convenient picks for setting commonly used values for the X and Y components. You can set a value by picking one of the boxes provided, or you can input the values from the keyboard. If you type them, remember to give both X and Y values, and to separate them with a comma, for example `0.5,0.25`. These commands are transparent and may be used within most other AutoCAD commands.

Numerics Group

This group contains two sets of boxes. The top six rows of boxes supply common numerical values as text strings when selected.

[DIMTXT HEIGHT] — These six boxes set the current DIMTXT height to the value shown.

Variables Group

The variables group of menu selections provides control of frequently used dimensioning variables.

[EXTENSION 1] [EXTENSION 2] — Toggles the suppression of extension lines 1 and 2. You can turn one or both extension lines off or on.

[SET DIMASZ] — Sets the size of dimension arrows.

[SET DIMEXO] — Sets the dimension line offset value.

[SET DIMDLI] — Controls the spacing between continuous linear dimensions created by the BASELINE and CONTINUE commands.

['SETVAR] — Sets system variables to your own value or selection. This is transparent and can be used while in most commands.

[LTSCALE] — Sets the variable for the global linetype scale factor. LTSCALE is a transparent command, included here for convenience. If REGENAUTO is off, however, an LTSCALE change will not be visible until you regenerate your drawing. Common linetype scale factor selections are provided.

[DIMCEN] — Controls the size and style of center tick marks placed within circles and arcs by the DIAMETER, RADIUS, and CENTER dimensioning commands. A positive DIMCEN value draws a simple tick, a negative draws a tick with center lines, and a zero value draws no tick mark at all.

[DRAG DIMTEXT] — Allows associative dimensioning text to be moved by employing the STRETCH command with OSNAP's Insert option and a Crossing window, to correctly select associative dimensioning text.

[HOMETEXT] — Redraws an existing associative dimension, replacing its text to the default location.

[NEWTEXT] — Replaces the text of an existing associative dimension with new, user-specified text, or with its associative measurement if a <RETURN> is entered instead of new text.

[UPDATE] — Redraws all selected associative dimensions using the current settings of all dimension variables as well as the current text style and units.

[DIMASO ON | OFF] — Sets dimensions created or updated with DIMASO on to be associative. DIMASO off draws the dimension text, arrows, dimension lines, and extension lines as separate entities, as in earlier versions of AutoCAD. The default value is on.

[DIMSHO ON | OFF] — Controls the associative dimension display when dragging. DIMSHO on causes constant recomputation and display of associative dimension measurements when dragging. Keep DIMSHO off unless you are using a fast (386-based or better) computer.

Layer Group

The layer menu group is organized alphabetically. The Y14.5 layers have been used in our prototype drawing, PROTO-C. The Y14.5 layers may be set, turned on and off, and frozen or thawed by selecting their corresponding boxes. Four boxes have been left unassigned for you to customize the tablet menu with layers of your choice.

[TITL-??] — Provides a wildcard combination pick for manipulation of the title box layers in the prototype drawing PROTO-C.

[????-CX] — Provides a wildcard combination pick for manipulation of the text layers associated with the title, part list, application, and specifications boxes in the prototype drawing PROTO-C.

[*] — Supplies the asterisk wildcard for layer commands.

[MAKE] [NEW] [SET] [SET BY ENTITY] [LTYPE] [COLOR] — May be used to create new layers and/or assign them names, linetypes, and colors of your choice. If you choose [MAKE], AutoCAD will also make the new layer the default. The [SET] box sets as default any layer not listed in the layers group. A [SET BY ENTITY] selection is provided to allow you to set the default layer by picking an entity from the screen. After the entity is selected, the default layer will be set to that of the entity chosen. [COLOR] changes the color assignment of layers, prompting you for the color and layer name.

[?] — Lists all layers in the current drawing.

[DIALOG] — Calls up the layer dialogue box.

[FREEZE] [THAW] [ON] [OFF] — Are used to freeze or thaw selected layers and to turn selected layers on or off. For example, pick the layer [OFF] box and then pick the box corresponding to the layer you wish to turn off.

Color Group

The color menu group provides convenient selections for setting layer color.

Plot Group

The print/plot group contains two macros for automated plotting and printer plotting as described below.

[AUTOPLOT] — Accesses a plotting script file. The sample script files PL-STD.SCR and PL-STD7.SCR are included with the Y14.5 Menu System. PL-STD.SCR plots a view named PLOT, at 0,0, on a B-size sheet, at a scale of 1=1, with colors 1-7 plotted by pen 1 at speed 16.

The PL-STD7.SCR file is the same as the previous plotting script except that it uses pens 1-7, respectively, for colors 1-7.

[AUTOPRINT] — Executes an automatic printing script named PR-STD.SCR which generates a printer plot of the view PLOT, at 0,0, on the maximum size sheet available for the configured printer, and scaled to fit the available area.

These are included as sample plotting scripts. Use a text editor to change the view name or other parameters supplied in the script files, and to create similar scripts for your own purposes.

Y14.5 Menu System Exercise

The following exercise instructions are written to show you how to use the Y14.5 Menu System with a digitizing tablet. If you are not using a tablet, the menu system commands and options may be accessed by the screen, pull-down, and icon menus. With a little experimentation and practice, you will be able to perform production Y14.5 drafting regardless of your system's input devices.

This exercise steps you through a few of the Y14.5 Menu System's options. We'll use the servo motor mount drawing from Chapter 5 that we saved under the file name MENUTEST for our menu demonstration. MENUTEST is also on the SIA DISK.

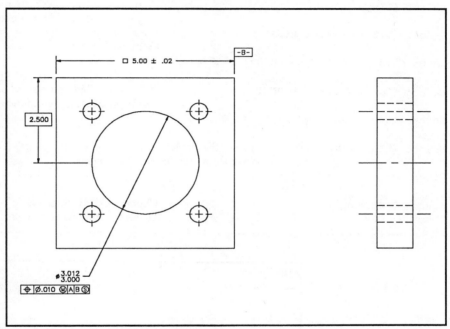

Y14.5 Menu System Exercise Drawing

Converting the MENUTEST Drawing to the Y14.5 Menu System

```
Enter Selection: 2.          Edit an EXISTING drawing named MENUTEST.

Perform SETUP for new drawing.
UNITS: eXit/Metric/<English>? X        Exit the setup procedure.
SETUP terminated

Command: MENU
Menu file name or . for none <acad>: Y14   Load the Y14 menu.
Command: END                               End the drawing.

Enter Selection: 2                         Re-enter the MENUTEST drawing.
```

This time, answer the setup prompts for English or metric units, select FULL for the drawing scale and 22 x 17 for limits size from the screen menu.

Let's try the [SETTINGS], [NUMERICS], and [VARIABLES] sections of the tablet menu.

Setting Tolerance Values and Dimensioning

Before dimensioning, set the current layer to DIM.

Select **[DIM]**   From the tablet LAYERS menu, or select
                                        [Layers] [Set] [DIM] from the screen or pull-down menu.

Select **[Set Tolerance PLUS]**   From the tablet menu, or select
                                        [Settings] [Plus] from the screen or pull-down menu.
Enter plus tolerance <0.0000>: **.012**

Select **[Set Tolerance MINUS]**   From the tablet menu, or select
                                        [Settings] [Minus] from the screen or pull-down menu.
Enter minus tolerance <0.0000>: **0**

Select **[LIMITS ON]**   From the tablet menu, or select [Settings] [Dimensioning Limits]
                                  from the screen or pull-down menu.
Dimensioning Limits is on

Select **['Setvar]**   Change LUPREC to 3.
Command: **DIM**   Diameter dimension the large circle as shown below.

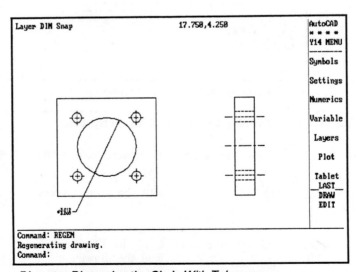

Diameter Dimension the Circle With Tolerance

Now let's use the [SYMBOLS LIBRARY] section of the tablet menu to build feature control symbols for the dimension you just completed. The following instructions take you through the manual construction of the symbols.

Manual Construction of a Y14.5 Symbol

Select **[Feature Control Frame]**   Pick point ①.
Select **[Position Symbol]**   The circle with the cross through it.
Select **[MANUAL CONSTRUCTION]**

Insertion point: Pick point ① again.

Select **[Diameter Symbol]**

Insertion point: Pick point ②.
Enter tolerance value: **.05**

Select **[Maximum Material Condition Symbol]**

Insertion point: Pick point ③.

Select **[Feature Control Frame]**   Pick small datum feature control frame.
Select **[MANUAL CONSTRUCTION]**

Insertion point: Pick point ③ again.
Datum?: **A**

Select **[Feature Control Frame]**   Pick the large datum feature control frame.
Select **[MANUAL CONSTRUCTION]**

Insertion point: Pick point ④.
Datum?: **C**

Select **[RFS Symbol]**

Insertion point: Pick point ⑤.

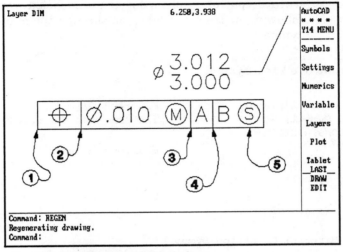

Completed Manual Y14.5 Symbol

Now let's try this same process using the automatic construction technique.

Automatic Construction of a Y14.5 Symbol

Command: **ERASE**	Erase the manually constructed symbol.
Select **[Position Symbol]**	The circle with the cross through it.
Select **[AUTO CONSTRUCTION]**	
Insertion point:	Pick point ①.
Diameter? Yes or <N>o: **Y**	Enter Y for yes.
Enter tolerance: **.010**	Enter or pick .010.
Enter Material Condition Symbol:	
None/Mmc/Rfs/Lmc/Prj : **<RETURN>**	
Add datum or <D>one: **A**	Add datum references.
Adding datum.	
Enter datum letter: **A**	
Datum modified? Yes/<N>o: **N**	No material condition symbol.
Add datum or <D>one: **A**	Add another datum reference.
Adding datum.	
Enter datum letter: **B**	
Datum modified? Yes/<N>o: **Y**	Modify this one.
Enter Material Condition Symbol:	
None/Mmc/Rfs/Lmc/Prj : **R**	Enter R for regardless of feature size.
Add datum or <D>one: **D**	Enter D for done.

Use the tablet menu to change the tolerance values, and add the 5.0 horizontal dimension at the top of the mount.

Select **[SET TOLERANCE PLUS]**
Enter plus tolerance <0.000>: **.02**   Pick from screen menu.
Select **[SET TOLERANCE MINUS]**
Enter minus tolerance <0.000>: **.02**   Pick from screen menu.
Select **[TOLERANCE ON]**
Command: **DIM**
Command: **HOR**
Pick the mount's upper left and upper right corners.

Enter dimension text: **5.00 %%P.02**   Pad the front of the text string with two or three spaces to leave room for the square symbol.

Select **[SQUARE]**   From the form and proportion symbols section of the tablet or icon menu and position it in the space you just made.

Enter dimension value: **<RETURN>** Notice that you could have entered the dimension text as an attribute of the SQUARE block also, but you would have needed to pad the entire text string when in the DIM command.

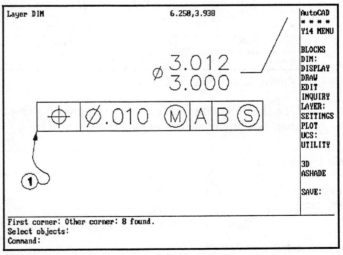

Completed Automatic Y14.5 Symbol

Finish the last dimension by adding the datum feature symbol to the end of the right extension line. The datum feature control symbol uses a floating insertion point, designed for maximum efficiency. It prompts you for the insertion point of the datum box, which helps you to easily insert it in its desired location. After the box is inserted, you are prompted for the datum letter. Let's do it.

Adding a Datum Feature Symbol

```
Select [-B-]
LL LR UL or UR <LL>... <RETURN>
```
Take the default, or pick LL for lower left from the screen menu.

```
Insertion point:
```
Pick point at the end of the right extension line.

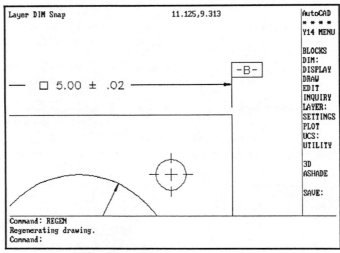

Adding Datum Feature Box [-B-]

Use the following instructions to generate the 2.50 vertical dimension, then add the basic dimension box around it.

Generating a Basic Dimension

```
Select [LIMITS OFF]
Select [TOLERANCE OFF]

Command: DIM
```
Vertically dimension the large hole center as shown below.

```
Select [BASIC DIMENSION]
Pick dimension text:
```
Pick a point at the center of dimension text.
Drag to stretch the upper right corner of the box above and to the right of the text, touching the dimension line, then pick a point.

```
Command: END
```
End the drawing.

After you pick the insertion point, the box will stretch as you move the cursor. Position the upper right-hand corner above and to the right of the dimension text.

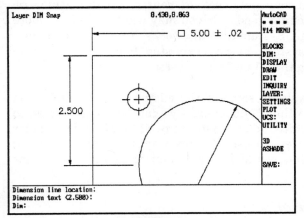

The Completed Vertical Dimension

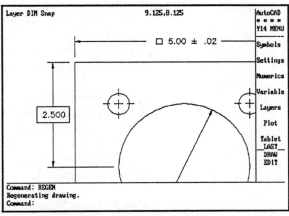

The Dimensioned Text With Basic Box

You can see how customizing AutoCAD's menus increases your drafting efficiency and productivity by automating many repetitive drafting tasks. Customization also increases consistency and reduces chances for errors.

Editing Older Drawings With the Y14.5 Menu System

If you use the Y14.5 Menu System to edit a drawing which was not originally created with the system, start AutoCAD with Y14.BAT and load the drawing normally (the same procedure used to edit the PROTO-C drawing). Respond to the units (English or metric) and scale setup parameter prompts. When you are presented with the sheet size selection, cancel. Next, load the Y14.5 menu as explained above. After you go through these setup steps, the Y14-SYS block (explained in the system startup section a little later in this chapter) is inserted into the drawing. When you end the drawing session, the drawing will automatically read the setup parameters the next time it is edited.

If you wish to edit a drawing which was created with an earlier version of the Y14.5 Menu System, delete the old Y14.5 symbols. You do not need to erase any other dimensioning features or text, just the old symbols. Then use the new Y14.5 Menu System to insert these symbols.

Taking a Closer Look at the Y14.5 Menu System

We hope you have found STEPPING INTO AutoCAD's ANSI Y14.5 Menu System easy to use, powerful, and maybe just a little fun. By applying the many customizing techniques available for AutoCAD, we have provided you with a means of making your job easier. But we also recognize that the Y14.5 Menu System may not meet *all* your particular geometric tolerancing and dimensioning needs. Or you may want to find out more about how the Y14.5 Menu System actually works. You can read on and learn more about the system, or you can stop here and return to production drafting using the Y14.5 Menu System.

The following section explains some of the customizing concepts and details incorporated into the Y14.5 Menu System. You may decide to come back to this section after you have used the Y14.5 Menu System for a while, and have a greater curiosity for the way it works, or a better understanding of how you would like to adapt it to your particular in-house standards.

Y14.5 Menu System Start-Up

When you use the Y14.BAT file to start AutoCAD with the Y14.5 Menu System, it sets the DOS environment variable ACAD (which tells AutoCAD where to look for menus, fonts, blocks, and other support files) to the \Y14 subdirectory. It also sets the environment variable ACADCFG to the \Y14 subdirectory to which you copied the configuration-related AutoCAD files. This allows you to run the menu system as a stand-alone product, independent of the STEPPING INTO AutoCAD configuration and example drawings. You can then safely erase the STEPPING INTO AutoCAD files from the SI-ACAD directory when you are through with them. The environment variables for ACADFREERAM, LISPHEAP, and LISPSTACK are next set to optimum values for coordination between AutoCAD and the Y14.5 Menu System.

Next, the batch file executes AutoCAD (assuming it is installed in an \ACAD subdirectory — you need to edit this entry if your installation is different) with replaceable parameters for default drawing and optional script execution. The final entries in the batch file release the environment variables after AutoCAD terminates, so as not to conflict with any other custom AutoCAD applications you may be using.

When AutoCAD starts a drawing (assuming you specified the prototype), it loads the customized ACAD.LSP file and begins to interpret its contents. This includes *pushing* several AutoLISP functions onto the LISPHEAP. These functions are:

SETLAY — Performs the setting of the current layer to that of an entity picked in the drawing (see the [SET BY ENTITY] explanation under the Layers Group subheading earlier in this chapter).

CONST and **CONST1** — Prompts the user through insertion of feature control frame symbols and options.

STATS — Displays the current DIMLIM, DIMTOL, DIMTP, and DIMTM values on the graphics display's status line.

SYMBLK — Prompts the user through insertion point options for the datum-feature symbols.

SETLIM — Changes sheet sizes in an existing drawing.

AUTOPL — Prompts the user for a plotting script to execute.

AUTOPR — Prompts the user for a printer script to execute.

S::START-UP — Upon startup, checks the drawing for the existence of a special block that stores drawing scale and dimension text with the drawing after it is initialized. This is an autoexecuting function (Release 9 users must manually execute this function by selecting [Release 9 Setup] from their opening menu).

After AutoLISP is done initializing, the Y14.5 compiled menu is loaded and the drawing scale factor is established by the S::STARTUP function and stored in #DWGSC, an AutoLISP variable. This one variable is then used to calculate proper sheet size (limits), line width, text size, symbol size, and linetype scale.

If you already use a customized ACAD.LSP file for functions you would still like available while using the Y14.5 Menu System, first rename the existing ACAD.LSP file to another name, such as MYFUNCS.LSP. Then add a line with your text editor near the end of the Y14.5 Menu System's ACAD.LSP file above the (princ) expression in the form: (load "drive:/path/myfuncs") where drive:/path/ is the actual drive and path of the renamed file. This will load your functions after those used by the Y14.5 Menu System.

If the renamed file includes an S::STARTUP function, you need to either combine the two functions into one function, or delete the S::STARTUP function from the renamed file.

Establishing the Drawing Scale

The Y14.5 Menu System uses an invisible block named Y14-SYS, which contains attribute definitions for the dimension scale factor and drawing units. When the Y14.5 Menu System is initiated, the S::START-UP routine searches the drawing database for this block. If the block is *not* found, the user will automatically be stepped through the Y14.5 setup routine. This routine prompts for drafting units (English or metric), drawing scale, and sheet size. Once the drawing scale is selected, the invisible Y14-SYS block is inserted into the lower left-hand corner of the current drawing. The attribute information is read and the #DWGSC variable is set. Also set at this time is another variable, #UNITS, which holds the English or metric unit system choice for the current drawing.

A smaller AutoLISP file is loaded next, either ENGLISH.LSP or METRIC.LSP, which contains AutoLISP expressions to establish dimensioning variables appropriate for the units selected.

If the block *is* found, the setup process is assumed to be unnecessary and therefore skipped.

ANSI Y14.5 Menu Anatomy

Now that the proper drawing scale has been established and saved with the drawing, actual drawing entities can be selected from the menus and created on the screen. AutoCAD uses the compiled menu file Y14.MNX to correlate picks from the tablet, screen, pull-down, and icon menus to a predetermined series of commands and responses called macros. You can explore these macros by viewing the non-compiled menu file Y14.MNU with a text editor or with a word processor in ASCII or non-document mode. Careful scrutiny of the Y14.MNU file will reveal that it is broken up into several sections as shown below. Menu items in boldface type indicate sections provided by the Y14.5 Menu System.

***BUTTONS	Designates the button menu.
***AUX1	Designates an auxiliary device menu.
*POPn	Designates pull-down menus 1 through 10.
*ICON	Designates the icon menu.
*SCREEN	Designates the screen menu.
*TABLET1	Designates the tablet menu for area 1.
***TABLET2	Designates the tablet menu for area 2.
***TABLET3	Designates the tablet menu for area 3.
***TABLET4	Designates the tablet menu for area 4.
**name	Designates a submenu name, (i.e. **Y14-LAY).

AutoCAD and Y14.5 Menu Designations

Each section of an .MNU file corresponds to a different menu type or area, and each line in a section corresponds to a particular selection within that area. Thus, the first line under the ***BUTTONS section designates the action to be performed when button 1 on a digitizer puck or mouse is pressed. The next line corresponds to button 2, and so on. A submenu section designates another menu to which control is transferred when that selection is picked.

If a menu selection is not blank, or does not contain a submenu name, then AutoCAD executes the characters, commands, and/or AutoLISP expressions that follow. Some of these macros can:

■ Use the AutoLISP variables mentioned above to scale and insert symbols.

■ Use AutoCAD commands to step through repetitive editing tasks.

■ Automate the keystrokes necessary to set various AutoCAD system and dimensioning variables.

■ Execute self-contained AutoLISP routines.

■ Supply commonly used values to other commands or macros.

You may be able to decipher what certain menu selections do by simply reading through the macros, and using a little imagination.

Bonus AutoLISP Routine

As an added bonus, we have included a more sophisticated AutoLISP function on the SIA DISK for you to explore and use. FLANGE.LSP is an example of the application of AutoLISP to the problem of designing and drafting a machinery shaft connection flange.

To try it out, simply load the routine once while in the AutoCAD drawing editor. The routine is then available any time during that drawing session, just like an AutoCAD command.

Trying the Bonus Routine

```
Command: (LOAD "FLANGE")
C:FLANGE
Command: FLANGE
```

You will be prompted for all the necessary properties of a safe flange. Then the routine will report its calculations to you, prompt for the center point of the flange, and draw the flange before your eyes!

The FLANGE.LSP file is heavily commented so that you can learn how it works by examining it with any text editor.

Summary

This chapter has shown you how the STEPPING INTO AutoCAD ANSI Y14.5 custom menu system was created and how to use it to increase your drafting productivity. With a custom menu system, you saw how easy it can be to set up a drawing and control its layers, its tolerance, limits, and other dimensioning variables, and to manually or automatically construct ANSI Y14.5 geometric dimensioning symbols.

If you are interested in exploring the programming of the ANSI Y14.5 Menu System further, load the Y14.MNU file into your word processor in ASCII (non-document) mode and take a look around. Use its anatomy as your guide to finding the ***POPn, ***ICON, ***SCREEN, and ***TABLET1 menu support sections.

We hope we've given you a taste for customizing AutoCAD to suit a particular drafting application. If you would like to learn more about how the menu systems operate and how to further customize the Y14.5 Menu System for your own system, we encourage you to pick up a copy of CUSTOMIZING AutoCAD, which gives in-depth coverage of the techniques used to develop the Y14.5 Menu System and much, much more.

In order to develop the Y14.5 Menu System to its full potential, it was necessary to develop and customize many of its functions using AutoLISP programming. If programming in AutoLISP appeals to you, get a copy of INSIDE AutoLISP. It covers AutoLISP in every detail, and will have you creating your own AutoLISP functions in very little time. Both INSIDE AutoLISP and CUSTOMIZING AutoCAD are available from New Riders Publishing.

STEPPING INTO AutoCAD's Expandable Tool Kit

STEPPING INTO AutoCAD has guided you through the vast array of production drafting tools which come with AutoCAD or can be created through customization. By using STEPPING INTO AutoCAD, you have begun to tap the potential of AutoCAD as well as your own potential as a drafter, designer, or engineer. AutoCAD is an ever-expanding program. As AutoCAD is revised, we hope you will look to our future editions to help you expand your drafting tool kit.

Now it's time to put your production drafting tools to work for you.

Good drafting.

MS-DOS, Batch Files, and Text Editors

This appendix describes common DOS (Disk Operating System) operations and AutoCAD file handling procedures to help you manage the AutoCAD program and drawing files. If you need additional information on DOS commands or syntax, refer to your DOS reference manual.

Working With Files

DOS refers to program or data information as a file. Think of a file as an individual document in your office's file cabinet. The folder that holds a number of related documents is the subdirectory, and the file cabinet itself is like the hard drive where the files and subdirectories are stored.

Each file requires a unique name to distinguish it from the many other files in the computer system. A file name can consist of up to eight characters, with an optional three-character extension that follows a period. AutoCAD drawing files use the extension .DWG. Some keyboard characters are invalid for use in file names. These include the " / \ [ ] : | + = ; , and . characters.

When specifying files for DOS operations, you can often save keystrokes and operate on several groups of files at one time by using the question mark and asterisk wildcard characters.

? — is a wildcard substitute for a single character.

* — is a wildcard substitute for multiple characters.

Using Wild Card Characters

`PART?.DWG`	All .DWG files beginning with PART, followed by any single character.
`PART*.DWG`	All .DWG files beginning with PART, followed by any other characters.
`???.DWG`	All .DWG files that have three-character file names.
`*.DWG`	All .DWG files.
`PART*.*`	All files that begin with PART.
`*.*`	All files.

Commonly Used DOS Directory Commands

Computer systems can access an unlimited number of files. Organize the files on your disk into meaningful groups, called subdirectories. Subdirectories are organized in a *tree* type structure similar to the AutoCAD menu hierarchy.

The *root* directory of a disk is at the most basic level. On tree diagrams where the elements branch in a downward direction, the root directory would be shown as the topmost entry. It can only hold up to 512 files and subdirectories, so it should only be used to hold the basic files the system needs to start up. Store all other files in organized subdirectories. This not only makes finding files easier for you, but also easier for DOS.

Subdirectories can hold as many files as disk space allows. They use the same naming conventions as files. The directory you are working in is known by DOS as the current subdirectory. DOS also remembers the last subdirectory you were in on the other drives in your system.

DIR (Directory)

The directory command will list all or specified files in a subdirectory.

Using the DIR Command

`C:\> DIR`	Displays a listing of the files in the current directory or subdirectory.
`C:\> DIR A:*.DWG`	Displays a list of all drawing files in the root directory of the diskette in drive A:.
`C:\> DIR \SIA-DWG`	Displays a list of all files in the subdirectory named SIA-DWG.
`C:\> DIR /P`	Displays a directory listing one screen page at a time for easier viewing.
`C:\SIA-DWG> DIR *.DWG /P`	Displays a directory listing of all .DWG files in the SIA-DWG subdirectory one screen page at a time.
`C:\> DIR /W`	Displays a directory listing in a wide list format.

MD or MKDIR (Make Subdirectory)

The make directory command creates a new directory. You can make as many directories as you wish, but each must have a different name. This name cannot be the same as a file name in the current directory. You can make a subdirectory in an existing directory.

Using the MD Command

C:\> **MD SIA-DWG**	Makes a subdirectory named SIA-DWG in the current directory.
C:\> **MD SIA-DWG\JOHN**	Makes a subdirectory named JOHN in SIA-DWG, the parent subdirectory.
C:\> **MD B:\DAVE**	Makes a subdirectory named DAVE in the root directory of drive B:.

Subdirectories can be nested. In other words, a directory can have subdirectories of its own, and they can have further nested subdirectories. In the SIA-DWG\JOHN example above, JOHN is nested in the subdirectory SIA-DWG.

CD or CHDIR (Change Directory)

The change subdirectory command is used to make another directory the current directory. This is similar to putting one folder away and taking out another. You must however, follow the directory tree structure (close the open folder) by first changing to a subdirectory's *parent* directory (the directory "above" the current directory) when traversing a file tree. It is not possible, in current versions of DOS, to jump across subdirectories in a single operation. The change directory command can also be used to display the name of the current subdirectory.

Using the CD Command

C:\> **CD \ACAD10**	Makes the ACAD10 subdirectory the current directory.
C:\APPS\CAD\> **CD ACAD10**	Makes the ACAD10 subdirectory, located in the parent CAD subdirectory, current.
C:\ACAD10> **CD **	Makes the root directory current.
C:\> **CD B:\SIA-DWG**	Makes the SIA-DWG subdirectory of disk drive B: current, while the current drive remains unchanged.
C:\APPS\CAD\> **CD**	
C:\APPS\CAD\	Displays the directory name.

Saving AutoCAD Drawing Files in Subdirectories

You can save AutoCAD drawings in any existing subdirectory by either specifying the subdirectory with the file name during the SAVE command, or by specifying the subdirectory with the file name when beginning a new drawing.

Enter name of drawing: **\DRAWINGS\ARM**   Places ARM in subdirectory DRAWINGS.

---

or

Save file name <PIN>: **\JOHN\PIN**   Places PIN in the subdirectory JOHN.

What Is a Path?

A *path* is one or more directories which must be "opened" to reach a specified file. For example, in \DRAWINGS\ARM.DWG and \APPS\CAD\PIN.DWG, \DRAWINGS and \APPS\CAD are the path names. Path names must be separated from file names by backslashes.

The DOS command, PATH, is used to specify a set of paths that DOS will search for executable files (COM, EXE, and BAT files). For example, PATH C:\;C:\DOS;C:\ACAD tells DOS to first look in the root directory of drive C:, then in the C:\DOS directory, and finally in the C:\ACAD directory when given a command or program name to execute at the DOS command prompt. The path is usually specified in the AUTOEXEC.BAT file.

➡ *NOTE: In the UNIX operating system, you must use forward slashes, not backslashes, in directory path names.*

RD or RMDIR (Remove Directory)

The remove directory command removes a subdirectory from a disk. A subdirectory cannot be removed if it contains files or other subdirectories. You must first delete all files and remove all subdirectories, and then make the subdirectory's parent directory current before you can remove the subdirectory.

Removing a Subdirectory

C:\> **RD \DRAWINGS**   Removes a subdirectory named DRAWINGS from the root directory.

Commonly Used DOS File Commands

The following DOS commands are commonly used on files. MS-DOS is not case-sensitive. It does not matter whether you input commands from the keyboard in upper, lower, or mixed case.

Disk drives are referred to as the source drive (where information is transferred from) and the target drive (where information is transferred to).

COPY

The copy command copies files from one disk or directory to another. When copying AutoCAD drawings or backup files, you must include the file extension or appropriate wildcards.

Copying a file to a destination that contains an existing file with the same name will overwrite the file at the destination, *without* any warning.

Using the COPY Command

C:\> **COPY PART.DWG B:**	Copies the drawing file named PART from the current subdirectory to the target diskette in drive B:.
C:\> **COPY *.* A:**	Copies all files from the current directory in drive C: to the target diskette in drive A:.
C:\> **COPY A:*.***	Copies all files from a source diskette in drive A: to the current drive and directory.
C:\> **COPY *.DWG A:/V**	Copies all .DWG files from the current subdirectory of drive C: to the target diskette in drive A: and verifies the copy.
C:\> **COPY \JOHN\PART.DWG A:**	Copies the drawing file named PART from the JOHN subdirectory to the target diskette in drive A:.

If you need to copy a file and rename it at the target destination, you can do so using the following example.

C:\> **COPY PART.DWG A:LATCH.DWG**	Copies the drawing file named PART to the target diskette in drive A: and renames the file LATCH.DWG.

COMP (Compare Files)

Use the compare files command (with the same syntax as COPY) to verify critical files. It is a better test than COPY's /V option.

Using the COMP Command

C:\> COMP *.DWG A:*.DWG   Compares all drawing files in the current directory with all drawing
                               files on the diskette in drive A:.

DEL (Delete File)

The delete command deletes a specified file.

Using the DEL Command

C:\> DEL PART.DWG   Deletes the drawing file PART from the current subdirectory.
C:\> DEL \SIA-DWG\ARM.DWG   Deletes the drawing file ARM from the SIA-DWG subdirectory.
C:\> DEL A:*.BAK   Deletes all backup files from the diskette in drive A:.
C:\ DEL \SIA-DWG   Deletes entire SIA-DWG subdirectory.

Notice that if you specify a subdirectory name without specifying any file
name, the delete command will delete all files in that subdirectory. Also,
DEL *XYZ.* is equivalent to *.* and will delete all files in the current
directory. The asterisk wildcard means all characters to the right, until
it encounters a period or the end of the file name. If the delete command
asks, "Are you sure?" be careful, because it is going to delete an entire
drive or directory.

REN (Rename File)

The rename command renames a designated file with a new file name.
Be sure to include correct file extensions such as .DWG so that AutoCAD
will be able to read the files.

Using the REN Command

C:\> REN PIN.DWG BLOCK.DWG   Renames the drawing file named PIN to the new drawing file
                               named BLOCK.
C:\> REN ARM.BAK ARM.DWG   Renames the backup file named ARM to the drawing file named
                               ARM.

Commonly Used DOS Disk Commands

Changing the Default Drive

Changing the default drive is like looking in another file cabinet. You can
change to any drive actually configured in your system.

```
C:\> A:                Changes from drive C: to drive A:
A:\> C:                Changes from drive A: to drive C:
```

CHKDSK (Check Disk)

The check disk command checks the file integrity of available drives or individual files and reports memory allocations.

Using the CHKDSK Command

```
C:\> CHKDSK            Checks the files on drive C: and reports the current memory
                       allocation.
C:\> CHKDSK D:         Checks the files on drive D: and reports the current memory
                       allocation.
C:\> CHKDSK /F         Checks the default drive and fixes any errors it finds (chains of lost
                       clusters).
```

Lost clusters are leftover pieces of files which may be recovered into a *readable* file named in the form FILE*nnnn*.CHK where *nnnn* is a sequential number for each file written. Once the lost clusters are converted into readable files, you can look at them to determine if they contain any useful information. If not, remove them from the disk. Do not use this option with AutoCAD's SHELL command. Repeat CHKDSK periodically to maintain free disk space.

DISKCOPY (Diskette Copy)

The disk copy command lets you copy a source diskette to a target diskette. DISKCOPY will copy all the files from the source diskette and, if necessary, format the target diskette in the process. Use DISKCOPY for copying floppy diskettes only.

Using the DISKCOPY Command

```
A:\> DISKCOPY A: B:    Copies all files from drive A: to drive B:.
A:\> DISKCOPY A: A:    Copies a diskette in a single drive system.
```

After the copying is complete, you will be asked if you want to make any additional copies.

DISKCOMP (Diskette Compare)

Use the diskette compare command (with the same syntax as DISKCOPY) to verify critical files (on diskettes only).

Using DISKCOMP

```
C:\> DISKCOMP A: B:
```
Compares all files on the diskette
in drive A: with all files on the diskette in drive B:.

FORMAT (Format Disk)

The format command initializes a disk so that files can be written to it.
The format process will also check a disk for bad tracks (created during
the manufacturing process). New disks must be formatted before use.

Formatting will delete all files that were previously on the disk. While
DOS 3.0 and later versions make it more difficult than earlier versions to
accidently format a disk, thereby destroying all existing data, be careful
with your drive letters!

Using the FORMAT Command

```
C:\DOS> FORMAT A:
A:\> FORMAT B:
```
Formats the disk in drive A:.
Formats the disk in drive B: (the diskette in drive A: must contain
a copy of the format program).

FORMAT /S (Format With System)

The format with system command creates a bootable disk (one that will
boot up the computer when it is turned on). You do not need to format
AutoCAD drawing diskettes or other data diskettes with the /S switch.

```
C:\DOS> FORMAT A:/S
```
Formats the diskette in drive A:, copying the operating system files
from DOS.

FORMAT /V (Format With Volume Label)

The format with volume label command labels drawing diskettes for good
file management.

```
C:\DOS> FORMAT A: /V
```
Formats the diskette in drive A: and prompts for a label (name) of
the diskette volume to display when other DOS commands are used on it.

TREE (Display Directory Tree)

The tree command displays the directory structure of a specified drive. If
no drive is specified, the default drive's directory tree is shown.

Using the TREE Command

C:\> **TREE**	Displays the directory structure on drive C:.
C:\> **TREE A:**	Displays the directory structure on drive A:.

SET (Set Environment Variable)

The set command sets program-specific DOS environment variables to values which can affect the way that program performs. Some programs use this method for controlling memory allocation, directory usage, and other program execution options. See the AutoCAD Installation and Performance Guide for more information on how AutoCAD uses the SET command.

Batch Files and How to Create Them

The concept of batch processing comes from the mainframe computer world where extremely large batches of records or transactions are processed overnight. A personal computer batch file is a simple text file containing one or more DOS commands that execute one at a time as if you had just typed them at the DOS prompt. Batch processing provides you with an easy way to program and execute many frequently used DOS commands to manipulate files, directories, and programs. Batch files are named with up to eight characters and .BAT, the DOS extension. A batch file is executed by the DOS command processor similar to the way it executes programs (when a command is entered at the DOS prompt, DOS first checks to see if it is an *internal* DOS command (such as DIR or COPY), and then *searches* the directories contained in the current path for files with the extensions .COM, .EXE, and .BAT). A batch file can be suspended by simultaneously pressing the control and break or the control and C keys.

Batch files can use *replaceable parameters* (a type of variable). In this way, one batch file can perform the same operations on different files, directories, or drives. A replaceable parameter is a character string that follows the batch file (or command or program) name on the DOS command line. For example, OLDFILES, \NEWFILES, and X: are parameters to the QUENCH command or batch file in the line: C:\> A:QUENCH OLDFILE \NEWFILES X:. Up to ten replaceable parameters can be used with one batch file before this capability needs to be expanded with the SHIFT command. Ten parameters should be sufficient for all but the most exotic needs.

Parameters can be used within the batch file. DOS substitutes the parameters you specify on the command line after a batch file name for corresponding variables *within* the batch file. These variables are specified by the names %0 - %9. For example, in our hypothetical batch file QUENCH.BAT, DOS would substitute the value of the drive letter and batch file name for %0, OLDFILE for %1, \NEWFILES for %2, and X: for %3, and so on up to %9. You would use the names %0-%9 within the batch file when referencing information to be supplied by the user in the order given above.

Much like menu macros automate AutoCAD, batch files can automate DOS. Batch files can execute other batch files, display messages, repeat DOS commands for groups of files, branch to specified sections in the batch file, perform conditional execution of commands, and test for the successful execution of other programs. This gives the DOS user plenty of power and makes working with DOS much easier. For a further explanation of batch file features, consult your DOS reference manual.

AUTOEXEC.BAT (Automatic Executing .BAT File)

When you turn on a DOS-based computer, the command processor searches for an AUTOEXEC.BAT file in the root directory of the disk it was started from. An example of an AUTOEXEC.BAT file that can be used for automatically running AutoCAD is described in Chapter 1, System Management.

Selecting Text Editors

A text editor is the easiest way to create batch and other text files. Any good text editor will work as long as it creates "pure" ASCII files that include the ASCII <ESCAPE> character. It must also be able to merge files and allow you to turn word-wrap off. Norton's Editor, our choice, includes all this and the following additional recommended features:

■ Quick loading, compact size. Quick saving and exit. Saves to another file name. Handles large files. Merges files.

■ Has line and column number counter display. Will go to line number. Has row mode.

■ Includes block copy and move. Has versatile cursor control, delete, and undelete text features.

■ Compares files for differences. Has versatile search and replace, and can find matching punctuation like: (([ ])).

If you have doubts about your DOS editor's ability to produce ASCII files, test it with the following steps.

Testing the Text Editor

With your text editor, create a few screens full of text. Save the file to the name TEST.TXT and exit to DOS.

```
C:\> COPY TEXT.TXT CON         Test it. All the text you entered scrolls by.
C:\> DEL TEXT.TXT
```

Your text editor is okay if COPY TEXT.TXT CON showed text identical to what you typed in your editor, with no extra ^L, åÇäÆ characters, or smiling faces! If you got any garbage, particularly at the top or bottom of the copy, then your text editor is not suitable, or is not configured correctly for ASCII output.

Setup, Memory, and Errors

Setup Problems With CONFIG.SYS

If your CONFIG.SYS settings do not run smoothly, your only indication may be that things don't work. If you get the error message:

```
Bad or missing FILENAME
```

DOS can't find the file as it is specified. Check your spelling, and provide a full path. If you get

```
Unrecognized command in CONFIG.SYS
```

it means that you made a syntax error, or your version of DOS doesn't support the configuration command. Check your spelling.

Watch closely when you boot your system. These error messages flash by very quickly. If you suspect an error, temporarily rename your AUTOEXEC.BAT file so that the system stops after loading CONFIG.SYS. You can also try to send the screen messages to the printer by hitting <CTRL-PRINTSCREEN> as soon as DOS starts reading the CONFIG.SYS file. Another <CTRL-PRINTSCREEN> turns the printer echo off.

Problems With AUTOEXEC.BAT

Errors in AUTOEXEC.BAT are harder to troubleshoot. There are many causes. Often, the system just doesn't behave as you think it should. Here are some troubleshooting tips:

■ Isolate errors by temporarily editing your AUTOEXEC.BAT. Try using a leading colon to disable a line:

```
: NOW DOS WILL IGNORE THIS LINE!
```

■ Many AUTOEXEC.BAT files have echo to the screen turned off by the command ECHO OFF or @ECHO OFF. Disable ECHO OFF to see what the AUTOEXEC.BAT file is doing. Put a leading colon on the line.

- Echo to the printer. Hit <CTRL-PRINTSCREEN> while booting to see what is happening.

- Make sure PROMPT, PATH, and other environment settings precede any TSR (memory resident) programs in the file.

- Check your path for completeness and syntax. Unsophisticated programs that require support or overlay files in addition to their .EXE or .COM files may not work, even if they are in the path. Directories do not need to be in the path unless you want to execute files in them from other directories.

- APPEND (DOS 3.3 or later) works like PATH and lets programs find their support and overlay files in other directories. It uses about 5K of RAM. All files in an appended directory are recognized by programs as if they were in the current directory. If you use APPEND, *use it cautiously*. If you modify an appended file, the modified file will be written to the current directory, *not* the appended directory. Loading an AutoCAD.MNU file from an appended directory creates an .MNX file in the current directory. AutoCAD searches an appended directory before completing its normal directory search pattern, so appended support files will get loaded instead of those in the current directory.

- SET environment errors are often obscure. Type SET <RETURN> to see your current environment settings. If a setting is truncated or missing, you are probably out of environment space. Fix it in your CONFIG.SYS file. Do not use extraneous spaces in a SET statement:

```
SET ACADCFG=\CA-ACAD .... OK. Sets "ACADCFG" to "\CA-ACAD"
SET ACADCFG =\CA-ACAD ... Wrong. Sets "ACADCFG "
SET ACADCFG= \CA-ACAD ... Wrong. Sets to " \CA-ACAD"
```

- If your AUTOEXEC.BAT doesn't seem to complete its execution, you may have tried to execute another .BAT file from your AUTOEXEC.BAT file. If you nest execution of .BAT files, the second one will take over and the first will not complete. There are two ways to nest .BATs. With DOS 3.0 and later, use:

```
COMMAND /C NAME
```

where NAME is the name of the nested .BAT file . With DOS 3.3, use:

```
CALL NAME
```

■ If you are fighting for memory, insert temporary lines in the AUTOEXEC.BAT to check your available memory. Once you determine what uses how much, you can decide what to sacrifice. Use:

```
CHKDSK
PAUSE
```

at appropriate points. Reboot to see the effect. Remove the lines when you are done. We use an alternative FREEWARE program called MEM.COM. It reports available RAM quickly.

■ If you have unusual occurrences or lockups, and you use TSRs, suspect the TSRs as your problem source. Cause and effect may be hard to pin down. For example, there is a simple screen capture program that, if loaded, locks up our word processor — even when inactive! Disable TSRs one at a time in your AUTOEXEC. Reboot and test.

These are the most common problems. See a good DOS book if you need more information.

Problems With DOS Environment Space

Running out of space to store DOS environment settings may give the error:

```
Out of environment space
```

An environment space problem also may show up in unusual ways, such as a program failing to execute, AutoLISP not having room to load, or a block insertion not finding its block. This occurs because the path, AutoCAD settings limiting EXTended/EXPanded memory, and AutoCAD configuration, memory, and support file settings are all environment settings.

To find out how much environment space you need:

■ Type SET at the DOS prompt.

■ Count the characters displayed, including spaces.

■ Add the number of characters for all SET statements you wish to add. Include revisions to your AUTOEXEC.BAT and startup files, like SIA.BAT.

■ Add a safety margin of 10 percent.

For STEPPING INTO AutoCAD, you need about 240 bytes (characters). DOS defaults environment size to 160 bytes or less, depending on the

DOS version. The space expands if you type in settings, but cannot expand during execution of a .BAT file, including your AUTOEXEC.BAT. Loading a TSR (memory resident) program or utility such as SIDEKICK, PROKEY, some Ram disks and print buffers, the DOS PRINT or GRAPHICS commands, and other utilities freezes the environment space to the current size.

Fortunately, DOS 3.0 or later versions can easily expand the space. Add this line to your CONFIG.SYS:

```
SHELL = C:\COMMAND.COM /P /E:nnn
```

Substitute your boot drive for C: if your boot drive isn't C. Do not use *nnn*; replace *nnn* with an integer value:

■ For DOS 3.0 and 3.1, *nnn* is the desired environment size divided by 16. If you want 512 bytes, use 32 since (512/16=32). The maximum for *nnn* is 62.

■ For DOS 3.2 and 3.3, *nnn* is the actual size setting. For 512 bytes, use 512. The maximum for *nnn* is 32768.

If you must use DOS 2, your solutions are more difficult. You have few choices. You can modify your COMMAND.COM file to allocate a larger environment.

Memory Settings and Problems

There are several DOS environment settings that deal with AutoCAD's memory usage. These settings are explained and shown in a memory usage chart in the AutoCAD Installation and Performance Guide. None of AutoCAD's settings affect other programs or tie up memory when AutoCAD is not running. The AutoCAD status command shows several memory values:

```
Free RAM:  9784 bytes        Free disk: 1409024 bytes

I/O page space: 109K bytes   Extended I/O page space: 592K
                             bytes
```

"Free RAM" is the unused portion of RAM for AutoCAD to work in. "I/O page space" is RAM used by AutoCAD to swap data in and out. An I/O page value of 60K or more is adequate for most use, and we've worked (slowly!) with values under 20K.

"SET ACADFREERAM=nn" reserves RAM for AutoCAD's working space. Too small a size can cause "Out of RAM" errors, slow down spline fitting, and cause problems with AutoCAD's HIDE, TRIM, and OFFSET commands. However, a large ACADFREERAM setting reduces I/O page swap space and slows down AutoCAD. The default is 14K, the maximum depends on the system, usually about 24 to 26K. A setting larger than the maximum is equivalent to maximum. There is no magic number. Try changing ACADFREERAM to a lower or higher setting if you get errors or want to increase I/O page space.

"Extended I/O page space" is another factor that affects I/O page space. Extended memory is IBM AT-style memory above the 1 Mb mark. It is commonly used as RAM disk (VDISK), a print buffer (PRINT), and by some sophisticated programs like AutoCAD. AutoCAD uses extended memory as "Extended I/O page space" to swap its temporary files into extended RAM instead of slower disk space. Expanded memory is Intel Above Board style memory above the 640K mark. It is also known as LIM and EMS memory. It is used for RAM disks and print buffers, and is designed for page swapping. AutoCAD uses it as "Extended I/O page space."

It may take some investigation to determine which type of memory you have. You often can configure Intel Above Boards and their imitators as expanded or extended memory. Expanded memory is relatively clean, with established techniques for programs to share it. Unfortunately, extended memory lacks protection. Programs wishing to use it are not always able to tell if it is already in use by another program.

If you use extended memory and sometimes get unexplained crashes, you may have a memory conflict between programs. Crashes may appear random. Check to see what, if any, programs other than AutoCAD may be using your extended memory. In particular, check for DOS VDISK and PRINT. Check your CONFIG.SYS and AUTOEXEC.BAT. Figure out what addresses are in use so that you can set AutoCAD to avoid the conflict. If you have extended RAM, and it is used by any other program like DOS VDISK (RAM disk) or DOS PRINT, you can use "SET ACADXMEM=start,size" to avoid conflict. See your AutoCAD Installation and Performance Guide for details.

Even if you do not encounter crashes, you may want to examine your memory usage. AutoCAD uses up some free RAM to enable "Extended I/O page space." If you have 2 Mb or more of extended or expanded memory, you may need to actually restrict AutoCAD's use of it. Each Kbyte of "Extended I/O page space" reduces free RAM by 16 bytes. You may also want to restrict your extended or expanded memory use if you run SOFTWARE CAROUSEL or another multi-tasking setup.

"SET ACADLIMEM=value" configures expanded memory usage (LIM-EMS). This setting is probably not critical, since EMS avoids conflicts. If you must restrict it, or wish to reserve some of your LIM-EMS RAM for other programs to use via SHELL, refer to your AutoCAD Installation and Performance Guide.

Using STEPPING INTO AutoCAD With a RAM Disk

Running AutoCAD from a RAM disk can be more efficient than using extended/expanded memory for I/O page space. If you want to run AutoCAD from a RAM disk, there are three things to look at: AutoCAD's program files, temporary files, and the drawing itself.

AutoCAD locates its temporary files on the same drive and directory as the drawing, unless you tell it otherwise. Using the configuration menu, select item 8 (Configure operating parameters). Then choose item 5 (Placement of temporary files). Item 5 defaults to <DRAWING>, for the drawing's directory. You can reset this to a RAM disk and locate your temporary files there. If you use a RAM disk, we recommend allowing about two times the size of your largest drawing.

Regardless of the temporary file setting, AutoCAD still locates the temporary file(s) that eventually becomes the new drawing file in the directory of the drawing file itself. This occurs because AutoCAD closes up the file(s) instead of copying it when the drawing is ended.

To speed drawing disk access, you can edit the drawing from your RAM disk. Make sure the finished drawing is copied back to a real drive. Use a menu macro, or redefine the END command for safety. If you have sufficient I/O page space, you won't gain much by putting the drawing on a RAM disk.

The easiest way to put the AutoCAD program on RAM disk is to copy all files to it. This may waste a little memory, but if you have plenty, it works. Make sure that you have set a real disk directory with SET ACADCFG=, ensuring any configuration changes are copied back to a real disk.

If you want to place AutoCAD on the RAM disk but need to make efficient use of RAM disk space, selectively copy AutoCAD program files to it. There is little advantage to putting support files or the ACAD.EXE file on a RAM disk. Start with the overlay files. They are listed in the Software Installation section of your AutoCAD Installation and Performance Guide. The most important are: ACAD.OVL, ACAD0.OVL, and ACADVS.OVL. The ACAD2.OVL and ACAD3.OVL contain ADE2 and ADE3 commands, and the ACADL.OVL is AutoLISP. If you have to decide between them, you can refer to the AutoCAD Reference Manual's appendix on commands. Decide whether you use ADE2 or ADE3 commands the most.

Make sure that the files copied to the RAM disk are not included in the \ACAD directory of your hard disk. Make an \ACAD\RAM directory to store the files. Let's assume that you have the following drives and directories:

C:	Hard disk.
D:	RAM disk.
C:\ACAD	Standard ACAD support files and program files except the .OVL files.
C:\ACAD\RAM	AutoCAD .OVL files to go on RAM disk.
C:\SUPFILES	Project-specific support files.
C:\PROJECT	Working drawing project directory.
C:\CFGFILES	Specific configuration.

If D: is on your path, and you have copied the .OVL files to D:, you start AutoCAD with the following:

```
SET ACAD=SUPFILES
SET ACADCFG=CFGFILES
C:\ACAD\ACAD
```

This works fine. AutoCAD will find all its needed files. The \ACAD\ACAD explicitly tells DOS to look in the \ACAD directory for the ACAD.EXE file. AutoCAD will also look there for .OVL files and remember it for support files. AutoCAD is a smart program, and it will also search the path to find its other needed support files. Since D: is on the path, it finds its .OVLs, and remembers D: as a possible source of support files.

If your path is wrong, or if a file is in neither \ACAD or D:, you will get:

```
Can't find overlay file ACAD0.OVL
Enter file name prefix (path name\ or X:) or '.' to quit=
```

Finding Support Files

When you ask AutoCAD to find a support file, like a menu file, it searches in a particular order. Given the above settings, you would get:

```
"STUFF.mnu": Can't open file
  in C:\PROJECT (current directory)      First the current directory.
  or C:\SUPFILES\                        Then the directory designated by SET ACAD=.
  or D:\                                  Then the .OVL directory found on PATH, if any.
  or C:\ACAD\                            Last the program directory, home of ACAD.EXE.
Enter another menu file name (or RETURN for none):
```

If you keep AutoCAD's search order in mind, it will help you avoid errors in finding the wrong support files. A common cause of finding the wrong support files is setting ACAD=*somename* in a startup batch file. Make sure to SET ACAD= to clear it at the end of the batch file. Clear your SET ACADCFG= settings.

Current Directory Errors

If you use SHELL to change directories (CD) from inside AutoCAD, you may get strange results. Parts of AutoCAD recognize the change and parts do not. New drawings will not default to the new current directory, yet drawings saved with SAVE will observe the directory change. Subsequent attempts to load support files, such as .MNX files, can cause AutoCAD to crash.

If you must change a directory on SHELL excursions, automate it with a batch file that returns to the original directory.

SHELL Errors

Here are some common errors encountered when using SHELL:

```
SHELL error swapping to disk
```

is most likely caused by insufficient disk space. Remember that AutoCAD's temporary files can easily use a megabyte of disk space.

```
SHELL error: insufficient memory for command
```

can be caused by an ill-behaved program executed during a previous shell, or before entering AutoCAD. Some ill-behaved programs leave a dirty environment behind that causes AutoCAD to erroneously believe insufficient memory exists.

```
Unable to load program: insufficient memory
Program too big to fit in memory
```

If SHELL got this far, these are correct messages. You need to modify your ACAD.PGP to allocate more memory space for your program.

```
SHELL error in EXEC function (insufficient memory)
```

can be caused by the shell memory allocation being too small to load DOS. Exactly how much memory you need to allocate depends on your versions of DOS and AutoCAD, and on what you have in your CONFIG.SYS file. DOS 3.2 and later versions must have at least 25000 bytes allocated in the ACAD.PGP. Use 30000 to give a little cushion.

Miscellaneous Problems

If you run under a multi-tasking environment like CAROUSEL or DESKVIEW, you may get an error claiming a file should be in a directory it never was in. For example, you may get:

```
Can't find overlay file D:\ACAD\ACAD.OVL
Retry, Abort?
```

Or any other .OVL or ACAD.EXE. Don't type an "A" until you give up. Try an "R" to retry. If that doesn't work, copy the file to the directory listed in the error message. Flip partitions. You may need to hit another "R" during the flip. Copy the file, flip back and "R" again.

```
Expanded memory disabled
```

When starting ACAD from DOS, this error message can be caused by a previously crashed AutoCAD. Sometimes a crashed AutoCAD does not fully clear its claim on expanded memory. This causes the program to think none is available. Reboot to clear it.

Insufficient File Errors

You may encounter file error messages due to AutoCAD's inability to open a file. This may be caused by too few files requested in the FILES= statement of the CONFIG.SYS file or by AutoLISP's OPEN function leaving too many files open. If you repeatedly crash an AutoLISP routine which opens files, you may see the following:

```
Command: (load "test")
Can't open "test.lsp" for input
error: LOAD failed
(load "test")
```

If you know the variable names SETQed to the files, try to CLOSE them before you get the message. Otherwise, you have little choice other than to QUIT AutoCAD and reboot the system to clean things up. This error can also show up as:

```
Can't find overlay file C:\ACAD\ACAD.OVL
```

Tracing and Curing Errors

You are your best source for error diagnosis. When problems occur, log them so you can recognize patterns. Here are some tips and techniques:

■ Use screen capture programs to document the text screen.

■ Dump the screen to the printer.

- Write down what you did in as much detail as possible, as far back as you can remember.

- Dump a copy of AutoCAD's STATUS screen to the printer.

- Dump a copy of the screen of the DOS command SET to check settings.

Avoidance is the best cure.

AutoCAD System Variables

AutoCAD System Variables

A table of AutoCAD system variables starts on the following page. Use this table to find AutoCAD's environment settings and their values. The table presents all the variable settings available through AutoCAD's SETVAR command or AutoLISP's setvar and getvar functions. The system variable name and the default AutoCAD prototype drawing (ACAD.DWG) settings are shown. A brief description is given for each variable, and the meaning is given for each code flag. All values are saved with the drawing unless noted with <CFG> for ConFiGuration file, or <NS> for Not Saved. Variables marked <RO> are read only, meaning you can't use SETVAR or the setvar function to change them.

AutoCAD System Variables

VARIABLE NAME	DEFAULT SETTING	DEFAULT MEANING	COMMAND NAME	VARIABLE DESCRIPTION
ACADPREFIX	"C:\ACAD\"			AutoCAD directory path **\<NS\>,\<RO\>**
ACADVER	"10"			AutoCAD release version **\<RO\>**
AFLAGS	0		ATTDEF	Sum of: Invisible=1 Constant=2 Verify=4 Preset=8
ANGBASE	0	EAST	UNITS	Direction of angle 0
ANGDIR	0	CCW	UNITS	Clockwise=1 Counter clockwise=0
APERTURE	10	10	APERTURE	Half of aperture height in pixels **\<CFG\>**
AREA	0.0000		AREA,LIST	Last computed area **\<NS\>,\<RO\>**
ATTDIA	0	PROMPTS		Insert uses: DDATTE dialogue box=1 Attribute prompts=0
ATTMODE	1	ON	ATTDISP	Attribute display Normal=1 ON=2 OFF=0
ATTREQ	1	PROMPTS		Insert uses: Prompts=1 Defaults=0
AUNITS	0	DEC. DEG.	UNITS	Angular units Dec=0 Deg=1 Grad=2 Rad=3 Survey=4
AUPREC	0	0	UNITS	Angular units decimal places
AXISMODE	0	OFF	AXIS	Axis ON=1 Axis OFF=0
AXISUNIT	0.0000,0.0000		AXIS	Axis X,Y Increment
BACKZ	0.0000		DVIEW	Back clipping plane offset - See VIEWMODE **\<RO\>**
BLIPMODE	1	ON	BLIPMODE	Blips=1 No Blips=0
CDATE	19881202.144648898		TIME	Date.Time **\<NS\>,\<RO\>**
CECOLOR	"BYLAYER"		COLOR	Current entity color **\<RO\>**
CELTYPE	"BYLAYER"		LINETYPE	Current entity linetype **\<RO\>**
CHAMFERA	0.0000		CHAMFER	Chamfer distance for A
CHAMFERB	0.0000		CHAMFER	Chamfer distance for B
CLAYER	"0"		LAYER	Current layer **\<RO\>**
CMDECHO	1	ECHO	SETVAR	Command echo in AutoLISP Echo=1 No Echo=0 **\<NS\>**
COORDS	0	OFF	[^D] [F6]	Update display Picks=0 ON=1 Dist>Angle=2
CVPORT	1		VPORTS	Identification number of the current viewport
DATE	2447498.61620926		TIME	Julian time **\<NS\>,\<RO\>**
DIMALT	0	OFF	DIMALT	Use alternate units ON=1 OFF=0
DIMALTD	2	0.00	DIMALTD	Decimal precision of alternate units
DIMALTF	25.4000		DIMALTF	Scale factor for alternate units
DIMAPOST	""	NONE	DIMAPOST	Suffix for alternate dimensions **\<RO\>**
DIMASO	1	ON	DIMASO	Associative=1 Line,Arrow,Text=0
DIMASZ	0.1800		DIMASZ	Arrow Size=Value (also controls text fit)
DIMBLK	""	NONE	DIMBLK	Block name to draw instead of arrow or tick **\<RO\>**
DIMBLK1	""	NONE	DIMBLK1	Block name for 1st end, see DIMSAH **\<RO\>**
DIMBLK2	""	NONE	DIMBLK2	Block name for 2nd end, see DIMSAH **\<RO\>**
DIMCEN	0.0900	MARK	DIMCEN	Center mark size=Value Add center lines=Negative
DIMDLE	0.0000	NONE	DIMDLE	Dimension line extension=Value
DIMDLI	0.3800		DIMDLI	Increment between continuing dimension lines
DIMEXE	0.1800		DIMEXE	Extension distance for extension lines=Value
DIMEXO	0.0625		DIMEXO	Offset distance for extension lines=Value
DIMLFAC	1.0000	NORMAL	DIMLFAC	Overall linear distance factor=Value
DIMLIM	0	OFF	DIMLIM	Add tolerance limits ON=1 OFF=0
DIMPOST	""	NONE	DIMPOST	User defined dimension suffix (eg: "mm") **\<RO\>**
DIMRND	0.0000	EXACT	DIMRND	Rounding value for linear dimensions
DIMSAH	0	OFF	DIMSAH	Allow separate DIMBLKS ON=1 OFF=0
DIMSCALE	1.0000		DIMSCALE	Overall dimensioning scale factor=Value
DIMSE1	0	OFF	DIMSE1	Suppress extension line 1 Omit=1 Draw=0
DIMSE2	0	OFF	DIMSE2	Suppress extension line 2 Omit=1 Draw=0
DIMSHO	0	OFF	DIMSHO	Show associative dimension while dragging
DIMSOXD	0	OFF	DIMSOXD	Suppress dim. lines outside extension lines Omit=1 Draw=0
DIMTAD	0	OFF	DIMTAD	Text above dim. line ON=1 OFF(in line)=0

VARIABLE NAME	DEFAULT SETTING	DEFAULT MEANING	COMMAND NAME	VARIABLE DESCRIPTION
DIMTIH	1	ON	DIMTIH	Text inside horizontal ON=1 OFF(aligned)=0
DIMTIX	0	OFF	DIMTIX	Force text inside extension lines ON=1 OFF=0
DIMTM	0.0000	NONE	DIMTM	Minus tolerance=Value
DIMTOFL	0	OFF	DIMTOFL	Draw dim. line even if text outside ext. lines
DIMTOH	1	ON	DIMTOH	Text outside horizontal ON=1 OFF(aligned)=0
DIMTOL	0	OFF	DIMTOL	Append tolerance ON=1 OFF=2
DIMTP	0.0000	NONE	DIMTP	Plus tolerance=Value
DIMTSZ	0.0000	ARROWS	DIMTSZ	Tick size=Value Draw arrows=0
DIMTVP	0.0000		DIMTVP	Text vertical position
DIMTXT	0.1800		DIMTXT	Text size=Value
DIMZIN	0		DIMZIN	Controls leading zero (see AutoCAD manual)
DISTANCE	0.0000		DIST	Last computed distance <NS>,<RO>
DRAGMODE	2	AUTO	DRAGMODE	OFF=0 Enabled=1 Auto=2
DRAGP1	10		SETVAR	Drag regen rate <CFG>
DRAGP2	25		SETVAR	Drag input rate <CFG>
DWGNAME	"TEST"			Current drawing name <RO>
DWGPREFIX	"C:\IA-ACAD\"			Directory path of current drawing <NS>,<RO>
ELEVATION	0.0000		ELEV	Current default elevation
EXPERT	0	NORMAL	SETVAR	Suppresses "Are you sure" prompts (See AutoCAD Reference Manual)
EXTMAX	-1.0000E+20,-1.0000E+20			Upper right drawing extents X,Y <RO>
EXTMIN	1.0000E+20,1.0000E+20			Lower left drawing extents X,Y <RO>
FILLETRAD	0.0000		FILLET	Current fillet radius
FILLMODE	1		FILL	Fill ON=1 Fill OFF=0
FLATLAND	0		SETVAR	Temporary 3D compatibility setting act like Release 9=1 R10=0
FRONTZ	0.0000		DVIEW	Front clipping plane offset - See VIEWMODE <RO>
GRIDMODE	0	OFF	GRID	Grid ON=1 Grid OFF=0
GRIDUNIT	0.0000,0.0000		GRID	X,Y grid increment
HANDLES	0		HANDLES	Entity handles Enabled=1 Disabled=0 <RO>
HIGHLIGHT	1		SETVAR	Highlight selection ON=1 OFF=0 <NS>
INSBASE	0.0000,0.0000		BASE	Insert base point of current drawing X,Y
LASTANGLE	0		ARC	Last angle of the last arc <NS>,<RO>
LASTPOINT	0.0000,0.0000			Last @ pickpoint X,Y <NS>
LASTPT3D	0.0000,0.0000,0.0000			Last @ pickpoint X,Y,Z <NS>
LENSLENGTH	50.0000		DVIEW	Length of lens in perspective in millimeters <RO>
LIMCHECK	0	OFF	LIMITS	Limits error check ON=1 OFF=0
LIMMAX	12.0000,9.0000		LIMITS	Upper right X,Y limit
LIMMIN	0.0000,0.0000		LIMITS	Lower left X,Y limit
LTSCALE	1.0000		LTSCALE	Current linetype scale
LUNITS	2	DEC.	UNITS	Linear units: Scientific=1 Dec=2 Eng=3 Arch=4 Frac=5
LUPREC	4	0.0000	UNITS	Unit precision decimal places or denominator
MENUECHO	0	NORMAL	SETVAR	Normal=0 Suppress echo of menu items=1 No prompts=2 No input or prompts=3 <NS>
MENUNAME	"ACAD"		MENU	Current menu name <RO>
MIRRTEXT	1	YES	SETVAR	Retain text direction=0 Reflect text=1
ORTHOMODE	0	OFF	[^O] [F8]	Ortho ON=1 Ortho OFF=0
OSMODE	0	NONE	OSNAP	Sum of: Endp=1 Mid=2 Cen=4 Node=8 Quad=16 Int=32 Ins=64 Perp=128 Tan=256 Near=512 Quick=1024
PDMODE	0	POINT	SETVAR	Controls style of points drawn
PDSIZE	0.0000	POINT	SETVAR	Controls size of points
PERIMETER	0.0000		AREA,LIST	Last computed perimeter <NS>,<RO>

VARIABLE NAME	DEFAULT SETTING	DEFAULT MEANING	COMMAND NAME	VARIABLE DESCRIPTION
PICKBOX	3		SETVAR	Half the pickbox size in pixels **<CFG>**
POPUPS	1			AUI Support=1 No Support=0 **<NS>**, **<RO>**
QTEXTMODE	0	OFF	QTEXT	Qtext ON=1 Qtext OFF=0
REGENMODE	1	ON	REGENAUTO	Regenauto ON=1 Regenauto OFF=0
SCREENSIZE	570.0000,410.0000			Size of display in X,Y pixels **<NS>**, **<RO>**
SKETCHINC	0.1000		SKETCH	Recording increment for sketch
SKPOLY	0	LINE	SETVAR	Polylines=1 Sketch with Line=0
SNAPANG	0		SNAP	Angle of SNAP/GRID rotation
SNAPBASE	0.0000,0.0000		SNAP	X,Y base point of SNAP/GRID rotation
SNAPISOPAIR	0	LEFT	SNAP [^E]	Isoplane Left=0 Top=1 Right=2
SNAPMODE	0	OFF	SNAP [^B] [F9]	Snap ON=1 Snap OFF=0
SNAPSTYL	0	STD	SNAP	Isometric=1 Snap standard=0
SNAPUNIT	1.0000,1.0000		SNAP	Snap X,Y increment
SPLFRAME	0		SETVAR	Display spline frame ON=1 OFF=0
SPLINESEGS	8		SETVAR	Number of line segments in each spline segment
SPLINETYPE	6	CUBIC	SETVAR	Pedit spline generates: Quadratic B-Spline=5 Cubic B-Spline=6
SURFTAB1	6		SETVAR	Rulesurf and tabsurf tabulations, also revsurf and edgesurf M density
SURFTAB2	6		SETVAR	Revsurf and edgesurf N density
SURFTYPE	6	CUBIC	SETVAR	Pedit smooth surface generates: Quadratic B-Spline=5 Cubic B-Spline=6 Bezier=8
SURFU	6		SETVAR	M direction surface density
SURFV	6		SETVAR	N direction surface density
TARGET	0.0000,0.0000,0.0000		DVIEW	UCS coords of current viewport target point **<RO>**
TDCREATE	2447498.61620031		TIME	Creation time (Julian) **<RO>**
TDINDWG	0.00436285		TIME	Total editing time **<RO>**
TDUPDATE	2447498.61620031		TIME	Time of last save or update **<RO>**
TDUSRTIMER	0.00436667		TIME	User set elapsed time **<RO>**
TEMPPREFIX	""			Directory location of AutoCAD's temporary files, defaults to drawing directory **<NS>**, **<RO>**
TEXTEVAL	0	TEXT	SETVAR	Evaluate leading "(" and "!" in text input as: Text=0 AutoLISP=1 **<NS>**
TEXTSIZE	0.2000		TEXT	Current text height
TEXTSTYLE	"STANDARD"		TEXT, STYLE	Current text style **<RO>**
THICKNESS	0.0000		ELEV	Current 3D extrusion thickness
TRACEWID	0.0500		TRACE	Current width of traces
UCSFOLLOW	0		SETVAR	Automatic plan view in new UCS=1 Off=0
UCSICON	1		UCSICON	Sum of: Off=0 On=1 Origin=2
UCSNAME	""		UCS	Name of current UCS Unnamed="" **<RO>**
UCSORG	0.0000,0.0000,0.0000		UCS	WCS origin of current UCS **<RO>**
UCSXDIR	1.0000,0.0000,0.0000		UCS	X direction of current UCS **<RO>**
UCSYDIR	0.0000,1.0000,0.0000		UCS	Y direction of current UCS **<RO>**
USERI1 - 5	0			User integer variables USERI1 to USERI5
USERR1 - 5	0.0000			User real variables USERR1 to USERR5
VIEWCTR	6.2518,4.5000		ZOOM,PAN,VIEW	X,Y center point of current view **<RO>**
VIEWDIR	0.0000,0.0000,1.0000		DVIEW	Camera point offset from target in WCS **<RO>**
VIEWMODE	0		DVIEW,UCS	Perspective and clipping settings, see AutoCAD Reference Manual **<RO>**
VIEWSIZE	9.0000		ZOOM,PAN,VIEW	Height of current view **<RO>**
VIEWTWIST	0		DVIEW	View wist angle **<RO>**
VPOINTX	0.0000		VPOINT	X coordinate of VPOINT **<RO>**
VPOINTY	0.0000		VPOINT	Y coordinate of VPOINT **<RO>**

VARIABLE NAME	DEFAULT SETTING	DEFAULT MEANING	COMMAND NAME	VARIABLE DESCRIPTION
VPOINTZ	1.0000		VPOINT	Z coordinate of VPOINT **<RO>**
VSMAX	12.5036,9.0000,0.0000			ZOOM,PAN,VIEW
				Upper right of virtual screen X,Y **<NS>,<RO>**
VSMIN	0.0000,0.0000,0.0000			ZOOM,PAN,VIEW
				Lower left of virtual screen X,Y **<NS>,<RO>**
WORLDUCS	1		UCS	UCS equals WCS=1 UCS not equal to WCS=0 **<RO>**
WORLDVIEW	1		DVIEW,UCS	Dview and VPoint coordinate input: WCS=1 UCS=0

<NS> Not Saved   **<CFG>** Configure File   **<RO>** Read Only

AutoCAD Command List

Each AutoCAD command is given below with a brief description of its action and the primary prompts it generates. A more detailed source of information on AutoCAD commands and system variables is available in Dorothy Kent's AutoCAD REFERENCE GUIDE from New Riders Publishing. INSIDE AutoCAD, also from New Riders, gives thorough coverage of the AutoCAD commands from a tutorial approach.

Object Selection Methods

AutoCAD's editing commands prompt the user to select objects for the command to operate on. This flexible selection process allows a set of objects to be constructed by the following options:

pick point — One object at the point picked.

Multiple — Multiple objects selected by picking.

Last — Last object created.

Previous — All objects in the previous selection set.

Window — All objects contained within a window.

Crossing — All objects within or crossed by a window.

BOX — Either Crossing (to the left) or Window (to the right).

AUto — By BOX if a single object pick comes up empty.

SIngle — One selection.

Add — Add objects which follow to selection set.

Remove — Remove objects which follow from selection set.

Undo — Undo the last option.

AutoCAD chooses objects in the order that they were added to the drawing database. In other words, if you pick the intersection of two objects, the newest of the two objects will be selected.

Coordinate Entry

Coordinate and point entry in AutoCAD can be accomplished by either absolute, relative, or polar methods. Absolute coordinate triplets separated by commas define a point in the Cartesian coordinate system (X,Y,Z). Relative coordinates from the last point picked are specified in a similar fashion, except the coordinates are preceded by the @ symbol (@X,Y,Z) and the values for X,Y, and Z define the distances in those directions from the last point. Polar coordinates are entered in the form @distance<angle, where distance and angle are values measured from the last point. If the Z coordinate is omitted, the current Z elevation is assumed. Polar coordinates have effect only in the X and Y axes.

AutoCAD provides a *filter* method to build a coordinate by using any combination of the X,Y, or Z components of an existing entity. The filter is invoked be preceding the coordinate letter(s) with a period (.X or .YZ) when prompted for a point. The remaining coordinate components are then prompted for and can be supplied by filtering or numerical means.

AutoCAD Commands

The commands shown with a leading apostrophe can be executed transparently from within another command. When entered this way, the current command is suspended, and the transparent command is executed. When the transparent command has completed its function, the original command is resumed. When executed from the command prompt, the apostrophe is not needed.

APERTURE The APERTURE command controls the size of the target box located in the middle of the crosshairs during object snap selection. You can change the size in pixels of the aperture box. The default setting is 10 pixels for most displays. The setting is half the height of the box, or the number of pixels above or below the crosshairs.
Object snap target height (1-50 pixels) <10>:

ARC The ARC command draws any segment of a circle greater than one degree and less than 360 degrees. Except for the three-point option, arcs are constructed in a counterclockwise direction. An arc or line can be drawn immediately tangent to the last arc or line by defaulting its Start point: or From point: prompts. The default is three-point arc construction, but you can use several other methods.
Center/<Start point>:

AREA The AREA command lets you calculate an area by picking a series of points or by selecting entities (circles and polylines). In addition to the area, you are also given the perimeter, and line length or circumference. You can keep a running total by adding and subtracting areas. The default picks points to define the area.
`<First point>/Entity/Add/Subtract:`

ARRAY ARRAY copies selected entities in rectangular or polar patterns. A rectangular array prompts for the number and spacing of rows and columns. A polar array prompts for center point, number of copies to make, the angle to fill with the copies, and whether to rotate each copy. By dragging a rectangle at the Unit cell prompt, you can show AutoCAD the X and Y spacing for rectangular arrays.
`Rectangular or Polar array (R/P):`

ATTDEF ATTDEF (ATTribute DEFinition) defines how attribute text will be prompted for and stored. Attributes are saved in blocks which can contain additional entities. Mode toggles are provided for Invisible, Constant, Verify, and Preset options.
`Attribute modes -- Invisible:N Constant:N Verify:N Preset:N`
`Enter (ICVP) to change, RETURN when done:`

ATTDISP ATTDISP (ATTtribute DISPlay) controls attribute visibility after insertion. ATTDISP overrides the ATTDEF invisible/visible settings. The default is Normal, which lets the modes set by ATTDEF control visibility individually.
`Normal/ON/OFF <Off>:`

ATTEDIT ATTEDIT (ATTribute EDIT) lets you edit attributes, individually or globally. The default setting edits attributes one at a time, allowing you to change value, position, height, angle, style, layer, or color. Global edits are confined to changing value. You can control your selection set by block name, tag name, or attribute value.
`Edit attributes one at a time? <Y>`

ATTEXT   Use ATTEXT (ATTribute EXTract) to extract attribute data from your drawing. This information is formatted into an ASCII text file in one of three possible formats: CDF, SDF, or DXF. (See below.) CDF is the default format. You can extract all attributes, or select certain entities to extract attributes from.
```
CDF, SDF, or DXF Attribute extract (or Entities) <C>:
```

AXIS   AXIS creates ruler marks, or ticks, on the bottom and right side of your screen. These marks are used as visual drawing aids. The Snap option sets the mark spacing equal to the current snap value. Aspect controls unequal horizontal and vertical tick values. The default setting is off and the default value is 0.0000.
```
Tick spacing(X) or ON/OFF/Snap/Aspect :
```

BASE   Any drawing can be inserted into another drawing. By default, every drawing file has a base point of 0,0,0, relative to which it is inserted into other drawings. The BASE command establishes an alternative insertion base point.
```
Base point <0.0000,0.0000,0.0000>:
```

BLIPMODE   BLIPMODE toggles the display of temporary marker crosses generated by point and object selection. The default in ON.
```
ON/OFF <On>:
```

BLOCK   The BLOCK command defines a group of entities as a block within the current drawing. (Use the INSERT command to insert blocks into your drawing.) You define a block by choosing an entity selection set which is deleted from the current drawing and stored as a block definition in the drawing. (OOPS will restore the entities.) You are prompted for a block name and insertion base point. The base point is a reference point relative to which the block will be inserted and scaled. Such blocks may only be inserted in the drawing within which they are defined.
```
Block name (or ?):  Insertion base point:
```

BREAK   BREAK enables you to split or erase portions of lines, arcs, circles, 2D polylines, and traces. When you select an object to break, the default assumes your pick point is also your first break point.
```
Select object:  Enter second point (or F for first point):
```

CHAMFER   CHAMFER creates a beveled edge for intersecting lines and contiguous segments of a 2D Polyline. CHAMFER trims or extends two lines or polyline segments at specified distances from their intersection or vertex point, and creates a new line to connect the trimmed ends. Alternatively, you can chamfer an entire polyline at once with the Polyline option. CHAMFER requires two distance values. The first distance value is applied to the first selected line, the second distance to the second line. The default for distances is 0.
`Polyline/Distances/<Select first line>:`

CHANGE   CHANGE lets you modify existing entities. You can change the endpoints of lines (the nearest endpoint is pulled to the change point). You can respecify the center and radius of circles. You can enter new text or you can enter new values for any text or attdef option. You can enter a new origin or rotation angle for a block insert. If you select multiple entities, you will be prompted appropriately for each. Once you have completed the CHANGE command, you may have to regenerate the screen to see the revisions.
`Properties/<Change point>:`

CHPROP   CHPROP redefines the layer, color, linetype, and 3D thickness properties of existing entities. Use CHPROP instead of CHANGE to change entity properties.
`Change what property (Color/LAyer/LType/Thickness) ?`

CIRCLE   The CIRCLE command is used to draw circles. The default method uses a <Center point> and <Radius>. If DRAGMODE is set to on or auto (the default), you can determine the size of the circle by dragging it on the screen. Other methods of construction are by 3 points on the circumference, 2 points indicating diameter, and tangent to 2 existing entities.
`3P/2P/TTR/<Center point>:`

COLOR   The COLOR command controls the color of new entities, overriding the default layer color. To change the color of existing entities, use the CHPROP command. To control layer colors, use the LAYER command. Use a color number or name to set a new color. You can also set the current entity color with the 'DDEMODES dialogue box. The default setting is BYLAYER.
`New entity color <BYLAYER>:`

COPY   COPY creates a replica of an entity or selection set anywhere in 2D or 3D space. The command uses standard object selection. The original entity or selection set remains unchanged. You can show and drag displacement by picking two points or by using an absolute X,Y displacement value. The multiple option allows repeated copying of the chosen selection set.
```
<Base point or displacement>/Multiple:
Second point of displacement:
```

DBLIST   DBLIST displays a listing of properties of all entities in the database of the current drawing.

DDATTE   DDATTE (Dynamic Dialogue ATTribute Edit) edits attribute string values with a dialogue box. You can only edit one block at a time. It presents the current value and lets you specify a new value.
```
Select block:
```

'DDEMODES   The DDEMODES (Dynamic Dialogue Entity creation MODES) dialogue box shows the current settings for layer, color, linetype, elevation, and thickness. You can change any of these variables. Layer, color, and linetype present another dialogue box when selected.

'DDLMODES   DDLMODES (Dynamic Dialogue Layer MODES) presents a dialogue box to control layer options. The options include setting the current layer, creating new layers, renaming layers, and modifying layer properties such as color, linetype, on/off, freeze, and thaw.

'DDRMODES   Dynamic Dialogue dRawing MODES controls the settings of the drawing aids: snap, grid, axis, ortho, blips, isoplane, and isometric mode with a dialogue box.

DDUCS   DDUCS (Dynamic Dialogue User Coordinate System) displays dialogue boxes that control the User Coordinate System. You can also use it to create or rename a UCS. The default setting is *WORLD*.

DELAY   The DELAY command is used in scripts to pause execution of the script primarily for the display of slides. The delay parameter is specified in approximately 1 microsecond increments (depending on the hardware used).

DIM/DIM1   DIM activates the dimensioning mode. The command prompt changes to `DIM:`, and only the subcommands associated with dimensioning are active. The EXIT command or a `<^C>` redisplays the normal command prompt. DIM1 activates the dimension mode for a single command and then returns you to the regular command prompt.
`Dim:`

DIST   DISTANCE is an inquiry command that determines the length of an imaginary 2D or 3D line, its angle in the XY plane, its angle from the XY plane if 3D, and the delta XY (or XYZ) between two points.
`First point:   Second point:`

DIVIDE   DIVIDE marks an entity into equal length segments. You can divide lines, circles, arcs, and polylines. The divided entity isn't physically separated; point entities (or optionally, blocks) are placed as markers at each division point.
`Select object to divide:`
`<Number of segments>/Block:`

DONUT   The DONUT (or DOUGHNUT, if you prefer) command draws solid filled rings and circles. The donut entities are closed wide polylines. You give an inside diameter value (or two points) and an outside diameter (or two points). DONUT repeats its `Center of doughnut:` prompt until you cancel or `<RETURN>` to exit.
`Inside diameter :   Outside diameter :`
`Center of doughnut:`

DRAGMODE   Dynamic dragging of objects during their creation or editing is controlled by the DRAGMODE command which allows three states.
`ON/OFF/Auto <Auto>:`

DTEXT   The DTEXT (Dynamic TEXT) command prompts for the same text justification parameters as the TEXT command, but DTEXT draws the text characters on the screen as you type them, and allows entry of multiple lines of text. DTEXT displays a rectangular character box to show where the next character will be placed.
`Start point or Align/Center/Fit/Middle/Right/Style:`

DVIEW   DVIEW is a display tool for viewing 3D models in space. DVIEW is similar to the VPOINT command. However, in DVIEW you can dynamically drag and rotate the 3D model with the aid of slide bars. You can display a perspective view of the model and toggle back and forth between parallel and perspective views. The DVIEW command is similar to the concept of using a camera to view a target. You can set a camera point, target point, lens length, and position front and back clipping planes. The default is for parallel projection.

```
Select objects:
CAmera/TArget/Distance/POints/PAn/Zoom/TWist/CLip/Hide/Off/
Undo/<eXit>:
```

DXBIN   DXB or Drawing Interchange Binary is a binary drawing file format. You can import binary drawing files with the DXBIN command. If AutoCAD is configured with an ADI plotter, the DXB file output option can be selected which will create a .DXB file.

```
DXB File:
```

DXFIN/DXFOUT   These commands are used to create and import DXF (Drawing Interchange Format) files for analysis by other programs or translation to other CAD programs. The .DXF file is an ASCII text file.

```
File name <drawing name>:
Enter decimal places of accuracy (0 to 16)/Entities/Binary <6>:
```

EDGESURF   EDGESURF generates a 3D polygon mesh by approximating a Coons surface patch from four adjoining edge entities. Each edge can be a line, arc, or open polyline, anywhere in 3D space. The endpoints of the edge entities must touch, combining to form a closed path. You can pick the edges in any order. The first edge or entity selected defines the M direction (controlled by SURFTAB1) of the mesh. The two edges that touch the M edge define the N direction (controlled by SURFTAB1).

```
Select edge 1:
Select edge 2:
Select edge 3:
Select edge 4:
```

ELEV   The ELEVATION command sets the elevation and extrusion thickness of entities you construct. The elevation is the object's base value on the Z plane. The extrusion thickness (negative or positive) is its height above (or below) the base elevation. The elevation setting only effects those entities whose Z value is not given. The default is <0.0>. You also can set the elevation and thickness with the DDEMODES Dialogue Box.
```
New current elevation <0.0000>:
New current thickness <0.0000>:
```

ELLIPSE   The ELLIPSE command gives you several methods for constructing ellipses. The default setting assumes a first axis defined by an `Axis endpoint 1` and an `Axis endpoint 2`; the other axis distance is defined as half the length of the other axis.
```
<Axis endpoint 1>/Center:
```

END   The END command updates (saves) the drawing file and exits to AutoCAD's main menu. The old drawing file becomes the new .BAK file.

ERASE   ERASE deletes entities from the drawing. The OOPS command can be used to restore the last entity erased.
```
Select objects:
```

EXPLODE   EXPLODE converts the selected block, polyline, dimension, hatch, or mesh into its component entities.
```
Select block reference, polyline, dimension, or mesh:
```

EXTEND   EXTEND lengthens the endpoints of a line, open polyline, and arc to a boundary edge. Boundary edges include lines, circles, arcs, and polylines. You can have more than one boundary edge, and an entity can be both a boundary edge and an entity to extend.
```
Select boundary edge(s)...
Select objects:
```

FILES   FILES activates the file utilities menu. It provides an alternative to DOS (or your operating system) for managing your files.

FILL   FILL, an on/off toggle command, controls whether polylines, solids, and traces are displayed and plotted as filled, or if just the outline is displayed and plotted. In either case, they will still hide as usual. The default setting is on.
ON/OFF <On>:

FILLET   FILLET creates an arc with a predefined radius between any combination of lines, circles, and arcs. FILLET extends or trims entities as needed to draw the specified arc, if geometrically possible. A *single* polyline can be filleted at selected vertices, or globally at all vertices, but not in combination with other entities. An arc entity is inserted at the preset fillet radius. The default fillet radius is 0, which causes the entities or segments to be extended or trimmed to their intersection point.
Polyline/Radius/<Select two lines>:

FILMROLL   FILMROLL produces a file containing a description of the entities that can be processed into fully shaded renderings using AutoShade. The filmroll file also contains camera, lighting and scene descriptions, that are created in the drawing using AutoShade tools. AutoShade is a separate program by Autodesk.
Enter the filmroll file name <*drawing name*>:

'GRAPHSCR   This command performs the equivalent of pressing the F1 toggle key on MS-DOS based systems by flipping the display screen to graphic mode.

GRID   GRID, a drawing aid, displays dots at any user-defined increment. It helps you to keep the space you are working in and the size of your drawing entities in perspective. GRID dynamically toggles off and on, as well as accepts numeric values. The default settings are 0.0000 and off.
Grid spacing(X) or ON/OFF/Snap/Aspect <0.00>:

HANDLES   The HANDLES command assigns a unique label to every drawing entity. This label, in hexadecimal format, is stored in the drawing database and is used to access entities with AutoLISP or external programs. The default setting is OFF.
Handles are disabled.
ON/DESTROY:

HATCH   The HATCH command cross-hatches or pattern-fills an area defined by a boundary. The boundary must be continuous and closed, formed by any combination of lines, arcs, circles, polylines, or 3Dfaces. The hatch patterns available are defined in a file named ACAD.PAT. You can also specify the spacing and angle for parallel or cross-hatched continuous lines. The HATCH command's default creates a block with a hidden name and inserts it. If you precede the pattern name with an asterisk, like *name,* the hatch will instead be drawn with individual line entities. You can also choose a style of hatching for nested boundaries: Normal, Outermost, or Ignore. Hatching is always defined and generated relative to the X,Y axes and plane of the current UCS.
Pattern (? or name/U,style):

'HELP or '?   HELP lists available commands and provides specific information about the operation of individual commands. The apostrophe prefix causes the command to be transparent, and therefor will execute within another command.
Command name (RETURN for list):

HIDE   When you work in 3D, you see all the edges of all entities. The HIDE command calculates solid areas defined by those edges and determines what would be hidden or suppressed from your viewpoint. HIDE only evaluates circles, polylines (assigned a width), solids, traces, 3Dfaces, meshes, and extruded edges of entities assigned a thickness as opaque surfaces. In addition, extruded circles, polylines (assigned a width), solids, and traces are considered solid entities, having top and bottom faces.

ID   ID identifies the absolute X,Y,Z coordinates of any selected point.
Point:

IGESIN/IGESOUT   These commands produce or import IGES (Initial Graphics Exchange Standard) files for translation to or from other CAD programs.
File name:

INSERT   INSERT inserts an image of a block definition into the current drawing. You pick the insertion point, X,Y,Z scale values, and the rotation angle. The insertion point is relative to the block's base point. The default X scale factor is 1, and the Y scale defaults to equal the X scale. Specifying a negative scale factor causes the image to mirror along that axis. Rotation angle defaults to 0. If you preface the block name with an asterisk, like *FRONT, then an actual copy of each individual entity in the block's definition is inserted instead of an insert entity image. This is often referred to as insert* (insert-star) or a *block (star-block).
```
Insertion point:  X scale factor <1> / Corner / XYZ:
Y scale factor (default=X):  Rotation angle <0>:
```

ISOPLANE   The ISOPLANE command lets you draw in an isometric mode. <^E> toggles to the next isoplane. When you draw isometrically, the grid and crosshairs are displayed isometrically. The default is the left plane. You can also set the Isoplane with the DDRMODES Dialogue Box.
```
Left/Top/Right/<Toggle>:
```

LAYER   The LAYER command controls layers which act like transparent drawing overlays. You can create (with the Make or New options) an unlimited number of layers and give them names up to 31 characters long. You can set any layer active (current), turn layers on (visible) or off (invisible), freeze or thaw layers, and control their colors and linetypes. When a layer is frozen, it is disregarded by AutoCAD, and will not be plotted, calculated, or displayed. You draw on the current layer. The default settings for new layers are white with continuous linetype. You can also control layers with the DDLMODES dialogue box.
```
?/Make/Set/New/ON/OFF/Color/Ltype/Freeze/Thaw:
```

LIMITS   LIMITS determines your drawing area or boundaries, defined by the absolute coordinates of the lower left and upper right-hand corners. With the LIMITS command, you can modify these values or turn limits checking on and off. The default settings are from 0,0 to 12,9 with limits checking off.
```
ON/OFF/<Lower left corner> <0.0000,0.0000>:
Upper right corner <12.0000,9.0000>:
```

LINE   LINE lets you draw straight line segments. You can enter 2D or 3D points by entering a From point and a series of To points. Entering C closes a series, U undoes the last segment, and <RETURN> at the first prompt continues the previous line or arc.
From point: To point:

LINETYPE   LINETYPE assigns linetypes to entities, loads linetype definitions stored in library files, and creates new linetype definitions. Linetypes are based on dash-dot line segments. You can control the linetypes of new entities explicitly or by their layer assignment. You can also set linetype with the 'DDEMODES dialogue box. The default setting is BYLAYER.
?/Create/Load/Set:

LIST   The LIST command provides information on selected entities within a drawing. This command lists layer assignment, XYZ position relative to the current UCS, and color and linetype (if not the default BYLAYER).
Select objects:

LOAD   The LOAD command is used to load new shape library files (.SHX) into the current drawing, or list those library files previously loaded.
Name of shape file to load (or ?):

LTSCALE   LTSCALE (LineType SCALE) determines the dash and space settings for linetypes. The LTSCALE is a global value. All linetypes (except for continuous) are multiplied by the LTSCALE. After altering the current value, a regeneration of the drawing will be necessary (if the current value of REGENAUTO is OFF) to make the change LTSCALE visible. The default setting is 1.0000.
New scale factor <1.0000>:

MEASURE   MEASURE marks an entity at predetermined segment lengths. You can measure lines, circles, arcs, and polylines. The entity isn't physically separated; point entities (or blocks) are placed as markers at each segment point.
Select object to measure:
<Segment length>/Block:

MENU   The MENU loads a new menu file (.MNU) into the current drawing which defines the actions performed by selections from the screen, tablet, pull-down, icon, button, and auxiliary menus. The default menu is ACAD.
Menu file name or . for none <acad>:

MINSERT   MINSERT (Multiple INSERT) is a combination of the commands INSERT and (rectangular) ARRAY. MINSERT lets you insert a multiple copy of a block in a rectangular array pattern. The command has the same prompts as the INSERT command for insertion point, X,Y scaling, and rotation angle, plus ARRAY-like prompts for rows and columns.
Number of rows (---) <1>: Number of columns (|||) <1>:

MIRROR   The MIRROR command creates mirror images of a selected group of entities. You can keep the original group of mirrored entities or you can delete it. The default does not delete the originals. MIRROR can also reflect text or keep it right-reading when mirroring an image, controlled by the MIRRTEXT system variable. The default setting for MIRRTEXT is 1 (on) to mirror (reflect) text.
Select objects:
First point of mirror line:

MOVE   MOVE moves an entity or selection set to a new drawing location anywhere in 2D or 3D space. See COPY.
Base point or displacement:
Second point of displacement:

MSLIDE   MSLIDE creates a "slide" file (.SLD) which is a snapshot of the active viewport. This file may be viewed with the VSLIDE command.
Slide file <drawing name>:

MULTIPLE MULTIPLE is a command modifier. To automatically repeat any command in a loop, enter MULTIPLE before that command. To end the command loop, cancel with <^C>. No prompt is issued when you enter the MULTIPLE command.

OFFSET   OFFSET lets you copy an entity parallel to itself, once you establish an offset distance. You can offset a line arc, circle, or polyline by giving an offset distance or a through point.
Offset distance or Through <Through>:

OOPS   OOPS restores the last entity, or group of entities, deleted by the most recent ERASE command.

ORTHO   ORTHO constrains your drawing lines, polylines, and traces to horizontal and vertical lines. ORTHO mode controls the angle at which you pick the second point in many drawing and editing commands. ORTHO is a toggle, and the default setting is off.
ON/OFF <Off>:

OSNAP   OSNAP (Object SNAP) lets you preset one or more running object snap modes. The default setting is off or NONe. You can override a running mode by entering a different transient osnap mode or modes when a point is requested. The STATUS command displays the current running osnap mode.
Object snap modes:

'PAN   PAN lets you scroll around the screen without altering the current zoom ratio. It is similar to repositioning paper on a drafting board to access a different drawing part. You do not physically move entities or change your drawing limits; you move your display window across your drawing. PAN is a transparent command. The default setting provides a displacement in relative coordinates.
Displacement: Second point:

PEDIT   PEDIT edits 2D polylines, 3D polylines, and 3D polygon meshes. Editing 3D polylines and meshes is a subset of 2D polyline editing with its own set of prompts. There are two basic sets of editing functions. The first set operates on the entire polyline; the second set lets you edit individual vertices. The default response is X to exit the command. The default for the vertex editing option is N for next vertex.
Close/Join/Width/Edit vertex/Fit curve/Spline curve/
Decurve/Undo/eXit <X>:
Next/Previous/Break/Insert/Move/Regen/Straighten/
Tangent/Width/eXit <N>:

PLAN   A PLAN view is defined as a view point of 0,0,1 in the selected UCS. It can be applied to the current UCS, a previously saved UCS, or to the WCS.
<Current UCS>/Ucs/World:

PLINE   A polyline is a series of line and arc segments that are interconnected because they share the same vertices and are processed as a single entity. The PLINE command draws 2D polylines. PLINE starts with a From point prompt. After entering the first point, you can continue in line mode or arc mode. Each mode has its own set of prompts. A polyline may also have a constant width or taper. To edit polylines, you can use PEDIT as well as most of the regular edit commands.

```
Arc/Close/Halfwidth/Length/Undo/Width/<Endpoint of line>:
Angle/CEnter/CLose/Direction/Halfwidth/Line/Radius/Second pt/
Undo/Width/<Endpoint of arc>:
```

PLOT/PRPLOT   PLOT directs your drawing to a plotter or to a plot file. If you plot from the main menu, you will be asked which drawing file you want to plot. If you plot from within the drawing, it's assumed you want to plot the current drawing. Only layers that are on and thawed will be plotted.

```
What to plot -- Display, Extents, Limits, View or Window <D>:
```

POINT   The POINT command creates a point entity at the coordinates chosen which can be snapped to with the OSNAP NODE option.

```
Point:
```

POLYGON   The POLYGON command draws 2D regular (all sides equal) polygons from 3 to 1024 sides. The size of the polygon is determined by specifying the radius of a circle in which the polygon is inscribed (inside), or circumscribed (outside), or by specifying the length of one of the polygon's sides. Polygons are closed polylines. Use PEDIT to edit polygons.

```
Number of sides:   Edge/<Center of Polygon>:
Inscribed in circle/Circumscribed about circle (I/C):
```

PRPLOT   PRPLOT directs your drawing to a printer plotter (such as a dot matrix or laser printer.) If you plot from the main menu, you will be asked which drawing file you want to plot. If you plot from within the drawing, it's assumed you want to plot the current drawing. Only layers that are on and thawed will be plotted.

```
What to plot -- Display, Extents, Limits, View or Window <D>:
```

PURGE   PURGE is the method for eliminating unused blocks, layers, linetypes, shapes, and styles from the current drawing. This may reduce the file's size, and reduce the number of object names displayed as lists by commands, or for selection by dialogue boxes. The PURGE command may only be used before the first command entered in a drawing session which alters the current drawing's database.
`Purge unused Blocks/LAyers/LTypes/SHapes/STyles/All:`

QTEXT   QTEXT (Quick TEXT) sets a mode that causes the screen to draw boxes in place of text strings and attributes. This saves time when redrawing or regenerating the screen. The box or rectangle is the height and approximate length of the text string. The default setting is off.
`ON/OFF <Off>:`

QUIT   QUIT terminates the drawing editor and discards all edits made in the current drawing session
`Really want to discard all changes to drawing?`

REDEFINE   The REDEFINE command allows you to substitute AutoCAD's built-in commands with your own commands created in AutoLISP or provided by external commands in the ACAD.PGP file. An original command may be invoked by prefixing the command name with a period.
`Command name:`

REDO   REDO simply reverses the last U or UNDO command. A group, the UNDO Back, or <number> options are treated as a single REDO operation.

'REDRAW/REDRAWALL   REDRAW cleans up the current viewport. REDRAWALL cleans up all viewports. Blips are removed and any entities or parts of entities that seem to have disappeared during editing are redrawn. Grid dots are redrawn if the grid is on. These are transparent commands. (If the grid is on, you can get the same effect by toggling the grid with two <F7>s or <^G>s.)

REGEN/REGENALL   REGEN causes the current viewport to be regenerated (recalculated and redrawn); REGENALL regenerates all viewports. When a drawing is regenerated, the data and geometry associated with all entities is recalculated. REGEN and REGENALL are not transparent commands. You can cancel a regeneration with <^C>.

REGENAUTO   REGENAUTO lets you control some (not all) regenerations. Some changes, such as block redefinitions, linetype scale changes, or redefined text styles, require a regeneration before they are made visible. Sometimes, particularly when making multiple changes, you do not want to wait for these regenerations. You can set REGENAUTO off and use the REGEN command to regenerate the screen when you are ready to look at the results.
ON/OFF <On>:

RENAME   RENAME allows you to rename existing blocks, layers, linetypes, styles, UCS's, views, and viewports.
Block/LAyer/LType/Style/Ucs/VIew/VPort:
Old (object) name:
New (object) name:

RESUME   The RESUME command returns control of AutoCAD to a script that has been interrupted by keyboard input or error.

REVSURF   REVSURF (REVolution SURFace) generates a 3D polygon mesh by revolving a selected profile "path curve" around a selected axis.
Select path curve: Select axis of revolution:
Start angle <0>: Included angle (+=ccw, -=cw)
<Full circle>:

ROTATE   ROTATE lets you rotate entities around a designated base or pivot point. The rotation angle can be entered as a numeric angle, by picking a point relative to the base point, or by a reference angle option. The reference option lets you specify the rotation angle relative to a base angle, usually on an existing entity.
<Rotation angle>/Reference:

RSCRIPT   RSCRIPT is used within a script to replay the script from the beginning, thereby creating a continuous loop.

RULESURF   RULESURF (RULEd SURFace) generates a 3D polyline mesh depicting the ruled surface between two entities. The two entities can be points, lines, arcs, circles, 2D polylines, or 3D polylines. If one boundary, such as a circle or closed polyline, is closed, then the other boundary must be a point or be closed. A point can be used with any another entity.
```
Select first defining curve:
Select second defining curve:
```

SAVE   The SAVE command writes drawing changes made since the drawing was last saved or ended to the disk file, and does not leave the drawing editor. Another file name may be specified, thereby creating incremental drawing documentation.
```
File name <drawing name>:
```

SCALE   SCALE changes the size of existing entities. The entities are scaled relative to the base point selected. The same scale factor is applied to the X and Y axes. Enter a numerical scale factor or use the Reference option to pick a reference and new length. A numerical scale factor is the default.
```
Base point: <Scale factor>/Reference:
```

SCRIPT   AutoCAD command scripts can be executed with the SCRIPT command. A script will execute until: a keystroke is input from the keyboard, a command error occurs, or the end of the script file is encountered.
```
Script file <drawing name>:
```

SELECT   SELECT lets you pick entities to retain as a selection set. At the next entity selection prompt, use the Previous option to reselect the retained set. You can create the selection set with standard object selection. SELECT is often used in menu macros.
```
Select objects:
```

'SETVAR   SETVAR retrieves and modifies system variables. Most system variables are also modified through AutoCAD commands. A few system variables are "read-only." Enter a ? for a listing of all variables.
```
Variable name or ? <default>:
```

SHAPE   The SHAPE command is used to insert a LOADed shape into the current drawing at user specified parameters, or list available shapes.
```
Shape name (or ?):
Starting point:
Height <1.0>:
Angle <0>:
```

SH/SHELL   SH suspends the drawing editor, and allows DOS *internal* commands to be executed. Responding with a <CR> at the DOS Command: prompt will display the DOS prompt with an appended right angle bracket C:\>. At this point, multiple commands may be executed. Entering EXIT will return to the AutoCAD drawing editor. SHELL suspends the drawing editor and allows DOS external commands and other programs to be executed. Entering EXIT will return to the AutoCAD drawing editor at the point where you left it.
```
DOS Command:
C:\>
```

SKETCH   The SKETCH command allows freehand drawing of line or polyline segments that track the pointing device similar to a pencil or pen.
```
Record increment :
Sketch.  Pen eXit Quit Record Erase Connect.
```

SNAP   SNAP lets you move the crosshairs at any defined increment. This command is dynamic. You can constantly modify the increment value and turn the setting on and off. It may be rotated to any user specified angle and given unequal X and Y increment values. The default setting is 1.0000 and off.
```
Snap spacing or ON/OFF/Aspect/Rotate/Style <1.00>:
```

SOLID SOLID draws solid filled areas or extruded volumes. If the FILL command (or system variable FILLMODE) is set to on (1), the solid is displayed filled. These areas can be triangular or quadrilateral (four sided). You enter points in a triangular or bow tie order to get a triangle or quadrilateral. The first two points are the endpoints of a starting edge; the next point defines the corner point of a triangle; at the fourth point prompt, you can <RETURN> to close the triangle or enter a fourth point to define a quadrilateral. The command repeats the third and fourth point prompts, adding on new solids with the previous third and fourth points as new first and second points, until you <RETURN> at the third point prompt or cancel it.
`First point: Second point: Third point: Fourth point:`

STATUS STATUS gives you current information on drawing limits, extents, the drawing aids settings, and some system information. When entered in DIM mode, it provides reporting of the current state of dimensioning variables. The status report is a text screen.

STRETCH STRETCH lets you extend (or shrink) certain entities by selecting them with a crossing window and picking a base and new point of displacement. You can stretch lines, arcs, traces, solids, polylines, and 3D faces. Entity endpoints that lie inside the crossing window are moved, those outside the crossing window remain fixed, and the lines or arcs crossing the window are stretched. Entities which are defined entirely within the crossing window (all endpoints, vertices, and definition points) are simply moved. The definition point for a block or shape is its insertion base point; for a circle, the center point; for text, the lower left corner.
`Select objects to stretch by window... Base point:`
`New point:`

STYLE The STYLE command lets you create new text styles, modify existing styles, and obtain a listing of defined styles. The style name is arbitrary; you can use up to 31 characters to name a style. Various appearance attributes may be employed to create unique text styles. A style is named by assigning it a text font. Font files have the .SHX extension.
`Text style name (or ?) <ROMANC>:`

TABLET   The TABLET command is used to calibrate a digitizer to input an existing paper drawing, or to configure the digitizer for up to four tablet menu areas, and define the screen pointing area.
Option (ON/OFF/CAL/CFG):

TABSURF   TABSURF, or tabulated surface, generates a 3D polygon mesh by projecting an entity (path curve) through space along a direction vector.
Select path curve: Select direction vector:

TEXT   TEXT lets you enter text in your drawing. An older command than DTEXT, TEXT does not dynamically show your text characters on the screen as you enter them. Several justification options can be specified. It places the text string when you end the text input.
Start point or Align/Center/Fit/Middle/Right/Style:

'TEXTSCR   TEXTSCR performs the equivalent of pressing the F1 toggle key on MS-DOS based systems by flipping the display screen to text mode.

TIME   TIME displays the following: current date and time; date and time the drawing was created; date and time the drawing was last updated; and the current amount of time in the drawing editor. In addition, you can set an elapsed timer. The default setting has the elapsed timer on.
Current time:
Drawing created:
Drawing last updated:
Time in drawing editor:
Elapsed timer:
Timer on.
Display/ON/OFF/Reset:

TRACE   The TRACE command allows you to draw solid-filled lines of a specified width. AutoCAD automatically miters the corners of adjacent trace segments entered during the same command.
From point:
To point:
To point: ...

TRIM TRIM makes it possible for you to clip entities that cross a boundary or cutting edge. You can have more than one cutting edge. Entities like lines, arcs, circles, and polylines can act both as boundary edges and as objects to trim.
`Select cutting edge(s)...  Select object to trim:`

U/UNDO The U and UNDO commands let you step back through your drawing, reversing previous commands or groups of commands. UNDO keeps track of the previous commands in a temporary file. This file is cleared at the end of each drawing editor session, or when you plot. U undoes a single command or group per execution. UNDO offers additional controls.
`Auto/Back/Control/End/Group/Mark/<number>:`

UCS The UCS (User Coordinate System) command lets you redefine the location of 0,0 and the direction of X,Y. The default UCS is the WCS (World Coordinate System). You can set your user coordinate system with the UCS command or with the DDUCS dialogue box.
`Origin/ZAxis/3point/Entity/View/X/Y/Z/Prev/Restore/Save/`
`Del/?/<World>:`

UCSICON The UCSICON marker graphically displays the origin and viewing plane of the current UCS. The default setting for the icon is on and Noorigin (displayed at the lower left corner). The ORigin option displays at 0,0,0, if possible.
`ON/OFF/All/Noorigin/ORigin <ON>:`

UNITS The UNITS command controls the format and display for the input of coordinates, distances, and angles. You specify the system of units, the precision, the system of angle measurement, the precision of angle display, and the direction of angles.

'VIEW The VIEW command lets you save, name, and restore the current display or a windowed area. The view name can be up to 31 characters.
`?/Delete/Restore/Save/Window:`

VIEWRES VIEWRES controls fast zooms and the display resolution of arcs, circles, ellipses, polyline arcs, and linetypes. The default setting is for fast zooms with a resolution factor of 100 percent. Fast zoom allows most zooms and pans at redraw, not regeneration, speed.

```
Do you want fast zooms? Y
Enter circle zoom percent (1-20000) <100>:
```

VPOINT VPOINT (ViewPOINT) lets you determine the direction and angle for viewing a drawing by selecting a 3D viewpoint. Issuing the command regenerates the drawing with a parallel projection from the 3D point that you specify. The original default is the plan view, looking from 0,0,1. The current default is the current viewpoint. You have three ways to define a viewpoint: by entering X,Y,Z values; by supplying an angle in the X,Y plane and from the X,Y plane; or by picking a point on the compass icon, using the axes tripod for reference.

```
Rotate/<View point> <0.0000,0.0000,1.0000>:
Enter angle in X-Y plane from X axis <270>:
Enter angle from X-Y plane <90>:
```

VPORTS The VPORTS command lets you divide your screen into several viewing areas. Each viewport can display a different view of your drawing. Each viewport contains its own drawing display area and can have independent magnification, viewpoint, snap, grid, viewres, ucsicon, dview, and isometric settings. You can independently ZOOM, REGEN, and REDRAW in each viewport. DOS-based systems let you define up to four viewports at any one time. Other systems let you define up to sixteen.

```
Save/Restore/Delete/Join/Off/?/2/<3>/4:
```

VSLIDE VSLIDE is used to display the contents of a slide file (.SLD) in the current viewport. A slide contained within a slide library created by the SLIDELIB utility program may also be viewed. The viewport is returned to its original state with the REDRAW command.

```
Slide file <drawing name>:
```

WBLOCK   WBLOCK (Write BLOCK) writes a drawing, a selection set, or a block definition to disk as a new drawing file (not a block definition). A "wblock" is not an entity; it is a command that creates an ordinary drawing file which can be inserted into other drawings, or can be recalled from the main menu option Number 2 – Edit an existing drawing. When wblocking, you are prompted to enter a file name, a block name, an insertion base point, and to select the wblock entities. An equal sign as a block name makes it look for a block in the drawing that matches the file name. It then writes the block to disk as individual entities in a new drawing file. A <RETURN> or space as a block name requires you to enter a base point and use normal object selection to select entities which are deleted and wblocked. No new block is created in the current drawing.

File name: Block name: Insertion base point:

' ZOOM   The ZOOM command magnifies (zooms in) or shrinks (zooms out) the display in the current viewport. It does not physically change the size of the drawing, but lets you view a small part of the drawing in detail, or look at a greater part with less detail. Entering a number for magnification is considered an absolute value in drawing units. Placing an X after the value defines the magnification relative to the current display. Several other methods of specifying the desired window are provided.

All/Center/Dynamic/Extents/Left/Previous/Window/<Scale(X)>:

3DFACE   3Dfaces are shapes defined by either three or four corner points. You can define nonplanar faces by varying the Z coordinates for the corner points, however only faces with co-planar Z coordinates will hide other entities. You can construct 3dfaces with visible or invisible edges.

First point: Second point: Third point: Fourth point:

3DMESH   3DMESH creates three-dimensional polygon meshes. Give the mesh size and specify the vertices as 2D or 3D points, starting with vertex (0,0) and ending with vertex (M,N). 3D meshes act like 3Dfaces fused together, and are treated as one entity. The meshes are created open. Close the mesh by editing it with the PEDIT command.

Mesh M size: N size: Vertex (0, 0):

3DPOLY 3-dimensional polylines can be created with the 3DPOLY command. These polylines may have vertices located anywhere in 3D space, but may only include straight line segments with no width.

```
First point:
Close/Undo/<Endpoint of line>:
```

AutoLISP 3D Programs

In addition to AutoCAD's built-in 3D polygon mesh commands, Autodesk programmers have developed many 3D construction and editing programs with the AutoLISP language. Each object construction program creates a single 3D polygon mesh. These programs are supplied on the distribution diskettes labeled "Support" and "Bonus."

➡ *NOTE: The Bonus diskette is only sent to those AutoCAD customers who mail in their registration cards.*

The program files must be present in your AutoCAD directory. The 3D object construction programs can then be accessed by either the [3D Construction] pick from the [Draw] pull-down menu, or by the [3D Objects] pick on the [3D] screen submenu. Other picks must be executed from the AutoCAD command line. All of the programs presented below are fully documented in the AutoLISP Programmer's Reference; those relevant to the concepts covered in this book are briefly discussed.

AXROT AXROT is the equivalent of the ROTATE command implemented in 3D space.

```
Select objects:
Axis of rotation X/Y/Z:
Degrees of rotation: <0>:
Base point <0,0,0>:
```

BOX This program draws a 3D rectangular box or cube to your specifications parallel to the current X,Y plane.

```
Corner of box:
Length:
Cube/<Width>:
Rotation angle about Z axis:
```

CHFACE   Allows moving of individual 3D face vertices.
```
Select entity to change:
1/2/3/4/Undo/Display/<Select vertex>:
```

CL   This program draws a pair of center lines through an existing circle or arc. The lines are drawn parallel to the circle, and on the layer CL.
```
Select arc or circle:
Radius is nnnn
Length/<Extension>:
```

CONE   Builds a cone from the dimensions and segments you supply.
```
Base center point:
Diameter/<radius> of base:
Diameter/<radius> of top <0>:
Height:
Number of segments <16>:
```

DOME or DISH   Creates the top or bottom half of a sphere from a center point and dimension. The number of segments in both directions can be specified.
```
Center of dome:
Diameter/<Radius>:
Number of longitudinal segments <16>:
Number of latitudinal segments <8>:
```

EDGE   Allows interactive toggling of 3D face edge visibility. The command highlights invisible edges for selection.
```
Display/<Select edge>:
```

MESH   MESH offers a simpler method of creating planar 3D meshes than the 3DMESH command. Specify four corner points in natural clockwise or counterclockwise fashion, and the mesh M and N sizes.
```
First corner:
Second corner:
Third corner:
Fourth corner:
Mesh M size:
Mesh N size:
```

PROJECT   This program can be helpful in creating 2D engineering drawings from 3D models. It creates 2D lines, arcs, circles, polylines, solids, and point entities in the current UCS from their 3D counterparts. 3D meshes, polyline width, and extrusion information are not supported, however.

PYRAMID   This program draws a three- or four-sided pyramid with the sides meeting in either an apex, flattened top, or ridge.
```
First base point:
Second base point:
Third base point:
Tetrahedron/<Fourth base point>:
Top/<Apex point>:
Ridge/Top/<Apex point>:
```

SLOT   SLOT constructs a 3D slot or hole and uses 3D faces with invisible edges to form a rectangular outline around the slot or hole on the top and bottom surfaces.
```
Hole or Slot? H/S <S>:
First center point of slot:
Slot radius:
Second center point of slot:
Depth:
```

SPHERE   Constructs a complete sphere as one polygon mesh.
```
Center of sphere:
Diameter/<radius>:
Number of longitudinal segments <16>:
Number of latitudinal segments <16>:
```

TORUS   TORUS builds a toroidal polygon mesh, or 3D doughnut, by drawing a tube around a center point.
```
Center of torus:
Diameter/<radius> of torus:
Diameter/<radius> of tube:
Segments around tube circumference <16>:
Segments around torus circumference <16>:
```

WEDGE Creates a wedge-shaped polygon mesh starting from a corner point.
```
Corner of wedge:
Length:
Width:
Height:
Rotation angle about Z axis:
```

3DARRAY Is the equivalent of the ARRAY command implemented in 3D space. The term *levels* is used to describe the Z element of rectangular arrays. Polar arrays are restricted to a single level rotated from the current X,Y plane.
```
Select objects:
```
Then for Rectangular arrays:
```
Rectangular or Polar array (R/P):
Number of rows (---) <1>:
Number of columns (| | | |) <1>:
Number of levels (...) <1>:
Distance between rows (---):
Distance between columns (| | |):
Distance between levels (...):
```
Or for Polar arrays:
```
Number of items:
Angle to fill <360>:
Rotate objects as they are copied? <Y>:
Center point of array:
Second point of axis of rotation:
```

Index

3D

A

B

**New Riders Library contains the best books on the best software—
Get the *inside story*!**

New Riders Library

There is a good reason why New Riders Publishing is the best computer book publisher — they consistently deliver the best tools for AutoCAD users and desktop publishers.

STEPPING INTO AutoCAD   Fourth Edition—Release 10
A Guide to Technical Drafting Using AutoCAD
By Mark Merickel
380 pages, over 140 illustrations
ISBN 0-934035-51-2, **$29.95**

This popular tutorial has been completely rewritten with new exercises for Release 10. The book is organized to lead you step by step from the basics to practical tips on customizing AutoCAD for technical drafting. Handy references provide quick set-up of the AutoCAD environment. Improve your drawing accuracy through AutoCAD's dimensioning commands. It also includes extensive support for ANSI Y14.5 level drafting.

Optional ANSI Y14.5 Tablet Menu Disk available.

AutoCAD for Architects and Engineers
A Practical Guide to Design, Presentation and Production
By John Albright and Elizabeth Schaeffer
544 pages, 150+ illustrations
ISBN 0-934035-53-9   **$29.95**

Master your AutoCAD project using high-powered design development with AutoCAD Release 10. Learn to construct working drawings using techniques from real life projects. Export crucial data for credible report generation. Generate stunning computer presentations with AutoLISP, AutoShade, and AutoFlix. The ONLY AutoCAD book specifically written for the architectural, engineering and construction community.

Optional Productivity Disk available.

INSIDE AutoCAD   Over 250,000 sold
The Complete AutoCAD Guide   Fifth Edition — Release 10
D. Raker and H. Rice
864 pages, over 400 illustrations
ISBN 0-035035-49-0 **$29.95**

INSIDE AutoCAD, the best selling book on AutoCAD, is entirely new
and rewritten for AutoCAD's 3D Release 10. This easy-to-understand
book serves as both a tutorial and a lasting reference guide. Learn to
use every single AutoCAD command as well as time saving drawing
techniques and tips. Includes coverage of new 3D graphics features,
AutoShade, and AutoLISP. This is the book that lets you keep up and
stay in control with AutoCAD.

CUSTOMIZING AutoCAD   Second Edition — Release 10
A Complete Guide to AutoCAD Menus, Macros and More!
J. Smith and R. Gesner
480 Pages, 100 illustrations
ISBN 0-934035-45-8, **$27.95**

Uncover the hidden secrets of AutoCAD's 3D Release 10 in this all
new edition. Discover the anatomy of an AutoCAD menu and build a
custom menu from start to finish. Manipulate distance, angles,
points, and hatches — ALL in 3D! Customize hatches, text fonts and
dimensioning for increased productivity. Buy *CUSTOMIZING
AutoCAD* today and start customizing AutoCAD tomorrow!

INSIDE AutoLISP   Release 10
The Complete Guide to Using AutoLISP for AutoCAD Applications
J. Smith and R. Gesner
736 pages, over 150 illustrations
ISBN: 0-934035-47-4, **$29.95**

Introducing the most comprehensive book on AutoLISP for AutoCAD
Release 10. Learn AutoLISP commands and functions and write your
own custom AutoLISP programs. Numerous tips and tricks for using
AutoLISP for routine drawing tasks. Import and export critical
drawing information to/from Lotus 1-2-3 and dBASE. Automate the
creation of scripts for unattended drawing processing. *INSIDE
AutoLISP* is the book that will give you the inside track to using
AutoLISP.

AutoCAD Reference Guide
Everything You Want to Know About AutoCAD — *FAST!*
By Dorothy Kent
256 pages, over 50 illustrations
ISBN: 0-934035-57-1, **$11.95**

All essential AutoCAD functions and commands are arranged alphabetically and described in just a few paragraphs. Includes tips and warnings from experienced users for each command. Extensive cross-indexing make this the instant answer guide to AutoCAD.

INSIDE AutoSketch
A Guide to Productive Drawing Using AutoSketch
By Frank Lenk
240 pages, over 120 illustrations
ISBN: 0-934035-20-2, **$17.95**

INSIDE AutoSketch gives you real-life mechanical parts, drawing schematics, and architectural drawings. Start by learning to draw simple shapes such as points, lines and curves, then edit shapes by moving, copying, rotating, and distorting them. Explore higher-level features to complete technical drawing jobs using reference grids, snap, drawing layers and creating parts. *INSIDE AutoSketch* will let you draw your way to succes.

The Autodesk File
The Story of Autodesk, Inc., the Company Behind AutoCAD
Written and Edited by John Walker
532 pages
ISBN: 0-934035-63-6 **$24.95**

The unvarnished history of Autodesk, Inc., the company behind AutoCAD. Read the original memos, letters, and reports that trace the rise of Autodesk, from start-up to their present position as the number one CAD software company in the world. Learn the secrets of success behind Autodesk and AutoCAD. Must reading for any AutoCAD user or entrepreneur!

AutoCAD Software Solutions

New Riders AutoLISP Utilities

Disk 1 — Release 10
ISBN 0-934035-79-2 **$29.95**

This disk contains several valuable programs and utilities and subroutines. You will find these useful to any AutoCAD drawing application. They include:

CATCH.LSP CATCH is great for selecting the new entities created by exploding blocks, polylines, 3D meshes, and dimensions.

HEX-INT.LSP is a set of hexadecimal arithmetic tools that make dealing with entity handles easier.

SHELL.LSP contains the SHELL function that executes and verifies multiple DOS commands with a single AutoCAD SHELL command execution (DOS only).

MERGE-V.LSP contains MERGE-V, which combines two files and verifies the copy procedure (DOS only).

PVAR.LSP provides functions for creating a personal variable system which can retain up to 254 variable values in a drawing's LTYPE table.

ISODIM.MNU implements an isometric dimensioning system as a TABLET1 menu. Using a tablet menu makes iso-dimensioning more intuitive.

GROUP.LSP contains functions to create and select *groups* of entities in AutoCAD drawings.

GRPT.LSP contains GRPT, a function that draws GRDRAW temporary points with any PDSIZE or PDMODE system variable setting.

FLATPAT.LSP is a program to generate flat pattern drawings of pipe end conditions.

XINSERT.LSP contains XINSERT, an external block extraction and insertion program.

STACK.LSP is a function loading program to minimize memory conflicts in using several moderate to large AutoLISP functions at once.

These AutoLISP programs and subroutines are not encrypted and are well documented by comments in the *filename*.LSP files.

For fast service, call a New Riders Sales Representative
at (800) 541-6789

The New Riders' Library also includes products on Desktop Publishing

Inside Xerox Ventura Publisher Version 2/2nd Edition
A Guide to Professional-Quality Desktop Publishing on the IBM PC
James Cavuoto and Jesse Berst
704 pages, 330 illustrations
ISBN 0-934035-59-8 **$29.95**

The best reference guide to Ventura Publisher is now even better! *Inside Xerox Ventura Publisher*, 2nd Edition, has been completely rewritten for Ventura Publisher Version 2 and includes more of what readers have asked for: more hands-on examples, more easy-to-use charts, and more time-saving tips and tricks.

Publishing Power With Ventura Version 2/2nd Edition
The Complete Teaching Guide to Xerox Ventura Publisher
By Martha Lubow and Jesse Berst
704 pages, 230 illustrations
ISBN 0-934035-61-X-9, **$27.95**

Unlock the inner secrets of Ventura Publisher Version 2 with this well-written tutorial. You'll learn how to create your own great-looking business documents by producing the "real world" documents presented in this book. These documents include reports, newsletters, directories, technical manuals, and books.

Companion software is available.

Desktop Manager   Software Program
ISBN: 0-934035-34-2, **$99.95**
Supports Versions 1 and 2

Desktop Manager is the desktop accessory software for IBM and compatible personal computers that helps you manage your Ventura Publisher documents, running transparently from within the Ventura Publisher environment. A multifunction software utility, Desktop Manager provides file management, timed-backup, document control, style sheet settings, and report generation. This utility program comes complete with an 180-page guide.

Managing Desktop Publishing
How to Manage Files, Styles and People for Maximum Productivity
By Jesse Berst
256 pages, over 100 ilustrations
ISBN: 0-934035-27-X, **$9.95**

The essential handbook for the modern writer and editor. *Managing Desktop Publishing* shows you how to save production time by preformatting documents. Learn to manage your files, styles and style sheets. Also presented are the elements of style you need to succeed in today's desktop publishing arena.

Companion software is available.

Inside Designer
Techniques for the Electronic Canvas
Frank Lenk with illustrations by Sû Allison
320 pages, 100+ illustrations
ISBN 0-934035-70-0 **$21.95**

A clear and concise introduction to Micrografx Designer, the powerful IBM-compatible graphics and design package. Dozens of real-world examples, suitable for users at all leve;ls. *Inside Designer* also includes an introduction to the Windows operating environment.

Optional Designer Disk available.

Inside Xerox Presents
A Guide to Professional Presentations

Martha Lubow
384 pages, 100 + illustrations
ISBN 0-934035-66-0 **$21.95**

Inside Xerox Presents teaches you how to turn this exciting new program into an indispensable business tool. Clear-cut, easy-to-follow instructions teach you the inside secrets of the Xerox Presents program.

Organize and produce top-notch presentations — add impact to your visuals, speaker notes, and audience handouts to create a complete presentation. Streamline the design process with tricks, tips, and shortcuts not available anywhere else.

Optional disk available for instant point and click productivity.

Style Sheets For Business Documents
(Book and Disk Set) **Supports Version 1 and 2**

Martha Lubow and Jesse Berst
320 pages, 150 illustrations
ISBN 0-934035-22-9, Manual/Disk Set **$39.95**

Introducing a cure for the common document— *Style Sheets for Business Documents.* This book and disk set contains more than 30 predesigned Ventura Publisher templates for creating top-quality business documents. Style sheets are presented for proposals, reports, marketing materials, ads, brochures, and correspondence. more than 100 pages of design tips and tricks are also included.

Style Sheets For Technical Documents
(Book and Disk Set) **Supports Version 1 and 2**

By Byron Canfield and Chad Canty
320 pages, 150 illustrations
ISBN 0-934035-29-6, Manual/Disk Set **$39.95**

Get the maximum out of Ventura Publisher with these advanced technical document formats. This book/disk combination presents more than 25 ready-to-use templates for creating technical documents and books. Also includes techniques for creating pictures and tables, plus advanced tips for modifying formats to fit your needs.

For fast service, call a New Riders Sales Representative
at (800) 541-6789

Style Sheets For Newsletters
(Book and Disk Set) **Supports Version 1 and 2**

By Martha Lubow and Polly Pattison
320 pages, over 150 illustrations
ISBN 0-934035-31-8, Manual/Disk Set **$39.95**

This book and disk set presents more than 25 predesigned Ventura Publisher templates for creating one-,two-, three-, and four-column newsletters. Just open the chapter template, load in your own text, and print. A complete description of every style sheet and key tag for all chapter templates is also included.

STYLE SHEETS VALUE PACK!

Order all three style sheets sets together for an over $19.00 savings. Complete your Style Sheet Library for only **$99.95**

Style Sheets for Business Documents

Style Sheets for Technical Documents

Style Sheets for Newsletters

(Includes all three!)

For fast service, call a New Riders Sales Representative
at (800) 541-6789

Order from New Riders Publishing Today!

Please indicate which release of AutoCAD you are using.

❏ **AutoCAD Release**

Yes, please send me the productivity-boosting material I have checked below. Make check payable to New Riders Publishing.

❏ Check enclosed.

Charge to my credit card:

❏ **Visa #**   ❏ **Mastercard #**

Card # _____

Expiration date: _____

Signature: _____

Name: _____

Company: _____

Address: _____

City: _____

State: _____ ZIP: _____

Phone: _____

The easiest way to order is to pick up the phone and call 1-800-541-6789 between 9:00 AM and 5:00 PM PST. Please have your credit card available and your order can be placed in a snap!

Quantity	Description of Item	Unit Cost	Total Cost
	Stepping into AutoCAD 4th Edition	$29.95	
	Stepping into AutoCAD 4th Edition Disk	$14.95	
	AutoCAD for Architects and Engineers	$29.95	
	AutoCAD for Architects and Engineers Disk	$14.95	
	The Autodesk File	$24.95	
	Inside AutoLISP	$29.95	
	Inside AutoLISP Disk	$14.95	
	AutoLISP Utilities — Disk 1	$29.95	
	Inside AutoCAD 5th Edition	$29.95	
	Inside AutoCAD 5th Edition Disk	$14.95	
	Customizing AutoCAD 2nd Edition	$27.95	
	Customizing AutoCAD 2nd Edition Disk	$14.95	
	AutoCAD Reference Guide	$11.95	
	AutoCAD Reference Guide Disk	$14.95	
	Inside AutoSketch	$17.95	
	Inside AutoSketch Drawing Disk	$ 7.95	
	Shipping and Handling: See information below.		
	SalesTax: California please add 6.5% sales tax.		
	TOTAL:		

Send to:

New Riders Publishing
P.O. Box 4846
Thousand Oaks, CA 91360
(818)991-5392

SIA

Shipping and Handling: $4.00 for the first book and $1.75 for each additional book. Floppy disk: add $1.75 for shipping and handling. If you need to have it NOW, we can ship product to you in 24 to 48 hours for an additional charge and you will receive your item over night or in 2 days. Add $20.00 per book and $8.00 up to 3 disks for overseas shipping.

New Riders Publishing ● P.O. Box 4846 ● Thousand Oaks ● CA 91360

1-800-541-6789
Orders

1-818-991-5392
Customer Service

1-818-991-9263
FAX

Order from New Riders Publishing Today!

Please indicate which release of AutoCAD you are using:

❏ **AutoCAD Release** _____

Yes, please send me the productivity-boosting material I have checked below. Make check payable to New Riders Publishing.

❏ **Check enclosed.**

❏ **Charge to my credit card:**

    ❏ **VISA** _____

    ❏ **MasterCard** _____

Expiration date: _____

Signature: _____

Name: _____

Company: _____

Address: _____

City: _____

State: _____ ZIP: _____

Phone: _____

The easiest way to order is to pick up the phone and call (818) 991-5392 between 9:00 AM and 5:00 PM PST. Please have your credit card readily available and your order can be placed in a snap!

SIA

Quantity	Description of Item	Unit Cost	Total Cost
	Stepping into AutoCAD, 4th Edition	$29.95	
	Stepping into AutoCAD, 4th Edition Disk	$14.95	
	AutoCAD for Architects and Engineers	$29.95	
	AutoCAD for Architects and Engineers Disk	$14.95	
	The Autodesk File	$24.95	
	Inside AutoLISP	$29.95	
	Inside AutoLISP Disk	$14.95	
	AutoLISP Utilities—Disk 1	$29.95	
	Inside AutoCAD, 5th Edition	$29.95	
	Inside AutoCAD, 5th Edition Disk	$14.95	
	Customizing AutoCAD, 2nd Edition	$27.95	
	Customizing AutoCAD, 2nd Edition Disk	$14.95	
	AutoCAD Reference Guide	$11.95	
	AutoCAD Reference Guide Disk	$14.95	
	Inside AutoSketch	$17.95	
	Inside AutoSketch Drawing Disk	$ 7.95	

Shipping and Handling: See information below.		
Sales Tax: California please add 6.5% sales tax.		
TOTAL		

Shipping and Handling: $4.00 for the first book and $1.75 for each additional book. Floppy disk: add $1.75 for shipping and handling. If you need to have it NOW, we can ship product to you in 24 to 48 hours for an additional charge and you will receive your item overnight or in 2 days. Add $20.00 per book and $8.00 up to 3 disks for overseas shipping.

New Riders Publishing • **P.O. Box 4846** • **Thousand Oaks, CA 91360**

1-800-541-6789
Orders

1-818-991-5392
Customer Service

1-818-991-9263
FAX

To order: Fill in the reverse side, fold, and mail